THE AUTISM DISCUSSION PAGE ON ANXIETY, BEHAVIOR, SCHOOL, AND PARENTING STRATEGIES

THE AUTISM DISCUSSION PAGE

ON ANXIETY, BEHAVIOR, SCHOOL, AND PARENTING STRATEGIES

A toolbox for helping children with autism feel safe, accepted, and competent

BILL NASON

Jessica Kingsley *Publishers*
London and Philadelphia

First published in 2014
by Jesscia Kingsley Publishers
73 Collier Street
London N1 9BE, UK
and
400 Market Street, Suite 400
Philadelphia, PA 19106, USA

www.jkp.com

Copyright © William Nason 2014

Library of Congress Cataloging in Publication Data
A CIP catalog record for this book is available from the Library of Congress

British Library Cataloguing in Publication Data
A CIP catalogue record for this book is available from the British Library

ISBN 978 1 84905 995 4
eISBN 978 0 85700 943 2

Printed and bound in the United States

ACKNOWLEDGEMENTS

This book and its companion, *The Autism Discussion Page on the core challenges of autism: a toolbox for helping children with autism feel safe, accepted, and competent*, were the result of ongoing support and encouragement from the members of the Facebook page I moderate, Autism Discussion Page. The outpouring of encouragement gave me the drive to put all these articles together in a two-volume set to provide a manual for the members as well as countless articles to share with friends, teachers, relatives, and caregivers. Special thanks go out to a handful of early members who have supported and shared my work across the world to spread awareness and understanding. For the early members who advertised and spread the word, without your support these books would never have happened. I owe you an endless debt of gratitude.

I wish to thank my wife and family for all their support and encouragement to enter this endeavor and stay with it through to completion. I am lucky enough to have a patient wife who has put up with me working countless hours to moderate the Facebook page and working endlessly to put these two books together. Thank you, LouAnne! Special thanks to my daughter, Carrie Aldrich, who has been a valuable sounding board for my ideas and has edited my manuscripts. Your support has been very dear to me.

Most importantly, there are many special families and friends with autism who have enriched my life over the years. For all the families who have allowed me into their lives, thank you so much for sharing this journey with me! Lastly, for all the adults on the spectrum who have shared with me all their comments, suggestions, recommendations, and experiences, thank you so much for providing me wich the feedback and guidance to share your unique perspectives. Understanding your world allows me to communicate that awareness to the rest of the world. Thank you so much, and keep advocating your perspectives!

CONTENTS

INTRODUCTION

This is a unique book in that the material was never designed to be a book in the first place. It is a collection of articles that I post on my Facebook page, Autism Discussion Page. I am a mental health professional, with a master's degree in clinical psychology and more than 30 years of experience in treating individuals with developmental disabilities and autism spectrum disorders. Over the years I began to specialize in autism spectrum disorders and developed a strong compassion for these children. In May of 2011 I started this Facebook page to share more than 30 PowerPoint (slide) presentations that I had created over the years of different strategies for supporting children on the spectrum. These PowerPoint presentations consist of a toolbox of strategies for helping children on the spectrum feel safe, accepted, and competent. These strategies provide guidelines for supporting the sensory, cognitive, emotional, and social challenges the children experience, and include parenting and teaching strategies. For those of you who go to the page looking for further information, these PowerPoint presentations can be found in the "Photo (albums)" section of the page.

In addition to these slide presentations, I started posting a variety of text articles on important areas of interest for parents, teachers, caregivers, professionals, and individuals on the spectrum. Little did I realize that this page would take off and grow so rapidly. What I thought would be a membership of a few hundred people blossomed into its current membership of more than 50,000 people from all around the world. In addition to the slide presentations, the members found my daily articles to be very valuable in both enabling them to understand the inner experiences of their children and giving step-by-step "how to" guidelines for helping their children feel safe, accepted, and competent. On this page we have a very supportive group of parents, teachers, professionals, and other caregivers who expand on my articles by sharing their comments, suggestions, and valuable experiences. We continue to grow at a rate of about 2,000 members a month, and with the help of their sharing, we reach an average of 90,000 to 130,000 viewers a week.

This book actually grew out of the members' encouragement to publish these posts in a book format so they could have a hard copy of all these articles in one collection which they could reference and share with others. It would also provide them with a manual for the page, so the members would not have to copy and paste the material and could reference it whenever they desired. So what you will find in this book is a series of short posts/articles that are arranged in chapters by common issues. Most of the posts are designed to stand alone (they do not need to be read in sequence), are written in easy-to-understand language, and can be read in just a few minutes. They provide an in-depth understanding of how the child perceives the world so that the supportive guidelines make natural sense. More than 300 posts are presented in two books:

1. *The Autism Discussion Page on the core challenges of autism: A toolbox for helping children with autism feel safe, accepted, and competent*

   This book provides an in-depth view of the four basic sensory, cognitive, social, and emotional areas of vulnerabilities for individuals on the spectrum. There is a comprehensive view of each area of vulnerability with detailed guidelines on how to support the child through these challenges. When readers are finished, they will have a good understanding of how their children perceive the world, process information, and act the way they do. The book takes you through all the sensory challenges that are common for those on the spectrum, how they process information differently, why they struggle so much socially, and how overwhelming their emotional world can be. From this awareness, it becomes easier to understand and accept those with autism, as well as help them regulate our world. Whether you are a parent, teacher, professional, or someone on the spectrum yourself, this book will be of value to you.

2. *The Autism Discussion Page on anxiety, behavior, school, and parenting strategies: A toolbox for helping children with autism feel safe, accepted, and competent*

   This book covers some of the major challenges that children and families experience during their daily routine and how to address each challenge. We cover stress and anxiety, addressing behavior issues, co-occurring conditions, stretching comfort zones, harnessing strengths and preferences, parenting and discipline strategies, teaching empowerment skills, and a host of mentoring strategies for coaching your child in basic life skills.

Each book, as well each article within, stands alone. Although the second book complements the first, they can be read and understood separately from each other.

Basic premises underlying these books

Before delving into the strategies for helping your child feel safe, accepted, and competent, it is best to outline the basic premises that provide the foundation for the strategies. Every author has their own biases that drive their approach, and it is important that you understand what they are. These premises provide the foundation for understanding the recommendations and suggestions. They may not dictate what procedures are used, but how we apply them. They provide the starting point, the values, and intentions that drive how we perceive the children, understand their needs, interrupt their behavior, and support their growth. The strategies in these books are based on the following premises:

1. *Assume the child is doing the best he can, given the situation he is in and his current skills for dealing with the demands.*

   Dr. Ross Greene, in his book *The Explosive Child,* outlines this basic premise that should drive all strategies designed for helping children. We have to assume that the children will act correctly if they have the right tools to respond competently. Therefore, if they are responding badly or incorrectly, assume that the demands of the situation outweigh the children's current skills for dealing with them. When faced with misbehavior or lack of progress, we have to change our expectations and teaching strategies to better match the child's abilities, build in better assistance to maximize success, and teach better skills for coping with the demands. It is up to us first to change our expectations and strategies, before expecting the child to change.

2. *Understand and validate first, before trying to change.*

   We often make the mistake of jumping in and trying to change the child's behavior before taking the time to understand how the child is experiencing the situation and the meaning the behavior has for him. All behavior has a functional purpose for the child. We must understand the behavior in light of the child's strengths and vulnerabilities before deciding how to change it. When we act without understanding, we often invalidate the child. Understand and validate first, then support and assist the child in learning.

3. *Help the child feel safe, accepted, and competent.*

   In the 30 plus years I have been in the field, I have learned that if I can create conditions so the children feel safe and secure, accepted and valued, and confident and competent, all children grow and develop. Everyone, children and adults, flourishes when we feel safe, accepted, and competent. We are all trying to reach these conditions. There is so much in this world that is chaotic and overwhelming for our children that they often feel unsafe, insecure, and inadequate. When designing strategies to teach the child, always ask yourself: "In what way does this strategy help my child feel safe, accepted, and competent?" If the strategy does not match this criterion, question its worth.

4. *Nothing for the child without the child!*

> The child's perspective and voice should be sought and respected at all stages of designing strategies. All behavior is communication, and we must listen to the child in all areas of training. Whenever possible, the child needs to be a working partner in identifying the goals and objectives, and in designing and implementing the strategies. Strategies should be based on the child's strengths, interests, and dreams, not simply focused on treating their vulnerabilities and weaknesses. Training is more effective when the child is an active agent in the learning process. When we try to impose, demand, and pressure, we force the child to avoid, resist, and mistrust our guidance. We must be a working partner with the children for them to respect us as a trusted guide.

Using these principles will help us understand and validate the child, help the child feel safe, accepted, and competent, and foster greater growth and development. These principles also direct how we set expectations, design treatment strategies, and avoid blaming the child when things go wrong. They also guide where to look when progress stops occurring. These premises give us a framework for identifying where to start, how to go, and what to fall back on when progress halts. At those moments when we are feeling lost and powerless, these premises keep us stable and secure, knowing where to turn and how to evaluate. They are the guiding principles that keep us on the right path. Never fear when momentarily confused. Take a deep breath, slow down, listen, and understand, then try another way! The journey is full of surprises and temporary setbacks, but many celebrations! These principles will provide the path for a fruitful journey! Have fun and support each other in helping the child. Place no blame when things go wrong, but share in the celebration when things go right! The greater the challenge, the sweeter the success!

How to read these books

These books can be read in a variety of ways:

1. They can be read from beginning to end to get a good understanding of all the issues and comprehensive strategies. Although each post can stand alone, they are clustered in series of related topics.

2. The reader can skim through the contents page and pick and choose areas that interest them, isolating strategies that are most relevant to their life and child. The posts do not have to be read in order and a post can often be understood without reading the material before it.

3. The articles are very condensed, packed with information, so it is important not to try to digest all the information at one time. It may be helpful to read the books from beginning to end, while checking off posts and strategies that you can come back to later to focus more on.

4. For parents, teachers, and professionals, these books can be used as reference books for looking up strategies for issues that arise as you move through this journey. These posts and strategies are laid out in an easy-to-find detailed format that provides you with a quick reference to comprehensive guidelines.

5. Since the books do not have to be read from front to back, you can take your time reading each post. If you only have brief moments to read, you can read one or two posts in a few minutes while taking a break from your daily living. You can read as little or much as you want, given the time that you have.

6. For the articles that you would like more information on you can go to our Facebook page, Autism Discussion Page, (www.facebook.com/autismdiscussionpage), view the different slide presentations and follow these same posts that are expanded on by our members sharing their comments, suggestions, and experiences, or message me privately for further information.

7. For members of the Facebook page, you finally have a manual for the page, giving you easy access to all the posts. You no longer have to stress about seeing every new post and trying to copy and paste them as you go along.

8. The appendices provide additional tools to help you support children on the autism spectrum. All the forms included can be downloaded at www.jkp.com/catalogue/book/9781849059954/resources.

Whether you are just starting out on this journey or have been following this ride for a while, you will find new and valuable information in these books. Whether you are a parent, teacher, professional, or a friend of someone on the spectrum, you will find that these books provide you with a better understanding, awareness, and acceptance of those you know on the spectrum.

How to use the strategies

As you read these books, it is easy to become overwhelmed by all the strategies that are compiled in these posts. You will recognize so many of these issues in your loved ones and want to implement many of the strategies. Trying to decide what to focus on and what to implement first can be very overwhelming.

I caution you to work on only one or two strategies at a time. As you read the posts, make a list of the strategies that are pertinent to you and your child. Do not try to implement them all at once. Go through your list and pick one or two to focus on until you have those strategies ingrained into your daily routine. Most strategies require you, as a parent, teacher, or professional, to make changes in your basic daily habits. This is not easy to do and takes time to accomplish. You only have energy to work on one or two at a time. When prioritizing these strategies, I would recommend that you first start off with a couple that would be the easiest for you to incorporate into you current routine. Do not start with the more difficult strategies to implement. Start small and easy and gradually build your way up. The greatest mistake that parents and caregivers make is jumping in and trying too much, never being successful with any of the strategies, and then giving up in despair. Keep it simple and build gradually.

Things to consider

- Like most literature in the field, when using terms autism and autism spectrum disorder I am incorporating Asperger's, PDD-NOS, and classic autism under this label. Occasionally, posts will refer to Asperger's when others are labeling their child that way. But most of the time autism and autism spectrum disorders encompass the whole spectrum.

- Most of the posts will refer to "him" as the person of interest. We use the male pronoun to include both males and females. It gets cumbersome and difficult to read when continually using him/her, he/she, etc. I am not excluding females on the spectrum.

- The material in these books will not flow as smoothly as other books. Since each post (article) was not necessarily written with the others in mind, one post may not easily flow to the next. Although every attempt has been made to group them by subject matter and fill in with material to help them transition together, the material will often read like independent posts. In addition, you may find some principles being repeated several times, since those principles were needed to explain the material of each post.

- Since these books are collections of posts from Facebook, they will not be filled with numerous citations, academic references, and empirical data. Most of the material is based on either common practice or best practiced procedures, but supportive citations will not be occurring here. Such information is way too cumbersome for Facebook posts.

- These books incorporate and integrate many different models of treatment. My work is heavily influenced by sensory integration; cognitive behavior treatment; Stanley Greenspan's Developmental, Individual Difference, Relationship-based (DIR®) Model; cognitive developmental models; Steven Gutstein's Relationship Development Intervention (RDI); Applied Behavior Analysis (ABA): TEACCH; and Ross Greene's Collaborative Problem Solving model. These books do not argue either all for or all against any one model. They incorporate a dynamic mix of many.

- *Disclaimer:* As the author of these books I do not know your child, what his strengths and vulnerabilities are, and which strategies would be appropriate for him. Each of these strategies will need to be individualized to the needs of your child, and I recommend that you seek guidance from those who have evaluated and know your child well. I am not prescribing any specific strategies for your child. Please seek professional guidance.

By reading these books you are taking your first steps into a very supportive, collaborative journey. I invite you all to join the thousands of people on the Autism Discussion Page (www.facebook.com/autismdiscussionpage), to learn, share, and receive supportive guidance. Hope to see you there!

Chapter 1

FAMILIES, CAREGIVERS, AND TEACHERS

As your child's voice, I "thank you"!

Parenting a child with autism takes courage and passion! It pulls out the worst in you, as well as the best in you. One minute you hate it, the next minute you embrace it. You steam with anger, and excel with excitement. You anguish over the challenges your children experience, but marvel at their endurance and passion. Your child teaches you to view love, life, and happiness in a different light.

The nice thing about doing this page is that I know that every parent, relative, teacher, and friend on here has a true love for the children. If you didn't, you would not be on here seeking to learn and share. The unique qualities of your children test your wisdom, nerves, and honesty. But the more challenging the task, the deeper the passion. For your children's sake, I thank all of you for being here for them, advocating for them, and most importantly loving them with so much passion! Without your love and guidance, they would never be able to navigate this chaotic world. In ways that you may not realize, you are truly blessed to see and feel the world with so much passion! For your children, I thank you!

Be a "working partner" to become a "trusted guide"

If you have been on the page for long, you probably have heard me say that phrase before. Before the child will trust following your lead, he has to perceive you as a supportive, working partner with him. What does that actually mean?

As a parent or teacher, you have to play many roles. You are a protector, mentor, provider, coach, and therapist all wrapped up in one. Given all these roles, for the child to learn to reference you for guidance and trust following your lead, he needs to feel safe that you are a "working partner" with him. The following are qualities I see as important in establishing yourself as a working partner:

- Listen and understand first before passing judgment and punishing behavior.

- Understand and respect your child's vulnerabilities and comfort zones.

- Always start where the child is at, while gradually stretching comfort zones.

- Teach through "we-do" activities, doing them together, framing and scaffolding the activity for success. Learn through relating! Be a model and a guide. Build competency by doing with you! Do less directing and instructing, and more mentoring.

- Even during rough times, communicate love and acceptance, but stay firm to your guidance. Focus more on what the child is doing right, highlighting his strengths and successes, and less on what he is doing wrong.

- When correcting, focus more on what you want the child to do than on what he is doing wrong. Don't tell him to stop doing something without specifying and reinforcing what you want him to do.

- Teach by example, demonstrating and modeling for the child to follow.

- When upset, focus first on acknowledging and validating the feelings before dealing with the behavior.

- With all the support above, yes, you want to show love, acceptance and validation, but you also need to provide very clear and consistent rules, regulations, and expectations. Don't lose sight of the need to provide clear boundaries and consistent consequences.

- Remember, discipline to teach, not to punish.

- Remember to teach respect by giving respect. Give him a choice, and honor his voice!

- You don't have to be perfect, or even close to it. Don't fret over what you do wrong, just learn from it. Your child is resilient and can handle your mistakes. As long as you love and respect the child, he will grow to love and respect you!

I am sure that people can add many other qualities, but please be aware that being a working partner and trusted guide for your child means not just loving, respecting, and validating him, but also providing clear and consistent boundaries, expectations, and consequences. Children want and grow from structure and firm guidance! So, be a loving, working partner with your child, and he will trust following your lead.

Don't beat yourself over the head!

Parents, please don't expect perfection of yourself. For any of these procedures, you will not always be consistent. Once in a while, you will lose your cool and yell, or say things that later you wish you hadn't said. That is common, natural, and to be expected. Principles such as validating feelings first before correcting behavior, focusing on the positive while minimizing attention to the negative, and staying calm and collected in the heat of the moment are all what we *strive for*, not what we can expect all the time.

I have parents who feel guilty, even horrible, when they lose their cool, yell, threaten, or react before thinking. It is going to happen occasionally, and usually it will not have a major impact on the child. It is our "posture" or "attitude" over the long run that matters. If your goals are to focus on the positive, understand and validate, set clear boundaries, and minimize emotional responses to negative behavior, you are on the right track. These procedures are difficult and exhausting, requiring tremendous patience and attention. It is impossible to implement them perfectly all the time. However, if you make them your objectives, you will continue to improve. When you slip up, try to identify why and seek to minimize the conditions in the future. These children are very resilient and can easily handle periodic slip-ups. It is your overall loving and compassionate stance that penetrates the child.

The fact that you are on this page and reading this article is evidence enough to me that you are a loving and compassionate parent, doing the best that you can given the situation you are in. Relax, take a deep breath, and pat yourself on the back for what you are doing right! Brush off your slip-ups and simply focus on what you are doing right!

Believe me, I would not be doing this page if I didn't feel that those participating were loving, committed parents, teachers, caregivers, and professionals. I do not implement these procedures perfectly, or even near perfectly. That is OK! Remember, it is the intent and general attitude and posture that you project that will eventually be successful! Please, pat yourself on the back and smile at yourself when looking in the mirror! You rock!

Don't take a back seat to anyone!

Parenting a child on the spectrum can be a bumpy journey to travel. If you are a parent on the journey of advocating for your child, you must stay in the driver's seat for the entire ride. Your child should be in the front seat, right along with you, to stay connected, read the road maps together, and navigate the crossroads. Along the way you will pick up passengers, but they should not drive from the back seat. You may pick up teachers, professionals, advocates, friends, and relatives to join you on the journey. Some will come and go, and a few may stay for the full ride. These people can be valuable, if supportive. They should add strength and clarity to the journey, help you navigate during the fog and rain, and help you shovel out during the snow storms.

Your first priority is who you take on the ride with you! If the people you pick up on the way do not support you, and hinder your progress, drop them off. Let them walk! If they don't make you stronger, they need to leave. Heavy baggage will only make the journey harder. They will try to take over the wheel and steer you off the road. They may take the wrong way and refuse to turn around when common sense points that you are getting lost. When you see this happening, pull over, let them out, and politely say goodbye! Save the space for an advocate who will be a working partner with you, rather than a thorn against you. Through this ride, you want the topics of conversations to be positive and strength-based, without any complaining, whining, or bickering. No fighting, just collaborating, seeing the positive, and relishing the gains.

For those who listen to you and your child, value your vision, and add to your journey, keep them on board. Most will not be able to stay forever, but their influence will provide valuable guidance throughout the journey. They have knowledge and experience that can be valuable for you and your child, but only you can be the driver of this ride. Only you understand, accept, and are totally committed to your child. You know the vulnerabilities, challenges, goals, and dreams for you and your child, but others can help provide the framework for making it happen. Keep them on board as long as you can, and replace them with care. Treat them with respect; appreciate and value their opinions. We want people who may agree or disagree respectfully, but allow you to make the decisions. If you start to steer off course, you need honest companions to guide you back. You navigate together, share the experiences, and enjoy the triumphs. They help you navigate, but you continue to drive. When you are worn out and tired, pull off the side of the road and rest a while. Do not let them drive! When you feel overwhelmed, stop off at a rest area, take a breather, go for a short walk, regroup, and collaborate. Talk it over, get on the same page, then continue on your journey.

As you start this journey, you will feel overwhelmed, scared, and confused. You will know very little, but you do know your child. You will need these passengers to help you navigate. However, with or without their support, you will become more knowledgeable and stronger as the journey moves on. You will gain experience, read the road maps, listen to the opinions, ask for directions, and navigate the road blocks. When no one in the car has an answer, call an experienced friend—one who has taken this trip already. A friend or another parent who has lived this journey, followed this road many times, made the mistakes already, and has more of the answers.

Stay in the driver's seat with your child right with you, the two of you navigating together, sharing the experiences, learning together, growing together, and getting stronger together. You want your child to learn by driving with you, learning by listening and observing, following your lead, and collaborating with you. Your child must learn how to read the maps, understand the signs, and navigate the crossroads. As he gets older, he will need to take over the steering wheel, a little at a time, as his competence and confidence increase. You will both be in the front seat together, but this time with you in the passenger seat and your child driving. You will still navigate together, share the experiences, and collaborate as usual. You will continue to grow together and become stronger together. You can look back at your passengers, smile and share the enjoyment of the accomplishments, and most importantly thank them for their support. Without them, this ride would have been a lot bumpier and the costs much higher. You will look back and see all the wrong turns and misfortunes, but enjoy the fact that you made it through the journey! Everyone is stronger, happier, and looking forward to the future.

Most importantly, realize it is a long journey, not a race. Take it slowly, navigate with purpose, and take frequent breaks to clear your head, collaborate, and stay on course. As you are driving, take frequent opportunities to look over at your child and enjoy the ride. Smile, give fives, thumbs up, and knuckles, and focus on the positives. You will find the ride much more enjoyable.

Anger after first receiving the diagnosis

How many of you felt anger when your child first received his diagnosis? Angry with the doctors for not recognizing and/or listening to you sooner, angry at yourself for not recognizing or advocating harder, angry with yourself for the missed opportunities that were lost in the time it took to finally get a diagnosis, and angry or guilty over how you handled situations in the past, knowing now what you didn't know then? There are a lot of emotions that flow when the diagnosis is first received. The post that follows is my response to a mother who is experiencing such feelings. I feel it is important, especially for parents of recently diagnosed children.

The anger you are feeling is natural and common among parents with a recent diagnosis. As a mother you feel directly responsible for everything that happens to your child. You are his protector, provider, emotional security blanket, social buffer, and essential lifeline. Now that you have a diagnosis, it is easy to think back and second-guess everything you did, didn't do, or possibly should have done. We all do that. Parenting takes a lot of guessing and second-guessing, regardless of any disabilities. You are not going to make all the right decisions and always respond as compassionately as you would like. You are a loving, very caring mother (otherwise you would not be reading this message right now). You will get angry a lot while parenting (both at yourself and others). You will experience frustration, anger, and, at times, embarrassment at what your child does or doesn't do. There is nothing wrong with those feelings! They are natural human emotions that will come and go. Just because your son has Asperger's doesn't mean you shouldn't feel frustrated, angry, or disappointed over his behavior or your and others' reactions to his behavior. Right now those feelings are intensified, because of the strong emotions you have over the recent diagnosis. You want to scream at times, "Why me! Why my child!" and you immediately panic about what life will bring, and how much of a struggle it is going to be for him. Then you panic about how much of a struggle it will bring for you, and then feel guilty over feeling that way. Although those emotions will stay with you, they will get better with time, especially once you realize Asperger's is a set of different abilities, rather than a blanket ticket to a horrible life.

One of the major problems I see young parents make is getting so wrapped up in the disability that they forget to enjoy their child. Remember that your son or daughter is a child first and a person with a disability second. Sometimes we get so wrapped up in the disability that we lose time for simply loving and enjoying the child. We tend to focus more on his disability than on his unique gifts. Yes, he will have some struggles that other children will not have, and it will require helping him to bridge those differences, but enjoy the little things and share the positive experiences. Don't let the "fight" overshadow the joys of childhood. As far as getting angry at yourself is concerned, all children are very resilient and easily handle all the slips-ups and emotional reactions we give out of frustration. As long as you love the child and share the little experiences with the child, these little moments of emotional reactions simply bounce off him. It is the underlying love and caring that stays with the child.

The very fact that you are on here and reading this post means that you love your child very much! Will you be a perfect parent? Do you need to be a perfect parent? No! Just slow down a little, pace yourself, build friendships with many families on here for support, and enjoy the ride. These children, all children, have so much to offer us that we want to make sure we experience it. There will be many ups and downs, joys and tears, but don't let them overshadow the good moments and the value of parenting. You will find that your child, with all his difficulties and unique abilities, will give you a deeper sense of life and a different, more compassionate view of yourself and others.

Family-centered planning

In the professional field, the emphasis is on the child. We assess, plan, design, and implement a variety of strategies for the child, under the label of "person-centered planning." We assume we know best what the child needs, and we often *instruct* parents in what to do to supposedly help their child. We often tell parents how they should parent, discipline, and teach their children. We tell them they need to build in structure to the day, implement behavior plans, use visual strategies, encourage engagement and communication, be a stronger advocate at school, and pattern their whole day around their child.

As professionals, when focusing on what we think the child needs, we often unintentionally ignore and/or invalidate the parents and caregivers. We tell them what they need to do, then we inadvertently blame them if they do not do it. We pick apart how they parent their child, tell them what they are doing wrong and what they need to change. "If only you do this, your child will grow!" We intrude upon their home and require them to fill out paperwork and meet with us regularly as we monitor their progress. The more challenging the child, the more intrusive we are in the family's life. They are held under a microscope and required to meet all kinds of demands in order to maintain services.

In my experience, in the narrow focus of person-centered planning, we are missing the boat. Without any conscious intent by us professionals, while we focus so heavily on what the child needs, we often miss what the family needs. We forget that the major change agents for the children are the parents, and that the family unit is the primary avenue for support. With all the stressors that the parents experience, the family is often drained and left totally exhausted. Often these families are single-parent households, or the main care of the child is the responsibility of one parent. The challenges often drain the family of time, money, and energy, while they frequently feel abandoned by other family members, friends, and outside support. Between trying to take care of the child, fighting for services, dealing with school issues, navigating government and professional services, and trying to meet the needs of everyone else in the family, parents are under constant stress. At this time, professionals coming in and asking them to make major changes in their life and implement sophisticated strategies is more than they can possibly handle.

I honestly feel that we should expand person-centered planning to family-centered planning. We should not be going in and telling families what they should do; we should be asking, "In what ways can we help you?" We should start with what help the family feels they need and how they would like us to help them meet those needs. How can we *assist* the family, rather than *change* the family? How can we help the family meet their needs and develop the strengths they already have, rather than focusing on changes we feel need to be made? If a family can handle a challenging child with special needs, obviously they have many strengths that have allowed them to persevere under such stress. How can we help them deal with their struggles, reduce the stress, and allow for all family members to meet their needs? These needs should be determined and driven by the family, not us clinicians, allowing them to direct how we can best assist them. It is not up to us to determine what is best for them or the child, but up to us to assist them in meeting their needs, goals, and dreams.

We should start our assessments by asking the family what they see as their biggest problems and what help they desire from us. We will meet the needs of the child by meeting the overall needs of the family, supporting the family's strengths to better meet their own needs. Our evaluation should begin by doing a strength-based assessment of the family and helping them to use these strengths to meet their overall needs. The family knows what they need and value. They may be dazed and confused from being exhausted, but they have a vision. If we can identify that vision, and ask them how we can assist them toward that vision, then they can feel supported. By letting the families determine what assistance they need, we can respect their values and empower them to meet their own dreams. We should not force a vision on them, but assist them in meeting their vision. Then they will see us as a working partner in their journey. So, let's expand person-centered planning to family-centered planning.

Help the children feel "safe and accepted" and they will be attracted to you; help them to feel "competent" and they will follow your lead!

We spend a lot of time and effort building in supports and accommodations to help the child feel safe and accepted. However, don't stop there! The greatest gift of all is helping him feel competent! Granted, it is a prerequisite step to feel safe and accepted in order to start the journey of building competency, but learning to tackle his challenges and advocate for himself is the ultimate goal! Once you identify and support his comfort zones, he needs to feel confident and competent stretching those comfort zones. Like all children, learning to tackle uncertainty and feeling confident tackling new challenges come from following the lead of a mentor (you)—a trusted guide who is more experienced than him. You, as a guide who can do it with him, frame and scaffold the experiences, so he (1) feels the challenge and (2) feels himself successfully tackling the challenges.

Until the child gains that confidence and trusts following your lead, he will stay insecure in the face of challenges, resist stretching his comfort zones, and fear facing uncertainty. It is very important that parents learn to teach through "we-do" activities (doing activities together, guiding and coaching for success), allowing the child to feel the new challenge and feel himself becoming more competent through following your lead. Once you establish that trust, the child will be confident stepping outside his comfort zone and feel connected in following your lead to mastery! So, take your parenting a step further than helping your child feel safe and accepted, and teach him to stretch his comfort zones and tackle uncertainty by following your lead!

Look at yourself in the mirror and smile

At the end of the day, as you drag yourself to bed, look in the mirror and smile! You made it through another day. Regardless of the challenges that were presented, how much you feel you accomplished or didn't complete, you made it through another day protecting your family, advocating for their needs, and scaffolding this chaotic world for your child. You may feel completely exhausted, that you are defeated, as if you said and did everything wrong, and left behind a million things you still have to do! However, if your family is safe, protected, and receiving your love, you have had a successful day!

Between running from one therapy to the next, meeting with professionals, advocating at school, dealing with a meltdown in the middle of Kmart, arguing with a family member who feels that you are parenting wrong, chasing your child as he escapes down the block, and watching as your child changes clothes 20 times before he finds the one outfit that feels comfortable, you may not feel like a success! Believe me, most parents of children with special needs are superhuman! They take on more challenges and stress, and have to multitask more than any other parents. It is a new battle every day and you tackle each one as a passionate soldier! You enter challenges for which people do not have answers. You are often alone, facing challenges that most of us would run away from.

Why do you do it? You have no choice! You are your child's voice, protector, mentor, source of love, and the only one who truly knows him. You are his link to the world, and with every day that passes you have served that role with honor and passion. So look at that face in the mirror each night and smile! You are one awesome person!

Are you a good parent?

All parents on here have times when they question what they are doing. They wonder if they are being a "good parent." Let me give you my professional criteria for a good parent, in your situation:

- Are you acting out of love?
- Are you trying to do your best?
- Do you question what you are doing?

- Do you seek out advice and try to learn as you go?

- Are you worried about being a good parent?

Answering yes to those questions makes you a good parent! Does it mean always making the right decision, never getting frustrated at your child, never feeling guilty about wanting some time alone, or having others (including members of this page) agree with you? No! There is usually no one right answer, and there is much that we do not know in this field. There are many different approaches and no right one. You are not always going to make the right decisions—no one will. Rarely, however, do the momentary decisions that you make have drastic or long-term effects on your child. If you were a "bad parent," you would:

- not be reading this book in the first place

- rarely question what you are doing

- rarely feel guilty over what you did

- rarely seek advice

- rarely worry if you are being a "good parent."

The fact that you are here puts you in the running for being a good parent!

Take a deep breath, hold each other's hands, laugh and cry with each other, and take note that you all are special people and loving parents.

My hat goes off to all you grandparents out there!

If you are a grandparent and viewing this message, I applaud you! Just reading this book means you are very committed to your grandchild and must be a very healthy element in his life. That is so very important, not just for the child, but also for the parents.

In the years that I have been involved with autism, I have met so many awesome grandparents. Many have had to step up and take on the majority of parenting responsibilities, and many have simply walked the path, right alongside your child. You are not only a support and role model for your grandchild, but also for his parents. Parents with children with special needs need that support, but many of you go way beyond the expected commitment to stand right along with the parents in offering social, emotional, and economical support.

Grandparents provide a perspective to the child that parents cannot. When providing services to the families, I gravitate to the grandparents, because they often have a more global view of the situation and challenges. They are often there to pick up the pieces and be the glue to hold things together during rough times.

Let me shake your hand; the world is so much better with such loving and committed grandparents. If you are a grandparent, please introduce yourself here! Don't be shy—stand up and let us recognize you!

Parents take the lead and drive the supports!

Take it from me. I have more than 30 years in the field, but I do not know your child like you know your child. Do not take a back seat to the teachers or professional opinions. It is a working partnership, and you should be facilitating it until the child is empowered to direct it himself. Empower yourself with knowledge, listen to your child, and trust your instincts. If it doesn't feel right, it probably isn't.

Don't allow others to do things to your child without informed consent. You need to know and understand what they are doing and why they are doing it, and, in turn, guide and modify what they are doing to match your child. Then observe and listen to your child's response. It should always be a working partnership, with you determining the direction. If the professionals do not ask for your assistance and opinion, and do not include you in the process, then don't let them do it. You are your child's voice.

As I tell parents, I cannot know your child better than you. I may have met hundreds of children with common vulnerabilities and have many ideas, but only you know your child. I can give you the different ideas and experiences I have seen, but you have to determine if they are appropriate for your child. If it doesn't feel right for you, question it until you are comfortable with it. If you are not comfortable with, do not allow them to do it.

Siblings! Let's celebrate them!

Siblings of children with special needs often get forgotten. They often have to take a back seat, since so much attention has to be directed to the child with special needs. They often feel neglected, angry, and starved of attention. They often develop emotional issues of their own, unless their physical and emotional needs are also met. It can be a delicate balance for parents to make. There have been a lot of sibling support groups developed over the past several years, which have been very helpful for those working through these issues.

On the other hand, many siblings rise to become the loving peer support for their brother or sister, to provide the peer-to-peer interaction that a parent, or other adult, cannot provide—the love and understanding that a child needs to feel from someone their own age. The sibling often can step up and provide the safety net for their brother or sister in social situations, and model more appropriate ways of responding. In looking at the negative aspects that autism has on siblings, we often forget to look at the strengths that siblings bring to the table. Just like all children, siblings of kids on the spectrum provide the child with numerous opportunities to emotionally relate with and learn from their siblings.

Siblings often have a more objective insight into their brother/sister than the parents do. I often try to elicit the perspective of the siblings when doing assessments. On some occasions, I have elicited the help of siblings to implement treatment strategies, such as engaging in a "we-do" activity with their brother/sister, creating opportunities for social engagement, modeling desired behaviors, and even implementing reinforcement procedures. They often enjoy the opportunity to be a mentor for their brother/sister. I have also had schools give extra credit for siblings who implement supportive strategies, since they are very educational.

Tell us your stories! Let's appreciate the struggles they often experience. However, just as importantly, let's celebrate the love, understanding, and acceptance that only a sibling can provide.

Mom/Dad, sleep well tonight!

With the challenges you face, and the limited knowledge and tools you have, rest well because you are doing a fantastic job! You question your actions and agonize over what you do, do not do, or cannot provide for your child. You are frustrated with the lack of services or the quality of services you have, the looks, comments, and questions from others, and the struggles you face to advocate for ongoing supports at school and from professional agencies. You see the challenges and pain that your child endures. Unfortunately, you probably see what you didn't do, what you could have done, or what you might have done differently, and miss seeing what you do right! You don't see the love, compassion, dedication, and determination you express day in and day out!

It is natural to question the "what ifs" and to ask "could I do more?" However, if you get too wrapped up in the maze of "what ifs," you will miss the positives that make parenting special. Sometimes we try to do too much, and obsess about what we are not doing, so that we miss the special moments that gleam with your love and devotion.

It is hard to see the fruits of your love when you are only looking at what is not occurring. Believe me, there is nothing healthier than your love and time spent simply enjoying your child. Don't let those little times pass you by, or be hidden by your feelings of inadequacy and drive to do more.

Autism brings out the best and worst in us, but self-doubt is what I see eat at parents the most. There are no givens, sure strategies, or "just right" decisions out there. We are still in our infancy in understanding autism. But I will assure you of one thing. Your children are children first and respond strongly to the same love and attention that all children need and respond to! Your love is so obvious to everyone but yourself. Try recognizing that, feeling good about that, and shielding the negative self-doubt with that.

It is a long journey, but one that you are tackling well. When going to bed at night, smile at yourself in the mirror and sleep well! If you can assure yourself of your love and devotion, you should rest well. Slow yourself down and give your child the two most important ingredients—time and love! They need that to feel safe and accepted. You also need that to feel loved and loving. You are doing it, so feel it! Good night, sleep tight, and give yourself a big hug!

Slow down, take a breath, and share the moment!

Parenting a child with autism often means wearing multiple hats (mother/father, therapist, teacher, researcher, advocate, social mediator, biomedical doctor, etc.). You have to continually multitask to keep up with the chaos. Parents of young children on the spectrum often have an overwhelming sense of urgency to do as much as possible to help their child overcome their challenges and develop and grow to their maximum potential. This is very understandable and recognizable in many parents of young children. However, we have found that often we move too fast in our urgency to provide for our children. The world moves way too fast for these children, and we need to slow it down to maximize learning.

The world moves too fast for children on the spectrum. They have trouble processing multiple information at one time and tend to have problems with delayed processing. Because of this, our world simply moves way too fast for them. Slow things down and savor the moment. Pause to let them process and think! Take little things in the day and slow them down, highlighting the important details, so they can reference the important things. When using language with children on the spectrum, there are three important factors:

1. Slow it down and shorten your sentences. Speak in two- to three-word phrases if the child only speaks in short phrases. It makes it easier for him to process. Try not to use sentences that are more than one word longer than the child uses. Use sentences only as long as the child speaks in return. However, even for very verbal children, using shorter sentences makes it easier for them to process.

2. Use fewer words and more nonverbal language (exaggerated gestures and animated expressions) to communicate. Most of the children have better visual processing than they do auditory. In addition, it gets the child referencing your nonverbal language for information. Children on the spectrum will usually listen to your words without referencing you

visually for information. This is one reason why they have a hard time reading body language. Slow it down and use more exaggerated gestures and animated facial expressions to convey meaning. When the child starts to forget to reference your nonverbal language, you simply pause the activity until he references you again. Once he picks this up, he will start to reference you more naturally.

3. When using words, use declarative language instead of imperative language. Under the teaching of Dr. Steven Gutstein, founder of Relationship Development Intervention (RDI), this was one of the principles that impacted me the greatest. Imperative language is any statement that directs a specific response from a child (questions, directives, instructions, prompts, etc.). Declaratives are statements that invite, but do not direct a specific response from the child (statements sharing information, ideas, thoughts, feelings, experiences, and perspectives). Normal interaction between two people usually consist of about 20 percent imperatives (questioning, directing) and 80 percent declaratives (sharing ideas and information). However, when we interact with children on the spectrum, the ratio is turned around: usually 80 percent imperative and 20 percent declarative (Gutstein S. 2002a, 2002b, 2009). Children on the spectrum tend to freeze up and resist imperative language. They tend to have strong performance anxiety and pull back from imperative (directive) language. Just like us, no one likes to be questioned, prompted, and directed all the time. In our experiences with families, changing (rephrasing) our language is probably the strongest tool we have. It is as simple as changing our language from "John, what is the matter?" to a descriptive statement such as "Wow, John, you really look upset to me!" You will find your child provides much more information. Try it on your teenager when he comes home from school. Instead of saying "How did your day go?"(which usually gets one word: "fine"), try "You look like you had a good day today (or bad one)" and watch the kind of reaction you get. Usually the child will go into much more detail. We find that we often get three times more interaction from the child when we use declarative language.

4. Learn to pause and wait! Children with delayed processing need time to respond. They have to process what is coming in, appraise what is needed, and formulate how to respond. In our haste, we often jump in and continue to prompt, or respond for them. Waiting is the hardest thing to do. It is much slower than our nervous system wants. It tasks patience and practice, but it is very important. Slow it down, and give them a chance!

You're the teacher, therapist, coach, and mentor!

Don't look around or turn to the phone book! Look in the mirror! Yep, it is you. Mom and Dad, you are the best, the most passionate, and most trusted guide your child has. You can go to many therapists, teachers, and other professionals until you are blue in the face, but the best learning comes from being by your side, doing with you, learning from you, and feeling competent through you! You don't have to be educated or know everything there is to know about autism. Just be you and engage your child!

The world is your classroom; the lesson plans are nothing more than the normal daily activities that fill up your day. As often as possible, do them together, giving your child as big a role as possible. Do them together, side by side, as you scaffold the guidance for success. Share the experience of doing it together, with minimal focus on performance. Talk as you go and "think out loud." Model how you *think*, as well as how you *do*. Pause at each step and ponder what is next. Point out the options and appraise which is best. Take a second to give your child a moment to think. Give clues, but allow him to think. Even if he is nonverbal, he is listening. Even if he is not looking, he is observing. He is learning, as you two are doing!

Celebrate doing it together, rather than how well he is doing. Help him feel safe and accepted, and he will be attracted to you. Help him feel competent through doing with you, and he will follow your lead forever. You don't need expensive therapists, extensive training, or hours and hours of private therapy. Just you and your child, doing together and growing together.

Teach by showing and "doing with," rather than telling and instructing. Place no pressure to perform and celebrate any and all engagement. Don't praise him for what he is doing—"Good job, Johnnie"—but celebrate doing it together— "We did it!" or "We rock!" Let him feel being competent by doing with you. Learning through relating is the key. It adds value to all that is done.

For a child who is hard to engage, find any and all ways to be together in whatever he is doing throughout the day. If the child will not follow your lead, incorporate yourself in what your child is doing. Be together, hang together, and share the experience together. Talk when he won't; don't take silence as rejection. Provide a narrative with moments of silence. Use your hands, gestures, facial expressions, and soft words to invite without guiding. Gradually include yourself in what has value to him, and he will eventually value your presence. Don't instruct, demand, or try to control; just listen, learn, and follow his lead. Once he trusts your engagement, then expand your involvement. Take it slowly but steadily, calmly but persistently. Slowly become part of his play—or silence if that's what he chooses. Stay patient and it will come. Eventually, he will be following your lead. Become a working partner first, and eventually a trusted guide. Being a good mentor means being a passionate coach. Most importantly, believe it will happen, stay passionate and persistent, and love every minute of it. You have to: you are his greatest gift and most passionate guide!

Types of support!

The grass roots movement within the autism community has grown in leaps and bounds over the years. Families who seek out and use support find the journey much easier to navigate. The following are sources of support that I have experienced being helpful.

- Government services: Each country has their own government subsidy and insurance programs that help families with special needs children. They often help pay for medical, occupational therapy, speech, psychology, and psychiatric services. They also will often provide respite staff to give parents a break, which is probably the most valuable service (if you can find reliable staff). Seek out your local developmental disabilities government agency to see if you qualify for these services.

- Some major universities are developing strong resource centers to provide social and recreational opportunities, and advice for local families. Their ability to establish grants and provide educational opportunities for their students makes the collaboration a good fit. Check out your local universities to see what they provide.

- Public parks and recreation programs in local communities often offer recreational opportunities to special needs children and their families. This is a great way for the kids to get together for fun play, and for the parents to network and support each other.

- Churches have started recognizing the need to support families with special needs children. They are forming family activity nights and kid drop-off nights, as well as religious activities for children with disabilities.

- Probably the greatest supports are local autism support groups. Families banding together and networking with each other provide great support among families who share the same challenges. Local support groups can provide a list of valuable resources, support in navigating the local government and professional services, advocacy with schools, family fun nights/activities, social groups for the children, and even group drop-off nights so parents can get away. Seek out and join your local support group, or get one started if your area doesn't already have one.

- Parents in local school districts have been grouping together to form special education groups to advocate for stronger school supports and provide advocates to attend IEP meetings with the parents. They can have a strong impact on the school systems when the parents come together as one voice.

- Especially good for families in rural areas where support groups are not available, the internet provides many parent support groups, message boards, Facebook pages, blogs, etc. If you cannot physically make it to local meetings, online support groups are very popular and offer great support and educational resources.

These are just a few of the options available to families with special needs children. Please help me add to this list. If you have other resources, please let us know what your area has to offer! What supports do you have available? What do you use?

When I think about being exhausted, I think of you!

I work full time, coach soccer and basketball three days a week for approximately 100 children on the spectrum, volunteer for the local autism support group on Tuesday evenings, spend 2–3 hours a day moderating this page, and still find time to work out. I am focused on these endeavors most waking minutes of the day. I get tired, worn out, and question the reasons why.

However, when I question the purpose, you are the reason. As much as I work, commit, and offer, I cannot begin to match the effort you parents put in every day, throughout the day! Parenting children with special needs requires constant multitasking, shifting gears, and fighting battles, whether they are with the schools, professionals, government, or your own families. You cannot stop when exhausted or quit when you feel defeated. You are often questioned by others, and receive minimal thanks or validation. You have to be a strong advocate at times when you are the only voice.

Sometimes you stand alone in your battles, licking your own wounds, with no one to soothe and support you. You go to bed questioning what you did and wondering how you will do it tomorrow. You often get little sleep and wake already exhausted. You may get hit, bitten, kicked, and scratched, but keep moving forward. You feel isolated, defeated, and inadequate, but do not give up! Why? You have no choice! You are your child's voice, protector, advocate, teacher, and loved one. You look into those vulnerable eyes and see how precious your child really is. Others may not see it, but you do! You pick yourself back up, get your second wind, and push on! You feel strong and weak, defeated and victorious, loved and hated, and angry and elated all in the same day.

Do I feel exhausted? How can I? When I think of you, I become energized! Thanks for feeding my energy! I hope what little I do can make you see how strong and powerful you really are! Parents, I admire you and salute you! You are true champions! Thanks for letting me be a small part of your and your children's lives!

Yes, I love you!

"I may not know how to show it, but I do love you!"

I do not want to assume I know what it is like to be a parent of a child with autism. However, I live in the world of autism in my work and leisure life. I have many friends on the spectrum and I value their friendship. I have learned to experience the world differently because of them. I have learned that most stereotypes of how people on the spectrum experience the world are misguided. Because they do not express emotion very well (or simply in a different way), they are often thought to not feel as deeply. In many cases, they feel more deeply and more intensively. They simply have difficulty expressing emotions the way we do.

Because they have difficulty relating with others, they are perceived as not being interested in others. When you chat with the adults who can share their experiences, they tell you that they have very strong feelings, often have a strong desire to connect with others, and love very deeply, just not in the same way that we do.

In working with the younger children, I feel the pain of mothers who want so desperately for their child to express affection for them, to love them. That often feeds the drive for a "cure." But I tell you, your children do love you very strongly. You just have to listen a little better and in a different way. Learn to read their subtle behavior better, and how they communicate. They have trouble expressing love the way we do, but they feel just as deeply. Often they do not know what they are feeling or how to label and control those feelings. If we stop trying to change them, and instead slow down, simply listen to them, and meet them halfway, we will help them feel safe, accepted, and valued.

Only by becoming a working partner with your child, can you become a trusted guide for him. If you slow down, and simply relate with your child (instead of prompting, directing, controlling), you will feel the love. Yes, his world needs structure, boundaries, and a lot of guidance, but spend a few minutes every day simply hanging with your child, saying very little, and simply sharing the experience. If he likes deep pressure, give it; if he likes movement, move together; if he likes smelling things, smell together. Slow down and share the simple pleasures. We often are so busy trying to "cure" the autism that we forget the special little moments. Believe me, even if he doesn't show it externally, your child feels and remembers those moments. Don't let those moments pass by unnoticed. Slow down; share the experience! There is plenty of time to teach and develop. Let him enjoy the moment, and let yourself enjoy the moment. Enjoy them together!

To parents and adults on the spectrum: "If they don't make you stronger, get rid of them!"

Life is too short and fragile to waste it on negative people who hold you back and drag you down. Whether you are a parent of a child on the spectrum or on the spectrum yourself, you are going to run into people who do not understand you, have negative attitudes, pressure you to change, or invalidate your self-worth. People who try to tell you what to do, what is best for you, and how you should act. These same people will make you second-guess yourself, make you feel weak, and can make or break you. Whether you are on the spectrum yourself or a parent of someone on the spectrum, the feedback you get from those around you drastically affects how you view yourself. Individuals on the spectrum, as well as many parents, often suffer from severe anxiety and depression, because of constant invalidation.

Given that we are all somewhat a reflection of the feedback we receive from others, it is vital to recognize the importance of building a network of people close to you who accept and validate who you are and what you are doing. Forget about comparing yourself with those around you who do not accept you and who do not help you feel stronger. Forget about changing to meet the expectations of those who do not value you. Your differences and challenges do not need changing; they need support and strengthening. Your differences can be strengths if developed correctly, and are only challenges because others define them as such. Those who focus on invalidating your weaknesses, trying to change you, and dragging you down—get rid of them!

You need to build a social network of a few good friends who understand, accept, and validate you. Who support you and help you to feel stronger. Negative, invalidating feedback will be all around you; however, it should not be part of your immediate support system. Whether you are a parent or individual on the spectrum, know yourself, define some goals and short-term objectives of what you want to do and where you want to go with your life, and keep your focus on this plan. Be very clear to people that you understand you have differences, but they are either with you or not worthy of you. You do not have time for those who invalidate you and try to pull you back or change you. First, try to explain your situation and direction; however, if they do not understand, then leave them behind. You can only succeed if you have strong support around you. We all need help and assistance from others to move forward. If the person doesn't match that need, then say "no thanks" and politely ignore them.

I know, easier said than done! We cannot always determine those around us, who are in power positions that affect us, and we cannot avoid much of the invalidating feedback that is constantly bombarding us. That is true, but I find that there are three main tools that we can use to avoid being affected by this:

1. Have a vision of who you are, where you are at, and where you are going. Know your strengths and weaknesses, and how to use your strengths to better your life. Have a plan of what you need and where you are going. Have some long-term goals and short-term objectives to help you stay focused on your vision. This becomes important when deflecting negative criticism. The more resistance you experience, the more important it is that you have concrete goals that keep you focused on what you need to do. Without those, you get sucked into all the negativity around you. When you have a clear vision, you can more easily deflect the negative feedback. Also, you have to have a concrete vision and plan in order to measure if others around you are there to help you or hold you back. They either validate or support your efforts (vision and plan) or they are not part of your vision.

2. You need to find a small group (only needs to be one or two people) who accept and validate you and your vision. It helps to have family members and close friends who support you, but often that is not the case. You may need to look outside your immediate network to establish support. For parents, I recommend local autism support groups of other families facing the same challenges; and for adults on the spectrum, seek out adult support groups or join clubs around your special interests. Find others who think like you and/or support your differences, others who define your differences as strengths and help you develop them. It is OK to be different, a little weird (different from others). In this day and age, many people find differences exciting! Seek them out and surround yourself with them. Different is good! You may need to step outside your immediate family to find these people. However, they will make you stronger, validate your vision, and provide the needed support to build strong confidence.

3. You cannot always choose who is around you. You may have invalidating family members, relatives, or co-workers whom you cannot escape, for one reason or another. However, if you have an image and vision for yourself (step 1), have developed a strong support system around you (step 2), then you can deflect and ignore the negative feedback you cannot avoid (step 3). You may not be able to choose all of those around you, but you can choose whether their feedback affects you. If they do not understand or accept you, they are not a "credible source." You don't have to be angry at them, just write them off as ignorant (not understanding) and unworthy of attention.

You cannot become stronger without understanding who you are, advocating for what you need, and choosing who will support you. You are always going to be a minority (as a parent or individual) and always going to fight negativity and invalidation, but you can choose to reject them and learn to build a stronger support system around you. However, you have to have a true vision and a plan of action to move you forward. You may need help with defining a plan. You may need to seek out a life coach or counselor to help you define that vision and plan. You do not need "therapy" for this. You need a counselor or mentor to coach you in identifying that vision and developing that plan of action. Whether you are a parent or an individual on the spectrum, having help in developing this vision can be very important.

If it doesn't feel right, avoid it! If it makes sense, try it!

While navigating through the maze of services, professionals, and therapeutic/educational strategies, make sure they (1) make sense to you and (2) feel right for your child. So often I talk to parents who (1) do not thoroughly understand what is going on or (2) do not feel comfortable with having it done. However, because the therapist, doctor, teacher, or administrator recommends it, they go along with it. They feel uncomfortable questioning what the "experts" say is needed.

Please, for your sake and that of your child, do not accept anything that doesn't make sense to you and that you don't feel comfortable with. This means (1) asking the professional to explain everything in easy-to-understand language, (2) asking for research references, (3) possibly doing some research yourself, and (4) judging the appropriate "fit" for your child. If a professional truly understands what he is doing and has effectively evaluated your child, then he should be capable of easily explaining it to you. When you question what he is saying, he should be comfortable (1) listening to your wishes, (2) validating your concerns, and (3) being flexible to accommodate the individual needs of the child. The ability to listen and collaborate with both the parents and the child is so vital to a long-term therapeutic relationship. You should feel good with both the strategies and the professional providing the service.

Characteristics to look for:

- Does the professional listen to you, answer your questions, and speak in a language you understand? If he provides quick, pat answers in complicated language which do not answer your questions, be skeptical. If he brushes off your concerns with the attitude that he is the professional and knows what he is talking about, walk away!

- Does the professional have the patience to work with you and your child, to increase your understanding, make the strategies comfortable and easy to implement, and model and coach you to learn them?

- Are you able to observe the treatment sessions so you can (1) see what the professional is doing, (2) see how your child is reacting, and (3) learn how to implement the strategies yourself? Be very skeptical of therapists who will not let you observe any of the sessions. If he does not want you physically present, then ask for him to videotape the session and sit down and review it with you.

- For almost all treatment strategies, the therapists and teachers should be giving you recommendations for implementing these strategies at home to expand the therapy throughout the day. Children on the spectrum need to have the strategies built into their daily routine with frequent repetitions to be truly effective. If you are taking your child to therapy once a week with no real understanding of what the objectives are and how to work on them at home, then the effectiveness of the treatment will be minimized. The therapist, at school or in the private clinic, should be encouraging and assisting the parents to use these strategies throughout the day at home. He should be training you, as well as working with your child.

- Most importantly, does the professional seem to listen to, accept, respect, and validate your child? Is the person patient, understanding, and respectful of your child's processing speed, sensory sensitivities, social and emotional vulnerabilities? He should be very flexible in working with your child (modifying and accommodating as needed), rather than molding your child to the technique. When observing, you should get a feel for how the therapist respects your child and how your child responds to the therapist.

In conclusion, what the therapist is doing should make sense to you and feel right. Do a little research, get references to talk to, and make sure that both you and the child feel very comfortable with the therapist. If it doesn't feel right, don't do it. Ask more questions, do more research, observe and investigate some more. If it still doesn't feel right, don't do it.

Chapter 2

STRESS AND ANXIETY

Anxiety on the spectrum!

Anxiety is the most common co-occurring disorder in people with autism spectrum disorders. It is understandable since their nervous system has to work so hard just to fit in with our world. The constant stress on the nervous system due to all the sensory, cognitive, social, and emotional vulnerabilities they experience naturally leaves them very prone to anxiety. Their nervous system is on "high alert," leaving them anxious and on guard. It is important to help the children feel safe and accepted, and to minimize the amount of stress in their lives.

For many children on the spectrum, anxiety is a daily experience. Anxiety is one of the most common conditions associated with autism/Asperger's. The nervous system is so fragile that simple day-to-day processing and regulating our world is very taxing for those on the spectrum. What comes naturally for us is hard work for them. Much chaos and confusion naturally results in anxiety. Studies have shown that even in a resting state, the nervous system is on high alert with greater levels of stress chemicals, compared with neurotypical (NT) people. Since the world can be very overwhelming, it makes sense that there would be stronger levels of anxiety for these children. This anxiety is often expressed in obsessive compulsive behavior, oppositional defiance, rigid/inflexible thinking, perseverations, rigid reliance on rituals/routines, compulsive need for sameness, mood swings, as well as a variety of other challenging behaviors. In providing proactive supports to lessen stress, it is important to isolate the type of anxiety your child experiences. Below, I have listed several of the types of anxiety that children experience.

Which of these does your child experience? How does your child express his anxiety? What supports/techniques have you found to be helpful in lessening the anxiety?

Types of anxiety

- *Anxiety of uncertainty*: fear of anything new or unfamiliar; seeks sameness; can be controlling and oppositional.

- *Social anxiety:* experienced when interacting with others, participating in social events; fear of not knowing how to act or fit in. The stronger the desire to fit in, the greater the anxiety.

- *Performance anxiety:* perfectionism and fear of being wrong. Occurs when ask questions or being prompted to do something. Any demand for performance puts them "on the spot."

- *Anticipatory anxiety:* becomes anxious over an upcoming event, either good or bad. May ruminate/perseverate on upcoming event.

- *Sensory/informational overload:* becomes anxious in settings that present strong sensory stimulation or informational processing demands.

- *Separation anxiety:* has to be next to mom or dad at all times; becomes highly anxious when parent leaves their sight.

- *Defused generalized anxiety:* an ongoing, pervasive anxiety that is not connected to a specific event. Seems to always be apprehensive and insecure.

In future sections we will look at different techniques (biomedical, sensory diet, exercise, meditation, graded exposure, desensitization, and medications) that are used to help reduce anxiety. First, it is important to isolate what types of anxiety the child experiences.

Anxiety is inevitable when you don't "fit in"

When you are a stranger in a strange land, always trying to fit in, making yourself something that you are not, and having trouble understanding what is going on around you, anxiety is inevitable. When you are constantly trying to guess what is needed, have trouble reading what is expected, and are continually out of sync with the world around you, your nervous system will naturally be anxious and insecure. When normal daily activities present constant uncertainty about what to expect and what is expected of you, you will always be on guard and anxious about "not getting it."

Because of processing differences, our world simply moves way too fast for most people on the spectrum. Our world is too vague, with too many invisible, unwritten social rules for them to feel safe and secure. Simply trying to figure out what comes naturally for most of us is very stressful and draining on their nervous system. When the nervous system becomes drained, it is more sensitive and anxious. In this state of disorganization, the nervous system becomes taxed and coping skills deteriorate, leaving the vulnerable nervous system weak and anxious. For many on the spectrum, simply trying to regulate and fit in to our world will create high anxiety.

Research has shown that people on the spectrum, even in their relaxing state, have much higher levels of anxiety chemicals in their nervous system. Their thresholds for fight or flight (panic) are much lower than ours. Because of their limited ability to understand our world, they are under constant anxiety just stepping out in our fast-paced world. When your processing abilities do not match the demands placed on them, the nervous system is bound to be stressed and taxed. When continually overwhelmed, your nervous system begins to habitually fear being put in situations that may tax it. Any new situation could be overwhelming. So, the nervous system stays on high alert for any situations that could threaten it.

To lower anxiety effectively, we need to better match the demands of daily living to the processing abilities of the person. We need to slow things down, make them more concrete and visible, and allow the child time to process at his own pace. We need to start by evaluating the processing abilities of the child and building the accommodations needed to better match the environmental demands to his processing abilities. As the child becomes older, we need to teach him to empower himself by recognizing what his nervous system needs and advocating for the accommodations he requires to stay regulated, and teach him effective coping skills for dealing with potentially overwhelming situations. Just being aware that the normal daily demands of our culture are overwhelming for the child allows us to better understand why he is so vulnerable and to be better able to support him in reducing his anxiety.

STRATEGIES FOR REDUCING STRESS AND ANXIETY

Start with the nervous system!

There are many strategies for combating stress and anxiety, but the first step is to ensure that the nervous system is taken care of. A disorganized nervous system will leave you prone to anxiety. This is part one of a series of articles on combating stress.

Anxiety is a major challenge for many people on the spectrum. Their nervous system is often out of sync with the rest of the world, constantly being bombarded with sensory, social, and informational overload. Part of this distress is caused by internal factors which create disorganization in the nervous system. One of the first steps in managing anxiety is to start with the foundation of feeding the nervous system what it needs. There are three factors important for the nervous system:

1. *Diet.* A healthy diet is very important for keeping the nervous system strong and organized. Many children have food intolerances, allergies,

and problems processing proteins, sugar, preservatives, food colorings, and other additives. Also, with food sensitivities and preferences, it is often hard to provide a well-balanced diet. Although difficult to follow, establishing a good diet is important to organizing the nervous system.

2. *Sleep and rest.* Sleep is also important for regulating the nervous system and keeping the immune system effective. Approximately 50 percent of children on the spectrum have sleeping problems. If the nervous system is not getting enough sleep, it will be taxed and easily fatigued, slowing down an already impaired processing system. The more drained the nervous system, the higher the anxiety. Also, because their nervous system is often stressed throughout the day, it is important for people on the spectrum to take frequent breaks to rebound and re-energize. Their nervous system drains quickly and needs frequent breaks to reorganize. As their nervous system becomes taxed, their processing abilities deteriorate very quickly.

3. *Exercise and physical activity.* Movement and physical exertion are paramount to an organized nervous system. This increases serotonin which organizes the chemistry in the nervous system, keeping it calm, alert, and organized. Exercise will also help stabilize sleep and mood. It releases stress chemicals from the nervous system, reduces anxiety, decreases depression, and increases mood.

These three fundamental factors are primary for the children's nervous system. Additional strategies below can also help the nervous system regulate better:

1. Provide a sensory diet that calms, alerts, and organizes the nervous system. Providing the nervous system with calming stimulation (deep pressure, calming music, slow rocking, etc.) can soothe the nervous system when over-aroused. In turn, when the nervous system is under-aroused and sluggish, providing it with alerting stimulation (swinging, physical exertion, chewy and spicy foods, fast-paced music, fidget objects, etc.) can keep it alert and organized. Keeping the nervous system at an optimal level of arousal is important to lessening anxiety.

2. Engaging in favorite activities can be very organizing to the nervous system. Focusing attention on reading, music, walking, or other favorite activities increases dopamine (the feel-good chemical) which helps calm and organize the nervous system.

3. Relaxation techniques (meditation, mindfulness, yoga, muscle/tension exercises, imagery, etc.), used a couple of times a day, can help release stress chemicals and help the nervous system rebound.

4. Back to nature! Being outside in the country, away from artificial lights, noises, and sounds, can help the nervous system rebound. Also, the sensory patterns of nature (sights, sounds, and smells) can be very organizing to the nervous system. Living in the country often gives people on the spectrum a chance to escape the overwhelming artificial stimulation of the city.

5. Self-stimulation, in the form of repetitive, rhythmic sensory patterns, can help regulate the nervous system by alerting it when under-aroused or calming it when overwhelmed. It also can be used to block out other uncomfortable stimulation. Whether it be movement patterns, vocal patterns, or tactile patterns, the controlled rhythmic patterns calm and organize.

6. Biomedical supplements can be used to change the chemistry of the nervous system and reduce anxiety. They can be used to increase digestion, strengthen a weak immune system, or directly reduce anxiety. These should be taken as prescribed by a medical professional trained in biomedical strategies for those on the spectrum.

7. Lastly, but only in combination with the above strategies, medications can be given to reduce severe, chronic anxiety. Anti-anxiety medication and anti-depressants (SSRIs) have been used effectively with many on the spectrum. These, however, often come with side effects and should be used with caution.

Change conditions causing stress!

Anxiety = environmental demands greater than your abilities to handle them! If the environmental demands (sensory, cognitive, social, or emotional) are greater than the nervous system's current abilities to handle them, anxiety will most likely occur. When the nervous system is constantly taxed by overwhelming stimulation and demands, anxiety will occur. If this situation is ongoing, chronic anxiety will develop. This is often the case for children on the spectrum. Whether it be sensory overload from the bombardment of overwhelming sensory stimulation, information coming too fast for them to process, pressure to perform faster than their ability to do so, or being placed in social situations that they cannot successfully navigate, the nervous system is continually being overwhelmed and taxed. Chronic, generalized anxiety is often the result. With chronic anxiety, the person is bordering on "fight or flight" panic mode. They are hyper-aroused from anticipation and quickly interpret even mild stressors as a threat. Such high arousal will not only drain mental energy but also create physical fatigue which can lead to additional physical vulnerabilities.

To help reduce this overloading stress on the nervous system, we need to better match the sensory, cognitive, and social demands of the environment to the processing needs of the individual. We need to tone down the stimulation that is bombarding him, break down and slow down the information flow to match his processing skills, reduce the intensity of performance demands, and respect his need to pull away and rebound. Be cognizant of the sensory and social processing demands that living in our social world can present for the child. When the nervous system is placed in a situation that it cannot adequately process, anxiety will escalate. This chronic anxiety in turn will reduce the child's current ability to process and cope. We need constantly to assess how the sensory, cognitive, and social demands compare with the child's current strengths and vulnerabilities. This is where modifications and accommodations need to be built in to help reduce the amount of overload attacking the nervous system. Keep these six strategies in mind when trying to accommodate situations for your child:

1. Reduce or modify demands to better match the child's current skill level. Shorten or simplify demands, break tasks down into smaller steps, give visual directions (written, pictures), and give more time to complete projects.

2. If the demands cannot be modified, try distracting or buffering the stimulation/demands with adaptations: sunglasses or rimed hats for bright lights, ear plugs and headphones for loud settings, seat cushions for hard seats, etc. When the environment cannot be modified to turn down the stressors, these adaptations become tools to cope with the challenges.

3. If you cannot modify or accommodate the environment or demands, then help support the child with extra assistance. Provide guided participation, assist with difficult steps, help soothe and encourage. Walk the scary path together; guide and protect.

4. Let the child "pace" the activity/demands himself, so he can better match the demands to his processing speed. Do not rush or pressure. Slow the world down! Give him control over how much and how fast the information/demands come. Do not force the brain to operate faster than it can.

5. Allow the child to pull back and temporarily escape the demands when he starts to become overwhelmed. Allow the child to escape and rebound, then regroup to tackle the situation with added support. Take frequent breaks, keep work sessions short, and allow for physical activity to calm and alert.

6. When you see the child start to shut down (stop responding, stare off in space, put his head down, squint his eyes, etc.), then back away and don't continue prompting. Give the child time and space to regroup. Minimize talking and interacting, and remove task performance demands.

By following these six basic strategies, you will be on your way to creating a less stressful life for your child. Most importantly, always observe and listen to what your child is communicating. Respect his need to slow down, break it down, and clarify the world for him. For a summary of the potential areas of stress and anxiety for people on the spectrum, as well as suggestions for lowering the stress, please see "Fragile World on the Spectrum" in Appendix A.

In summary, start with the fundamental basics (diet, sleep, and exercise) and then add in other strategies as needed to calm and organize the nervous system. An organized nervous system is the first step to managing anxiety.

Make the world more understandable!

In the first post in this chapter, we discussed making sure that we first meet the needs of the nervous system (calm and organize) in order to reduce anxiety. In the second post, we focused attention on changing or modifying the environment demands (sensory, cognitive, and social) to better match the child's processing needs. In this post we will look at reducing uncertainty and providing structure, predictability, and understanding to reduce anxiety.

When your world is very chaotic and confusing, there is a lot of uncertainty, which leads to strong insecurity and anxiety. People on the spectrum require a very concrete, literal, and predictable world to feel secure. Unfortunately, our world is filled with many unwritten, invisible rules, which fluctuate based on situational context. Something can have a specific meaning in one situation and mean something totally different in another situation. A given action can be acceptable in one situation but be rude or unacceptable in another situation. It is hard to be confident in your actions if you cannot accurately read the expectations. The world is just too vague, relative, and unreliable for many on the spectrum. This uncertainty creates ongoing anxiety. For this reason, many children on the spectrum have a strong need to control all activity and interaction around them.

To help deal with this insecurity and anxiety, we have to decrease the uncertainty in their lives. The following strategies can help do that:

1. *Build structure to daily routine.* The more structured and predictable the daily routine is, the less uncertainty there is for the child. When he knows what is coming up next and how his day is going to flow, there is less anxiety. Unfortunately, for many of us, our life is very scattered and disorganized, with little predictable pattern to it. This can cause severe anxiety for children on the spectrum. Using visual strategies such as

written checklists and picture schedules can help make the world clearer and more predictable.

2. *Routine "habits" use less energy!* Keeping familiar routines throughout the day also allows us to skate smoothly through our daily activities without much cognitive effort. We do many routine activities without thinking about them. We do these daily tasks out of habit with little effort. This frees up our mental energy for more important matters. The same is true for our children on the spectrum. Since the world is often chaotic and confusing for them, keeping the simple routines consistent allows children to know what to expect and to perform them with minimal effort. This helps reduce both uncertainty and cognitive effort. This adds predictability and certainty to their world.

3. *Define a path to provide a map!* Many kids on the spectrum go through the day essentially lost, with little concrete direction to lead the way. Since they cannot read the invisible rules that help us make sense of our world, they often do not know what to expect or why they are doing what they are doing. It's the same for all of us: if we do not know how to navigate in our immediate world, we feel anxious. If possible, provide visual (pictures, written) schedules so the kids can *see* what is coming up next and what they are doing. This provides predictable order to their day. These visual schedules provide a nice detailed path to follow. It lets them know what to expect and when to expect it. This alone can drastically reduce anxiety.

4. *Prepare by previewing!* We often lead children into tremendous, unnecessary uncertainty by not previewing for them what is going to happen. We move them from one event to another without much preparation. To reduce uncertainty, it is important that we prepare the children before entering events, by previewing (1) what they can expect, (2) what is expected of them, (3) how long it is going to last, and (4) what is coming up next (afterwards). Lay things out very concretely so the child clearly understands what he is walking into. This helps to reduce uncertainty and anxiety.

5. *Describe as you do!* Since the children often do not understand the invisible rules, and especially the thoughts, feelings, and perspectives of others, it is important for us to describe what is happening (what they don't see) as you are go through the day. Increase understanding by filling in the empty holes from what the children miss. Give the information to complete the understanding. If we are walking through a foreign country, it helps to be with someone who can describe and interpret

for us. So, when doing something together, verbally describe what is happening, why it is happening, and highlight what is invisible. Be the social interpreter for your child.

6. *Don't assume; clarify and verify!* We often assume; since we know, they know! Or, since the child is bright and verbal, he automatically understands. This is bad mistake to make. The child often cannot read the invisible assumptions we make. To maximize understanding, first clarify very literally what to expect, and then verify that he understands.

7. *Ease transitions, prepare for change!* For many children, their brains have difficulty rapidly shifting gears. They do much better if we make out a concrete schedule for what is coming up, and they have warnings or reminders when the one activity is ending and another is beginning, especially if the current activity is a strongly preferred activity. To ease transition difficulties, try to (1) ensure that the child always knows what will be coming up next (watch TV, then bath), and (2) give the child five-, three-, and one-minute reminders that the current activity is going to end (watching TV) and he will move to the next activity (bath). When there are a few minutes before the end of the TV show, say, "Johnny, remember once the movie ends we are taking your bath." This way, the brain is prepared for what is coming up next, and the reminders help bridge the transition.

8. *Have a plan B!* When a favorite activity is cancelled abruptly, the child can explode. For activities, especially preferred activities, that may be cancelled or postponed, discuss a plan B. "If it rains and we cannot go swimming, then we can go bowling instead." This way, the child already is prepared for what may happen and what will happen instead. This works well for common activities that are dependent on weather or factors that you cannot control.

In summary, help reduce anxiety by decreasing the uncertainty in your child's life. Provide predictability to his daily routines, use visual strategies (schedules, directions, etc.) to define a path to follow, prepare him by previewing ahead of time, provide information as you go, verify that he understands, and prepare for change! It may exhaust you, but it will drastically reduce his anxiety. In all seriousness, these strategies may seem overwhelming at first. Do not try to learn these strategies all at once. Use one strategy at a time until it becomes habit for you (remember, habits use little energy, because you do them without thinking about it). Build in one strategy at a time until you do the whole sequence out of habit, without thinking about it. Don't worry, when you forget, your child's reactions will remind you!

Identify, label, and cope with stress!

Since stress is an inevitable aspect of autism, we can empower the children, especially as they get older, to recognize and cope effectively with stress. Stress management is something we all can benefit from; however, we have to make it very concrete for people on the spectrum. Since these children usually have problems accurately identifying, labeling, and evaluating degrees of stress and their emotional/physical response to stress, it is hard for them to cope with it. Parents can help the child understand degrees of stress and help them recognize how they specifically react to them. From there, it is easier to help the child recognize the first signs of stress and learn how to lessen or cope with it.

1. *Rating your stress.* Children on the spectrum have a hard time gauging relative degrees of stress. They live in a world of all or nothing! They are either calm or upset, with little in between. The do not understand that they can be a "little bit" anxious. Once they start to feel anxious, they panic. They do not understand the relative gray area between calm and really upset. For these children, it often helps to create a graded scale to rate the intensity of stress. This consists of creating a visual scale to rate events along a dimension of degree of stress—minimal (a little bit stressful), moderate (somewhat stressful), or intense (very stressful)—and the emotional reactions associated with each degree of stress (annoying, irritating, upsetting, angry). We often make a thermometer to represent the scale. Using such a visual tool can be helpful. Probably the most popular visual rating scale used today is the 5-Point Scale by Kari Dunn Buron and Mitzi Curti (2012).

   Sit down and take examples from the child's daily life, and discuss where they would fall on the scale. Is this event #1 (annoying), #2 (irritating), or #3 (really upsetting)? This helps the children to recognize that not all events involve intense stress. Some are a little annoying, but can be handled with ease. Kids on the spectrum often exaggerate the degree of stress. Take small Post-its and write common daily stressors on them. Place each one alongside the grade scale, based on the degree of stress it causes. This helps the child identify events that are stressful for them, as well as evaluate the degree of stress. Also, as the child goes through the day, you can ask the child, "Is this a little bit stressful or *really* stressful?" Make sure to use the labels you use on the scale. Often, the child will learn not to overreact by cognitively rating the stressor as not that intense (big a deal).

2. *Adequately evaluating the stress.* Whether or not an event is stressful for a person is determined by his evaluation of the event in terms of two factors: the degree of threat the event has for him and the amount of

control he feels he has over the stressor (event). For the first factor, since many children on the spectrum have difficulty evaluating the degree of threat, they automatically respond as if it is a major threat (black and white thinking). This often makes minor snags into major ones. Using a scale (thermometer) to assess the degree of stress can help here.

Regarding the second factor, children with ASD often feel very incompetent in controlling stressful events. Uncertainty and lack of control often produces very strong anxiety and insecurity. This is where knowledge and practice comes in. By discussing the event and rating its degree of intensity, you can begin talking about how to handle the situation. The child learns that in many situations he can have greater control of the event. For example, if he has a fear of vacuums, you can start by showing him how a vacuum cleaner works and what it is used for, and then you can allow him to operate and use it. If the child learns how to control the feared object, the fear reduces. Many children with ASD immediately see the event as something they cannot control. This produces an immediate exaggerated response. Once you feed them the information and let them experience the control they can have, the fear reduces.

3. *Learn strategies for coping with stress.* Children on the spectrum often have very poor emotional regulation and weak ability to calm themselves once upset. Stress management often consists of two calming tools: strategies for coping with the immediate threat, and strategies to use following the event to calm and organize the nervous system. The child may learn to use deep breathing, progressive muscle relaxation, positive self-thoughts, deep pressure techniques, power cards or cue cards, ask for help, play with fidget toys, or ask for a break in order to rebound. This gives the child several tools to use when stressed. Have the child practice the tools and role-play what situations to use them in. Going back to the visual scale with degrees of stress (thermometer), you can identify which strategies to use (fidget toy, deep breathing, etc.) for each level of stress (for mild stress, calming thoughts; moderate stress, deep breathing; intense stress, pull away and take a walk). This way, the child learns not only how to rate the intensity of his stress but also which calming strategies to use with each intensity. From there, role-play and practice the techniques. As the stress occurs during the day, intervene early and cue the child into which strategy should be used. Do it with him and help guide him.

Self-calming tools:

- Physical outlets for energy release: jumping on trampoline, playing drums, riding exercise bike, pushing/carrying, swinging.

- Relaxing techniques: deep breathing, slow rocking, muscle relaxation, meditating, solitude, sleeping, calming self-stimulation.

- Organizing thoughts: writing in journal, diary, intensity scales, feelings book, problem-solving sheets, self-calming statements.

- Favorite activity: listening to music, reading, drawing, focus on topic of interest. Many children can rebound when allowed to engulf themselves in a favorite activity.

Although learning to manage stress is an ongoing project, it is one of the most effective strategies you can teach your children. Throughout their lifetime, stress will be an inevitable component of life. Teaching them to identify, label, evaluate, and cope with stress will be essential tools to learn.

Teaching new coping skills

Most acting-out behavior from children on the spectrum is an attempt to escape or avoid situations that they do not immediately know how to handle. Because the world is filled with so much uncertainty and chaos for the children, they are hyper-alert and "on guard" in any situations in which they do not automatically know what to expect and how to handle them. Consequently, when put in situations of uncertainty, they go into panic and the fight-or-flight stress response. At first, we can help them by making the world more understandable and predictable. We can help lower anxiety and uncertainty by providing strong structure and predictability to their day and by preparing them before heading into events by previewing what they can expect and what is expected of them. This helps avoid some of the uncertainty that freaks our kids out. However, the world is very dynamic and represents continuous change and uncertainty, and the children eventually need to learn how to cope with uncertainty and to deal with anxiety. These are some of the most important tools that we can teach the children: to feel competent in the face of uncertainty, to feel confident tackling anxiety, and to learn coping skills for regulating their emotions.

In order to tackle uncertainty, you need two primary strategies: (1) teaching coping skills to deal anxiety and (2) providing gradual exposure to uncertainty, to learn how to use the coping skills successfully. There are several steps with each strategy that need to be considered.

Learning coping skills

1. First, you have to choose one or two coping skills that might fit well for the child. That will depend on the age, interests, cognitive abilities, and sensory preferences of the child. These can include deep pressure calming

techniques, deep breathing, muscle relaxation, positive distracting thoughts, counting, singing to self, fidget items, focusing on special interests, power cards.

2. Next, the child needs to learn how to use these techniques when not under stress. He needs to practice with you when calm, role-playing situations and learning to feel competent before testing them under fire. We make the mistake of discussing the coping skills with the child, and then expecting the child to use them in the heat of the moment. Even though the child may have intellectually understood what to do, he is not able to perform under fire, leaving both the child feeling more incompetent and the parents feeling confused ("He knew what to do, we discussed it ahead of time. Why didn't he do it?"). Knowing what to do and being able to do it are two different things. The child has to rehearse the technique in role-playing situations to become skillful in implementing it. The role playing has to be lifelike, with coaching from the parent. We usually do this by having the parents and child list recent situations that have caused stress, and write them on index cards. Each day they pick out a couple of cards and role-play the situations, practicing the coping skills. The parents and children do it together, often switching roles and having fun practicing the coping skills.

3. Finally, we often create little snags during the day to practice the coping skills. This creates real-life situations during the daily routine, which produce mild stress in order to practice the coping skills on the spot. There are two aspects to this. (1) Parents will often create little snags for themselves when their child is with them, so the parents can highlight themselves using the coping skills. For example, while doing something with your child, make a simple mistake. While talking out loud, display initial frustration, "Oh no! I just tore the paper! OK…I need to take a deep breath, count to five, and say 'I can handle this.'" This way the child can see you successfully using the technique under stress. Then (2) create simple, mild snags in the child's day where you can immediately pause and coach the child in using the coping techniques.

Gradual exposure to uncertainty

1. Once the child learns how to successfully use the coping skills, then it is time to up the ante. Make a list of common stressful situations for the child, creating a hierarchy of least to most anxiety-provoking situations. The beginning of the list consists of very minor snags that will cause some stress for the child, but not overwhelming stress. Schedule and plan

out frequent situations on the "easy" list, so the child has lots of practice using the coping strategies in easy situations.

2.   If possible, prepare the child ahead of time: "OK…we are going to the store. Now, remember the noise and activity sometimes bothers you. Remember the coping skills we use for this?" If needed, briefly practice them before going into the situation.

3.   When in the event, watch your child closely. As he starts to look a little stressed, pause and coach him: "OK…we are getting a little stressed. Let's practice our deep breathing and counting." Focus on how successful you both are at handling the situation.

4.   As the child becomes skillful in using the techniques in mild events, he is building feelings of competence and confidence in using the skills. As he learns to cope with the mild events, start to gradually work your way up the hierarchy, keeping the anxiety low enough so he can feel it but it is not overwhelming ("just right" challenge). Focus on doing it together and feeling the mastery of tackling the anxiety. This helps build strong feelings of "I can do it!"

By using these two strategies, the child starts to feel more confident and comfortable in tackling stressful situations. You will notice that as the child learns better ways of coping, he becomes less anxious in these situations. His fight-or-flight response gets reset to a higher level, so he does not panic at the first signs of anxiety. He begins to feel more competent facing uncertainty and anxiety. This will help the child learn to cope with the daily stressors that will be inevitable in his life.

Anxiety: distortion of two appraisals

Cognitively, anxiety is often the result of two distorted appraisals. How we perceive the potential threat of an event and how competent we feel in tackling it will determine how anxiety-provoking it is for us. How we cognitively appraise our experiences drastically affects how anxiety-provoking they are for us. Anxiety is often caused by two faulty cognitive distortions: (1) appraising the situation as being a greater threat than it truly is and (2) appraising yourself as being incapable of handling it. The further these two appraisals are apart, the greater the anxiety. If we both over-exaggerate the actual threat of the situation and underestimate our ability to tackle it, our anxiety will increase. When we have poor ability to read situations to accurately appraise the event, we tend to over-exaggerate the potential threat. In addition, as a result of not understanding everything that is expected, if we tend to experience a lot of failure, we tend to feel inadequate in tackling the challenge.

For example, a young child is scared to pet the neighbor's small dog for fear of being bitten. Even though the dog is pretty harmless and unlikely to bite, the child over-exaggerates the chances of the dog biting, and feels pretty helpless in protecting himself if the dog does bite.

Cognitive treatment strategies

To lessen anxiety, cognitive strategies often work by teaching people to more realistically appraise (1) the actual threat of the event and (2) their abilities to handle the situation. Let's look at both appraisals separately.

1. Appraising the threat of a situation.

    a. You can learn to change your appraisal of the "feared" event by having repeated, non-punishing exposure to the situation, so that you learn that it is not as threatening as you thought.

    b. Or you can learn to "question and test out" your faulty belief system that over-exaggerates the threat. There are two questions to explore: (1) What is the probability of the threat occurring in the first place (how likely is it that the threat is going to happen)? (2) How bad would it be if the threat actually occurred (realistically looking at what it would be like if the worse result actually happened)? This strategy can only be used effectively for those with strong cognitive abilities. For those with more severe impairments, the primary strategy is to use the repeated, non-punishing exposure in step (a).

        For example, for a child who is scared of the neighbor's small dog, if he has strong cognitive abilities, he could watch the dog with others and learn that (1) the dog is not likely to bite and (2) if the dog does attempt to bite, it will not be that bad (step b). This, paired with providing the child with repeated exposure of successfully petting the dog (step a), will show the child he can do it without being anxious. If the child is more cognitively impaired, we could only use step a to lessen the anxiety, providing frequent attempts at petting the dog without being bitten.

2. Appraising ability to handle the situation.

    At this step, we want to teach the child that he can effectively master the situation. We would teach the child what to do so that he can successfully tackle the event. We would provide repeated practice so he feels more competent in tackling the challenge. With the example of the dog, we could teach the child how to approach the dog slowly and pet the dog gently, so the dog does not get scared and bite. This way, the child learns to feel more competent tackling the potential threat of the challenge.

By pairing the two steps together, the person learns to more realistically evaluate the situation as less threatening, and also learns that he is more competent in dealing with the challenge than he first thought. You can lessen anxiety by effectively dealing with step 1 or 2, or both together.

Since anxiety will always be present for many people on the spectrum, part of lessening anxiety is to learn to feel competent in the face of anxiety. Many children on the spectrum panic as soon as they begin to feel a little anxious. They can learn to not panic when a little anxious by experiencing repeated exposure of successfully mastering the situations causing the anxiety. To do this, the child needs to learn how to cope with anxiety, and then feel himself successfully mastering his anxiety with these coping skills.

In these situations, the child has to feel the anxiety, so that he can feel himself master the anxiety with the coping skill. So, tackling the anxiety consists of two parts: (1) providing gradual exposure to the stressful event, while (2) using coping skills to master the anxiety being felt. That way, the person learns that these situations are not as threatening as first thought and that he is more competent in dealing with them. The more practice he gets in tackling stressful situations, the more accurate he becomes in appraising the actual threat of situations, and the more capable he becomes in handling the stress. He then becomes confident in tackling future situations.

Physical activity and stress management

Unfortunately, over the years, schools in America have reduced the available time they allow for physical activity during the day. In favor of more time spent on academics, schools have reduced the time the child is engaged in structured physical activity (gym, recess, etc.). Especially in the early years, teachers need to start the school day with at least 10–20 minutes of physical activity that provides movement and physical exertion, and then provide another 10–20 minutes of physical activity at midday. Combining vestibular movement (running, jumping, etc.) with proprioception (pushing, pulling) alerts and organizes the nervous system for concentrating and learning. Healthy movement alerts the nervous system and increases focus, while exertion organizes the nervous system (both releasing stress chemicals and organizing neurotransmitters) by enhancing serotonin. Physical activity is a win–win solution for both calming the hyperactive child and arousing the sluggish child.

In addition, physical activity is a great coping skill for reducing anxiety and dealing with stress. Physical activity releases stress chemicals from the nervous system and better organizes the neurochemistry. It is a great coping skill for both children and adults, on or off the spectrum, who experience ongoing anxiety or depression. Exercise reduces anxiety and enhances mood. The greater the anxiety, the more important the physical exercise. The two 10–20 minute sessions of vigorous exercise are so important for both children and adults, and should be emphasized and established early in life.

Many children on the spectrum have poor muscle tone, coordination, and motor planning. Some avoid physical activity with a passion. They need to be encouraged to get up and move. It will increase their muscle tone, coordination, and self-esteem, as well as lower their anxiety and alert their nervous system. Children on the spectrum, like many of us, are creatures of habit. They need physical activity built into their daily routine, consistently implemented each day. Do it with them, turn it into a fun, sharing activity, and model the value of being active. You will see a calmer, more alert child, as well as the same benefits for yourself. Physical activity is one of the best and least expensive therapeutic tools you can use. Unfortunately, it is not used enough.

Chapter 3

COMFORT ZONES

Novelty and uncertainty: essence of learning

Neurotypical (NT) infants and children are motivated to seek novelty. Mastery of new things becomes a great motivator to learn about the world around them. NT infants are motivated to seek out novelty and master uncertainty. This seeking novelty and mastering uncertainty is the essence of learning and developing. It is also the foundation for feeling competent and developing strong self-esteem. The more novelty (learning) we master, the more competent we feel tackling more. For NT children, the world is a place to explore and learn, continually developing new skills from seeking out and mastering novelty.

For many infants and children on the spectrum, because their sensory systems are so sensitive and their processing is delayed, the novelty and uncertainty of the world can be very chaotic, overwhelming, and frightening to them. Since they tend not to use their parents as a trusted guide and as a "buffer" from the scary world (like NT children), they often feel very vulnerable in the face of uncertainty. These children naturally are motivated to escape and avoid novelty and uncertainty, unless it is static and easy for them to control (lining up cars, spinning things, fixating on repetitive patterns, shiny objects, counting things, playing video games, repetitive behavior patterns, etc.). They want the world to be the same and very predictable. So, instead of being motivated to seek novelty and master uncertainty, which is the essence of developmental learning, they seek to build behavior strategies (rigid thinking, obsessive rituals, compulsive interests, etc.) to escape and avoid the scary novelty and uncertainty. They tend to withdraw into a static world of rigid rituals and routines that is sameness and predictable.

As they mature, although they become a little more competent in tackling the uncertainty, they still do not feel confident taking on the dynamic uncertainty or our world. They continually have to fight the tendency to avoid and escape into a safe world of sameness and predictability, into a world that they can control and keep predictable. Of course, these children vary in their degree of competency in tackling new learning, but that tendency to avoid it is often still there. They seem to have a natural tendency to want to revert to their world of sameness and predictability. They build very structured comfort zones, which can be difficult to stretch.

That is why I teach parents how to start where the child is at (comfort zones) and gradually stretch these comfort zones. By doing so, you don't overwhelm the child and you teach him how to master uncertainty (become competent at learning). The secret is to not keep him in his comfort zone for too long. You want to be continually, but gently, stretching his comfort zone, so he continues to build confidence and competence in tackling novelty and uncertainty. The more successful the exposure to tackling uncertainty, the more his confidence will grow. Mastery is motivating for everyone; however, children on the spectrum just do not experience mastery enough to feel confident tackling the world that is confusing and overwhelming for them.

In essence, many children on the spectrum, because of their fragile nervous system, are steered onto a different developmental path. The NT child gets off on the path of seeking dynamic novelty (learning and developing), and the child with autism goes on an opposite path of learning how to escape and avoid the dynamic novelty by building a world of sameness and predictability. They are two opposite ends of the motivational ladder (seek or avoid).

In this chapter we will be discussing how to stretch these comfort zones. However, we must first build their trust in following our lead, so we slowly guide them through the uncertainty. They need to first feel safe holding our hand while we ease them into the scary world. This is accomplished through the use of apprenticeship mentoring, using "we-do" activities as the vehicle for engaging! Meeting the child where he is at, building that reciprocal engagement, and slowly stretching his trust into new learning. Only through you can the child learn to build the competence and confidence to face and master uncertainty, and take the risks needed to grow. The work of Steven E. Gutstein, Ph.D., founder of Relationship Development Intervention (RDI), has been instrumental in developing this apprenticeship model of teaching. For those seeking further information, please visit RDI's website, www.rdiconnect.com. The concepts of comfort zones have also been expanded upon by Dr. Stanley Greenspan, the founder of the DIR/Floortime Model (www.icdl.com).

Safety in comfort zones! Define them, respect them, but slowly stretch them!

Comfort zones are where children feel safe and secure, with minimal anxiety. They are the zones of familiarity, predictability, and control that serve to buffer the child from the chaotic, confusing world around them. They minimize uncertainty and anxiety. They often include rigid, ritualistic routines. The children can strongly resist stepping outside these comfort zones. Stepping outside these comfort zones usually causes strong anxiety.

Although there can be numerous comfort zones, the following five are very common ones that must be respected.

Sensory

We need to be familiar with what the children's sensory preferences and vulnerabilities are: what overwhelms them, what stimulation alerts them, and what stimulation comforts and soothes them. The child may be hyper-sensitive (sensory avoiders) in some areas and sensory seekers in other areas. They may have sensory issues that set off panic, which must be respected and accommodated for. Because of their sensitivities to bright lights, loud noises, strong smells, and various touches, the world can be very overwhelming and scary for the child. We need to be keenly aware of what their sensitivities are and help soften the sensory bombardment they experience.

In turn, these children will also have sensory preferences that they are attracted to and seek out, and that can be used to engage them. These preferences can also be used to build learning experiences around. They can be used to calm and organize the child. Many of these children also have one preferred sense that they explore their world with and use for learning (tactile, visual, or auditory learning styles). It is important that we identify and use that preferred sense to maximize teaching. By identifying these sensory experiences, we can use these attractions to motivate both relating and learning.

Social

Social anxiety can be very strong for people on the spectrum. Since they have difficulty reading social cues, understanding unwritten social rules, and co-regulating interaction with others, these children are often apprehensive and anxious interacting with others. Since over 80 percent of new learning comes from social learning (watching, copying, and following the lead of others), it is important that we identify the interaction style that works best with your child—the style of relating with the child that helps him feel safe, accepted, and engaged.

Does your child respond best to an animated, jolly approach or to a slow, gentle approach? Does your child crave physical contact or avoid it with a passion? There can be several different comfort zones for the child: (1) the personal interaction style they feel most comfortable with, (2) the amount of social stimulation they can handle at one time before being overwhelmed, (3) the type of social activity (one on one, group of two or three, larger group activities) they can comfortably process, and (4) the level of participation (passively watch, follow along, actively participate, or lead) the child can comfortably handle. After sensory issues, social demands are the next greatest stressor for those on the spectrum. Please identify and respect their comfort zones in these areas.

Emotional

This comfort zone has to do with the general flexibility in emotionally adjusting to variability, novelty, and change around them. It includes how your child experiences and handles his own emotions. Many children have very poor emotional regulation. They get upset very easily, escalate very quickly, and take a long time to calm down. They often are scared of their emotions and can get overwhelmed very easily. They go from 0 to 100 quickly, often in situations that present minimal frustration. It is important to know how your child responds to his emotions and what are the best ways to calm and soothe him. In addition, some of the children are very scared of the emotional reactions of others. If others are upset, agitated, or being criticized, the child may act as if the emotional reactions are his. He may become upset at any intense emotion coming from those around them. The people important in your child's life need to know what helps him feel safe emotionally, and what to avoid in order to keep him feeling safe.

Cognitive

Autism is an information processing difference. Every child on the spectrum has difficulty processing multiple information simultaneously. Much of what we process intuitively, at a subconscious level, children on the spectrum have to process consciously. This can be very taxing and mentally draining. All children have different thresholds for how much and how fast the information can come before they hit information overload. Many children have delayed information processing and need to have information presented visually and sequenced out in small portions at a time, and be given more time to process it.

Many children have auditory processing problems, and do better with visual information (pictures, written directions, demonstration, etc.). If the teaching doesn't match their processing style, then they will often pull back and shut down. It is important to know how much information your child can process at one time, what his best learning style is, how often he needs breaks to rebound, and what strategies help calm and organize him for learning. We must protect the child from becoming mentally drained and overwhelmed. Know how to give it, how much to give, and how fast to give it to keep learning fun.

Uncertainty

This comfort zone has to do with the child's ability to handle uncertainty, not overreact with panic, and rebound quickly once agitated. The more rigid and inflexible the children are, the greater the degree of familiarity and control they need. Children with weak flexibility need strong structure with very predictable routine. Uncertainty scares them extensively, and they will panic when things don't match their expectations. They do not feel competent tackling the normal snags that occur in their daily routine. They will demand to control everything around them to feel safe. So, it is important to define what degree of certainty has to be built into your child's life to feel comfortable. What type of uncertainty, novelty, and new learning can he handle? Does he need rigid routines to feel safe? Does novelty scare him? Does he need to lead everything to feel secure? What degree of certainty does he need to feel safe and secure? It is important to know what rituals and routines help him feel safe and secure, and how much you can stretch them at one time.

Children have a variety of other comfort zones that are very important to them feeling safe, accepted, and competent. You as a parent can best identify these comfort zones and advocate for others to know and respect them. It is very important that, as a parent and strongest advocate for your child, you define your child's comfort zones so that all people working with him can understand what your child is comfortable with, what his fears are, and how to help them feel safe, accepted, and competent. It is very important that you provide teachers, therapists, and any support persons with this information and then demand that they respect the child's comfort zones. If you don't, everyone will be guessing at what is appropriate for the child, often demanding that he conform to their expectations, and pushing the child into panic or shutdown mode.

The Comfort Zones Profile, in Appendix B, provides a document that you can use to help define your child's comfort zones, what vulnerabilities to avoid, and how to engage, teach, and soothe your child when he's upset. Please take the time to fill out this profile and provide it to all the important people (teacher, therapists, support staff, relatives, etc.) in your child's life. Start where the child feels safe, respect his vulnerabilities, and help him feel competent, slowly stretching these comfort zones. Keep it simple, stretch slowly, and continually redefine the child's comfort zones. He will feel safe, accepted, and competent in learning and growing!

Rigidity in comfort zones

Autism comes with strong rigidity in comfort zones. Once they define their comfort zones, children often rigidly hold on to them at all costs. They will actively fight anyone who tries to push them past these boundaries. Their sense of safety and security is very rigidly defined by these boundaries. This has nothing to do with cognitive functioning. Some of the brightest children I know on the spectrum have more rigid comfort zones than the less capable children. These children go into panic mode very easily when presented with new situations or expectations that do not match these comfort zones. They will actively resist anyone who rigidly expects them to suck it up and do it anyway. For most of these children, avoiding uncertainty is of the upmost importance to their security. You need to slowly stretch your child's comfort zones, as he begins to trust you and feel more comfortable with new challenges. However, do it at his pace, not yours. Each child has his own pace for stepping into new challenges. For him to feel comfortable, you have to let him pace the new learning.

The mistake that many make when working with these children is to not identify the children's comfort zones as the first step. Then they unintentionally push the children past these comfort zones. If we try to pressure or push them past these comfort zones, they often freeze and panic, become resistant, or shut down. However, once you understand what their comfort zones are, learn to respect them, and then slowly stretch them, the children can learn and grow like everyone. You cannot learn unless you feel comfortable and confident in tackling the challenges facing you. If the child is pressured past these comfort zones, the brain is in survival mode, rather than receptive to new learning. If this happens frequently, the brain is apprehensive to all new learning, ready to panic with minimal uncertainty. Learning how to identify, respect, and gradually stretch their comfort zones is a major tool in mentoring kids on the spectrum.

Stretching comfort zones

In order for your child to grow and develop, once you define and respect your child's comfort zones it is important that you teach him to feel safe stretching his comfort zones. The biggest mistake we make in respecting the child's comfort zones is allowing him to rigidly hold on to them. The comfort zones help the child feel *safe and accepted*, but stretching the comfort zones helps him feel *competent*. The longer the child stays in his comfort zone, the harder it is to get him to stretch it. The longer he avoids stretching, the more rigid the comfort zone becomes. So, helping the child learn and grow is a constant balance between respecting the comfort zones while continually stretching them. The two biggest mistakes we tend to make are either ignoring or not respecting the child's comfort zones or going the other way and allowing the child to stay in the comfort zones too long without stretching them.

So, mentoring children on the spectrum consists of guiding them to safely stretch their comfort zones, so that they eventually feel more and more confident stepping outside their comfort zones. The secret to stretching is to add just a small amount of new challenge at a time, so that the child feels the challenge, but not so much that it overwhelms him, thus setting off his fight-or-flight panic response. This is part of the comfort zone profile: identifying how much can you comfortably stretch, while allowing the child to feel the challenge but keeping it simple enough to successfully master. This is accomplished by two factors: (1) only adding a little challenge at a time and (2) providing guidance and support to maximize success in mastering the new challenge. By providing numerous trials of successfully stretching their comfort zones, the children begin to feel

(1) more confident in risking and (2) more trusting of following your lead when stepping outside their comfort zones.

To teach the child to feel safe when stretching and learning, it is important to keep the stretching going. Don't stop. Don't allow the child to stay in his comfort zone too long. Once you learn how to stretch and how to keep him feeling competent in stretching, do not allow him to stay in a comfort zone very long. Once he has assimilated the new learning (challenge), up the ante again. Keep upping the ante, small amounts at a time, as long as the child is experiencing success. If success breaks down, back up and break the new challenge down into smaller, safer amounts, or add extra support to help the child succeed. Also, keep in mind that it is OK for the child to experience frustration at times, so he can feel himself mastering the frustration. He cannot succeed every time, and he needs to learn that sometimes you have to fail to succeed.

"Just right" challenge

All learning is tackling uncertainty. So, in order to learn and develop, the child has to become more confident in facing and tackling uncertainty. The "just right" challenge is the small band of new learning (uncertainty) that the child can feel confident handling, with needed support. It provides a little anxiety, but not enough to overwhelm him. Again, the child needs to feel comfortable trusting your support and guidance in scaffolding the new learning so that he can (1) feel the challenge (a little anxiety) and (2) feel himself master the challenge. You must feel the challenge (anxiety) in order to feel the mastery. This way, the child learns to feel competent in the face of a little anxiety, and confident in tackling the anxiety. This comes from your ability to:

- frame the new learning to be within the "just right" range (enough to feel the challenge, but not enough to overwhelm the child), plus frame the new learning so it maximizes the chance of success.

- provide guided participation to support the child in maximizing success. However, avoid providing so much guidance that the child doesn't feel himself mastering the challenge. He has to be actively engaged, with you guiding his active engagement, to feel himself mastering the challenge. As the child feels the mastery of tackling the challenge by following your lead, he will gain greater trust in following your lead in the future. This mentoring relationship becomes vital in the child's confidence in risking uncertainty. So, the mentor has to become competent in adding new challenges, as well as guiding the child so that he feels himself mastering the challenges. This builds confidence and trust in following your lead for further learning.

Principles of stretching

1. Start where the child is at:

    a. start in the child's comfort zone

    b. where the child feels safe.

2. Keep it simple:

    a. start with small steps

    b. steps that will be easily mastered with support ("just right" challenge).

3. Build gradually:

    a. build one step on a time

    b. add greater challenges, just outside child's comfort zone.

4. Maximize success:

    a. provide support to maximize success

    b. when snags arise, back up and make steps smaller.

These four steps to successful stretching are good for setting up new learning, as well as troubleshooting when teaching breaks down. If you start in the child's comfort zone, he can feel safe. New learning often fails because we immediately throw the child into too much, with not enough support, and the child does not feel competent tackling the uncertainty. Repeated failure results in panic when faced with new situations. So, make sure you start in the child's comfort zone where he already feels competent, before adding new learning.

Once the child is feeling comfortable, then add a little new learning (challenge). Keep it small and within the child's capabilities of mastering. Keeping it simple is adding enough new learning to stretch the child's abilities, while not overwhelming him by eliciting his fight-or-flight response. As long as you are continually stretching, you can stretch just a little at a time and learning can move forward smoothly. While stretching, it is important to provide guided support as needed to help the child experience mastery. I prefer doing it together, side by side, with the parent assisting and supporting the child. As the child becomes more competent, you give him a bigger role. By doing with you, task performance anxiety is decreased and the child learns to feel competent and trusts following your lead. This solidifies the mentoring relationship.

If the child starts to struggle, more than likely you made the new step too large or didn't provide enough support. When progress stops or the child resists, back up to the last successful step and break the new challenge down into simpler steps. Remember, the mentor needs to take responsibility for the breakdown, not the child. When in doubt, go back and evaluate all four of the principles above to see where the breakdown in progress occurred.

Tools for stretching: exposure plus support!

Effective stretching consists of a balancing act between gradual exposure to the new challenge and gradually fading out support during the exposure. While slowly stretching, the child will need more support when first facing the uncertainty, needing less and less as he feels more competent handling the challenge.

Graduated exposure

1. Provide gradual exposure to uncertainty or new learning.

2. Provide just enough new learning to stretch the comfort zone, but not enough to overload.

3. Continue to stretch, gradually increasing the uncertainty.

Supportive assistance

1. Provide assistance and support to help the child through the new learning.

2. Provide just enough assistance for the child to feel supported, but allowing the child to feel the mastery.

3. Provide repeated mastery of tackling uncertainty to build greater confidence.

As you can see, effective mentoring consists of (1) gradual exposure to new learning and (2) supportive assistance in guiding the child to success. With any guidance, you want to be continually grading the assistance so the child feels himself doing it and mastering it. Effective guidance involves continually fading the assistance as the child becomes stronger. It is a balancing act of guiding and fading as competence is established.

THE ART OF STRETCHING

Below is an example of using the four principles of stretching (start where the child is at, keep it simple, build gradually, and maximize success), as well as the two tools of stretching (graded exposure and guided participation) to help a child tackle his fear of crowded places. Stay true to these principles and you maximize success!

Example #1: Fear of crowded places

- Problem: Jamie will frequently melt down in crowded settings in the community.

- Comfort zone: Jamie can handle familiar events with no more than one or two strangers.

- Stretching: Start with brief outings to familiar stores during low-activity times. Gradually increase time and number of people.

- Procedure: Start by going into a small convenience store to buy no more than three predetermined items and a sucker.

- Supports: Prepare the child before entering; hold his hand; end the event with a reward; briefly leave the event if he becomes anxious.

- Stretching: Gradually add a few more settings (gas station, library, dry cleaners). Gradually expand to larger stores with greater numbers of people. Gradually move from familiar settings to novel settings.

In this example, the principles of stretching are displayed. Jamie has difficulty going out into the community. He gets overwhelmed by the activity, noise, and novelty of dynamic settings. His parents have tried keeping him in these situations to try to teach him how to handle the outings, but the more they pressure, the more problems he has. In further analysis, we looked at outings where he was successful, as compared with ones where he wasn't. Two variables stood out: he did better (1) in familiar settings that they visited frequently and (2) if the setting only had one or two people in it. This defines his comfort zone (familiar settings with no more than two extra people in them). The third variable we considered was time spent in the event. Jamie's parents figured that he does pretty well for about the first 15–20 minutes, and then the uncertainty gets too much for him. So, we decided to keep the first outings at 15 minutes or less to maximize success.

So, looking at our four principles of stretching, we started with the child's comfort zones (familiar setting, with fewer than three people, and for 15 minutes or less). From that, we then made a hierarchy of the settings (events) based on the likelihood of them producing anxiety for Jamie (starting with the least likely, moving toward the most likely). Since the local convenience store is a place that he has had some success in, we decided to start there. The parent could gauge how many people were in the store by how many cars were in the parking lot. We wanted to frame and scaffold the outings to maximize success. We wanted to lessen the uncertainty by previewing with the child what he was going to do, how long he would be in there for, what they were going to purchase, and that he could buy a sucker when leaving. They also discussed that if he got overwhelmed, they could leave the store briefly to rebound, and then go back into the store if he desired. We felt that if he knew what to expect, how long he could expect it to occur, and reassured him that he could escape at any time he was overwhelmed, he would be less anxious. We gave him the job of checking off each item on the shopping list as his mom found them. He mentioned that he would feel more comfortable holding mom's hand, so we built that in. This allowed Jamie to feel that his mom was a working partner with him, and helped him to trust following his parent's lead. He handled this step with ease, which we figured he would. We wanted him to experience easy success with the first step.

Once successful at this step, we decided to start stretching by gradually increasing the number of people who were in the store. Mom would time their entrance for when there were a couple more people in the store, which also increased the time he would have to stand in line. We continued to prepare him ahead of time by previewing what they were going to buy and had him check off the items. We stayed with this step, gradually going at busier times. Once Jamie was successful with this setting, we added the grocery store, which was larger, busier, and more chaotic. We started with only ten minutes at first because we knew it would be harder for him. However, he was feeling pretty competent with the procedures of previewing everything ahead of time, and then allowing him to check off the items on the list. He eventually became familiar with some of the staff at the store and looked forward to talking to them. He still had anxiety over the size and number of people in the store, but focusing on the list allowed him to handle it.

For the first trip, he requested to go to the car three minutes into the trip. However, once the anxiety subsided, he wanted to go back in to finish the trip. We think this "testing" established better trust that he could leave if he got overwhelmed, which in turn lessened his anxiety. Jamie started feeling really good about mastering his anxiety. He was feeling more competent. From there, we began gradually adding more settings (with his approval), increasing the size and activity level of the setting. He had a couple of slip-ups, but he was able to leave the setting, regroup, and then re-enter. This led him to feel more comfortable entering new situations because he realized he could simply leave if he became overwhelmed. With each successful trial, he was experiencing greater mastery and stronger feelings of confidence. If at any time Jamie was unsuccessful, we dropped back to the last successful step and made the next step smaller. We continued to increase the types of settings, length of time in the settings, and the number of people in the setting. The procedures of previewing ahead of time, giving him a role to play (checking-off list), and allowing him to briefly leave the setting if overwhelmed continued in all the settings.

Example #2: Rigid/inflexible thinking

- Problem: Brad melts down when things don't go exactly the same way all the time.

- Comfort zone: Family has to do everything the same way (set rituals/routines) to pacify Brad.

- Stretching: Gradually build in greater variations into the child's day.

- Procedures:

    ○ Add simple variations to what you do; do things in a slightly different way, make little changes to the way you do things. Develop plan B(s).

    ○ Make a hierarchy of least to most anxiety-provoking routines in your child's day. Start with very small, simple variations and gradually work up the hierarchy.

    ○ Teach "same but different" and "more than one way."

Brad has rigidity issues that are common for many on the spectrum. He has moderate generalized anxiety and is fearful of uncertainty. He needs to keep his world very predictable; hence, he does better when his day is very routine and predictable. Unfortunately for the family, he holds tight to some very rigid routines (dressing, mealtime, before bed, leaving the house, doing self-care, etc.) and dictates that the entire family follow his desire for sameness. If any variation occurs, it has to be initiated and controlled by him.

To keep peace and some calmness in the family, the members basically learned to give in to Brad's demands and allow him to control everything that went on in the household. If the family resisted, he would get upset, holler and scream, slap himself, and sometimes hit others or throw things. The longer this went on, the harder it was to stretch Brad's comfort zones. Brad and his family members became captive to the demands that he needed to feel safe and secure.

So, for Brad the starting point was in his comfort zone, where he felt safe. We used the Comfort Zone Profile to determine what his comfort zones were, so we could begin to slowly stretch his need for rigid routine. The two main variables were (1) having very familiar, predictable routines and (2) being in control of the activity in order to make everything according to his expectations. We started by respecting his two comfort zones, letting him keep his rigid routines and allowing him to control what was happening to him. We had the parents turn these routines into "we-do" activities (parents engaging with him) during his daily routine, in order to start developing a trusted mentoring role. Once Brad felt comfortable engaging with his parents, we started having the parents put in little variations into the activities, to start stretching his comfort zones a little.

We wanted to program in little changes throughout the day (e.g. doing things a little differently, at a different time, in different order).

We developed a hierarchy of least to most anxiety-provoking changes that we could make in his routines. For example, he did better when things did not occur at the exact same time, as compared with doing things a different way. He also handled snags better in the morning routine than he did in the evening routine. He was more flexible with handling variations at bathtime, than he was at dinnertime. So, we made a list of variations that produced minimal anxiety, those that represented moderate anxiety (acting out 50% of times), and those that were high anxiety. We started by picking three events at the minimal-anxiety level to start building in little variations (used a different soap at bathtime, then a different towel, then a different shampoo, etc.).

In addition, since we wanted eventually to build in variations to his routine, we wanted to give Brad a tool to provide him with structure and predictability but also allow variability. We decided to use a picture scheduling board to structure out his time. Then, when changes in routines were going to occur, we made the changes on the picture board to allow him to see the change, talk about the change, and see how everything would continually flow by what was on the schedule board. This way, his need for predictability was maintained by the picture schedule, even though we would change the sequence of how things were being done. He knew what was coming up and when it was occurring. Eventually, he was allowed to make changes in his routine and we were allowed to make changes, as long as we (1) represented the change on the picture schedule and (2) previewed this with him ahead of time.

To help Brad tackle changes and events being cancelled, we started preparing him ahead of changes by previewing and reviewing what was going to happen. For events that were not certain to happen (may get cancelled because of rain, time, etc.) we always discussed a plan B, which reviewed what would happen if the event got cancelled (what else he could do). This alleviated a lot of stress for both Brad and his family. Although sudden changes would still overwhelm him, he started learning how to use his written lists, schedules, previewing, and making plan Bs to minimize his anxiety over the variations in his life. Over time, we worked on using counting and deep breathing, with a problem-solving worksheet to deal with major episodes of anxiety arising from change. This way, he started to feel less anxious when unexpected change came his way.

This approach successfully used our four main principles of stretching. We started where the child was at (his comfort zones), kept it simple by slowly stretching without overwhelming him, provided assistance and added support with a picture schedule, previewed expectations ahead of time, and used plan Bs for unpredictable events. We increased trust in his parents by engaging together in "we-do" activities, which allowed him to feel more comfortable with little snags that came his way. Also, if the planned variations overwhelmed him, we immediately pulled back and broke the changes down into smaller steps. We immediately made changes, rather than requiring him to change.

Trying new things: stretching comfort zones

One of the common complaints I get from parents is that the children are reluctant to try new things. It's almost as if the kids need to be pushed into new things. Many parents and professionals interpret this as a lack of motivation. However, often it is the children's fear of uncertainty that keeps them from trying new things. When you don't feel competent tackling uncertainty, then trying new things is scary and you fall back into the sameness of your comfort zones. These children need the predictability of sameness to feel safe. No one wants to feel vulnerable and inadequate, so they fight being placed in situations of uncertainty. The following are tips that I have used to teach children to try new things and stretch their comfort zones:

1. Some kids on the spectrum will give you an "automatic no" to anything you ask of them, especially if it is a request to try something new. Try not to give them an option of participating. Do not word your directions with "Do you want to _____?" or "Would you like to _____?" Use language that expects participation: "It is time to _____." Give them a choice of a couple things to do, but not whether they participate. Throw the expectation out there.

2. If uncertainty is what is scary for them, then lessen the uncertainty by preparing them. Start by preparing what they can expect before entering the event. Go over what they can expect to happen, what will be expected of them, how long it will last, and how they can escape the event if it is too much for them to handle. Discuss it, have them watch it before participating, and talk about what aspects make them nervous. This often helps a lot.

3. When working with children who have siblings, I will often ask the sibling to participate with me to demonstrate what is expected, so the child can see it vicariously. Once the child sees what he can expect and what is expected of him, plus how much fun it is, then he is more willing to participate.

4. To increase motivation, I will use the "Premack principle," which is rewarding participation in a non-preferred activity with a preferred activity. If the child's main interests are videos and trains, then I use access to videos and trains contingent on short participation in the other activity. First we do *this* (activity you want them to participate in), then

you can do *that* (video or trains). You use the activity that they are fixated on to increase participation in the other activity. Keep the new activity short and easy at first. This makes obtaining the preferred activity easy. Gradually lengthen (stretch) the time as they become used to participating.

5. If the child needs support, offer to do the activity with him, providing guidance as needed. Take the task performance anxiety off the child by doing it with him. Do the task together, bridging the difficult parts and maximizing success.

6. Some children have a hard time with unpredictability and transitions. If that is the case, use a visual (picture or written schedule) so the sequence of activities throughout the day is very concrete. This way, he can see the activities that will be coming up. We usually space a preferred activity (videos, trainings, etc.) after every couple of non-preferred activities (homework, self-care, chore, etc.), so the child can see when the fun activities are occurring and what he needs to do to get to them. For each activity coming up, let him know what it is and what activity will follow it. For example, if he is going to watch TV for 30 minutes (favorite show), then let him know that once the show is over, it is time to brush his teeth. This way he knows that when TV time ends, then he brushes his teeth. Use visual timers to help him gauge how much time he has. Now, help bridge the transition by giving him warnings before it is time to end the current activity and go on to the next activity. For example, "Ben, in three minutes you will have to end TV time and brush your teeth." Then remind him at one minute, and then end it on time. This way his brain is being prepared to switch from the one activity to the other. Now, once he starts to transition into brushing his teeth, tell him what will follow brushing his teeth. By telling him what he is going to do, and then what will follow it, you are preparing him for these transitions.

7. Build new activities different from the child's current interests so that he has natural motivation. If he likes race cars, then do as many different new activities as you can think of using race cars. Read about them, research them on the internet, take him to car races, buy a race car set, keep a scrapbook about different race cars. This way, you are stretching his comfort zones by expanding on his preferred interests!

8. Slowly stretch his interest by starting small and gradually building greater variability in activities, as well as the amount of time participating. Start with the most likely activities to gain responsiveness, and gradually add more difficult ones as he gets used to stretching his comfort zones.

Every child has different levels of comfort zones. If you allow your child to withdraw into these comfort zones for long, he will actively resist stepping outside them. Keep the expectation within a reasonable challenge, but keep the expectation just the same. Unless he expands, it is difficult to grow. Over time, he will become less anxious about trying new things. However, always expect that you may need to use an external reward and concrete structure to keep it happening.

Don't pressure me or shield me; support me!
Moving from feeling safe and accepted to feeling competent!

It is not enough to help the children feel safe and secure by shielding them from uncertainty; help them feel competent in tackling it! Many people think that confidence and self-esteem come from praise and validation. Although praise is important, words from others cannot build confidence and self-esteem. Confidence and self-esteem come from facing and tackling challenges. Feeling competent can only come from successfully tackling uncertainty.

The secret is to provide the right balance of risk versus support. It seems as if people want to either push the children into situations that are too demanding (sink-or-swim mentality) or want to protect them from anxiety by shielding them from the challenges. The secret to challenges is not to push them forward unprepared or have them avoid the challenge altogether by shielding them from it; it is to match the challenge to the child's current abilities. We can either modify the demands to better fit the child, provide added assistance to support the child, or a combination of both. Either way, you want the child to feel the challenge and then support him through it. To build competence and confidence, the child needs to feel himself mastering the challenge. Avoiding the challenge will not build competence and serves to maintain low self-esteem ("I cannot do it, I have to avoid it").

To build strong confidence and self-esteem, the child needs numerous experiences of successfully mastering realistic challenges. He needs frequent, successful opportunities of mastering uncertainty. Uncertainty represents strong anxiety for many on the spectrum. To build confidence, the child needs numerous experiences tackling situations of low anxiety. To risk is to grow! When risking is successful, the child learns not to fear risking but to tackle it.

So, provide the child with countless opportunities to master small challenges in all areas of life. Whether it is homework, field trips at school, family events, or birthday parties, we need to continually stretch the child by presenting new challenges, a little past his comfort zones. Enough challenge to create low doses of anxiety, but not strong enough to overwhelm the child—the "just right" challenge. That may mean lowering the demands to just a step above where the child is at, or providing just enough support to maximize success, but not so much that the child doesn't feel himself mastering it.

When providing assistance, we want to support the child, not do it for him! He has to feel the challenge to feel the mastery. Mastery is intrinsically rewarding for all children. Once they feel it repeatedly, they will be motivated for more. Throughout the day, build in these little challenges by holding back and letting the child take "baby steps" to experience frequent mastery. Pause and give the child a chance to tackle it. Frame the activity to maximize success. Pause and then provide guidance, but let him do it. For the daily challenges that we typically tackle for him, frame the demands to match the child, or provide the support to make exposure to such challenges successful. It is OK for him to feel the anxiety, so he can learn to tackle it. Otherwise, he will learn to avoid every time he is faced with a challenge.

Let's all make a resolution not only to help the child feel safe and accepted, but also to help him feel competent. Don't just praise and validate, but provide supported challenges that will allow the child to feel competent mastering them!

Chapter 4

CHALLENGING BEHAVIOR

It comes as no surprise to anyone that individuals with autism can present a variety of challenging behaviors. With all the struggles they face, with often limited skills, their lives are filled with ongoing stress, frustration, and anxiety. Often these challenges are due to being overwhelmed by the sensory, cognitive, social, or physical demands that are placed on them, not having the ability to communicate a need or want, when they do not understand expectations or how to meet them. We have discussed how most challenging behavior (self-abuse, aggression, noncompliance, property disruption, tantrums, etc.) occurs when the children are placed in situations where the demands of the situation are greater than their ability to deal with them. Consequently, many of the tools discussed in this book are designed to help lessen or modify the demands, provide supportive accommodations, teach functional skills for dealing with the demands, or provide extra assistance to support the child through the demands.

Before discussing some of the most common behavior challenges in autism, there are two points that I would like to make. First, to gain a good understanding of behavior issues, a functional behavior assessment (FBA) by a person trained to complete them should be obtained. Although a comprehensive description of functional behavior assessment is beyond the scope of this book, it is briefly described in Chapter 8, Effective Discipline. Also, Appendix C includes a more detailed look at completing comprehensive behavior assessments, combining both functional behavior assessments and core deficits assessments for a comprehensive understanding of challenging behavior. Appendix D includes a brief Functional Behavior Assessment Scale for those seeking a questionnaire form.

Although a variety of challenging behaviors is discussed in this chapter, the common challenges of meltdowns are not included here. Emotional regulation challenges and meltdowns, as well as detailed strategies for supporting them, are discussed extensively in the companion book *The Autism Discussion Page on the core challenges of autism: A toolbox for helping children with autism feel safe, accepted, and competent* (Nason 2014). Also included in that book is a detailed analysis of self-stimulatory behavior.

Do you think I am having fun?

From the child's perspective!

Do you think I am having fun when I scream, fall to the floor, and repeatedly slam my head?

Do you think I am enjoying it when I melt down in the middle of a classroom with the other kids staring at me?

Do you think I am having fun when I cannot sit still, and am running around the room, bouncing off the walls, ignoring your assistance?

Do you think I am having fun when I am staring into space with glassy eyes, and turning away to block you out because I am overwhelmed and shutting down?

Do you think I am having fun when I repeatedly hit my face with my fists until all the frustration is gone?

Do you think that I enjoy hitting, kicking, and biting you when I love you?

When I hear people discussing my behavior, what is there that leads them to believe that I like to do this; that I find enjoyment in creating havoc, stress, and anxiety for myself and others? Do you think I would do this if I had better ways of dealing with the problem? When I am continually acting out to gain your attention, you say I am "seeking attention" (as if I enjoy it) and then put me on extinction (ignore me). Do you ever think about why I need constant attention in the first place? Why am I acting inappropriately to obtain attention? Instead of ignoring me, try to listen and understand why I have the need to act this way. Seeking attention may be the obvious reason, but ask yourself (1) why do I need so much attention, and (2) why am I using this behavior to get it? Don't just ignore me. It doesn't teach me anything, but makes me feel isolated and unwanted. It does not deal with the reason that I need the attention, or teach me better ways of getting it.

When I act out because of the demands you place on me, you force me to comply so my acting out is not rewarded by allowing me to escape. You say I act out to manipulate you to avoid things I do not like. Have you asked yourself, "Why does he feel the need to escape or avoid?" "What is there about the demand that makes him want to run?" If most children willfully comply, why am I resisting so adamantly? Don't you think if I had the tools and felt confident enough to do it successfully, that I would also want to do it? If my brain is overwhelmed, how can I think and cope?

When I become overwhelmed in events with overpowering sounds, sights, and smells, why would you think that forcing me through it is somehow helping me? If my brain becomes overloaded with stimulation, how can I be expected to handle it? What is that teaching me, if my brain doesn't allow me to learn during those moments? How can forcing me to be overwhelmed help me learn to handle it?

I wonder why you do not ask these questions. You call me a manipulator, lazy, disrespectful, oppositional, as if I somehow intentionally choose to act this way, assuming I know how to act differently. At your meeting, you sit at a table and discuss among yourselves how I must learn to act better, to not be spoiled, learn to respect others, and comply with your demands; as if I am somehow having "fun," intentionally choosing to act this way. You do not look at what you might need to change, but try to force change on me. You scold, force, punish, and restrain me, as if I purposely want to be this way. Are you that DUMB to not think that if I knew how to do it right, and I felt confident doing so, I wouldn't have more "fun" being cooperative and receiving the positive attention and rewards like all the other children. Look at my face! Look at my actions! Look at my emotions! How do you assume that this is fun?

Please let me tell you, if I felt good about myself, confident in what I am doing, and safe and accepted by you, I would not be acting this way. Either the demands of the situation are greater than I can handle, the way you are supporting (or not supporting) me is overwhelming me, or I do not feel safe in doing it. I do not mean to "piss you off"! I do not find joy in making you angry and lash out at me in frustration. I am not having fun in watching everyone stare, scold, and ridicule me into submission. How do you think that timing me out, taking away privileges, and restraining me helps me to feel safe, accepted, and competent in your presence?

Please, when you look at me struggling, assume that I am feeling anxious, insecure, and, most importantly, "inadequate" at the moment. The stronger the opposition, the more insecure and inadequate I am feeling. Then, ask yourself how can you (1) change the expectations and demands to better match my abilities, (2) provide greater assistance to support me, and (3) teach me better skills for meeting these expectations. And most importantly, in the heat of a meltdown, think "How can I help him feel safe?" not "How can I control him?" And when it is over with, ask yourself how you can change the conditions next time to avoid setting me into "fight or flight," rather than how you can punish my behavior into submission. You are the one placing me in these conditions; you are the one who has to learn to change! Yes, like all children, I need realistic boundaries and consequences to learn to be successful; however, meet me where I can realistically succeed, be a supportive mentor, and please do not assume that I am having fun and prefer to act this way!

Thank you for listening to me. Please do it more often!

Irrational behavior!

Often the behavior of children with autism makes little sense to us, and even appears irrational. However, all behavior is rational (makes sense) if we can see the world from the eyes of the child. When you can see the world from how the child experiences it, the behavior usually makes sense!

I learned this lesson when I was an intern. I was working with a young man who was referred to me for running down the street screaming and stripping his clothes off. At first thought, this behavior seemed truly irrational; there was no apparent reason for its occurrence, no obvious adaptive function that it served. However, after gaining the person's trust, he relived the experienced for me, telling me that his clothes were on fire and he was screaming and trying to get the burning clothes off of him. He was, in his words, "freaking out" because his clothes were burning. So, what initially looked like very irrational behavior now made more sense. Although he was hallucinating and delusional, he was responding to an experience that was very real for him. From that moment on, I realized that we must first see the world from how the person is experiencing it to truly understand the behavior and eventually help the person.

Once we understand what function the behavior serves and what the child is trying to communicate with the behavior, it makes sense. We need to make sense of the behavior, identify the function the behavior serves, in order to truly help the child. Once it makes sense, then it is a lot easier to support the child and teach more appropriate alternative responses. We must listen, observe, and investigate closely in order to understand and make sense of the behavior. We must be able to see the world the way the child does to truly understand his behavior.

We have to know the child's sensitivities, vulnerabilities, and current skill level to grasp how he is experiencing the world. We often make the mistake of jumping in and trying to change the behavior, before understanding it. Not only do we often guess wrong, but we also invalidate the child by trying to change him rather than teach more appropriate ways of meeting his needs. So, when you first see a behavior that seems irrational, take your time to listen, observe, and understand it before trying to change it.

Change conditions first, before trying to change the child

When the child is acting out, behaving inappropriately, or not progressing as expected, it is very tempting to blame the child. The first tendency is to expect the child to change to meet our expectations, instead of changing our expectations to match the child. We somehow assume it is the child's fault if they don't match our expectations; therefore, it is the child's responsibility to change. This can be very damaging to children, especially since they often do not have the skills or abilities to make those changes.

To avoid this trap, we must start with the premise "Assume the child is doing the best he can, given the situation he is in, and his current skill level in dealing with it." Most often, if the child is behaving inappropriately or not meeting expectations, then the demands of the situations are greater than his current abilities to deal with them. Given that assumption, then it naturally leads us to (1) re-evaluate our expectations and the demands we are placing on the child, in light of his current skill deficits and (2) either lower the demands (expectations) or provide greater supports in helping the child meet the demands (or a combination of both). When the demands match the current abilities of the child, the child will learn and grow.

So, when faced with either behavior challenges or learning difficulties, we need to evaluate three primary conditions to support the child:

1. *Change the demands and expectations.* First look at gaining success by changing the demands. In light of the child's physical, sensory, cognitive, social, and emotional vulnerabilities, could the expectations and demands be changed to better match the child's current skills? The sensory demands of the environment could be overwhelming for the child, the

social demands may be way too confusing for the child, or the task demands may be way above what the child can handle. Break it down, make it simpler, and build in extra support to help the child out.

This is where modifications and accommodations are important to match the environmental and task-related demands to the child. First, look at the physical settings that the child is in (classroom, cafeteria, gym, music room, hallways, etc.). Are they too loud? Is there too much activity? Is there too much sensory stimulation that overloads or distracts the child? Are there modifications that can be built in to lower the sensory noise in the room, or accommodations that can be made, such as seating arrangements, ear plugs, sunglasses, or other tools to mask the interfering sensory noise? Second, are the task demands too overwhelming for the child? Is there too much work, is the work too difficult, or is it presented in the wrong way? Can the work be broken down or presented more visually? Can assistance be provided to lower the demands to match the processing needs of the child? Can the child handle the ongoing demands for a full school day? Once his mental energy runs out, he will become overwhelmed quickly and often shut down.

2. *Change our interactions with the child.* Once the demands/expectations are modified to match the child, then look at how we interact and teach the child. Does the child need assistance or guided support? Am I presenting the information favorably? Does the child feel supported and validated by me, or am I being too demanding? Does the child welcome my support? If the child is to be successful, we need to find the right approach that helps support his learning. We need to ask, "Does the child feel safe, accepted, and competent with me?" If the child is anxious, fearful, or insecure in our approach, he will naturally try to escape and avoid our guidance. Many behavior challenges are directly related to how the adult is interacting with the child. What interaction style (slow and quiet, upbeat and animated, etc.) does the child respond best to? How others are interacting with and teaching the child will have a lot to do with him feeling safe and learning.

3. *Teach the skills needed to be successful.* Once we have lowered the demand, provided needed support, and changed our interaction style, then we need to concentrate on teaching the child better skills to deal with the demands. If the child is struggling socially in school, then we need to teach better social skills. If he is having trouble with controlling his emotions, then we need to teach coping skills. If he is having trouble reading, then work more on teaching reading skills. This way, we are giving the child the tools necessary for meeting the environmental demands. Start

simple, build gradually, provide support as needed, and develop the skills necessary for success.

Once we meet these three conditions, rarely do we need to blame, force, or punish the child. When the child is struggling, we are the ones who need to make the changes, not the child. We are the ones who are placing the child in situations that he cannot handle. So, let's first look at changing what we are asking of the child and how we are supporting the child, before looking to blame or change the child. Everyone will be successful and feel competent about what they are doing!

Validating emotions before punishing behavior

When a child is upset and acting out, we tend to focus on stopping the behavior as our first priority. When doing so, we often punish the behavior, without first understanding why it is occurring. Frequently, the children don't have good abilities to control their emotions, nor the impulse control needed to check their impulses before acting on them. So, when we punish the behavior, we are punishing their emotions as well. This tends to invalidate the children (punishing them for something they do not have control over); also it does not teach them better ways of handling their emotions. I often recommend that whatever technique you use to reduce problem behavior, first acknowledge and validate the child's feelings, then deal with the behavior. Try starting out the intervention this way:

1. Acknowledge that the child is upset: "Wow…Johnny, you really look upset to me!"

2. Next, validate that is OK to be upset: "I understand that you are upset because you cannot have _____ right now. That might make me upset too." This does not mean you have to agree with him or approve of his behavior; just acknowledge and validate how he feels.

3. Finally, help the child problem-solve or understand when or how he might get what he wants. Focus on what you want the child to do, not on any negative behavior.

4. If the child is too upset to talk reasonably with you, simply say, "You are too upset to talk right now. That's OK; you let me know when you are calm enough to talk." Then minimize any attention given to the upset behavior. Do not try to reason with a child who is acting out. Show little emotion, speak matter-of-factly, and only reason and problem-solve once the child is calm enough to talk.

5. After the child calms down enough to talk, then return to steps 1–3.

This respects the child, even if we are punishing the behavior (I am not recommending punishing the child). Focus first on the feelings, not the behavior: "It is OK to be upset, but not OK to hit." In order to reduce a negative behavior, you need to focus on training a better alternative response to take its place. How do you want the child to respond when he is upset? Sit down with the child and work together to identify alternative ways of responding. Once you identify one or more, then practice and role-play the desired response, until it becomes more automatic. Then, when the child is upset, validate his feelings and coach him to use the new response. You will find that you are then teaching the child, rather than simply punishing him. The child views you as a working partner with him, and will try harder to develop more appropriate ways of acting.

Hyperactivity and autism

Individuals with autism typically have executive functioning problems which are shared with those diagnosed with attention deficit hyperactivity disorder (ADHD). These problems include poor impulse control, working memory, and organizational and problem-solving skills. Children on the spectrum can have difficulty concentrating, but become hyper-focused on an activity of interest. They can be bright but cannot organize themselves to get through the day. You may tell them what they need to do once they arrive at school, but they never remember to follow through with it. They may impulsively act without thinking, even though you discussed the consequences ahead of time.

In addition, they often share problems in arousal that are common with hyperactivity in ADHD. When you combine low arousal with poor impulse control, you get very disorganized behavior. Now, if the child has overlying ADHD with the autism, he will have very poor ability to focus, control impulses, and organize his behavior. The frontal lobes of the brain are not getting enough stimulation. In such cases, stimulants (medication) are used to arouse that area of the brain. When that part of the brain is stimulated correctly, the child can focus and organize his behavior. However, for many on the spectrum, stimulants (Ritalin, Adderall, etc.) may make them more active, or even aggressive. However, if the symptoms are truly ADHD, these medications will probably show good results.

It can be difficult to tell at first if the child's hyperactive behavior is the result of his autism or possible ADHD problems. How does your child seem at home, in class, and in other settings? If his behavior seems pretty scattered across settings, he has difficulty maintaining focus, and he cannot seem to benefit from instruction and guidance due to very poor ability to regulate his behavior, then I would consider ADHD. Don't be fooled by the child's ability to focus for hours on something that he enjoys, such as video games. The child with attention deficits can often focus in activities of strong interest or high stimulation. This is because the prefrontal lobes of the brain (executive functions) are stimulated and aroused. If the task is not stimulating (boring) or has no meaning for him, then the child cannot maintain attention. This is not a willful or intentional response. It is actually a brain wiring or neurotransmitter issue. The three most common ways to calm, alert, and organize the nervous system are using biomedical methods (digestive, dietary, immune system, etc.), sensory techniques to calm and alert, and, if needed, a possible trial period on medication. If you try medication, you should see good results if it is truly an ADHD problem. If you don't see good results, stop using it.

Sensory diet, biomedical, and structure for hyperactivity

Many people automatically think of medication for ADHD when treating hyperactivity in children with autism. However, there are many other strategies for organizing the nervous system. These techniques should be tried first or used alongside medication when dealing with scattered, disorganized behavior in children with autism. I have found that the following strategies can have good effects with children on the spectrum who display hyperactivity and other disorganized behavior.

1. *Structured daily routine.* I try to evaluate the child both at home and at school. Children can present differently in different settings. Children who show fewer symptoms at school, but more hyperactive, disorganized behavior at home, may be responding to the less structured environment at home. These children need predictable structure to their routine to give them boundaries to pattern their behavior. Without the structure, the child is anxious and disorganized. At school, the day is highly structured with predictable routines, activities, and boundaries. Often the child gets home and his time and activity are not as organized. His time is too loosely structured to direct his attention and behavior. He needs ongoing stimulation, but doesn't know how to appropriately organize his time to get it. Without the structure, the child simply bounces haphazardly from one activity to another. When the structure is not there, he is lost without boundaries. Try providing a visual (picture) schedule with a highly structured sequence of activities to see if the boundaries funnel the child's attention into constructive activity.

2. *Sensory diet.* Many children are hyperactive due to their nervous systems being either under-aroused or over-aroused. Our nervous system needs a certain amount of stimulation to stay aroused. When we are over-aroused, our nervous system is overwhelmed, scattered, and disorganized. We cannot focus and may seek out increased activity to gain predictability to the chaos. However, if our nervous system is under-aroused, it will seek out increased stimulation to alert itself to stay aroused. Many children on the

spectrum have trouble regulating the arousal level of their nervous system. For many children with hyperactivity, their nervous system often filters out too much stimulation, leaving the nervous system under-aroused and seeking out intense stimulation. Hence, they are always moving to stay aroused. When not moving or feeding their nervous system excitatory stimulation (e.g. video games), they become under-aroused and cannot sit and focus on a task that is not highly stimulating. I highly recommend these children be evaluated by an occupational therapist trained in sensory processing disorders, to see if they have an arousal problem. If so, the therapist can design a sensory diet of stimulating activities throughout the day to alert the nervous system if under-aroused, or calm it if over-aroused. Often these diets consist of frequent up-and-moving, gross motor activities periodically throughout the day to arouse the nervous system, and then sensory tools (chewing gum, sitting on an air cushion or therapy ball, chewy tubing, fidget toys, etc.) to keep the child aroused during activities that require concentration. When in doubt, physical activity in general—whether raking leaves, pushing a grocery cart, carrying heavy items, playing ball, or jumping on a trampoline—is very organizing for their nervous system.

3. *Stable sleep!* Autism is a neurological disability. The nervous system of those on the spectrum is fragile and vulnerable to being disorganized very easily. Any insult to the nervous system (lack of sleep, not feeling well, hunger, or being overwhelmed by too much activity/stimulation) can make the child hyperactive. Approximately 40–50 percent of children on the spectrum have disrupted sleep patterns. Many do not get more than a few hours of sleep at a time. Many of these children keep moving literally to stay awake! The less sleep they get, the more taxed and disorganized the nervous system becomes. Sleep problems can be the side effect of the other factors listed here, and in turn can further augment hyperactivity. The next post will list helpful suggestions for stabilizing sleep.

4. *Biomedical issues.* Some children have dietary intolerances, mineral deficiencies, metal toxicities, and other allergies that irritate the nervous system and cause it to seek out constant movement. Many of these children feel wound up and irritated, but do not know why. They cannot focus, are very active, and become agitated when others try to interrupt their activity. They may need supplements, special diets, or other medical interventions to remove the irritants and heal any internal damage. Discussion of these strategies is beyond the scope of this book. However, most families seek consultation from a doctor trained in biomedical interventions. A thorough medical evaluation is also recommended because many children have digestive/dietary issues

and weakened immune system problems that can cause hyperactivity and other challenging behaviors.

5. *Medications.* As a last resort, if the above strategies fail, or to augment the above strategies, medications can be used to stabilize the nervous system. If the child's nervous system is over-aroused, then a mild sedative may help. However, if the child has an under-aroused nervous system, then sedatives will only lower the arousal level and force the child to be more active. If the nervous system is under-aroused, as with most children with ADHD, then stimulants often have positive effects. However, many children on the spectrum react negatively to stimulants. They can become irritable and aggressive. Sometimes mood-stabilizing medications are tried, but they also are hit and miss. For most children, medications are a trial-and-error type of strategy. They all come with possible negative side effects. You try it; if it works, you will see a "wow" effect. If not, take them off! Even if they have positive effects, please incorporate a sensory diet and structured daily routine in combination with their use.

Hyperactivity is typically a sign that the child's nervous system is anxious and disorganized. There are many different strategies for calming, alerting, and organizing the nervous system. However, until the nervous system is calm and organized, it is continually seeking ways to pacify itself. Hyperactivity is one of those ways.

Difficulty sleeping

Difficulty sleeping is a very common problem with children on the spectrum. As many as 50 percent of children on the spectrum experience some difficulty sleeping. This can be a real problem for both the child and parents getting their needed rest. For the children, who already have a fragile nervous system, lack of sleep will compound any other difficulties (sensory, emotional, behavioral, etc.) they are experiencing. Steady sleep patterns are essential to keep the nervous system calm and organized. Listed below are several of the common strategies used to stabilize sleep patterns:

1. *Consistent bedtime routine.* The body needs to calm down and relax in order to sleep effectively. One of the best ways to stabilize sleep is to establish a consistent, relaxing routine before going to bed. The child should go to bed and rise at the same time every day. This helps establish a consistent sleep cycle for the body. The bedtime routine should consist of a sequence of relaxing events that lower the child's arousal level. This means avoiding video games and highly stimulating activity for the last 45–60 minutes of the evening. Common activities in bedtime routines are

taking a bath, brushing teeth, toileting, getting out clothes for tomorrow, getting a drink of water, reading a story, snuggling in bed, saying prayers, etc. Keep the same sequence of tasks each evening to build a consistent routine. This helps prepare the body for sleep.

2. *Lessen any environmental distractions.* If the child is a light sleeper, noise and activity going on in the house can disturb his sleep. Also, common noises occurring outside can be distracting for him. If needed, try using a consistent background noise (environmental tapes, soft music, white noise machine, fan, etc.) that will mask any other noises. Next, lighting can be an issue. If the child is scared of the dark, then a night light may be needed. Or, are there outside light sources that are disturbing your child's sleep (street lights, house lights, etc.)? If so, make sure they are blocked out. Another factor that could disrupt sleep is temperature. If the room is too cold or too hot, the child's nervous system will stay on high alert and he will not be able to sleep. Lastly, be aware of any tactile sensitivity that may present problems for your child. Are the pajamas a material that he feels comfortable in? How about the sheets and blankets? If any of these are too scratchy for the child, the nervous system will not relax.

3. *Favorite video or song.* Although you want to limit electronics that actively engage the child, for some children, having the same favorite video playing in their room each night often calms and soothes them. They typically do not watch it, but just having the familiar scripts in the background relaxes them. These favorite videos or music can represent security in something they love, block out other noise, and give them a familiar sensory pattern that calms and regulates them.

4. *Deep pressure and snuggables.* Deep pressure calms the nervous system and can promote sound sleeping. Provide large pillows, stuffed animals, or a body pillow to snuggle with. Lots of heavy blankets or a weighted blanket can assist with sleeping. Also, some children love the feeling of being wrapped up in a sleeping bag. Snuggling with a pet, or simply having one sleeping in the same bed, will often soothe and relax the child.

5. *Diet and exercise.* The three basic components of an organized nervous system (sleep, diet, and exercise) all affect each other. A good diet and lots of physical activity will help stabilize the nervous system so the child will sleep better. However, try to avoid arousing physical activity for the last hour before bedtime.

6. *Avoid frequent napping during the day.* If your child is having difficulty sleeping at night, try to avoid a lot of napping throughout the day. If a

nap is needed in the middle of the day, try to keep it short (30 minutes or less) and occurring at the same time every day.

7. *Medical concerns.* If the child has gastrointestinal problems, upper respiratory problems, or any other acute medical concerns, these can keep the nervous system on high alert, thus stopping the child falling asleep. Sleep apnea could also be a factor. If your child has any of these difficulties, seek medical help to lessen their impact.

8. *Sensory integration problems.* If the child has sensory processing issues, he will often have problems modulating his arousal level, making it difficult to fall or stay asleep. His nervous system may be too "wound up" to fall asleep. A good sensory diet throughout the day can help calm and organize the nervous system.

9. *Sleep aids.* Melatonin has been an effective sleep aid for many children on the spectrum. It is used very frequently with minimal, if any, side effects. There are a host of other sleep-inducing supplements and medications that can be prescribed, but these should be used as a last resort. Seek out your doctor's advice when using these.

Dealing with oppositional behavior

Many children on the spectrum have a strong resistance to following the lead of other people. Because of their anxiety and fear of uncertainty, they have a strong need to control all interaction and activity around them. Controlling makes the world very safe, consistent, and predictable. They simply feel too vulnerable to give up this control. One of our members posted this question a while back. I thought you might find the suggestions helpful.

? Question

Hi Bill, I have a question for you. My six-year-old nephew is living with us, along with my parents, temporarily. He has autism too and his behavior is defiant. Everything has to be done on his time and he has to be the boss of everything and everyone. When given consequences for his behavior (i.e. time-out), he becomes very aggressive. He hits people, destroys things, he will grab you and not let you go or follow you around and continue to try to hit you. This is relatively new behavior (the aggressiveness) and he has only been here with us for four months. We have tried lots of things, but nothing seems to work. Do you have any advice on how to deal with him? Thanks a bunch!!

AUTISM DISCUSSION PAGE

It is very common for young children with autism to need to control everything around them in order to feel safe. This will also increase when their routine is disrupted, more confusing, and chaotic. If your nephew recently moved in with you, plus your parents are living there, then my guess is that there is a lot of variability in your household; it is pretty chaotic, without much structure to the daily social patterns in the home. Children on the spectrum need structure, consistency, and predictability to their routine to feel safe and secure. When this is not there, they are often disorganized and anxious, resulting in them dictating what is occurring around them. This is a poor attempt to gain control to make life more predictable and safe. This may be contributing to the child's aggression. I might try the following:

1. Build a predictable pattern to his day. Try to set up a structured daily routine of predictable activity so that he will know what is coming up and when it will occur.

2. Try using a picture daily routine, with Velcro pictures so you can plan out the day in sequential order. This way, he can see what he is going to do in order of how he will do it. It allows him to mentally prepare for what is coming up and when he is going to do things. Even if your routine looks different every day, the child can mentally prepare himself by knowing what his day will consist of. The picture schedule will map it out for him. Go over it the night before, and then again in the morning, so he has a clear idea what is coming up in his routine.

3. Make a list of preferred activities (computer, TV, favorite snacks, outside activities, etc.) and make a picture reinforcer menu. As you are scheduling the day, sit down with him and, for every couple of events on his routine, have him pick a preferred activity to do. Lay it all out on the picture board, at least for the first couple of hours, so that he sees what is going to happen. This way, for every couple of daily activities, he gets a preferred activity. By using the picture board, he knows what he has to do first before getting the preferred activity. If he is really resistant, then build in a preferred activity for each non-preferred activity. First take a bath and then play computer.

4. Keep the activities brief and easy, so he can easily earn the preferred activity. You want to maximize the likelihood of him doing the non-preferred activity (bath) to earn the preferred activity (computer). That he can have what he wants, after following what you want. Provide lavish praise when he cooperates.

5. When he is oppositional and defiant, you want to avoid scolding, bribing, or counseling. Do not get angry or emotional. Acknowledge that he is upset and validate that you understand; however, stay very clear and concise about what he needs to do. If he is acting out, avoid scolding, counseling, or drawing attention to the negative behavior.

Focus your attention on what you want him to do. At that point you can do one of two things:

a) Keep restating the short instruction, with little emotion, while blocking and ignoring any problem behavior until he complies.

b) Let him know that it is OK if he doesn't want to do it right now; however, all the preferred activities are put on hold until he follows through with the activity. "Johnny, I understand you don't want to take a bath right now. That's OK. Take a break and let me know when you are ready." However, access to any preferred activity (e.g. computer) is restricted until he takes his bath. Do not argue; make it his choice. "Sorry, Johnny, you can play the computer once you take a bath. Let me know when you are ready and I will help you out." Back away and try to ignore his negative behavior until he calms and is ready to follow through with activity. Show little emotion; do not argue, scold, or bribe. Validate that you understand and that he can have his computer once the bath is completed. This is hard because you have to be prepared to hang in there a while, and the behavior will escalate before it gets better. Remember, show minimal emotion and give him the choice.

6. If he simply throws a tantrum, then I would try to ignore it, walk away, and let him calm down on his own. If he typically escalates to the point of aggression and property disruption, I would take him to a safe spot (bed or couch) where he should stay until he calms down. Again, show very little emotion, do not yell, but firmly repeat the prompt. It is OK to validate how he is feeling, but simply repeat what you want him to do (e.g. stay on the bed until calm).

7. Remember, he cannot have access to his favorite activities until he calms and follows through with the scheduled activity. It is very important that you stay consistent and don't overwhelm him. Keep his routine simple and very consistent. Expect to see worse behavior at first. He is used to throwing tantrums until he can gain control. So once you tell him what he needs to do, stay with that directive until he complies.

8. There is no negotiating when he is upset. If he will not let you soothe him, then give him a safe place and let him know that it is OK to be mad, but he has to stay there to be safe. You will keep him safe. Then stand back, say very little, and keep physically redirecting him back to the safe area if he tries to leave.

9. It is important to always communicate that you understand and validate that it is hard and he is upset, but he cannot hit, throw things, or hurt himself or others. You want to support him but remain firm and consistent about (1) what he needs to do and (2) that you will not let him assault others or destroy property.

10. Make sure to review the situation after everyone is calm to (1) acknowledge that he was upset, (2) validate his feelings, and (3) talk about how he should handle the problem.

11. You might also want to add in a sticker chart where he earns stickers for completing the events on the picture schedule. Once he earns a predetermined number of stickers, he can earn a special reward.

There are many different strategies that you could try, depending on what functions the behavior is serving for him, what events are creating distress for him, and what supports are needed to lower his anxiety. For example, if some tasks are too long or too hard, modify the tasks to make them easier for him, or build in assistance to help him out. He also may need frequent breaks to relax and regroup periodically throughout the day. You always want to match what you are asking him to do with his current abilities to do them.

Impulsive or oppositional? Purposeful or intentional?

For all children, the executive functioning part of the brain is one of the last parts to develop. It is the part of the brain that allows us to inhibit our impulses, think before we act, monitor and evaluate our behavior, and organize a plan of action. For most children on the spectrum, this development is often very delayed and some functions are always weak. Because of this, the children often have poor ability to control their impulses (even with consequences), think before they act, and consider how their behavior is affecting others. So, when parents and teachers tell them "don't do that" or "do this instead," they often cannot do it. Consequently, we often read this as purposeful intent and label the child as oppositional.

This part of the brain develops slowly over time and is often still developing into the early 20s. The frontal lobe of the brain gets some renewed growth in the early teen years, so your ten-year-old still has a lot to develop in that area of the brain. Research has recently found that this part of the brain is still developing up into the mid-20s. This explains why older teens often act without much forethought and will do dangerous things for excitement that they would never do when they get older. Using forethought to inhibit dangerous behavior is another one of the executive functions. Some of the adults on the spectrum have told me they keep learning better skills in these areas way into their 40s.

One of our members posted this comment, which is a good example of this delay in development that is often confusing.

> ### ? Member's question
>
> Sometimes our daughter (6, PDDNOS) tends to do the opposite of what would be expected by a neurotypical person. For example, if her brother is crying, she may laugh. When we point out that this is not appropriate, she starts to laugh even more, sometimes hysterically… She doesn't seem to hesitate in doing so, which is confusing if it's expected that she'd simply needed time to process?

AUTISM DISCUSSION PAGE

Laughing is often a nervous response to uncertainty (anxiety). It doesn't necessarily represent happiness. Most likely, your child has not yet developed the part of the brain that allows her to inhibit a response long enough to think before she acts.

This part of the brain is responsible for monitoring and evaluating your own impulses and actions. For her, this area of the brain is not well developed, so self-regulation of her emotions and actions is poor. She may not be able to (1) inhibit her impulse to laugh when anxious, (2) be able to hear your directions and apply it to her actions at the moment, (3) think about the consequences of her behavior before she acts, (4) think about (monitor) what she is doing, while she is doing it, and (5) evaluate how effective her actions are. Her development in these areas is probably delayed, but will develop over time. Be patient and continue to describe, explain, and model appropriate thinking and behavior.

Another example from one of our members:

> ### ? Member's question
>
> Do these impulses include hitting? My 3.5-year-old son is doing a lot of hitting throughout the day, almost like it's sub-conscious. He does this when he's excited, happy, normal, sad, and angry, directed at his mom and two younger sisters, or me. We've been giving him "time outs" as discipline. Before and after time out we explain to him it's not nice to hit and that you could hurt your sisters. Guess what the very first thing he does after time outs—yep, he goes around hitting. Very frustrating.

AUTISM DISCUSSION PAGE

Hitting can occur for a variety of reasons, including to communicate the need for attention, a way of initiating interaction, a means to escape and avoid events that he dislikes, and when overwhelmed, confused, or scared and anxious. This will frequently occur in your children before they develop effective ways of communicating. You can "time out" the child, but unless the child knows what to do (how he should respond appropriately to meet his needs), punishment will not work. In such cases you need to teach the child more appropriate ways to communicate what he wants.

However, it sounds as if your young one is seeking proprioception to help regulate his nervous system. Especially if he hits when happy, excited, and upset. When his nervous system gets excited, it seeks strong stimulation to the joints, tendons, and muscles, which is probably why he is hitting. Punishing the child (time out) when he (1) does not have another way of regulating his nervous system and (2) does not have the ability to inhibit his impulses will not help. At age three and a half, that is really young. Ability to control impulses and emotions is hard even for neurotypical kids at this age. I would focus on substituting another response that serves the same function—possibly hitting a pillow or the arm of a couch, or slapping his hands together. He is probably seeking out the jarring and resistance to his wrists and hands. When he gets excited, redirect him to hitting something else (or other replacement behavior) and do it with him, praising and reinforcing compliance. When trying to stop an undesirable behavior, first ask yourself, "What do I want the child to do?" Before punishing a child for doing an undesirable behavior, first ask yourself, "How should he respond (when upset, excited, etc.)?" and "Does he know how to do it?" If he doesn't know how to do it, practice it together.

Assume your child is either seeking out stimulation to regulate his nervous system or using the hitting as a way of initiating, maintaining, and controlling the attention of others. If hitting appears to be more seeking and maintaining attention, then focus on deciding how you want him to respond instead—another way of communicating (e.g. touch person lightly on the arm). Then have him practice this frequently throughout the day when seeking attention. Also model this when you approach him for interaction. Make it fun and use it all day long. Then, when he hits, interrupt and redirect him to touch the person lightly on the arm to get their attention. Focus on teaching, rather than punishing.

Help, my child is always resistant, oppositional, and non-compliant!

This message is long and includes a lot of strategies. As you read through the problems and strategies, simply check off the ones that may apply to your child.

Many children on the spectrum have problems with following the lead of others, and are frequently viewed as oppositional. This is frequently seen as "intentional" noncompliance, and the child is often labeled with oppositional defiant disorder (ODD). These children frequently have to control all activity and interaction, lead the activity their way, and refuse to follow the lead of others. If we press the issue, they will often act out to re-establish control. This reaction can occur if they do not get something that they want, are pressured to do things they wish to avoid, and whenever someone is trying to lead what they are doing. There can be a variety of reasons why a child on the spectrum will be so resistant. Here are several reasons why and strategies to support them. This list is not exhaustive, but includes common issues.

Reason

1. Because of the variety of processing problems (sensory sensitivities, delayed information processing, auditory processing difficulties, etc.), many children on the spectrum feel safe only when they are controlling and leading everything they are engaged in. Uncertainty scares them, so they need to control everything in order to maintain predictability in their world.

Suggestions

a. Respect and accommodate for sensory sensitivities and use a sensory diet to calm and organize the nervous system.

b. Break tasks down into smaller parts; make them concrete with visual strategies; provide information in small bits that are clear and concrete.

c. Let the child pace the speed that information is provided and how he expresses what he knows.

Reason

2. Because of the processing issues listed above, these children can become overwhelmed very easily. By resisting and controlling what they are engaged in, they can pattern how much stimulation they have to process, avoiding overload that overwhelms them. They can pace the information to meet their nervous system's needs.

Suggestions

a. Use strategies listed earlier under number 1.

b. Respect, avoid, and/or accommodate for situations that tend to overwhelm the child.

c. Teach the child coping skills for dealing with overload.

    d. Teach the child (and those around him) how to appropriately escape situations that overload him (break card, say "no," ask for help, etc.).

Reason

3. Difficulty understanding what is expected. Children on the spectrum have difficulty appraising what is needed, so they are either anxious about entering into new situations, or dive into new situations without understanding what is needed (then acting out when they struggle). These children (1) do not know what to expect and (2) do not know what is expected of them. They need the world to be very predictable so they know exactly what to expect.

Suggestions

    a. Preview, clarify and verify. Prepare the child before going into situations with (1) what they can expect to occur, (2) what is expected of them, (3) how long it will last, and (4) what will come up next. Also, anticipate any problem areas and discuss how to handle them (e.g. withdraw and regroup when overwhelmed). Don't assume the child understands; clarify and verify that he understands.

    b. For new situations, while knowing the child's vulnerabilities, try to make modifications and accommodations to reduce the impact. Again, preview these ahead of time.

    c. During activities/tasks, think out loud! Provide a narrative of what is needed and how to do it. This can help guide and coach the child through the tasks.

    d. Use visual schedules to help provide predictability and understanding.

    e. Ease transition by preparing ahead of time: "Johnny, when this TV show is over, you will take a bath." Then provide five-, three-, and one-minute reminders before transitioning between tasks: "Johnny, in three minutes we will need to put the Game Boy away and have your snack."

Reason

4. From a history of constantly being placed in situations where the demands are stronger than their skills to handle them, the children have learned that it is simply safer to escape and avoid any activity that is not initiated and led by them. So, they have to control all activity.

Suggestions

    a. By understanding the sensory, cognitive, and performance issues of your child, always look at how the demands can be lowered or presented differently, or provide more support to make them match the current skill level of the child.

    b. Do the tasks/activities as "we-do" activities (do them together, helping each other out) to frame and scaffold the activity to maximize success. Match the demands to the child's skill level, and do them together to support the child through it.

Reason

5. Many on the spectrum have strong task performance anxiety. So when we ask them to perform, they will resist unless they know that they will be perfect at doing it. Because of their black and white, all-or-nothing thinking, unless they feel completely competent (which is often just in their preferred, self-directed activity), they will pull back and resist. It is an all-or-nothing response; they resist any activity that will take some time to learn.

Suggestions

    a. Understand the child's comfort zones and stretch these slowly.

    b. Start where the child is at; keep it simple, build one step at a time, and maximize success.

    c. Find the "just right" challenge and stay within it. Providing too big a challenge may overwhelm him.

    d. When possible, do the activity together ("we-do" activity) so you can take the pressure off the child, thus lowering the task performance anxiety.

Reason

6. Some children have a hard time initiating a task. They simply cannot get themselves started. This is due to weak executive functioning (brain wiring). They need you to "jump start" them.

Suggestions

a. Assist them in starting the activity, then fade out the assistance as they get going.

b. Some of the kids with executive functioning issues cannot remember multistep directions. You may need to provide visual prompts for each step. When you give the child verbal instructions for a task and then walk away, he may not be able to organize what is needed to carry it out. Don't label this as noncompliance. Provide the necessary support.

c. Give written directions and a written outline (worksheet) to lead them from one step to the next. Be nearby to redirect and assist as needed.

Reason

7. Lack of motivation. Many children on the spectrum have low motivation to do things that are not exciting for them.

Suggestions

a. Increase motivation by following non-preferred activity with preferred activity. Simply use the activity that they enjoy to reinforce completion of the other activity. First do homework, then watch TV.

b. Catch them being good! Provide three times more praise and positive attention for being cooperative than for being resistant (scolding, coaxing, etc.). Minimize attention for noncompliance.

c. Build in token systems, star charts, or sticker programs only if needed to increase motivation.

d. Some children are resistant when tasks are boring. Try to build new learning around their strengths and interests to increase motivation.

Reason

8. Compulsively resistant to any request or directive! Feels insecure and defensive to all requests or directives.

Suggestions

a. Pick your battles. Reduce 80 percent of all requests, demands, and directions. Telling them or asking them to do things will elicit an automatic no! They will resist all imperative statements (questions, prompting, instructions, directions, requests, etc.). It just gives them ammunition to be noncompliant.

b. Use more declarative language to invite engagement. For example: "Wow…I could really use help with this!" or "I bet you are better at this then me!" rather than "Billy help me do ___." Invite without asking. It allows the child to feel himself volunteering to help, being in control, of his own volition.

c. Provide no negative emotion to refusal. The two main things to avoid when children are resisting is strong emotion or getting upset and any scolding, negotiating, coaxing, or bribing. They feed off the negative emotion (helps them feel powerful) and the attention that we give counseling, scolding, and coaxing. However you choose to respond to noncompliance, do it with little emotion and with minimal talking.

d. For requests that the child *has to* do, use the following:

    i.   Get the child's attention, face to face, at eye level.

    ii.   State the prompt in short, clear, concrete language.

    iii. Give the child ten seconds to respond (longer for delayed processing).

    iv.   Repeat the prompt in a firm manner, using the same language.

    v.   If there is still no response (as long as you have been using the strategies above to support all vulnerabilities), then continue to stand your ground, saying nothing but repeating the same statement every 30 seconds.

    vi.   For some children, increase the assistance with physical guidance (unless it agitates them more), or simply wait until they are ready to respond.

    vii. Once the child responds, provide support as needed and reinforce all cooperative participation.

e. Often these children respond negatively to positive praise (just the opposite of most children). They read praise as you controlling them to do things. So, for these children, do not praise performance, just let mastery be motivating.

Reason

9. Because of our wish to avoid a fight, many children on the spectrum have learned that, if they resist, people back off and withdraw the demands in order to avoid a meltdown or destructive behavior. By doing so, we often get to the point where we pacify the child so he will not get aggressive. We coax and bribe the child to do things. Consequently, the child learns that by being noncompliant and acting out, he can manipulate the people around him to give him what he wants and he can escape and avoid everything he wishes to avoid.

Suggestions

a. Of course, build in above proactive strategies to match the demands to the child's current skill level.

b. Use a visual schedule so the routine is consistent and predictable for the child, with preferred activity built into the schedule every two or three activities.

c. Do the activities as "we-do" activities as much as possible, providing support and praise as you go along.

d. When the child is resistant, do not argue, negotiate, or justify your request at that time. Take away the battle and let the consequences teach the behavior. Tell the child, "You are too tired to do it right now. That's OK. You let me know when you are ready, and I will help you." Show no emotion; simply back away and ignore noncompliance. However, the child cannot do any preferred activity until he follows through with the routine task.

e. If he complains, simply remind him that it is his choice and you are there to help him when he is ready.

f. It is important that you are very clear in your expectations and consistent in following through with "life stops" until the child becomes responsive again.

As you see, there are different reasons why children on the spectrum are oppositional. However, assume that the child is doing the best that he can, given the situation he is in and his abilities to deal with it. Also, assume that the more oppositional, the more incompetent the child feels. Focus on helping the child feel competent, and responsiveness will increase. We tend to focus too much on forcing compliance, when we need to be assisting the child by taking away the fight, lowering the demands (at least at first), providing increased supports, and focusing on what he is doing right. Help him feel more competent, and he will follow your lead.

Making transitions easier!

Transitioning between activities and events can be difficult for many children on the spectrum. This can often be a trigger for acting-out behavior. This is especially hard if the transition means leaving a preferred activity to do a non-preferred activity. To help ease times of transitions, try the following:

- Creating a visual schedule (pictures or written) is probably one of the best tools to use to make life predictable and manageable for many children on the spectrum. Uncertainty represents anxiety for many on the spectrum. Structure and predictability lessens anxiety and makes transitions predictable and more manageable. Knowing what is coming up and the order of events is so important. As each activity is completed, have the child check it off or remove the picture, so he can see what he has accomplished and what is coming up next.

- With each new activity, identify what activity will follow next: "Tommy, now you can read for 15 minutes, and then we will wash our hands for dinner." You want to always prepare the child for what activity will follow the current one. This starts preparing the child for that transition in advance. The brain is previewing what will happen when this activity ends.

- Knowing how long the activity will last and how much time is left is important for children on the spectrum. Preview with the child how long the activity is going to last and what activity will follow. Use a visual timer to show the child how much time is left, and keep a picture of the next activity next to the one he is currently doing.

- Ease into the transitions by giving early warnings. Start with five-minute warnings: "Tommy, in five minutes we are going to stop reading and then wash your hands for dinner." Include how much time he has and what is coming up next. Remind him at three minutes, then one minute. By using a visual timer and giving warnings, these strategies prepare the brain for the transitions.

- Teachers have found that creating little routines and/or transition songs/chants helps ease the transitions. Creating routines for transition between activities (e.g. putting materials away, washing hands, taking picture up to the board, etc.) adds continuity to the transitions. Also, creating little songs/chants about putting the materials away and moving on to the next activity can make transitions fun.

- Celebrating (give five, thumbs up, declarative statements, etc.) while switching the pictures on the schedule and moving on between activities adds strong reinforcement to transitioning. Concrete reinforcement systems can also help. If at school the child likes computer time, then give him a token card with three or four squares in a row. Upon completing each activity he gets a computer sticker to place in one of the boxes. Once he fills up all four boxes, he gets to cash in for computer time. This motivates the child to want to move on to earn the stickers and computer time.

- Be careful with how much activity you give a child for a specific period of time. Many children need to finish the task before moving on. If they are interrupted before completing, they will oppose moving on. If it is a big project, break it down into smaller steps. If there is a chance that the activity may not be completed, then discuss in advance when the child can come back and complete it. Then, when it is time to end, remind the child that he can come back and complete it at the time discussed.

These are several strategies that can help the child transition from one activity to another. At first, these strategies take a lot of mental energy on your part to do consistently. However, you will find that once you do them regularly, you will begin to do them naturally without much effort.

Repeated questioning!

Many children on and off the spectrum engage in repeated questioning. Many parents find this very exhausting and hard to decrease. Children can engage in repeated questioning for a variety of reasons:

- If they are insecure, some children will ask questions for reassurance about an issue. Uncertainty of the immediate future is very anxiety-provoking. These children need to constantly know what is coming up to feel secure. Questioning becomes a way of making the world more clear, consistent, and predictable.

- Some children experience strong anticipatory anxiety (strong excitement about what is coming up) and will continually question as a way of coping with anticipation. If the behavior is driven by severe anxiety, they will get very upset when you try to redirect or not answer.

- Some children simply get stuck on a particular topic or interest and cannot get past it. They may be seeking out more information but not know how to do it. In these cases, it is best to try to expand the conversation by providing more information.

- Some children who want attention will repeatedly ask the same question as a way of interacting. This occurs especially if they do not know how to get attention in other appropriate ways, or if the intensity of the reaction they get from questioning is much stronger than that from appropriately initiating interaction. Some children prefer initiating attention with questions that have predictable answers.

As annoying as the repeated questioning can be, it is important to look at what function the behavior seems to serve for the child before extinguishing it. If the behavior tends to reduce anxiety or make sense of the world, then we need to gently redirect it by trying to calm the anxiety or providing the information they need. Also, be careful not to invalidate the child's attempt to communicate, since we are trying to encourage communication as much as possible. My first recommendation is for parents to try to work with the child to expand his questioning into reciprocal interaction. Provide an answer to his question, and then expand on it with further information, asking him questions about what he is seeking, and building expanded interaction around the initial question. For example, the child questions, "Going to the park?" and the parent responses with "Yes, Johnny, we are going to the park after lunch. Going to the park is fun. I like to swing. Do you like to swing?" This is adding to and expanding on the topic of the question. Take whatever answer the child gives you and expand on it. This answers the child's original question, redirects him to other aspects of the topic, and teaches him how to expand on the conversation. If the child has limited language, you can simply expand on his question "Going to the park?" with "Yes, swing!" (since you know he loves to swing at the park). Adding on to the question provides further information and redirects the child's attention past the initial question.

There are a few other behavioral techniques that have worked successfully for me with several children I have worked with in the past; however, they do not build on the child's communication.

1. Answer the child once when he repeats a question, and then tell him that this is the last time you will answer. From then on, the parent gives no verbal response. She may shake her head no, but not give a verbal answer. In all cases, the parent's verbal answer is what reinforces the child to ask again. This is discussed with the child ahead of time, so he knows the parent will not verbally answer anymore.

2. For some children, answering only once is not enough, so you might try answering no more than three times. Then with each answer you count them off. When you hit three, that is it.

3. Some children will inhibit the questioning if you repeat the question to them. So the second time they ask the question, "Are we going to

McDonald's for dinner?" you say "Bobby, are we going to McDonald's for dinner?" They will usually give you the answer, and stop repeating the question.

4. For an older teen who can read and write, we would answer the repeated question one time and then have him write down the answer and carry it with him. If he asked again, the parent would refer him to his note. Another technique that has worked is writing the answer down on a note board and referring the child to that board. This worked well since the verbal response is what reinforces the repeated questioning.

5. This next technique is for children who find it really difficult to stop, so we gradually decrease the behavior as the child becomes more controlled in refraining from questioning. It is more complex but has worked well.

   a. The parent keeps track, for a couple of days, of how frequently the child repeatedly questions during the day (let's say an average of six times a day) and how many repetitions of a question the child averages (let's say five repetitions of a question). Then from there we write a plan to start gradually decreasing those frequencies (the number of repetitions of each question and the number of times a day repeated questioning occurs).

   b. To decrease the number of times the child gives a question, if the average frequency is five, we would start by answering the child up to four times. We would tell the child that we can only give up to four responses. Each time the child repeats the question, the parent responds, "This is number one" and answers the question. Then each response starts with, "This is number two, three, or four" and answers the question. At the fourth time, the parent reminds the child she cannot answer it again. If the child stops asking, the parent will praise the child: "Billy, you really pleased mommy by not questioning after I told you no." If the child asks again, the parent shakes her head no, and gives the child the manual sign for "no." The parent does not give another verbal answer to the question, regardless of how intense the child gets. When the child gets used to asking only up to four times, then we decrease to three times. We gradually decrease to twice and only once. This way we start where the child is at, and gradually expect him to control his asking.

   c. Now, we want to reward the child for stopping at the predetermined number of repetitions (as above), as well as decrease the number of times repeated questionings occur throughout the day. In this example, the child averages repeated questioning six times a day. We start at that number and gradually reduce the frequency as in the step above. We make a laminated reinforcement chart with six boxes on it. We also post a picture of a few rewards that the child can earn next to the board. For each time the child engages in repeated questioning, when he doesn't stop at four, the parent puts a cross or frown face in one of the boxes (with an erasable marker). The parent tells the child that if there is at least one box left by a certain time of the evening, the child will get his choice of one of the rewards. So, in this case, if the child has four or fewer times when he doesn't stop repeated questioning, he will earn a reward. This way, we start with where the child is at, teach him how to earn the reward, and then slowly start reducing the number of boxes (chances) he has to earn the reward. So for step b above, when the child asks for the fifth time, the parent shakes her head no, gives manual sign for no, and walks over and crosses out one of the squares. If the child has at least one box left at the end of the evening, he gets his choice of reward. If he has all five boxes crossed off, the parent shows him the filled-in squares and tells him he cannot get the reward tonight, but he can try again tomorrow.

Another way you can work a reinforcement board is to give the child a star in each box each time he stops the questioning at the predetermined amount without going over. So, if the child stops at four repetitions, the parent praises him and gives him a star to put on his chart. Once he earns the right number of stars, he earns a reward.

6. Another technique is to answer the child once or twice. Then the next time the child asks, you tell him you will not answer that question again, and ask him a simple question to redirect him. This way, you are redirecting him to talk about something else. If he doesn't answer, but asks his question instead, you continue to ignore his question and continue to ask him your question until he answers. If he answers your question and goes back to his, you simply ask another question about the issue you want to talk about and keep focusing on what you are asking him. Eventually, he will learn to take the redirection and converse on what you want to talk about.

Remember, almost all of these techniques focuses on (1) eliminating verbal answers that reward the child's repeated questioning and (2) rewarding him for responding the way you want him to do.

Self-abuse

Hand/arm biting, slapping self, and head banging are very common with children with emotional regulation problems. All three behaviors result in strong stimulation that releases stress chemicals when the nervous system is overloaded. Hand/arm biting is especially effective because of the strong proprioception (resistance to joints and tendons) that it gives. The child gets both strong proprioception into the jaw, as well as into the hand or arm. When the child gets frustrated, the stress chemicals build up to boiling point and the child seeks out strong proprioception through self-abuse, aggression, or property destruction to release stress chemicals from the nervous system. To reduce self-abuse, you have to do several things:

- Identify conditions that cause the stress and help reduce them. Keep track of the events that precipitate the agitation and build in proactive strategies to reduce the stress. More times than not, the demands (sensory, task performance, social, emotional, etc.) of the situation are greater than the child's current skills for dealing with them. Eliminate, modify, or accommodate these conditions to lower the demands on the child, or provide greater assistance to support the child. Often, sensory overload, too much uncertainty, or physical pain is at the root of self-abuse. Use the Fragile World on the Spectrum (Appendix A) to help identify and accommodate for the conditions that commonly cause problems for your child.

- Young children, until they develop speech, will engage in self-abuse as a means of communicating distress. Self-abuse becomes their major way of communicating pain, discomfort, or the need to escape the situation they are in. If your child is nonverbal, try to teach him to use picture communication, manual signing, or standard gestures to help him communicate.

- Identify the function that the behavior serves. All behavior serves a function for the child (to escape something he doesn't like, communicate frustration, gain something that he wants, etc.). Once you determine the function, then teach another behavior to take its place. If the child is engaging in the behavior to escape or avoid something, then identify another way of escaping (using break card, asking to leave, etc.). If he is doing it for proprioception, then give him another way of getting it (biting tubing, chewing gum, etc.). If the child bites himself when upset, how do you want him to react when upset? If he hits himself to say "leave me alone," how do you want him to communicate this?

- Once the replacement behavior is determined, have the child practice it when calm and reinforce heavily. You cannot teach new behavior when the child is upset. Practice the new response and, if possible, role-play common situations to practice the response. When the child starts to get upset, prompt the replacement behavior and reinforce the child for choosing that behavior over the biting.

- If the child has good control over his behavior, you can simply reinforce the lack of biting behavior. For example, develop a sticker chart with four or five boxes in a row on it. Have the child pick out a reward that he wants to work for (e.g. rent a video). Place a picture of the reinforcer at the end of the sequence of squares. Each day that he displays no incidences of biting, praise the child and have him put a sticker on his chart (in one of the boxes). Make a big deal over it and have him count how many stickers he needs to earn the video. Once he fills up the boxes with stickers, he gets to rent a video. If he doesn't earn a sticker for the night, then take him to the chart and let him know he cannot have one tonight but he can try again tomorrow.

- If it is harder for the child to control the behavior, you can use the 1–2–3 approach. Once he starts to bite, you count one, then two…, and if you have to say three, he loses his sticker. This way, it gives him a chance to regroup. If the child has multiple incidents of biting each day, then it would be unrealistic to expect the child to go the whole day without biting. First, start by decreasing the frequency of biting per day. If he averages four episodes of biting a day, put up a board with four tags. Each time he bites himself, have him take one tag off the board; if he loses all four tags, then he doesn't earn his sticker at the end of the night. However, if he has at least one tag left, he gets his sticker for the day. Once the child learns to hold himself to just three biting incidents a day, then you reduce the tags to three, then to two, and so on until the behavior is infrequent.

Severe self-injurious behavior

A small percentage of people with developmental disabilities engage in frequent self-injurious behavior. My first 12 years in the field were spent in an institutional setting providing services to severely impaired individuals with multiple behavior challenges. During this time I had the opportunity to work with some very fragile individuals with severe physical and emotional vulnerabilities. Self-injury took a variety of forms including biting, digging, hitting, slapping, kicking, gouging, head banging, and ingesting inedible items. During that time I learned that self-injurious behavior occurs for several reasons:

- Self-abusive behavior is more common with individuals who are nonverbal and have no consistent way of expressing themselves. Consequently, self-injurious behavior often is communicating pain, discomfort, frustration, task demands, need for attention, etc. Self-abuse can be used to communicate any intense emotional reactions. Once the child begins to develop language (or other form of communication), self-abuse tends to decrease to only those times when coping skills break down.

- Self-abuse occurs most frequently in those children who have very poor impulse control and poor emotional regulation. Consequently, you will see more self-abuse in young children or severely impaired individuals with poor executive functioning skills. However, many adults report the occurrence of self-abuse when extremely overwhelmed. The emotional centers of the brain overpower the thinking centers of the brain. They react with intense emotion without the ability to inhibit the impulse.

- Most self-abusive behavior involves strong proprioception (tension to joints, tendons, and muscles), which reduces stress chemicals (cortisol) in the nervous system. Hitting, kicking, biting, and head banging provide strong proprioception that reduces stress chemicals during times of emotional outbursts. When the stress chemicals accumulate to boiling point, the fight-or-flight stress response is activated, seeking strong proprioception to reduce the stress chemicals.

- Self-abuse produces strong reactions from others and these reactions can increase its frequency. The person learns that self-injury gains a lot of attention, and also allows him to escape situations that he wants to avoid. People around him will do anything to stop the self-abuse. The individual learns that the behavior can create a lot of control over his social environment (people let him escape unwanted situations, give him what he wants, let him have his way in order to pacify him).

- Self-abusive behavior can be used to mask or dull pain. Individuals may bang their head to mask pain from headaches and ear infections. They may hit themselves in the jaw to distract from toothaches. When self-abuse begins, or increases significantly, medical evaluation is important.

- Self-abusive behavior can occur for self-stimulation, to help regulate the nervous system. It can alert the nervous system when under-aroused and release stress chemicals when over-aroused. This behavior frequently occurs during times of no activity or when overwhelmed by too much activity.

In my experience, frequent self-abusive behavior occurs most often in individuals with poor communication skills, weak impulse control, poor emotional regulation, and inadequate coping skills. When it starts all of a sudden, suspect some medical/physical problem. Internal discomfort and agitation can elicit self-abusive behavior.

Severe and persistent self-injury (from biting, hitting, scratching, digging, etc.) can start for any of the above reasons, but can become addictive over time.

The pain from self-injury stimulates the body to release endorphins, the body's natural pain killer. Endorphins act like opiates which feel good, and the person can get addicted to the "feel good" endorphins. Not only do endorphins help dull the sense of pain, but they also feel good. The individual self-injures to stimulate the release of endorphins to maintain the feeling. Since the endorphins act to dull the pain, the behavior is not felt as painful.

Self-abuse that occurs for this reason can get worse over time. Like all addiction, the body begins to "habituate" (gain tolerance) to the stimulation, requiring the individual to do it more intensively to stimulate the pain to release the endorphins. The brain has a defense mechanism to dull the sense of pain over time, making it necessary to increase the intensity to stimulate the endorphins. In addition, scarring that can occur from the injury dulls the pain, requiring the individual to dig or bite deeper to stimulate pain. These individuals will gradually go from minor injuries to creating severe injury as the skin becomes more and more scarred. The individual then has to gouge or tear out tissue to get deeper for pain. In such cases, the medication naltrexone can be used to block the body's release of endorphins. If this works, the self-abuse begins to hurt more and doesn't release the "feel good" chemicals that are addictive.

In many cases chronic, persistent self-injurious behavior ends up being maintained by several of the above functions. It can start for only one reason, but once started can gain many secondary values by the addition of several of the other functions. In most cases, professional help is needed to isolate the functions and develop effective strategies to treat each function.

Treating self-injurious behavior

Self-injurious behavior can come in many different forms in children with autism. For some, it can be an expression of frustration or sensory overload, or it simply communicates a need or want. For others, persistent self-injury can become compulsive and even addictive, becoming very damaging to the body and self-esteem. Over the years, I have treated many forms of self-injurious behavior with the following strategies:

1. Treating self-injurious behavior usually starts with doing a functional behavior assessment to identify the functions that the behavior serves (communication, stress release, escaping unwanted events, self-stimulation, etc.). Functional behavior assessments involve tracking and identifying the situations in which the behavior occurs (when, where, with whom) and observing the immediate effects that the behavior produces. By identifying what triggers the behavior and what occurs immediately after the behavior, we begin to get an idea of which function it provides. (See Chapter 8, Effective Discipline, for more discussion on functional assessments.)

2. Treatment then usually proceeds with changing the conditions (lowering demands, reducing stimulation, increasing support, etc.) that trigger the behavior, and teaching another, more appropriate, replacement behavior that meets the same need (function). For example, if the child self-injures himself when difficult demands are placed on him, then we can initially lower the demands while teaching a more appropriate way of escaping (say no, stop card, etc.) and/or asking for help.

3. First, we look at what environmental demands are overwhelming or lacking for the person. This may require modifying the environmental demands, building in accommodations to lessen their impact, or providing greater assistance to support the person when faced with these conditions. If the person has too many demands placed on him, we look at providing fewer demands, making the demands easier, or providing added support in the face of the demands. We want to better match the demands of the situation to the skill level of the person.

4. If the function of self-abuse is to communicate needs and wants, then we focus on teaching the child communication skills. If the person is nonverbal, then we teach an alternative means of communication, such as pictures, gestures, or signing. We identify what the person is trying to communicate and then try to teach another, more appropriate way of communicating.

5. If the behavior is occurring to escape or avoid unwanted situations, we often need to look at why the person is trying to escape or avoid the situation in the first place. From there, we build in added supports or lessen the demands. In addition, we need to teach another way to communicate "stop" or "help." Teach the child another behavior to appropriately escape the situation. Practice and role-play the new response until it is well learned. Once the new response is learned, then during demanding situations, encourage the child to use the replacement behavior and immediately allow him to escape. It is important that the new, more appropriate way of escaping is immediately reinforced with successful avoidance.

6. If the self-abuse occurs for proprioception to release stress chemicals, then we look at (1) developing a sensory diet that gives frequent physical activity and other forms of proprioception (chewing gum, squish balls, weighted vest, etc.) to release stress chemicals throughout the day, and (2) teaching an alternative replacement behavior to substitute for the self-abuse. For example, if the child bites his wrist, then we might provide a chewy tube to bite on. This would provide an appropriate form of biting/chewing, substituting one form of proprioception for another.

7. If the person is engaging in self-abuse to mask pain, then we identify the source of pain and treat it. We also try to teach the person a method of communicating to others that he feels pain.

8. If the person is self-abusing to get strong reactions from others, we (1) lower the intensity of our reactions and (2) provide stronger attention for more appropriate behavior.

9. If the person is engaging in self-abuse for self-stimulation, then we try to increase the stimulation the person is receiving (keep him busier, provide an environment rich in stimulation) and teach other forms of self-stimulation that either calm or alert the nervous system. We also build in a sensory diet to provide the person with frequent stimulation.

10. If the behavior is the result of high anxiety, and the above doesn't help, then medications are often used to calm the nervous system.

11. In rare occasions when the self-injurious behavior may be maintained by endorphins (as discussed above), then we give naltrexone to block the release of endorphins.

As stated in the first step, most successful strategies for reducing self-injurious behavior start with completing a functional behavior assessment. To help with this, there is a brief functional behaviour assessment questionnaire form in Appendix D.

Treating acting-out, escape behavior

Explosive behavior (head banging, biting, slapping self, attacking others, destroying property, etc.) is often a form of "escape" behavior. It often occurs under conditions of frustration, anger, discomfort, sensory overload, or pain, and serves to help the person escape or avoid unwanted events. It often means we have placed the child in a situation in which the demands of the situation outweigh the child's current skills to deal with them. The child acts out and we take away the demands, allow them to escape the demands, and/or avoid giving these demands again in the future. Consequently, the child's use of acting out is reinforced to occur again under situations of frustration. Often, once the child learns to use explosive behavior to escape unwanted situations, it can become an automatic response to even simple frustration. He may start acting out whenever anything doesn't go his way—demands, not getting what he wants, discomfort, delay, waiting in line. It can become a conditioned behavior in all situations of distress.

Unfortunately, we often try to change the child's behavior without first looking at changing the conditions that lead to it. If the child is acting out to escape or avoid a situation, we must ask ourselves, "Why does the child feel the need to escape?" "What is it about the situation that is causing distress?" If we assume that the child is doing the best that he can, given the situation that he is in, and his current skill level for dealing with it, then our first step should be to change the demands of the conditions to match the abilities of the child. This usually means we (1) lower the demands of the situations that are overwhelming the child or (2) build in greater assistance to support the child in these situations. To do this, it is important to understand what the child's vulnerabilities are and how they impact the situation he is in. What are his sensory challenges, processing problems, and social and emotional needs? Often we are pushing the child too fast or too much and overwhelming him. Does he have the skills needed to meet the expectations? If not, what do we need to teach these or how do we need to assist the child?

Often, it may not be the demands of the task but the way people are approaching the child. The adult may be too demanding, too directive, moving too fast, or not listening to the child. Some children respond better to a soft, quiet voice and others to a more upbeat, animated style. Some respond better to a gentle, understanding approach, others to firm, matter-of-fact delivery. Not only do we have to match the task demands to the child, but we also have to match the interaction style to that which helps the child feel safe and accepted. The way we present the demands can have a lot to do with the child's response. Often we try to command and demand, when we should invite and support. If the child does not feel safe with the person, when pressured he will often freeze and not follow their lead. If he does not view the person as a working partner, he will not take them as a trusted guide.

After analyzing and changing the conditions that trigger the need to escape, we also need to teach the child alternative ways to appropriately escape unwanted situations. This is where it is important to teach the child a method of communicating "stop" and "help." If the child doesn't know how to appropriately protest and ask for help, then he will have to revert to acting out to protest and escape. If the child does not know how to appropriately protest, or people are not listening to him and ignore his protest, then acting out will still occur. We need to teach appropriate methods of communicating "stop" and "help," and then immediately stop and provide support when he is communicating this. More times than not, we ignore his protest (because we want him to do it) and force the issue. The appropriate protest loses its value, while acting out takes its place.

Once you have changed the conditions to better match the child, and taught more acceptable means of protest, then you need to make sure that it is more reinforcing to use the appropriate protest than to act out. Usually, (1) we practice using the appropriate means of protest (say "stop," put out hand to gesture "stop," ask for help, etc.) when not under stress, role-playing as appropriate, then (2) once the behavior is learned, we coach the child to use it when in situations of stress. Since the acting out behavior is so automatic, it will take a while to subside. When the child is experiencing frustration, we need to supportively interrupt the inappropriate behavior and redirect the child to use the newly learned response. Try to avoid allowing the child to escape the situation until he uses the appropriate way of escaping. "Tommy, if you want to stop this say 'stop.'" Then immediately allow him to escape. This way, he sees that the acting-out does not allow escape, but communicating "stop" or "help" either gets him out of the situation or gets help in dealing with it.

For example, Johnny will bite his wrist when presented with situations from which he wants to escape. We might teach him to say the word "stop" and/or put the palm of his hand up to gesture "stop," when faced with situations that he wants to escape. While being supportive, we would gently interrupt the wrist biting and prompt him to say "stop" and/or to put his hand out to gesture stop. We would support the child, but try not to let him escape until he produces the newly learned response. Once he protested appropriately, we would immediately praise him and pull away the demand. Escape would come from appropriate protest, not the biting. Once we pull away the demand, we might ask him if he wants help and teach him a sign, word, or gesture for communicating "help."

To make learning easier, we might preview communicating "stop/help" with him before doing tasks, or take him into situations that commonly caused wrist biting. Before asking him to do something, we may remind him to use the replacement behavior if the event becomes too hard and he wants to stop. Or we may remind him how to ask for help. Preview the desired response before doing the task, so it is fresh in his mind. While doing the task, if we see that he is getting distressed, before he starts to bite his wrist we might remind him, if it is getting too hard for him, to say "stop" or ask for help. In essence, we remind him before doing the task, while doing the task, and review how well he did after doing the task. This way, we are supporting the use of the new response from all sides. Once the child learns that the acceptable protest gains escape (or help) and the biting does not, then the acceptable protest will start to take the place of biting.

Occasionally, the acting out is too injurious to avoid blocking "escape" until the acceptable protest is used. It is just too dangerous, or the child is too upset to interrupt and redirect. In these situations, we may not be able to avoid the child gaining escape by acting out. This means you are unable to block escape, or the behavior is too dangerous to block, until the child uses the newly learned protest. In these situations, we may need to add in extra reinforcement (other than praise and escape), to make it more reinforcing to interrupt the inappropriate behavior and use the appropriate response. Often we will reinforce the child with a reward if he uses the acceptable protest and withhold it if he does not. This way, he is getting added reinforcement for using the acceptable protest. Or, if he can understand a token system, he might earn two tokens (points, stars, etc.) for using acceptable protest without acting out, one token if he uses the acceptable protest when redirected from biting, and no tokens if he refuses to use the acceptable protest at all. By using this reinforcement procedure, we are trying to make the acceptable protest more rewarding than the acting out.

Also, for the very intense behavior, in addition to the above, we will use exposure therapy to provide numerous trials to events that are only "mildly frustrating" before moving on to more frustrating events. Often we fail at these attempts because we immediately try to teach the new form of protest during very heated situations, where the child is simply too upset to learn new behavior. Even if the child learned the new protest during practice, these situations are just too overwhelming to try out new behavior. For exposure therapy, we make a hierarchy (list) of common events that set off the negative behavior, from least frustrating to most frustrating. Usually, this list will be broken down into events that sometimes present acting out (less that 50% of the times), events that are 50/50, and events that produce the negative behavior most of the time. We start out by creating frequent incidents of minor irritation in which it will be easier to support the child to use the acceptable protest. This maximizes the chances the child will work with us and learn to use the acceptable protest. Once he can reliably produce the acceptable protest under minor frustration, then we start tackling more frustrating events.

Depending on the frequency, intensity, and length of history using the negative behavior to escape, it can take a while to gradually replace it with an acceptable form of protest. However, usually if we stay with (1) changing the conditions to better match the child and (2) teaching and reinforcing more acceptable forms of protest, the acting out will eventually decrease.

Finger picking

One of our members presented concerns with her son's finger picking and how to help him decrease this behavior. Picking at one's fingers can become injurious, lead to bleeding, and occasionally result in infections. It can become a very habitual response that is hard for the child to control.

? **Member's question**

My son is a flapper and a twirler. It has decreased over the past couple of years but instead of doing that, which is harmless, he is now picking at his nails and cuticles until they bleed and hates having to have the injuries cut off and band-aided up (which he pulls off anyway). He does this when stressed or unsure. I would much rather him flap and twirl than hurt himself. Is there any way to re-direct him from this behavior? We prompt him each time he comes for first aid that it's not a good idea to do this, as it hurts. He promises every time he won't do it again but I think it is now an unconscious activity. Any ideas?

AUTISM DISCUSSION PAGE

Thanks for sharing. The picking of the fingers, like nail biting, is difficult to stop because it often occurs with minimal conscious awareness. It becomes an automatic, habitual response. The child himself often wants to stop the behavior (it injures him), but finds it very difficult. It becomes a habit that is difficult to break.

I would try to shape another automatic, habitual response to replace it. For example, in looking at the function that picking fingers provides, it seems to involve tactile stimulation to both hands and fingers (one set of fingers doing the picking, the other receiving the sensation of being picked). To decrease this behavior by substituting a replacement behavior, we need to meet three primary qualities: the replacement behavior needs to (1) provide tactile stimulation to the fingers of both hands, (2) be portable so it is with the person at all times, and (3) be able to be performed as discreetly as finger picking can be. In this case, we might consider working with the child to find some fidget items that he can keep in each of his pockets, which he can feel, rub, or fidget with to provide repetitive tactile stimulation to the fingers of both hands. This can be a piece of felt to rub between his fingers, piece of string, several paper clips hooked together—whatever feels good for him. You can buy little fingertip feelies that are placed on a finger and can be used for other fingers to rub against or for the finger to rub across the other fingers. The child can provide ongoing tactile stimulation in "fidget fashion" to soothe or alert his nervous system.

How do we teach the child to use the replacement behavior in place of the finger picking? Often where people go wrong is they try to teach the new behavior (fidget item) by redirecting the child to do it when they see the negative behavior (picking) occur. However, this will not usually work. Simply redirecting to the replacement behavior when picking is observed will not be powerful enough to override the picking behavior. Since the picking is an automatic habit, we first need to teach the new behavior to also be an automatic habit. To do this we need to provide very frequent practice of the new behavior and reinforce its use (not just wait until the negative behavior occurs). So, in your son's case, you want to do the following:

1. Have your son keep the items with him at all times, and prompt him frequently to fidget with them and then praise his use of them. We want him to establish a new habit with frequent use. If it feels good, it will become an automatic habit. While sampling a variety of fidget items, usually the child will land on a preferred one that can become the item. Make sure he is carrying the item on him at all times and cue him to use it frequently throughout the day. This gives him frequent trials (exposure) to fidgeting with it. Another member on this page shared that she replaced her little one's picking behavior with buttons. Her daughter fiddles with and rubs them. Mom also sewed them on to her clothes, toys, pillowcase, and other items dear to her daughter. This way, her daughter always has the buttons available to fidget with. Again, this substitute has to be portable—with the child at all times.

2. If the child is older or cognitively aware enough to understand, discuss with him the positive effects that using a fidget item will have on soothing him when anxious and alerting him when under-aroused. Teach him how stimming like this will help him stay calm and organized.

3. Prompt him to use the item frequently throughout the day and praise him heavily for calming himself by fidgeting. Another positive strategy is for the parent to model this by having their own fidget item that they frequently use throughout the day. The parent can also use it themselves during times of stress when the child would typically need to use theirs.

4. During times when you expect the behavior to occur the most (situations that often bring on picking), prompt him to use the fidget before the picking has a chance to occur. Again, praise him for doing so. For example, if this behavior occurs when he first goes to bed, before falling asleep, then you tuck him in each night, give him the fidget item(s), and encourage/reinforce him to fidget until he falls asleep. He can carry them in his pockets at school and everywhere he goes.

Do not scold him for picking his fingers, but encourage him that once he feels the urge to pick this is a cue for him to fidget. Over time, you want to empower him to recognize when he feels the urge to pick and to fidget instead. Of course, each time you do see finger picking, redirect to fidget and reinforce him.

Finger picking can occur at any age. It is important to teach these children as young as possible easy ways to pacify their nervous system with safe sensory stimulation. Remember, the tool needs to be portable (always on them) and as discreet as possible. Many adults learn to use alternative fidgets and other self-stimulation to keep their nervous system regulated and to avoid injurious behaviors such as finger picking. It is empowering to learn simple tools for keeping your nervous calm and organized.

Finger (or skin) picking can also be stimulated by dry or rough skin, hang nails, scabs, or other abnormalities of the skin that the child hyper-focuses on. Sometimes treating the underlying cause of the dry skin can help. Keeping the nails filed (not cut) and cuticles cut can help. Many of the children are hyper-sensitive to any little imperfection that constantly draws their attention. On the opposite side, some of the children are hypo-sensitive (dull sensations) and may hyper-focus on picking scabs, nails, and skin, while seeking intense stimulation that they can feel.

Teaching "soft hands"

How many of you have children who are overly rough with people and objects? Many children on the spectrum tend to be very rough with physical contact. Their sensory system does not give good input on how hard they are grasping, pushing, pulling, and tapping things or people. They often do not have good control of their bodies. They tend to do everything very roughly, often intruding in the space of others. Because it can be intrusive to others, and often gets negative reactions or rejection from others, it is important to teach the child "soft touch."

Teaching soft touch, or gentle hands, often requires a lot of practice. It requires the parents to model soft hands and have the child practice it. Flood a lot of attention around it and take every opportunity to prompt soft hands throughout the day. For a week or two, the parents provide numerous opportunities to model and practice soft touch. I will often play a game with the child where we both go around and touch things with soft hands (be careful with children who are tactile defensive; light touch is very discomforting for them, so do not force soft touch on them). We walk together, holding hands with gentle pressure. We walk to different objects in the house and tap on things softly, pick up and put things down gently. The child tries to copy what I am doing. I will pick a few things and we will practice soft hands. Then I have the child pick a few things and I follow his lead. So we go back and forth, and add mom or dad into the game.

Often the problem is poor emotional regulation. As the child becomes excited or upset, he loses his ability to regulate his behavior and becomes overpowering. By teaching the child what soft hands feel like, you are giving him a tool to learn to regulate his emotions. As the child becomes excited and his touch becomes rougher, you redirect the child to soft hands and do it with him if needed (praising cooperation). As the child focuses on appropriate touch, he gains better control over his emotional regulation. The important thing is making sure you focus on his attempts to use soft hands and take the focus off when he slips up. The more competent you can help the child feel, the more confidence he gains in controlling his emotions and behavior.

Children with autism often have difficulty measuring degrees of relativity (hard/soft, loud/quiet, fast/slow, etc.). I will play regulating games, with the children trying to follow my lead. One of the fun ones is banging on a drum. The parent and child each have a small drum and a drumstick. The child tries to follow the parent's lead in drumming. The parent will drum soft, soft, soft, soft, hard, hard, hard, hard, soft, soft, soft, soft (repeatedly back and forth) until the child is effectively copying the drumming of the parent. Then we will do fast and slow, loud and quiet. These kinds of games help the child follow the lead of the parent to learn what it feels like to regulate his behavior. All children learn regulation from another more experienced person (parent) before learning self-regulation. Once the child learns how to regulate his behavior, his emotions are easier to regulate.

Problems in the community

Many families who have children on the spectrum frequently feel like prisoners in their own homes. Because their children are often overwhelmed and act out in public, they are confined to the safety of their homes. However, for children to grow and develop, they need exposure to be part of the community. At the same time, we need to frame these outings to maximize success for both pleasure and learning. Like all exposure to novelty, we need to develop very structured boundaries, build in supports, add guided participation, and maximize the success of the outing. Instead of saying "no" they cannot do this, we need to ask "how." What are the barriers and what supports are needed to lessen these barriers? Listed below are potential challenges and possible strategies to support them:

- *Sensory.* If your child has sensory issues and becomes overloaded easily, then add in ways to lessen, filter, or distract auditory and visual stimulation. With knowledge of your child's sensory challenges, keep a sensory toolbox in the car to accommodate for these sensory challenges. Often having the child wear ear plugs or use an iPod to mask noise, wear sunglasses to dim bright lights, sit in enclosed booths or with his back to the crowd to minimize visual stimulation, and use fidget toys and other items to distract can greatly reduce stress for the child.

- *Spatial concerns.* Try to consider physical arrangement to maximize success. How much space does your child need? Does the child need to sit between two adults or between an adult and the inside of the booth, sit away from items of temptation, or close to the door or bathroom if a quick exit may be needed?

- *Waiting is always an issue.* Standing in line, waiting a long time for food, and waiting for others to finish eating are often issues. Do not simply expect the child to patiently wait. Bring fidget toys and simple activities (e.g. electronic devices) to distract and occupy time. Also try shortening the time by calling in advance, waiting to take the child into the restaurant until the group is seated, taking the child outside to play after he has finished eating, and discussing the menu in advance so the child knows what to order.

- *Clarify and verify.* Uncertainty is the child's worse enemy! Don't assume the child knows what is occurring and what is expected. Discuss each step of the activity, what will happen, the order of events, and what is expected of him just prior to going in. Clarify concretely what is happening and, if possible, verify that the child understands. Visual supports are often good for this. Use a Velcro board or picture story to visually sequence the order of events (waiting in line, sitting down, ordering, eating, paying, leaving, etc.).

- *Preview and review.* If you go to the same places a lot, make picture stories to prepare the child. Take a digital camera and take several pictures of the child going through the steps in the setting. On the computer, make a picture story by placing four pictures in sequence, with a note under each picture to tell the story. Before going to the event, use the picture story to preview what is expected, and if necessary, take it along. The picture page can also be used to review between trips. I like to create a "me" picture book of the various community events that the child frequently attends. This way, the parent and child can review them frequently, talk about how much fun they have, and instill further confidence about integrating into the community.

- *Sense of control.* Many children can bridge the uncertainty if they are actively a part of the process (planning the outing, taking orders for the family, paying at the end, etc.). The best way to tackle uncertainty is to have some control over it.

- *Have a backup plan.* For children who get overwhelmed, discuss with them before going into an event what to do if they start to become overwhelmed. Many children will freak when they start to get overwhelmed. They don't know what to do or how to escape the situation. This sets off panic and they act out, and then they get more furious when told that they have to leave. This often can be anticipated ahead of time. Discuss what problems might occur in the setting, what supports you can provide when this occurs, and how the child should handle it when overload happens. For example, if you discuss the need to pull back, leave briefly, rebound, and return when the child starts to get overwhelmed, then the child will be more likely to follow that plan once this situation arises. Since you discuss it as a proactive support, the child feels more competent in using it once the situation arises. I also find that the child's anxiety, as well as that of all family members, lessens when they have a plan worked out ahead of time. With less initial anxiety, there is less likelihood of a meltdown. Also, once overload starts to occur, the child understands that, by pulling back to regroup, it doesn't mean ending the activity altogether.

- *Reaction strategies.* Even with all the supports built in, unanticipated problems will still arise. Always have a reaction plan set up for immediately dealing with behavior challenges when they occur. I have found that members of the public are more annoyed with families that do not quickly intervene and block, redirect, or otherwise diffuse the situation. Part of being proactive is to brainstorm what you going to do *if* these behaviors occur. For most children, setting boundaries and intervening very early in the episode is more successful.

- *Graded exposure.* Start simple, build gradually, and maximize success! For some of my very challenging clients, we start by making a hierarchy of least to most challenging events. For example, we may start with going into a restaurant at a very slow time of the day and gradually work our way up to busier times. Or we may start by going in and just buying a quick snack to make it a short trip and give the child familiarity with the event. Gradual exposure can a build strong sense of safety and competency. Like any new learning, it can be successful; it just takes time, effort, and patience from parents and the public.

When using gradual exposure, we usually make three lists: (1) a list of events that rarely present problems, (2) a list of events that sometimes present problems, and (3) a list of events that usually represent major problems. From that list we isolate factors that make the events difficult and those that make the events more successful. By doing so, we can make a hierarchy of events from least to most challenging and start with frequent, but brief, outings in the least anxiety-provoking settings to maximize success and teach the family the supports. They learn to preview and review ahead of time, have a plan for when times get rough, and implement the plan under easy conditions. Once everyone feels more competent in implementing the supports, then we gradually stretch the outings up the hierarchy, as long as they remain successful. By doing so, everyone feels more relaxed and confident that they can handle the situations that may arise.

Going out in the community can cause significant stress for both the child and the family. However, integrating with others and inclusion in the community are ultimate goals for all of us.

WANDERING

Running or wandering off is probably one of the most dangerous behaviors for children on the spectrum. It is one of the leading causes of death and one of parents' greatest worries.

Wandering is also one of the most difficult behaviors to control. Many of the strategies involve controlling the environment, using technology to monitor the child, and building in as many protection strategies as possible.

Wandering: safety and protection first

Since wandering, or eloping, is the biggest threat to the safety of many children on the spectrum, the first line of programming is maximizing safety and protection. Common protective strategies consist of the following:

- Locks and other barriers to deter the child from leaving the house.

- Motion detectors and cameras to monitor the child's movement both in and out of the house.

- Alarms to notify us if the child does leave the house.

- Fences to keep the child in the yard.

- Personal tracking devices for locating the child when he does elope.

- Harnesses and strollers to restrain the child from running when in the community.

- Personal identification located on the child.

- A profile to give to first responders who may be called when eloping occurs.

- Notifying neighbors in case they see the child away from the yard.

Although the frequency of wandering/running will vary from child to child, the best stance to take is to assume that your child will wander at any chance available to him. Be prepared at all times by putting up barriers (locks, etc.), alarms to notify you if he does leave, motion detectors at night, and personal tracking devices to track him if he does elope. The Autism Speaks website's toolkit for wandering has a list of resources for personal tracking devices, alarms, and motion detectors (www.autismspeaks.org).

Wandering: personal observations

In my experience with children who run or wander, I have seen a variety of conditions that seem to lead to children to engaging in this behavior. There are often many executive functioning and sensory processing issues that can facilitate eloping.

Executive functions may include the following:

- The child often has poor awareness of boundaries and only sees what he is immediately attracted to. He does not realize that he is overstepping boundaries.

- The child has poor impulse control, with limited ability to inhibit his impulses; he acts without thinking.

- The child has poor awareness of dangers that are involved. He has poor ability to appraise the safety issues involved and seems oblivious to dangers.

- The child acts so impulsively that he has poor ability to monitor what he is doing, while doing it. This child usually moves faster than he can monitor what he is doing, and thus does not see the situation he is placing himself in (e.g. goes right into the water, even though it is going over his head).

- The child has limited ability to use forethought, to think about the consequences of his action before acting. Even though he may have had a close call last time, it doesn't seem to affect his actions now.

- The child becomes fixated on something that attracts him and cannot shift attention from it.

Other characteristics which are common in many but not all cases:

- Seems to occur the most between ages four and nine, and seems to subside as the child gains better regulatory skills (impulse control and emotional regulation).

- Seems to occur more in children with strong sensitivities, usually to escape sensory overload.

- Seems to occur more in children who are hyperactive, seeking excitement and stimulation. These children are usually very active, disorganized, and need ongoing stimulation to stay aroused.

- Seems to occur more in children who have very strong hyper-focus issues, where they have trouble shifting their attention (become stuck on) from the attraction.

- Occurs more in children with limited verbal skills, most likely because they do not see other avenues to get what they want.

- Seems to occur more with children who have difficulty following the lead of others. They tend to do what they want, when they want, with little referencing of others for direction. These children are often at the stage where they resist following the lead of others and have to control everything happening to them.

Again, these are my own experiences, not based on research. Obviously, each child is different, and some may include many of the above or none at all. Often, if we can identify some of the underlying variables involved (sensory issues, arousal problems, etc.), we can reduce the desire to run by addressing these vulnerabilities—for example, providing a strong sensory diet for a child who has an under-aroused nervous system, or providing the child with an MP3 player to mask the noise level when going into a noisy setting.

In future articles we will look at possible strategies that may help lessen the running. However, this is dangerous behavior and these should only be implemented under the direction of a professional and with all the safeguards put in place. No strategy I recommend should be tried without the assessment and guidance of a professional.

Wandering: proactive strategies for seeking behavior

As previously discussed, the first line of defense for children who wander is protection strategies to maximize the child's safety (locks, alarms, monitors, harnesses in the community, etc.). The second line of programming is to proactively tackle some of the conditions that motivate the child to wander. There are a variety of reasons why children elope, one of which is seeking something of interest (attraction). Listed below are some proactive strategies for lessening seeking behavior.

Reminder: Wandering is a very dangerous behavior. Only use these techniques under the guidance of a professional following a thorough assessment.

Strategies for use at home

- Some children become fixated on an interest (e.g. water, woods, food, etc.) and the attraction is so strong that they will elope to seek it.

- At home, if the child has an attraction that he always runs to, try to provide frequent exposure to the event. This way he doesn't have to sneak out to get to it. Provide easy access to it, and later have him earn it by first doing simple things around the house.

- Visit the attraction frequently at first. Schedule it into the child's daily routine by using a picture schedule or calendar to make it predictable. If using a visual schedule for the day, place a picture of the attraction on the schedule so the child sees that it will happen. At first, if the event is nearby, you might want to go twice a day for a short walk to the attraction. Each time you return, go to the picture schedule and discuss when it will occur again. This way, the child understands that it is coming up again soon. (For example, after dinner we will go again.)

- Also, it is good to have a picture schedule so the child can see the structure of the day. He can see the sequence of events that will occur before going for the walk. This will motivate him to stay busy doing the routine so he can go for the walk. The routine will also help occupy his time during the wait.

- In addition, give the child a way to request the desired event. If the child is nonverbal, and you do not use a picture schedule, then place a picture of the attraction on the refrigerator so he can easily obtain it. Always have the child hand you the picture before leaving so he learns to associate the picture with the event. At first, each time he brings the picture to you, take him to the event; later on delay by telling him when you two can go (soon after the request). We want to teach the child to ask to go, rather than elope. The picture becomes the center of communication.

- Try to identify a safe walking path to the attraction, and follow that route each time. This way, if he does run, you know which route he is taking and can maximize safety.

- Focus heavily on the two of you going together, not him going alone. Use a picture story teaching this concept (we-do, not you-do) or have one picture of the two of you at the event, and one picture of him alone, with the "no" sign (red circle with diagonal line through it) over the picture. Frequently talk about how he has to do it with you, not by himself.

- If possible, connect an item that you use together at the attraction to take with you, then keep it out of sight. For example, if the child likes to play in the sand near the pond, then take a bucket and play together. This bucket becomes associated with doing it with you rather than going alone. Then keep that item out of reach, so he can only do it with you. Next, take a camera with you and take pictures of you two having fun doing it together; make a scrapbook. This gives the two of you something to talk about, take pictures of, and build strong memories around. It changes the positive value from just the attraction alone to doing it with you. He is going to be less focused on going alone and more on going with you.

EXAMPLE

Jimmy has an attraction to water. There is a pond close by that he likes to run to when he can slip away. His mom decided to make this interest into a daily walk so Jimmy could enjoy the pond, learn a variety of activities while he was there, begin to understand safe rules around the pond, and learn a safe way of getting there. Since it was summer time, and Jimmy wasn't in school, mom decided to go there twice a day—once after breakfast and again after dinner.

Mom made up a picture schedule of the fun events in his day. She placed the pictures in sequence, so Jimmy could see what he was doing, what was coming up next, and when the walks were going to follow the meals. Mom focused on the picture schedule, having Jimmy take off each event as it was completed, and frequently discussed how close he was getting to the walk. The picture schedule kept him busy and gave him frequent avenues for attention and stimulation.

Mom had a one-page social story briefly discussing that going for a walk is a "we-do" activity (do with mom or dad) and not a "me-do" (doing it alone). She also had two pictures at each door, one picture of the two of them smiling, and one of just Jimmy alone with the "no" symbol covering it. This was a reminder for them to discuss that Jimmy does not go outside alone, but only with mom or dad.

Mom laid out a route to take that would be safe from traffic, in case Jimmy was to try to go alone. It provided a safer route and would always lead him to the same place in case they had to look for him.

Jimmy and mom had two buckets with small hand shovels that they took with them down to the pond. They would frequently do water and mud activities, and collect stones. They both loved doing this together. Mom took her camera and took pictures for them to make a picture story to review frequently at home. This way, Jimmy began to associate going to the pond with mom and taking the buckets. Mom kept the buckets out of sight at home, so the only way he could do these activities was with mom or dad.

These procedures worked with Jimmy's attraction to visiting he pond; it made it into a positive event, taught him how to do it safely, and taught him to enjoy doing it with someone rather than doing it alone. Mom also enrolled Jimmy in swimming lessons just in case he wandered into the pond. However, they never went swimming in the pond, because she did not want him associating the pond with swimming. Swimming was only for the pool.

Strategies when in the community

- Children who are attracted to certain things in the community (e.g. elevator) want to run to that attraction each time they are there.

- If possible, visit that attraction when you first get there and put boundaries on it ("We are going up and down the elevator two times."). Then tell the child that he can revisit it again before leaving.

- If possible, use a portable picture sequence board with pictures of what you will do. The first picture is the attraction, which occurs again after several other events in the outing.

- As at home, make the attraction a "we-do," not a "me-do."

These strategies provide a mental map for the child by previewing what is going to happen and when he will visit the item of interest. Remember, no matter how many proactive strategies you build in, occasionally the attraction is just too irresistible to resist. You may drastically reduce the incidents of eloping, but most likely the child will try on occasion. Keep safeguards in place to minimize the attempts and maximize safety. For some children, what they seek may be hard to identify and may be anything that draws their attention. These children will need constant supervision and safeguards until they mature to the point that this self-control develops. Remember, I recommend using these strategies only with professional consultation to maximize safety.

Wandering: proactive strategies for escape/avoidance

In the previous post we discussed proactive strategies for reducing running/wandering when the motivation is to seek out something that attracts the child. Another major reason for children to run is to escape or avoid something that is uncomfortable for them. This could include being overwhelmed by sensory overload, information overload, or intense excitement. This would also include trying to escape unwanted demands, uncertainty, or when the child doesn't understand what he can expect or what is expected of him. My experience is that many of these children will get anxious when faced with uncertainty and not knowing how to act. These same children may also run when they get excited and overwhelmed.

Reminder: Wandering is a very dangerous behavior. Only use these techniques under the guidance of a professional following a thorough assessment.

General procedures

1. Try to note what the child is escaping from (e.g. sensory, confusion, demands, etc.) and in what settings running is most likely to occur. The more we know, the more we can prepare for.

2. Look for ways either to modify the setting or demands to lessen the overload (turn down the noise, dim the lighting, go to the store at less congestive times, etc.) or to build in adaptations to mask or distract the overload (ear plugs, sunglasses, iPod, fidget toys, etc.).

3. Be aware of the high probability times (noisy settings, increased social demands, high excitement) and increase supervision and support to help the child regulate and cope, as well as minimize the chance of running.

4. Increase understanding and lower anxiety by preparing the child ahead of time. Preview what the child can expect to happen, what is expected of him, how long it will last, and what will come next. Running will occur more frequently when the child is not prepared for what is happening. The more the child understands what to expect, the less anxiety he has, and the less probability he will run to escape.

5. Also preview what the child should do if he starts to become overloaded (leave event, go to bathroom or car, etc.) or how he should ask for help if tasks get too hard. Discuss ahead of time how he should react if that situation occurs.

6. Give the child another way to communicate that he needs to escape (say "stop" or "go," gesture or sign, use picture card, etc.) instead of running,

and remind him of this before and during the event. Encourage this form of communication whenever he seems overloaded or excited.

7.   Look for early signs of overload, excitement, or agitation (increased motor movement, stimming, dilated pupils, etc.) and remind him to use his replacement behavior (alternative way of communicating) to briefly escape or end the activity.

8.   Give frequent breaks during events with longer durations, so the child has a chance to rebound before getting overloaded.

9.   Make a hierarchy of low- to high-stress situations that would predict possible running. Start with frequent visits to the low-probability events first, so he can practice his replacement behavior (alternative way to escape or ask for help). Provide brief exposure to the event, then gradually increase the time of exposure as long he is successful. Once he learns to use the replacement behavior, gradually work up the hierarchy of events most likely to elicit running.

10.   While in events, if he tries to run, block his escape and prompt him to use his replacement behavior. Try to make it so he cannot escape by running, only by communicating appropriately. Redirect him to communicate appropriately and then allow him to escape.

11.   Reinforce heavily for not running and for using his replacement behavior.

Running/wandering can be a very dangerous behavior. You must always have the safeguards built in (locks, alarms, harnesses, holding hands, strollers, etc.) because no matter how hard you try to be proactive, running/wandering can occur at any time. In summary, when dealing with running to escape unwanted events, try to lower the stressors, build in added assistance to support the child, and give him another way to communicate the need to escape to take the place of running.

Wandering: proactive strategies— focus on what you want them to do!

Often the best way to decrease a problem behavior is not to focus so much on what we don't want the child to do, but to focus our attention on what we do want the child to do. Usually, this means scripting for the child exactly what he needs to do, framing it so that it happens, and then reinforcing the child for doing it. By focusing on what you want the child to do, you set the path for him to follow, which may decrease the chance of wandering/running.

Reminder: Wandering is a very dangerous behavior. Only use these techniques under the guidance of a professional following a thorough assessment.

Reinforcing behavior incompatible with running

1. Example: When shopping in a grocery store, the parent gives the child the responsibility of pushing the grocery cart. Since the child also tends to impulsively grab things off the shelves, mom tells the child before going in that his hands need to be on the cart at all times. This sets an expectation of the child's role when in the store ("My job is to hold onto the cart with both hands"). This lessens the likelihood not only of running but also of grabbing items off the shelves. As long as the hands are on the cart, it is unlikely that the two inappropriate behaviors (running and grabbing) will occur. Mom praises the child every few minutes by making reference to and praising him for having his hands on the cart. The secret is keeping it a concrete rule! Once mom sees the child take a hand off the cart, she immediately "stops the action" until he puts his hands back on the cart. This way, it becomes very clear to him that the main objective is keeping his hands on the cart. Mom can also build in extra rewards, such as getting to buy a treat at the end of shopping if he cooperates. Mom needs to stay focused on "both hands on cart," "stopping the action," and redirecting hands back on the cart. Do not to wait until the child is grabbing or running to try to redirect. Nip it in the bud before it gets that far.

2. Example: Mom is waiting for a doctor's appointment with the child in the waiting room. Usually, this can be a real struggle because the child often is pacing around the room and running out the door. Instead, we have mom focus on reinforcing the child for sitting down. If he is sitting, he cannot be running around disrupting others or running out the door. Mom sits her son next to the wall, with her sitting on the other side. This makes it easier to block and intercept the child from getting up and taking off (framing). Mom tells him that he is expected to sit in the chair while they wait for the doctor. Mom gives him his Game Boy to play with while waiting. Mom praises him frequently for remaining seated. If he cooperates, he can get a special item from the doctor. When the boy forgets and impulsively attempts to get up, mom immediately prompts him to sit back down again. Mom doesn't wait until he is up and running around the room to redirect him back. She redirects immediately when he attempts to get up.

Teaching child to walk alongside you

1. For children who run or wander away, it is important to teach them to walk alongside you and to stop when prompted. We usually teach this first in a distraction-free setting, away from others (hallway in school or sidewalk near the house)—somewhere that is less tempting for the child and also less embarrassing for the parent.

2. The objective is for the child to walk alongside the parent. Begin by telling the child he needs to walk alongside you, and that the two of you will hold hands while walking down and back. Make it fun and have a good time with it. Let him know that if he gets too far ahead, or doesn't listen, then you will stop the action until he complies. Praise frequently and have a concrete reinforcer for him at the end if he complies with redirection.

3. When walking, pause occasionally to discuss or point out something. This requires the child to reference you to stop when you do and stay coordinated with you. If the child tries to walk away from your side, stop the action and prompt him back. If he doesn't listen, stop the action until he does comply. If he acts up too intensively and does not cooperate, simply end the trial without the reward or attention.

4. Be sure to praise frequently for walking alongside you. If praise is not effective, then possibly use a concrete reward such as a small treat.

5. Once he learns to walk alongside you while holding hands, try it without holding hands. Remind the child that he still needs to walk alongside you and stop when you do. Also let the child know that if he doesn't walk alongside you, then he will have to hold your hand. While walking, if he moves up too far, then stop walking and prompt him to stop and return. If he complies, then praise and continue. If he does not comply, then he must hold your hand for a short time before trying again.

6. Once he understands and cooperates successfully in the controlled setting, move out into community outings. Because of the distractibility of these settings, you may need to start off with holding hands again, until he can control his impulses well enough. Start in the parking lot and practice him walking right alongside you. Follow the same steps as above, praising all cooperation. If he pulls away, prompt him to stop and hold his hand if he is not cooperative. If he resists this, then stop the action and tell him that you two cannot enter the store if he cannot comply with walking alongside you. If he still doesn't comply, then go back to the car and try again some other time.

7. Remember, no matter where you two are, you have to keep your mind on the objective (walk alongside you). At first, don't let him stray even a little in front of or behind you. Even if he is being good, you two need to stay side by side. Keep the rule literal and very clear and consistent. Don't wait until he runs off to focus on the rule.

Setting boundaries at home

1. It is important that you define very clear, visual boundaries for the child to wander within. Outside, either use a fence or line the ground with a visual border that is easy for the child to see. Place stop signs along the boundaries to give visual cues to stop and go no further. It is very important that the boundaries and signs are very concrete and visual.

2. At least once a day, more often if needed, walk with the child along the boundaries, pointing them out and explaining that he cannot go past these boundaries unless with mom or dad. After a few days, have the child walk you around the boundaries, letting him point out the boundaries for you. This way, you are sure he understands. Make it fun and praise him frequently for cooperating.

3. When the child is outside, parents should be close by, observing, reminding the child to not cross the boundaries, and being ready to redirect and end the activity if he does not cooperate. Remind the child of the boundaries and rules just before going outside, and remind again during the activity if needed. If he begins to cross the boundaries, then prompt him to stop and redirect back within the boundaries. If he does not comply, immediately bring him inside and end the activity. He cannot be outside unless he is respecting the boundaries.

4. If needed, reinforce the child with a preferred item/event when the activity is over, if he did not cross the boundaries. Remind him of what the reinforcer is (better to let him choose) before going out to play. If you have to end the activity early because he was not cooperative in staying within the boundaries, then he does not get the preferred activity.

These are just a few positive strategies that focus on what you want him to do rather than focusing on not running. When focusing our attention on "don't run," it sets the expectation and running usually increases. When just focusing the attention on "no running," it doesn't tell the child what to do instead. Usually, when it is not clear what you *want* them to do, the children will focus on what you *don't* want them to do. So let's put most of our emphasis and attention on what we want the child to do, and often that is what we will see.

Wandering: proactive strategies for calming the nervous system

Some children run when they are excited and over-aroused, and some run for excitement when under-aroused. Some children run for the sake of running (find it enjoyable), some like the freedom of escape, and some enjoy the attention of having others chase them. The child may run for one of these reasons or for several of them. Often running can serve multiple purposes, each requiring different strategies. Some of the strategies below can help with these children.

Reminder: Wandering is a very dangerous behavior. Only use these techniques under the guidance of a professional following a thorough assessment.

1. If the children are sensory-defensive and over-sensitive to stimulation, they may run when their nervous system is overloaded in events where there is a lot of uncertainty or too much stimulation. If the child is anxious about the uncertainty of the event or because of sensory bombardment, he will run to escape the unpleasant situation.

2. For the sensory-sensitive child, you need to be aware of his sensitivities and provide accommodations for them. Such strategies as wearing a brim cap and/or sunglasses to mask bright light, or ear plugs or headphones to muffle noise, or using fidget toys to soothe the anxious nervous system will often help. Other strategies would be to avoid highly stimulating events, go late and leave early to cut the activity short, and/or take frequent breaks.

3. If children are overactive or under-aroused, they are likely to enjoy the excitement of running. Some kids will get very anxious when they are under-aroused, setting them off to run to create strong stimulation. I find a strong sensory diet of a lot of movement (bouncing on a trampoline, running, jumping, climbing, etc.) for 20 minutes at a time will help calm and organize the nervous system. Some kids require extensive amounts of movement and exertion to satisfy their nervous system. I have found that a good sensory evaluation, with a sensory diet tailored to the child's nervous system needs, can be very effective in reducing running.

4. Find a large fenced-in area that is safe for the child to run free. Many elementary schools have large fenced-off property, and some parks also have large fenced-off areas. This allows the child to run freely without restrictions. Allow the child to run as he pleases with little interruption.

5. For a child who loves the attention of others chasing him, if possible try not to run after him. Follow him, but minimize your emotional reaction so as not to provide strong excitable reactions. Take the bang out of the bite! When redirecting, focus verbally on what you want the child to do, not on what he is doing wrong (running). React very calmly so as not to reinforce the running with strong attention.

6. Sometimes if the child does not get out much, he is eager to test the extremes. Providing frequent exposure to being outside and in community outings can lessen the novelty and excitability, minimizing the child's excitability in community events. Since parents with a child who runs tend to minimize the child's access to out-of-home events, the novelty of going out will often stimulate more excitement to run. Sometimes, providing increased exposure to events that stimulate running will lessen the novelty and excitability.

If your child runs because it is fun and exciting, then the above strategies should help to lower the excitability factor of the event, as well as calm the child's nervous system. These children are often difficult to watch because you don't know when they will dart off. There is often little warning that running will occur.

This ends our series on wandering. Usually, a comprehensive plan will include several of the strategies listed in the above posts. It is important to work with a professional to evaluate the function(s) of the wandering/running and build a plan with strategies that meet the specific needs of your child.

Frustration during video games

Videos games can be very addictive, actually changing the neurochemistry in the brain. This can be for any person, on the spectrum or not, especially if there is any attention deficit disorder (ADD) involved. People with under-aroused nervous systems and attention deficit problems need excitability in order to focus. Video games provide excitation both at the visual, sensory level and at the cognitive (challenge) level. Kids on the spectrum, since they struggle regulating in the real world (especially relating with others), enjoy living in a fantasy world which brings them a sense of control and competence. They can control (or feel they control) what happens and this builds strong excitability. Then, as the game gets harder and they begin to fail, it takes them from an immediate high to an immediate low. Their brains cannot switch gears that quickly.

Mastery is rewarding for every living being. Unfortunately, children on the spectrum often only experience mastery when they are focusing on their obsessive interest or playing a video game. They start off the video games at the easier steps, gradually building confidence as they work up the levels. This mastery builds greater and greater excitement—and then suddenly they fail! What a letdown! Adding fuel to the fire, children with autism have trouble shifting gears and ending something that is very exciting for them. Once into it, it is difficult to for them to pull themselves away from the excitement. They get hyper-focused on the game and do not want to pull away.

The sensory excitability, feelings of mastery and competence, and ability to control what is happening are all very attractive to children with autism. They can withdraw from the real world and enter a world where they can feel more competent. Adding fuel to the fire, children with autism are also "all or nothing," and see failure as catastrophic. They have a difficult time with "good enough" thinking and see all failure as devastating. Since they have problems with regulating emotions anyway, video games obviously set them up for problems.

Now, given all these issues that video games can bring, it is good to limit the amount of time children on the spectrum spend with video games. You need to put very clear boundaries, rules, and expectations on their use. However, you may need to do this gradually. If your child is used to playing hours at a time, and you take it away for a week, expect to have withdrawal effects. Most children on the spectrum cannot handle this. Gradually cut back on how long they can play it and how often during the day. Build in other activities they have to do first, before playing the video games. It is important to teach children structure and routine, so get your child used to a routine filled with constructive activity, with video games built in periodically. Also, video games can be used to reinforce completing the less preferred activities. "First you do this and then you can play games!" So build in approximately 90 minutes or more of other activity to earn 30 minutes of video game time.

The two variables that I find affect emotional regulation with video games are the length of time the child can play them before becoming emotionally dysregulated and the complexity of the game that builds greater emotional excitement. Try to keep track of how long the child can play before becoming dysregulated, then limit playing time to a safe duration. Use a visual timer and give three- and one-minute warnings before ending the play. This gives the brain a chance to prepare for the transition of stopping and moving on. "Johnnie, you can play video games until 8 o'clock and then you will have your snack." This way, Johnnie knows what is coming up after video games. Make sure to give five-, three-, and one-minute warnings before transitioning to the snack: "Johnnie, in five minutes we will end the video game and have your snack."

Also, keep track of which games seem to be less intense (or easier) and which games are harder, thus causing emotional dysregulation. Talk this over with him. When the child throws a fit during one of the harder ones, then for the next session he has to play one of the easier ones.

Now, video games also can be used to teach the child how to deal with frustration, learn "good enough" tolerance, and teach emotional regulation. For the more difficult games, try to get the child to talk about what parts are easy and what parts are frustrating for him. Have him explain how he is working through the easier parts, and talk about how the game is built around "failing to succeed." You often have to fail numerous times before learning how to successfully beat it, and sometimes you may never be able to make it through all the steps. Try to get him to realize that is the strategy of the game.

Also, realize that as the child moves further and further along the complexity of the game, it will become more emotionally intense and he will become more drawn into the game. Have him pause at different steps of the game, take a minute or two break, and then go back to it. His nervous system needs a minute to rebound and collect itself, especially at the harder steps. Teach him to take a few deep breaths and do a few wall push-ups to settle himself. You want to identify with the child what he should do when the game starts getting intense, and then have him practice it at the easier levels while he has better self-control. Then, as the intensity builds, he is used to using the coping skill.

For the game that is very difficult for the child, tell him he must play it with you to help coach him through the tough stages. This is a good time to teach him how to gauge his level of emotional intensity. If he is older, have him grade his emotional level on a gradient of 1–5, with 1 being calm and 5 being too intense to handle. Have him pause periodically in the game and rate how he feels. Give him feedback on the level you would rate him at. For older children, have them sense how their bodies feel when upset. Together, figure out what he should do at each level to keep his cool (take deep breaths at low levels, get up for a break at higher levels, etc.). Once he allows you to be a working partner with him during these more intense games, coach him along as you see his intensity build. Have him pause briefly between levels to talk about how he feels and to use simple techniques to regroup. Once you identify the higher steps that cause him the frustration, build in concrete rewards for playing those steps while regulating his emotional reactions (win or lose). This way, he sees that the reward comes not for winning or losing but for controlling his reactions during the step. Let him feel the "mastery" of keeping control when losing. First, talk together about what coping skills to use when frustrated, coach him to use them during the game, and reward him for using them when things go wrong. Make the pay-off bigger for keeping his cool than for winning the game. Make the main goal/objective of the game dealing with losing without acting out! This changes the nature of the game.

If he becomes overwhelmed and acts out, back up the next time and end the game sooner. If you need to build in a consequence, either take five or ten minutes away from the next session (also add minutes if he ends on time without fuss) or lose the next session (keep it simple). Focus on building competency in the face of frustration (using coping skills and tackling the frustration) rather than punishing him for losing it.

Actually, there are other ways you can use video games to teach regulation, but it is too much for one article. Remember, however, video games can be a great teaching tool, since they require maintaining emotional control, which is hard for these children. It is a safe place to teach frustration tolerance and emotional control. Video games will only mirror other real-life times of frustration.

Chapter 5

LABELS, DIAGNOSES, AND CO-OCCURRING DISORDERS

High functioning, low functioning, cognitive impairment, anxiety and depression, obsessive/compulsive disorder (OCD), attention deficit hyperactivity disorder (ADHD), oppositional defiant disorder (ODD), seizures, and bipolar disorder are all frequently seen labels co-occurring with autism spectrum disorders. They can be very confusing and misleading, frequently leaving parents overwhelmed by what they mean and how to treat them. This chapter helps identify some of the common diagnoses and the reasons why they frequently occur with autism.

All a matter of degree!

For many of the symptoms of autism spectrum disorders, if you look closely at yourselves you will notice many of these common characteristics in you. Whether it be some quirky sensory sensitivity (we all have them), a few excessive worries, exaggerated reactions to certain snags or imperfections (especially in others), strong adherence to routine, favorite fixations, difficulty reading the mental or emotional states of others, misreading the effects of your behavior on others, or holding to rigid, inflexible ideas, we all have various characteristics that are often labeled as symptoms of autism.

All these characteristics occur on their own continuum, from very mild to extremely severe. Each one of us falls at different spots on the continuum. We all have our own profile of where we lie on each one of these dimensions. How many of these symptoms, and where you are on each of these dimensions, will determine whether you are diagnosed as being on the spectrum. It is the cluster of characteristics, severe enough to interfere with daily living, that usually ends up getting the diagnosis.

This is why it should not be hard for us to identify with these characteristics and to empathize with the struggles of those on the spectrum. We all experience them to lesser degrees. Most of the strategies I post on here can apply to all of us, not just people on the spectrum. People on the spectrum live in the world of extremes on many of these dimensions, whereas most of us live in a world of moderation somewhere between the two extremes. This allows us to be a little more flexible in our reactions to the world of gray relativity. We are a little more flexible in going with the flow, shifting gears, and handling little variations that occur throughout our day. Some of us are more flexible and more adaptive than others. Some of us struggle with many of these issues, but just not to the degree that would warrant a diagnosis.

We are all human! Each of us has our own little imperfections. We are definitely more alike than we are different. So, recognize your own vulnerabilities, rigid inflexibilities, and social weaknesses, and you can see how, if they were more exaggerated, they would affect your world. It makes understanding and being more tolerant a lot easier. It allows us to meet in the middle and compromise with each other better, relate with each other, and cherish each other's differences.

Asperger's: the often hidden social disability

I think what neurotypical people (especially teachers and parents) need to realize is that part of the main reason why people on the spectrum have difficulty relating is the neurological differences. Our brains have strong neurological connections between the different brain centers that allow these centers to simultaneously communicate with each other. This is what allows us to process multiple information simultaneously, most of which is done at a subconscious level, requiring minimal mental energy.

On the other hand, for people on the spectrum, the neurological pathways between the brain centers are not well developed, making it harder for the centers to communicate with each other. This makes it difficult to process multiple information simultaneously. Whereas we rapidly process this information at a subconscious (intuitive) level, people on the spectrum have to process sequentially, a little at a time, at a conscious level. They have to think through what we do intuitively without thinking. They can eventually arrive at the same understanding, but it is going to take longer (delayed processing) and require a lot more mental energy (since they have to consciously process it).

This drastically affects interacting with others (relating). When we interact with someone, we have to rapidly process multiple information simultaneously. When listening to others, we are processing the words they are saying, the context in which they are spoken, the tone and inflection in voice, facial expressions, physical gestures, and body language to understand what the person said and meant. We rapidly read all this information to understand the person's thoughts, feelings, and intentions. At the same time as we are processing what the other person is saying, we are formulating how we think and feel about it, plus how we are going to respond. At the same time we are replying, we are also reading their nonverbal cues to see if they understand and are staying interested.

In order for us to focus on the topic of conversation, we have to process most of this nonverbal information (facial expressions, body gestures, fluctuation in voice, etc.) subconsciously, with minimal mental energy. This allows us to relate with others without much effort. However, people on the spectrum have to process bits of this information sequentially and at a conscious level, thinking it all through. Since they cannot process this information simultaneously, the processing is delayed and often inadequate, making it difficult to read the big picture. To try to keep up with the conversation, they can process a small portion of this information, often missing much of the meaning. Sometimes by the time the person has processed what was said and formulated a response to it, the interaction has moved on to different content. Consequently, between not getting all the information and having delayed processing, their responses are often out of sync with others. For people on the spectrum, this can be very mentally and emotionally draining. This inability to rapidly process multiple information simultaneously is a major reason for many of the social struggles that people on the spectrum experience.

Although this is common for everyone on the spectrum, for children with Asperger's this deficit can be difficult to read. They can be very bright but still have this processing problem. This is hard for people to understand. They assume that since the child is bright and very verbal, they must intentionally choose to misinterpret instructions and act differently from others. Much of Asperger's is a hidden disability, masking their difficulties. That's why awareness training for significant people in the child's life can be important.

IQ and autism! Are they valid and reliable?

Many assessments, especially in schools, rely heavily on IQ tests (tests of intelligence). Often, the child gets a secondary diagnosis of cognitive impairment, in addition to autism. Or the child may be diagnosed as intellectually impaired, but not with autism.

Unfortunately, intelligence testing is often very unreliable with children with autism. The scores are frequently much lower than their true cognitive abilities. There are many factors for this. People on the spectrum often have complex processing problems, including sensory processing issues, auditory processing problems, and delayed information processing. These processing issues interfere significantly with being able to understand what is expected, respond to verbal questions/directions, and interpret the intent of the questions. People on the spectrum often have verbal communication problems (both receptively and expressively), and many of these tests rely heavily on auditory processing and verbal skills. Also, these tests require socially regulating, face to face, with an examiner, which is often extremely difficult for children on the spectrum.

In addition, task performance anxiety for many on the spectrum is very high in situations that put them socially on the spot. They tend to freeze and panic under such conditions, or misinterpret what the examiner is expecting.

Added to these are the problems with attention, hyper-focusing on detail, or being very distracted, which will significantly interfere with task performance. Lastly, many children on the spectrum have behavior interference in the form of repetitive, stereotypic behavior, which often increases under pressure. With all these conflicting variables, the chances of getting an accurate read for people with autism is unlikely.

Given the many variables autism creates for intelligence testing for children on the spectrum, please be very careful in interpreting these results, especially when making diagnostic decisions from them. These tests historically underestimate the child's true cognitive abilities, resulting in misdiagnosis of cognitive impairments, misplacement in schools, and lower expectations for them cognitively and adaptively. Often children with autism have higher scores on the nonverbal sections and lower scores on the verbal sections. Children with Asperger's may show the opposite, with high verbal scores but lower nonverbal scores. In conclusion, the more severe the impairment, the autism, the more unreliable intelligence testing is. If testing is needed for those with autism, try to use a nonverbal test such as the Leiter International Performance Scale or the Raven Progressive Matrices test. However, even with these, be suspicious if your child's results are low. If your child has communication and processing problems, there is a greater possibility the scores are suppressed. Be very suspicious of the intellectual impairment label. There is a good chance that it does not accurately reflect your child. The tests do not match the processing, communication, and learning style of your child.

Labeling: high and low functioning

We start this process when we first seek a diagnosis. For parents with young children (1–3 years of age) who are seeking a diagnosis, I often recommend that they do not wait for the diagnosis. Forget about the label and begin supporting whatever developmental delays the child is showing. The diagnosis of "autism" doesn't say much about the degree of disability. There is too much variability in strengths and skills. When a diagnosis is not descriptive enough, people look for more specific ways to categorize the severity of the disability.

In the medical field, diagnoses are categorized by symptoms and how much they impact the person's daily functioning. It is the impact the disability has on the person's functioning that drives a lot of the services. For the most part, "high functioning" usually refers to good expressive speech, fair to good receptive understanding, and fair ability to function independently in their daily settings. "Low functioning" is usually reserved for those with very limited verbal skills, lower intellectual abilities, extreme difficulty understanding daily instructions, and usually requiring a lot of assistance in their daily routine.

The confusion among parents and professionals is between "level of functioning" (intellectual ability) and "severity of autism." I know children who are labeled "high functioning" who have severe autistic traits (rigid/inflexible thinking, very resistant to change and uncertainty, and meltdowns over simple snags in their day). However, they are considered "high functioning" because they are verbal, get good grades in school, and can do personal care independently. I have also met children who are considered "low functioning" because they are nonverbal, have difficulty with performing personal care, and may struggle with academics. However, their autism traits are less severe; they are more flexible in their thinking, handle daily transitions more easily, can reference others better, and have fewer meltdowns. So, level of functioning does not always correlate with the severity of the autism. Just because a child is labeled "high functioning" does not mean he doesn't have severe autism. Many people confuse the two, which can exclude some children from the treatment they need and/or lower the expectations of others.

We also have to be very careful when we equate lack of verbal skills with low intellectual abilities. The single largest characteristic used in labeling children high or low functioning is the degree of spoken language they have. This also can be very deceiving! Although there is a positive correlation, there are many children who are nonverbal but have much higher cognitive abilities than we first recognize. They simply cannot express it in our customary ways. Once we find them a voice, whether through pictures, written words, manual signs, or electronic devices, we find that they have much stronger cognitive skills than we had anticipated. It isn't until we find the right mode of expression that we begin to understand what they truly know. So, our best bet is to always assume competence to learn, if the right supports and teaching style can be identified. Try not to get too hung up on low- and high-functioning labels.

Low/high functioning vs. severe/mild autism

The last section discussed the problem with labeling someone high or low functioning with regard to their diagnosis. The problem comes from the fact that a person can be high functioning (verbal, good academic skills, fair to good personal care) but have moderate to severe autism (rigid inflexible thinking, strong sensory issues, poor emotional regulation, delayed processing, and impaired ability to relate with others). Also, a person can be considered low functioning (poor verbal skills, limited academic skills, and minimal personal care skills) but only have mild autism (more flexibility, calmer emotions, fewer sensory sensitivities, and more socially connected).

This appears contradictory at first, but when we look more closely, we can see that these labels actually represent two different dimensions. The first, the level of functioning dimension, represents the degree of cognitive functioning or intellectual disability. The second dimension represents the severity of autism symptoms. You could look at these two dimensions as crisscrossing on perpendicular planes, with the dimension of intellectual abilities (high, moderate, low) running vertically and the dimension of autism symptoms (severe, moderate, and mild) running horizontally. The moderate levels of each dimension meet at the intersection of the two dimensions. Consequently, you can have people who are very high functioning verbally and intellectually, and be moderately to severely impaired in autism symptoms. This can be confusing for many people who initially see the very bright, verbal child and do not initially see the severity of the autism. Or they assume that the nonverbal child is severely autistic. It is not that easy to diagnose.

Making matters even more complicated is the variability of verbal skills. Although verbal skills are highly correlated with intelligence, it is not always the case. Do not assume that the child who is nonverbal has poor intellectual abilities. There are some children who find it difficult to talk due to auditory processing and motor planning difficulties, not lack of cognitive skills. People often assume that nonverbal children are severely impaired and place lower expectations on them. The same is also true for children who are very verbal, but for whom most speech is hidden in scripting and echolalia. They may appear to have higher cognitive abilities than they actually may have. Even for the two basic dimensions (intelligence and autism symptoms), the mixing in of verbal abilities can be deceiving.

Labels such as high and low functioning, and severely and mildly impaired, are not diagnostic terms, but are used more as descriptors when people try to categorize level of impairments. It is to be hoped that the diagnostic criterion in the new DSM will be more descriptive and accurate. Until then, and probably for some time, people will be adding their own descriptive labels to the diagnoses.

Differences vs. disabilities!

In previous posts, regarding the controversy over the labels high and low functioning, and IQ and autism, we explored that there are two main dimensions that have to be taken into consideration when talking about autism. There are two dimensions that interplay in how the person's ability to function will play out: (1) autism symptoms (sensory processing issues, rigid, inflexible thinking, processing differences, executive functioning problems, communication differences, social and emotional difficulties) and (2) intellectual or cognitive impairment (limitations in being able to cognitively process information, understand, learn, and adapt to environmental demands). As discussed in previous posts, a person can be higher functioning intellectually, but still have severe symptoms of autism; on the other hand, a person can be more impaired cognitively (lower functioning) but with less severe autism traits (more flexible, fewer sensory issues, easier time socially connecting, etc.). The whole confusion over low and high functioning has been a result of the misunderstanding of how these two dimensions overlap. Granted, these labels are misleading and only tend to devalue the person. However, having a good understanding of these two dimensions (autism traits and cognitive impairments) is needed to truly understand how to help the individual.

There have been a lot of discussions and arguments about whether autism traits are a disability or simply differences (different abilities). For purposes of discussion here, let's define "differences" as a different way of processing and adapting, and "disabilities" as limitations in being able to adapt. For example, there are both sensory differences in autism and sensory disabilities. Common sensory differences in autism are better acuity of sensory detail, heightened sensitivity to sensory stimulation, strong perception of sensory patterns, unbiased perception of sensory stimulation, and strong sensory memory. Granted, some differences (e.g. sensory sensitivity) can be a strength in one situation but a deficit in another (sensory overload). Whereas there are strong sensory differences in autism, there are also sensory disabilities. Deficits or disabilities can occur if the person has strong fragmented or distorted sensory integration difficulties, which interfere with the person's ability to integrate his senses effectively. This can greatly affect the person's ability to adapt to the world around him in any environment. When you cannot consistently integrate your senses effectively, it greatly affects all other functioning. In autism, individuals almost always have sensory differences, but sensory integration disabilities (distorted, fragmented perceptions, integration problems) vary substantially in severity.

The same holds true for cognitive differences. People on the spectrum process information *differently*. They are often more concrete, factual, detailed thinkers, with strong associative and static memory. In these areas, they are stronger than the global, more inferential, thinking patterns of neurotypical (NT) people. NT people tend to process from general to specific, and people on the spectrum tend to process from specific to general. People on the spectrum tend to be more factual and less biased in their thinking than NT people who have more global, inferential thinking. NT thinking tends to be more abstract, whereas spectrum thinking tends to be more literal and concrete—neither good nor bad, just different.

However, there are some processing disabilities that affect autism in varying severities. People on the spectrum can have strong disabilities in rapidly processing dynamic, multiple information simultaneously. They have difficulty processing information coming rapidly from multiple sources (or multiple senses) at one time. Once the information flow slows down and is given sequentially, the processing improves drastically. Also, people on the spectrum have varying degrees of weaknesses in the areas of executive functions, which consist of the abilities to control attention, inhibit impulses, organize, plan, and monitor a course of action, and multitask. These can be seen as a disability because they greatly limit the person's ability to adapt. These too can vary in severity among people on the spectrum.

We all have strengths and weaknesses, which come packaged a little differently. Unfortunately, since autism affects a minority in society, these differences tend to be quickly labeled as deficits (disabilities), because they do not fit the general norm. Different often stands out as a deficit or weakness. This is where, as for many minorities, society can severely limit people on the spectrum. We need to embrace the differences and foster their development, not interpret them as deficits. Since these differences can be strengths that we do not have, their value to society can be great. All we have to do is look at some of the major contributions people on the spectrum have made to art, science, and technology. The more we can learn from the way they view the world, the better our world can become. Their strong perceptual and detailed qualities can and have dramatically improved the quality of living for all of us.

So, in bridging the two cultures, since the mainstream culture is neurotypical, we need to help those on the spectrum accommodate and compensate for their disabilities (more sensory-friendly modifications, changing the information flow for them, respecting their tendency to become overwhelmed in our environment, avoiding strong social demands, etc.) and foster their valuable differences. By embracing everyone's differences, we can all benefit more. We have to be open to these differences meaning strengths, not weaknesses.

Co-occurring disorders in autism

How many of your children carry multiple diagnoses?

In addition to anxiety disorder and depression, ADHD, OCD, ODD, seizure, and bipolar disorder are common co-existing disorders diagnosed in autism. All of these co-existing disorders have common elements with autism. For example, children with autism have executive functioning problems (attention difficulties, poor organizational skills, impulse control problems, etc.) which they share in common with those with ADHD. It is also common for them to have under-aroused nervous systems that can cause hyperactivity, which, again, is common for ADHD. In addition, many children on the spectrum have very rigid/inflexible thinking (rigid adherence to rules, rituals, and routines), which is commonly seen as OCD. With the rigid/inflexible thinking comes strong anxiety to control all activity around them, leading to strong oppositional behavior common in oppositional defiant disorder (ODD). Finally, frequent anxiety, irritability, hyperactivity, meltdowns, and other emotional regulation difficulties are commonly seen with bipolar disorder.

Usually, children with bipolar disorder will exhibit cycles of extreme irritability and mood swings, racing thoughts, inability to concentrate, very rapid, pressured speech, uncontrollable rage episodes, and very driven hyper-motor activity. The big difference between bipolar and symptoms of autism is in the intensity and duration of episodes. Usually, with bipolar the child's extreme irritability, hyperactivity, rage, and racing thoughts are not specific to any event (trigger). The mood/behavior can last longer and seems driven by anxiety. The child obviously appears to have no control over the behavior. These same symptoms can also occur with severe biomedical conditions.

As you can see, it often can be difficult to separate out the signs and symptoms of autism from other co-existing disorders. It is very important that you have a doctor who understands autism well, in order to differentiate between what are symptoms of autism and what is symptomatic of other co-occurring disorders. Once these labels become fixed, it usually means long-term use of many different medications.

So, how do you tell? Usually, with the co-occurring disorders there is a generalized nature to the symptoms; this means they tend to occur across settings and situations, and are not specific to identifiable triggers. Usually, for autism, if you look closely, the symptoms (behaviors) can be tied to specific events. Often you can tie the behavior episode to sensory, informational, or emotional overload, transitions, uncertainty, and so on. However, since some of the symptoms can be very constant, it is often difficult to tell. Usually, if the symptoms are truly the result of another co-occurring disorder, then medication is warranted. However, at this time there are no medications to treat "autism."

I think often the problem is trying to isolate what underlies the child's anxiety, OCD, and irritability. Some behaviors are the result of their rigid, inflexible thinking, poor impulse control, sensory issues, and executive functioning difficulties. These can often be misdiagnosed as bipolar disorder and other psychiatric disorders. I have often seen that many children on the spectrum suffer from ongoing anxiety, partly because of their difficulties regulating in a world that is overwhelming for them. Others suffer from a mild depressive disorder, which is often masked by the anxiety. These cases seem to respond best to the SSRIs. Another thing to consider is that many of these children respond best to low doses of medications, rather than higher doses.

Bipolar and autism

Many children with emotional regulation problems are diagnosed with bipolar disorder. As well as anxiety, depression, ADD, and OCD, bipolar is a common co-occurring diagnosis for children on the spectrum. Because of the emotional rollercoaster these children can experience, these emotional reactions can be misinterpreted as bipolar disorder. There can be many similarities that can lead to a misdiagnosis.

It can be difficult to diagnoses bipolar disorder in autism unless the psychiatrist is very experienced with ASD. Many children with autism have a very fragile nervous system that is constantly anxious and on high alert, leaving the children hyper-vigilant and defensive. Because of sensory issues, biomedical vulnerabilities, difficulties processing the world around them, and poor emotional regulation, the stress chemicals in their nervous system are at high levels. Because the stress chemicals are so high, and the nervous system is continually being taxed, normal daily stressors can often set the child into meltdowns.

One of the problems for children with ASD is poor emotional control. They have difficulty identifying their emotions, let alone controlling them. Emotions come on very quickly and intensely, like a tidal wave. Since they do not feel in control of these emotions, all strong emotional reactions are experienced with "panic," fight, or flight. This can be very scary for children on the spectrum. Because of their rigid, inflexible thinking, they have difficulty shifting gears and going with the flow when met by normal changes and snags in their daily lives. This is why seemingly little snags can set them off into emotional turmoil. You often get over-exaggerated emotional responses to minor frustrations.

In addition to having difficulty identifying and controlling their emotional responses, the children often have difficulty understanding what events are causing their strong emotions. They have difficulty connecting their feelings with the events that are causing the feelings. We NT people can feel emotion and stress building up in ourselves. This leads us to step back and take some precautionary measures to calm ourselves, before hitting overload. Most children on the spectrum do not recognize that they are getting stressed until they hit overload. Once in overload, it is too hard for them to organize and cope with the stress.

Finally, the world presents a lot of chaos for these children. Essentially, our world moves way too fast for their way of processing information. Much of what we process is at a subconscious level, allowing us to consciously focus on what is important at the moment. However, people with ASD have to consciously process what we process subconsciously. This takes a lot of mental and emotional energy, often draining the energy and creating ongoing anxiety.

From these struggles, you often get children who have frequent mood swings and rapidly go from 0 to 100. They become frustrated and lose control very easily, resulting in an inability to control the flood of emotion. This is also common in bipolar disorder. The difference I see is that is in bipolar disorder the problem is more biochemical, whereas in autism it is more to do with how the brain is processing information. I often see bipolar diagnosed when it appears to me to be more emotional regulation issues from the ASD. However, there are definitely children with both.

Differences between tics, compulsive behavior, and self-stimulation

Are your child's repetitive behaviors tics, compulsive behaviors, or self-stimulation? The repetitive behaviors in all three conditions serve different functions. Tics are neurologically driven. They can be very jerky, not in a smooth rhythmic pattern, and are often involuntary. They usually involve motor muscle groups (eye blinking, facial twitching, etc.) or vocal noises, sniffing, throat clearing, or snorting type patterns. Usually, the child has multiple motor patterns and at least one vocal tic. They seem to serve no functional purpose for the child. The child may feel the "urge" coming on, but have a very difficult time stopping them. The child does not enjoy the tics and often feels frustrated in not being able to control them. Tics may come and go, and often increase during times of stress.

A true "compulsive behavior" (as compared with a fixation) is driven by anxiety and often results from obsessive thoughts—hence, the "obsessive (thought) compulsive (behavior)" link. The person feels driven to do it because of anxiety and will become more anxious if you block its occurrence. He is aware of and has some control over the behavior, but feels "compelled" to do it. He will often feel very anxious if he doesn't engage in the behavior. The person frequently does not like the behavior but feels driven to do it. If he doesn't do it, he will feel more anxious. The disorder can consist of strong repetitive obsessive thought patterns (intense worries, exaggerated fears, etc.), compulsive behavior patterns (washing hands over and over, repeatedly opening and shutting doors, compulsive orderliness, etc.), or both.

Self-stimulation is more voluntary, controlled sensory seeking to calm and organize the nervous system. These repetitive behaviors are used to soothe and calm the nervous system when over-aroused, alert the nervous system when under-aroused, and block out unwanted stimulation when overwhelmed. They usually consist of repetitive "rhythmic" movement, auditory, or visual patterns. Self-stimulation is usually a voluntary pattern the child uses to help regulate his nervous system. Usually, if the behavior has a repetitive pattern, is rhythmic in nature, and feels good, it is not tics or OCD, but self-stimulation.

OCD or autism?

OCD is often misdiagnosed in autism. OCD is not a core deficit of autism, but is a co-occurring disorder, usually driven by anxiety and/or associated with depression. In autism, repetitive, perseverative, and fixated behavior is often an adaptive strategy for reducing chaos and minimizing overload by seeking sameness, routine, and predictability in the midst of the chaos. These behaviors are qualitatively different from OCD.

Repetitive behavior, over-exaggerated interests, and need for predictability/ routine/sameness are by-products of poor relative information processing, rigid/inflexible thinking, and difficulty with shifting gears (cognitively and emotionally). These are all cognitive differences of autism. They are attempts to decrease overwhelming stimulation and provide some order to a confusing, overwhelming world. The self-controlled stimulation can be soothing and organizing. It can help the person provide organization, order, and control over the uncertainty that is driving anxiety and insecurity. Often the person has some conscious control over these fixations or repetitive behaviors, although he may do them out of habit.

Obsessive/compulsive disorder is an "unwanted" fixation on a specific thought or behavior pattern that is driven by anxiety. Usually the person has a strong worry or apprehension that he is preoccupied with and cannot stop the thoughts. These *obsessive* thoughts create strong anxiety, resulting in unwanted *compulsive* behavior that tends to reduce the anxiety. The individual has little control over it and often does not know why he is doing it. He does not enjoy the thoughts and behavior and usually wants them to stop. These thoughts and actions are not pleasurable for the person, only producing despair. Since the thoughts and behavior are driven by anxiety, if you try to block the compulsive behavior, the anxiety usually increases and the person becomes extremely agitated. So it is important to be careful to distinguish between adaptive behavior that is a functional by-product of the cognitive differences of autism and behaviour which is obsessive-compulsively driven by anxiety, causing great distress for the person. Because they are driven by anxiety, these patterns are very resistant to change.

Questions to ask: Does the child self-initiate the behavior for pleasure or as a tool to escape or avoid unpleasant stimulation around him? Does the child engage in the behavior to increase arousal, provide pleasurable stimulation, or assist him to block out stimulation? Does the child have some control over the behavior? Can the child be redirected, even though just briefly, without showing extreme distress? If you answer yes to these questions, then the behavior is probably not OCD.

Does the child feel compelled to engage in the behavior, does not enjoy it, wishes he could stop the behavior, and become severely distressed if you interrupt it? Does the child seem to have a very strong fear, worry, or generalized anxiety that seems to compel the unwanted behavior? More than likely, this is OCD.

PTSD and autism

This post was also included in companion book, *The Autism Discussion Page on the core challenges of autism: A toolbox for helping children with autism feel safe, accepted, and competent* (Nason 2014), in the chapter on sensory challenges. It was too important to leave out here, so it is in both books.

It has amazed me how long it has taken for the field to accept sensory processing dysfunctioning in autism spectrum disorder. For years, the field of psychology practically ignored sensory issues. Applied Behavior Analysis ignored it while forcing children to obey and stay in situations that were overwhelming for them. If the children acted out, we made them stick it out, so their acting-out behavior was not reinforced by escaping the unwanted situation. More than 20 years ago when I first started incorporating sensory processing strategies into my behavior plans, the behavioral psychologists all looked down on it because you could not observe it and measure it. Agencies would try to stop me from using the strategies because they were not evidenced-based. Sensory processing problems were not real. The agencies were in the business of changing behavior. Treating autism was nothing more than changing their behavior. The child's internal experiences were not recognized, considered, or valued. The ends (changing behavior) justified the means (punishment, forcing compliance). Sensory processing issues were not "real." Even though adults on the spectrum were writing extensively about these traumatizing experiences, the behavioral psychologists still claimed they were not real.

Sensory dysfunction in autism is being recognized now. Finally, after many years of people on the spectrum speaking out and demanding to be listened to, these experiences are being taken seriously. However, another topic not mentioned much in autism spectrum disorder is post-traumatic stress disorder (PTSD). Since most PTSD is caused by extreme sexual or physical abuse and wartime emotional trauma, it is not often suspected in ASD. However, I see evidence of it, and many of the reports from adults on the spectrum relate experiences that seem very similar to post-traumatic stress. Post-traumatic stress occurs when there is severe insult to the nervous system. It results in both changes in brain chemistry and in suspected structural changes in the brain. The person exhibits generalized anxiety, depression and isolation, panic attacks for no apparent reason, and sometimes rages.

PTSD can come from one or more emotional traumas, or long-term distress from severe sensory processing dysfunction. Many nonverbal people on the spectrum, who also experience severe sensory defensiveness, are often experiencing intense physical and emotional trauma from the overwhelming sensory insult to their nervous systems. The child never knows when the sensory bombardment is going to occur, and it often attacks without warning, leaving the child helpless in defending against it. The constant fight-or-flight panic reaction has long-term effects on the nervous system, leaving the individuals battling stress and anxiety for many years. Each time the nervous system experiences intense sensory bombardment, the stimulus characteristics of the event become associated with the severe panic response. At other times in the future, when these common stimuli occur again, it can produce an immediate panic reaction that was originally associated with the traumatic event. For these individuals, immediate panic occurs for no apparent reason. Neither the person nor those around him may understand why the panic reaction occurs. This response can occur in response to a given sound, color, or smell that was originally associated with the traumatic event. Our sensory memories are very intense. When your sensory experiences are very intense and inconsistent, like those of people with sensory processing disorders, such overwhelming emotion can be associated with, and set off easily by, simple sensory memories.

So, when working with severely impaired individuals on the spectrum, tread very lightly. Be very respectful of their comfort zones. Be very careful how you touch them, talk to them, and press them. Their nervous systems are very vulnerable and easily traumatized. Their reactions can be very guarded and intense. They can be very emotionally reactive and need you to be very calm, gentle, and compassionate. Always be looking for defensive reactions and immediately pull back when you see them. Never press children into situations they are scared of. Guide them, but let them pace their actions. Let them feel in control so they can immediately end any situation of panic. Learn what touch, words, actions, and stimulation help them feel safe and secure. Always listen and understand first, before intervening and redirecting their actions. Always assume that underlying their defensive reactions is intense emotional upheaval. Be respectful and compassionate, allow them to pull back, escape, and rebound. Teach them coping skills for dealing with these intense experiences, but most importantly teach them to feel safe in your presence and to trust in following your lead.

Medication: when, what, and how?

There is no medication at this time that treats the core deficits of autism. However, medications are frequently used to treat co-occurring disorders of anxiety; depression; attention deficit; mood disorders; and severe agitation, irritability, and aggressive/self-injurious behavior. Whether to use medication or not is a hard decision. Most of the medications have not been studied well in children, and all medications come with risks of side effects. You need to research the side effects and weigh the costs/benefit factors before using medication. However, for children who are so emotionally unstable and very behaviorally challenged, medications often need to be used temporarily until the underlying factors influencing the behaviors are identified and treated.

Anxiety and depression are the most common psychiatric symptoms in autism, and especially in Asperger's. There are many types of anxiety: social anxiety, task performance anxiety, anticipatory anxiety, sensory overload, separation anxiety, and generalized anxiety. The anxiety can drive obsessive compulsive behavior, frequent tantrums or meltdowns, rigid adherence to rituals, resistant/oppositional behavior, and constant need to control everything. There are many ways to attack anxiety, especially with sensory diets, biomedical supplements, and behavioral strategies; however, for some children, the anxiety is so debilitating that the use of medication is needed to calm and organize the nervous system. The most frequently used medication for anxiety in children on the spectrum is SSRIs (Prozac, Zoloft, Luvox, Anafanil, etc.). This class of medication is used frequently to treat anxiety, depression, and obsessive compulsive behavior. Occasionally, an anti-anxiety medication (Ativan, Xanax, Klonopin, etc.) is added with the SSRIs for supporting effect. However, most anti-anxiety medication can be addictive. Probably the most effective medications have been the SSRI anti-depressant medications.

Bipolar disorder is frequently diagnosed in children on the spectrum, but this is often confused with the frequent emotional dysregulation seen in autism. With frequent, uncontrolled mood swings, irritability, and hyper-manic activity, lithium or anti-convulsant medications (Tegretol, Depakote, etc.), as well as aripiprazole (Abilify), are frequently tried to stabilize mood. For more severe acting-out behavior (aggression, self-abuse, etc.), anti-psychotic medications (Risperdal, Seroquel, Zyprexa, Abilify, etc.) have been used successfully. They all come with potential side effects and must be evaluated closely.

Many children on the spectrum often have ADD/ADHD and may need typical stimulants (Ritalin, Adderall, etc.) or atomoxetine (Strattera) to improve concentration, impulse control, and reduce overactivity. However, be careful because many of the children react negatively to stimulants.

When using medication, please consider the following:

1. Use medication as a last resort, first trying sensory diets, possible supplements, and positive behavior supports to treat the underlying causes of the anxiety.

2. Work with the doctor to try only one medication at a time, starting with a low dose and gradually increasing the dosage until effectiveness is established. Try to avoid using multiple medications, especially starting them at the same time. It is hard to tell what is working and what is not working when using multiple medications.

3. Many children are very sensitive to medication and only respond favorably to very small doses. Also, the younger the child, the more vulnerable the nervous system is to possible negative side effects.

4. Try to find a psychiatrist or neurologist who specialize in or has frequent experiences with autism. Also find a doctor who listens and works with you. Remember, you know your child better than anyone.

5. Watch very carefully for any changes in behavior or mood when starting any medication. Children react very individually and very differently to medication. What works for one child may have the reverse effect with others. Many of the medications that are used to treat anxiety can create increased anxiety.

6. More often than not, you may have to try several medications before finding one that has a good treatment effect. It is definitely not an exact science.

7. Most importantly, only stay with a medication if it is having a "wow" effect. If the medication is truly therapeutic, you will see significant improvement in your child's mood, attention, or behavior. If you only see small changes, it is not worth putting chemicals into the child. If the medication is truly treating a biochemical imbalance in the child, you will see significant changes.

8. Once you start medication, try to keep working on identifying and treating the factors causing the anxiety, mood dysregulation, and behavior challenges. Never use medication alone. Always work on implementing proactive strategies to lessen stressors and teaching better coping skills for dealing with the stress. Medication should be seen as a temporary strategy to calm and organize the nervous system enough to learn more effective coping strategies. As the problems stabilize, start to gradually reduce the medication in hopes of eventually discontinuing if possible. Although some individuals may need medication all their lives, many do not.

The decision to use medication is a hard one to make. However, if the child's nervous system is too disorganized for the child to focus, learn, and be emotionally stable, then medication can be a strong support.

Wow effect

Medication has been used to treat irritability, anxiety, attention deficit, and depression in neurological disorders for years. At this time there is no medication to treat autism, but medication is usually prescribed to treat co-occurring disorders that often times are associated with having a disorganized nervous system. If a child with autism also has severe ADHD, then it would greatly reduce the child's ability to focus and learn. For autism, it is important to calm and organize the nervous system as best as possible, so the child can be receptive to learning. Learning is difficult enough for these children; we want to maximize their receptiveness to learning. Sometimes the child's behavior is the direct result of chemical imbalances in his nervous system. There are a variety of tools (sensory diet, dietary changes, supplements, medications, etc.) that can help calm and organize the nervous system. Finding the right balance is the key. However, if the person's behavior is very dangerous, and/or the person is so disorganized that he cannot focus to learn, then it is important to try what tools are available.

As I tell parents, you need to be very careful when using medication and do some research on the medications you are using. If the medication is not having the "wow" effect, then it probably is not therapeutic. However, if you do get a "wow" effect, it is probably having a positive organizing effect on the nervous system. Also, as the child matures and develops better coping skills, the medication can often be discontinued.

The problems I see with medication are the possible misuse of it to sedate children, and the use of multiple medications, adding one on top of another until no one knows if any of the medications are having a positive effect. However, if you try one medication at a time, evaluate the positive and negative effects, and discontinue if you do not see a "wow" effect, then medication can be used safely.

Chapter 6

MENTORING CHILDREN ON THE SPECTRUM

As many parents can confirm, children on the spectrum often require different teaching strategies for developing life skills. Children on the spectrum process information differently; what they value is different, and how they learn is different. The same teaching strategies that are usually used with neurotypical (NT) children have to be modified to match the learning style for children on the spectrum. The following articles provide a variety of strategies for mentoring children on the spectrum.

Conditioned dependency

Conditioned dependency is something that I see very frequently in children, teens, and young adults on the spectrum. It is a condition of becoming overly dependent on others to do for you, because they haven't expected you to do it for yourself. The person actually has the potential to do it, but we do not expect it of him. Conditioned dependency is very common in developmental disabilities, because we often feel that the person cannot do things, so we never give him the expectation.

This condition occurs for three main reasons: (1) we lower the expectation because of his disability, thinking he is not capable, often holding the child back; (2) because of his opposition, anxiety, and fear of meltdowns, we are scared to push him; or (3) with our busy lives, it is simply faster to do it ourselves than to teach him. These three things are always a balancing act when raising a child on the spectrum.

We should be very careful to not assume that the child doesn't have the ability to learn something, regardless of his current skill level. I think we should always assume competency, meaning that the child may not know how to do it now, but has the potential to learn it. If the child is not learning, then we need to change how we are teaching. If we start with this premise, then we are always holding the bar a little higher, and not letting the child's autism lower our expectations. I have found in more than 30 years of working with people with developmental disabilities that our greatest disservice to them is the low expectation we assume. We get what we expect, and that often holds the child back.

"We-do" activities

To avoid conditioned dependency, think of using daily routine activities as "we-do" activities. Instead of doing *for* them, do *with* them. Include them in the activity. In "we-do" activities, the child learns to be competent by doing together with you, helping each other out and learning by doing with you. In "we-do" activities, you do not teach by standing back and prompting the child to do it. You teach by doing it together, side by side, assisting each other. We tend to either prompt the child to do it or do it for him. We need to take the time to do it together, allowing the child to learn by following our lead and doing it together. Simply guide and assist, rather than do it for him. Always expect the child to be an active participant (learner) in the activity. Scaffold the activity (bathing, dressing, putting dishes in the dishwasher, raking leaves, etc.) to provide only the support needed to maximize success, fading that support as the child becomes more independent. You teach the child to feel competent by following your lead, learning by actively engaging with you. By turning daily activities into "we-do" activities, the child learns that he is expected to be an active participant in everything and gains greater feelings of competence.

Many children on the spectrum are scared of uncertainty and avoid risking and learning new things. If you allow them to fall into this comfort zone of avoidance, it becomes difficult for them to grow. Children on the spectrum have strong comfort zones for everything (participation in activity, social interaction, sensory sensitivities, emotional security, avoidance of "thinking," etc.). We want to teach children to feel safe, accepted, and competent. To do this, we need to gradually stretch these comfort zones, keeping the children feeling safe by slowly stretching a little at a time, always expecting participation. By doing so, the child learns to feel comfortable risking and learning new things, over time experiencing mastery and building self-confidence.

Expect active participation

Learning by doing! Research has shown that active learning (actively engaged in the learning) is much more effective than passive learning (being told or simply watching). The single biggest factor in learning is being an active participant in the learning task. If the child passively allows others to do things for him, he will not learn to do them for himself. The child becomes conditionally dependent on others doing for him, and doesn't expect to be an active participant in his life.

To avoid this problem, it is important to expect the child to be an active participant in everything that occurs for him during the day. If you get used to including the child in everything you do, and expect him to play an active part, the child will learn by doing with you. Learning comes from doing with you while you provide guidance as needed to ensure success. From the earliest years possible, include the child in everything you do for him, expecting him to play a small role, taking responsibility for making it happen. You are *assisting* the child, rather than *doing for* the child. For very young children, we might have to start by doing 90 percent of the task, while the child takes on a very small role. As long as the child is actively involved and playing a role, he is learning. Three primary principles occur during this process:

1. The child learns to be an active agent in his world, and is empowered to do for himself. He learns to enjoy the power of independence, of mastering new skills, and building feelings of competence. Once he gets used to doing, he begins to expect to be an active participant. He beings to automatically expect to take an active role in everything that happens to him during the day.

2. While being an active participant in these functional tasks, he is learning important life skills. From the very early ages, begin teaching personal care skills (bathing, oral care, etc.), household chores (laundry, cooking, making the bed, washing the car, etc.), and community skills (shopping, banking, pumping gas into the car, etc.). It may take longer for the child to learn, so start early and give many years of practice.

3. While doing with you, the child learns important relating skills (referencing others for information, coordinating actions with others, co-regulating roles with another, etc.). These relating skills are difficult for children on the spectrum, so learning by doing together provides numerous daily opportunities for learning not just life skills but also relating skills. He is learning how to engage with others—learning through relating.

Unfortunately, we tend to do *for* the child, rather than do *with* the child. Over time, the child becomes conditionally dependent on others doing for him, and develops "conditioned dependency." Lack of expectations lead to lack of participation. In turn, lack of participation leads to stronger avoidance of participating. Inactivity breeds further inactivity, resulting in active resistance to participation. The child then expects and demands others to do everything for him, and actively fights attempts to engage. Consequently, the child becomes an adult who cannot do for himself and will not try doing for himself.

There are a number of reasons why we get used to doing for the child: (1) our low expectations of the child, (2) the child actively resists participation and we want to avoid the fight, and (3) it is easier to simply do it for the child. Our limited expectations often hold the child back more than his disability. In addition, children on the spectrum get used to routine. If their routine is not to be an active participant but to have others do for them, then they will stay in that mode. If we set the routine and expectation early to actively engage, it becomes routine to be an active participant.

Turn it around! Start expecting active participation, regardless of how little, in everything you do for the child. Don't do *for*, do *with*! Once the child expects to participate, he starts to learn. If the child is used to doing very little, start with small amounts of participation. Give him small roles and provide support as needed to make them successful. Even if you do most of the task yourself, give him a small active part to play. If the child feels himself being an active participant, he will start to learn. With guided participation, the child feels himself gaining greater competency and gradually takes on greater responsibility.

Once the child begins to consistently expect to be an active participant, he becomes an active learner. With greater participation grows greater competence and stronger confidence. Participation becomes rewarding, increasing motivation for further participation. This does not come naturally for children with autism, but will develop with us expecting and encouraging them to participate!

Don't do for me; do with me!

Doing for children with special needs is doing them a disservice. Not only does it give them feedback that they cannot do it, but it is setting the children up to feel entitled, expecting that others will always do for them. Inactivity breeds inactivity, which breeds conditioned dependency. If the child is not expected to be an active participant in his life, he does not learn the daily life skills needed for adulthood and doesn't learn to tackle and master simple challenges. He becomes scared to risk and stretch his comfort zones; he never develops a sense of competency and healthy self-esteem. Over time, this fosters strong tendencies for depression. Activity breeds further activity, which breeds a strong sense of competency and positive self-esteem. Encouraging the child to be an active participant in everything happening to him gives him the sense of being an active agent in controlling his life. It gives him the confidence to do for himself, speak for himself, and advocate for his needs.

Get the child engaged with you in almost everything you do for him. Don't do for him without him. The best therapeutic opportunities are sitting right in front of you: the numerous activities (cooking, laundry, shopping, bathing, etc.) that make up your day. You don't have to artificially set up "therapy" sessions; just turn all your little interactions into numerous learning opportunities. Take whatever things you're currently doing for your child and give him a simple role he can comfortably play. If the child is used to doing nothing, start very small. Any role, regardless of how small (hold the pillow and place it on the bed while you make the bed, put one or two dishes into the dishwasher, drop a few articles of clothing in the washer, raise his arms to put his shirt on, etc.), is a start. These little daily tasks give you a vehicle for teaching your child to engage, relate, and follow your lead. It teaches him to reference you for information, to stay coordinated with you, and to learn from you. By doing with him, you frame and scaffold the task so his little role is successful, and he feels himself being competent. You celebrate doing it together with praise, giving fives, thumbs up, and other gestures of companionship. The child feels productive and competent, driving a desire to learn more. Over time, the child learns to feel good about doing, and the typical daily challenges that are now a major struggle will start to melt away. The child becomes more eager to learn, rather than driven to avoid. Have fun with it, knowing that you are setting a path toward greater independence.

Start simple and build gradually. If your child is not used to doing much, start with a couple of activities a day, when you can block out the time to slow it down and do it together. This will give you practice in how to guide, assist, and engage your child. Once it starts to feel natural, expand the "we-dos" into many daily activities, including personal care, household tasks, leisure activities, shopping, banking—you name it! Do them together, giving him a little part to play and gradually expanding his role as he builds more competence. Start now and pattern a more independent future!

Don't tell me; show me!

In the hope of teaching, we tend to tell kids what to do. We verbally prompt, instruct, direct, and correct the children into learning. For most children on the spectrum, this creates strong anxiety and resistance. We become the "instructor" and they become the "doer." This places strong task performance anxiety on them. They often freeze under pressure when put on the spot, and resist as we increase the prompting. This instructional style of teaching is not very effective with children on the spectrum, although we do it all the time. We prompt, direct, correct, and then reinforce. We tell and they do!

We need to be mentors and coaches, rather than instructors. We need to teach by doing it with them, right alongside them, scaffolding the activity to maximize success. Avoid standing back and instructing them every step of the way, making them do it as we prompt and correct. Do it together. When the child is doing with you, it takes the pressure off and minimizes task performance anxiety. You let him *feel* how to do it by doing it with you. He follows your lead, learning *through* you, by doing *with* you. He starts by assisting you, while you scaffold the guidance so he feels himself tackling the challenge. As the child becomes more competent, you gradually transfer more and more responsibility to him. This guided participation lowers the anxiety, teaches by showing and doing, and maximizes success with skillful guidance. The child sees you as a working partner with him, and you become a trusted guide for him. Stop being an instructor—be a mentor!

Get me started, but let me finish!

Many children on the spectrum suffer from self-initiation and sustained attention difficulties. These two functions are part of the executive functioning skills located in the frontal cortex of the brain. This explains why many kids appear to lack motivation and need to be jump-started to do everything. The ability to initiate an action, especially if it is task-related, is often impaired. These children have difficulty taking the first step to get started. They tend to blank out and freeze. However, once the first step is made, then they move forward with the action or task. This is the person who needs to be continually prompted to get up and do. Unfortunately, such children are labeled as lazy, unmotivated, or, worse yet, incapable.

Many of these same children also have problems with sustaining attention: staying on course until the task is completed. They become distracted very easily and have difficulty concentrating long enough to follow through with sequential tasks. Again, they are often labeled as lazy, unmotivated, and incapable. Unfortunately, what helps to reinforce these labels is the child's ability to initiate and sustain attention for video games and other special interests. "He can sit in front of video games for hours, so I know he can initiate and sustain attention!" The reason for this paradox is that the preferred interest is highly stimulating, alerting the executive functioning part of the brain, allowing it to focus. The problem comes when tasks (1) have a low level of excitement and (2) are not a preferred activity.

Both of the above problems are also augmented by another executive functioning issue called "shifting gears." This is the ability to leave one activity and transition to another. This overlaps with the initiating function. This is especially evident when it comes to ending a preferred activity (video game) to do a non-preferred activity (feed the dog). The child has a hard time not only starting an activity but also stopping the activity. Not only do you have to nag him to do something, but you may also need to "nag" him to stop.

So, the message is don't assume incompetence or laziness because your child needs to be supported to start doing everything. Stop nagging and getting angry. Most importantly, don't assume your child is incapable of doing and begin to jump-start his participation. Try the following:

1. Build a structured schedule into your child's day, so many of his routines stay consistent from day to day. This builds structure and predictability for the child. Over time, develop visual schedules (pictures or written) and activity lists, so the child has a visual reminder of what he is doing and what is coming up next. Check off each task when finished and cue him into what he is to do next. Task lists (or picture routines) can also help cue the child into the steps for each task.

2. To help the child stop one activity and move to the next (shifting gears), prepare him with a warning. First, let him know what is coming up next, once the current task is completed. "First, you can watch TV, and then it will be time to shower." Then, with three minutes left to go with the current task, remind the child, "In three minutes we will be ending ___ and doing ____." Then remind him again with one minute left. This helps prepare the brain for what is coming up.

3. For a child who has initiation problems, assist him in starting the first step to jump-start his participation. Try not to give repeated verbal prompts (nagging). If he does not respond on the first try, use a visual (hand him the toothbrush, point to the object, or demonstrate the action). Provide support as needed.

4. If he has problems with sustaining attention, you may need to stay nearby and provide occasional prompts to move from one step to another. For new tasks, until he learns the steps, try doing it together, assisting as needed, but expecting the child to actively participate. By turning the tasks into "we-do" activities, you can bridge the brain's weaknesses until the task becomes automatic.

Over time, as the routines become more automatic, you can fade out many of the supports. However, these functions (initiating, sustaining attention, and shifting gears) will always be weaknesses. The person will need to use such techniques to learn new routines. However, as he gets older, he will learn to use lists and schedules to keep himself organized.

In conclusion, do not lower your expectations of the child; just provide the supports needed to compensate for the brain weaknesses that interfere with the child's participation. Always expect active participation and foster independence. Help him get started, but let him finish!

How much do you expect; how hard should you push?

It is not surprising that the greatest limitations for these children are our own limited expectations. Whether it is reduced academic expectations from teachers or learned helplessness from parents doing for the children, we tend to let the disability become a liability for the child. I am still amazed at the development these kids can make when the growth is expected, then supported. You cannot support something that you do not expect. It is much better to set high goals and then build in supports to make them successful. The secret is how much you expect and how much support you give.

It can be difficult to tell how much you should push your child. Often, I find that one parent, in attempt to reduce all anxiety, builds in so much support that the child never has to step outside his comfort zone. Then, the other parent often refuses to accept the child's vulnerabilities and pushes the child too hard. The secret is to understand your child's comfort zones and then teach him to step outside these comfort zones by gradually stretching them. If allowed to, children on the spectrum will hold tight to their comfort zones. You don't want the child to stay in his comfort zone too long. The longer he stays in his comfort zone, the harder it will be to stretch him.

The secret is teaching a child to feel competent stretching his comfort zones. This comes from repeated, non-punishing exposure to tackling uncertainty. You stretch just enough to create a little uncertainty (anxiety), but not so much as to overwhelm the child. Once the child feels comfortable mastering that uncertainty, you stretch a little more. This way, you provide repeated exposure to mastering uncertainty, building greater confidence in tackling new learning. The child learns and grows, and becomes more competent in facing, coping with, and tackling new challenges. Parents can provide this by (1) continually nudging their child gently forward and (2) providing guided participation to ensure he safely succeeds in tackling the uncertainty. It is important that the child feels the challenge, which means a little anxiety, and then feels himself tackling the uncertainty.

When it comes to school, we often fight so hard to gain extra supports/accommodations that the child becomes overly dependent on them. The secret to effective teaching is to build in methods to fade the assistance or accommodations as soon as you implement them. As soon as success is established and maintained with the supports, begin to fade out the reliance on them. I rarely see this in IEPs. We build in extra supports with no guidelines to fade them. Over a year or two, the child becomes dependent on the supports. Inevitably, the school suddenly wants to end the supports all at once—as if the child magically does not need them anymore. This often happens when the child transitions to a new school year and/or to a higher grade. Or, worse yet, the child becomes overly dependent on the supports through grade school, and then once he leaves school there are no longer any supports. We should build in supports in the early years and then fade them out while in high school. By the time the child graduates, he should have learned how to build in his own supports to make it on his own. Only use accommodations and compensations to help bridge learning, not to become dependent on them.

Unfortunately, there are very few schools that actually know how to provide graduated assistance with built-in fading as the child becomes more competent. With the use of guided participation, the amount of support and assistance provided is continually faded as the child becomes more competent. The assistance varies from day to day and moment to moment, providing only the amount of support needed to maximize success. This type of guidance/support always stretches the child by allowing him to *feel* the challenge, to *feel* the mastery. The child needs to feel just enough challenge to motivate learning, but not too much to produce performance anxiety (freeze).

"Affect" (emotion) is the glue for learning!

Stanley Greenspan (1998, 2009) reminded us of the important link between emotion and learning. It is rarely talked about, but is important for people to know and use. Any experiences that are associated with strong affect (emotion) are encoded more effectively. When the event is connected with strong positive affect (feeling), it is remembered more strongly. The child's attention to something of strong interest is greater, and the information presented during times of strong affect is more thoroughly encoded in long-term memory. Things that make you feel good are remembered better. If the learning occurs in activities that are exciting and fun for the child, it will be remembered more easily. Learning that is associated with emotion is remembered. If the child enjoys rolling a ball back and forth, then build in counting the turns. For example, if you are rolling the ball back and forth, provide strong affect in your face. With an excited voice, count out each turn as you roll the ball back and forth. If you are teaching him to count to ten, then each time you reach ten you say, "Again!" and start the count over again. Pairing the new learning (counting to ten) with fun will be remembered more effectively. This is why teaching new words in speech can be most effective when singing or participating in a preferred activity. Affect (emotion) provides stronger meaning to the new learning, which in turn strengthens the memory.

When presenting information during activities of little emotional value, the child will have trouble attending to the important elements, and this information will not have the glue to stick in memories. Much of the teaching we do might have great importance to us, but may have little value or emotional impact for children on the spectrum. It does not have the glue to stick or provide the motivation to seek out more of it. That is why it is important to include the child's interests and preferences in the new learning and add strong affect to the teaching.

In most developmental models of social/communicative learning (DRI, DIR, Son-Rise, etc.), the importance of establishing strong emotion sharing is crucial for further social learning. Once I get a child to enjoy my attention and seek my excitement, I have no trouble teaching him. If you make children feel good, they will follow your lead and be excited to learn from you. Emotion sharing (the ability to share emotional experiences with another) is the glue behind social learning (learning by copying others). That is why, with the little ones, I usually start with their sensory preferences. When I build my interactions around the sensory preferences that excite them, they attend to and soak up the learning that is associated with it. They are motivated for more and actively participate. My interactions make them feel more competent and good about themselves. When they feel good in your presence, they *want* to learn from you. So, learn how to build in strong affect into your activities to build strong memory and learning. Make learning fun and purposeful, and the child will remember it!

Basic training principles

When training new skills or behavior, keep these five training principles in mind. They help frame successful training:

1. Start where the child is at.

2. Break it down, build gradually.

3. Keep it simple, maximize success.

4. Do it together, scaffold the learning.

5. Keep it fun! Mastery is motivating and builds confidence!

When beginning to teach a new skill or behavior, it is important to include all the basic principles. Regardless of the teaching strategies you are using, each principle, other than doing it together, will apply. Let's look at these five steps a little more closely:

1. *Start where the child is at.* Before starting to teach a new skill or behavior, we need to assess the child's current skill level and start where the child is at. You want the level of expectation to start at the level where the child can be expected to produce the desired response with little difficulty. If the child has very little skill in the area being taught, then the teacher/ parent's expectations should be minimal at first while providing guidance and assistance to support as needed to ensure adequate completion.

2. *Break it down, build gradually.* By starting where the child is at (skill level matches the expected demands), successful teaching begins by breaking the new learning down into small, easy-to-obtain steps. We want to gradually build the skill, while allowing the child to continue to experience success. If the child is failing to learn a step, then assume the step is too difficult for him. Back up to the last successful step, and (1) break the next step down into smaller steps and/or (2) provide stronger assistance in supporting the child to do it successfully. When children are not succeeding, it is usually because new expectations require too much for the child's current abilities. Either break it down into smaller steps or provide greater support. This is called "task analysis" and will be discussed in more depth a little later in this chapter.

3. *Keep it simple, maximize success.* The child should be successful at least 80 percent of the time to experience mastery and stay motivated. Learning is about gradually increasing the challenge within the comfort zone of the child's current abilities. Gradually add a little more new learning, enough to challenge the child, but not too much to overwhelm the child and break down successful performance.

4. *Do it together, scaffolding the learning.* I prefer to do the task with the child, providing guided participation to support the child until he is competent to do it on his own. This way, (1) the child feels less task performance pressure, (2) the child is provided with a mentor to model and coach him through it, and (3) the mentor scaffolds the new learning so it remains successful for the child. The mentor varies the guidance, from moment to moment, so the child is challenged but successful, with little performance anxiety. By doing it together, the adult can provide the necessary "just right" amount of assistance to maximize the chance of success. This may include doing parts of the task the child cannot do himself, or providing graduated guidance to help the child perform each step. Graduated guidance will be discussed more thoroughly later on in the chapter.

5. *Keep it fun!* Learning is fun when the children feel competent in what they are doing, trust following the lead of the mentor, and experience the success of mastering the new learning. Mastery is motivating for all children. When children are not excited about learning, more than likely they (1) do not feel competent, (2) have a history of repeated failure, and (3) do not trust the teacher to guide and support them to success.

Use these five principles when designing new training programs or when troubleshooting training programs that are not successful. They provide us with the criteria for staying on a successful track!

Task analysis

As stated earlier, one of the first steps in program development is to break the task or behavior down into an easily obtainable sequence of steps. Most tasks consist of a chain of simpler steps linked together to make a complex task. Task analysis is the process of dividing the task into a chain of discrete behaviors. Training usually consists of teaching one step at a time, until the whole sequence is learned and the objective is met. Task analysis is important to the basic training principles of starting where the student is at, building gradually, keeping training simple, maximizing success, and minimizing frustration. By breaking the task into a sequence of simple steps, the student gradually builds the skill by learning small increments of new material at a time. By keeping the steps simple, frustration is minimized and training progresses more smoothly. Frequency of reinforcement is enhanced, and probability of success is maximized.

One of the easiest ways to analyze a task is to have one person perform the task, while another person notes each discrete behavior in sequence as it happens. For example, eating with a spoon usually includes the following steps:

1. Pick up spoon.

2. Move spoon to plate.

3. Scoop food onto spoon.

4. Bring food to mouth.

5. Place food into mouth.

6. Put spoon down on table.

7. Chew and swallow food.

The same task many be divided up into several steps or into many steps, depending on the learning ability and frustration tolerance of the student. For example, tooth brushing can be broken down into the following steps:

1. Wet toothbrush.

2. Put toothpaste on brush.

3. Brush all teeth.

4. Rinse out toothbrush.

5. Rinse out mouth.

6. Put brush away.

However, for a student with more cognitive limitations, this skill may be broken down into smaller steps:

1. Pick up toothpaste.

2. Unscrew cap off toothpaste.

3. Pick up toothbrush.

4. Place paste on brush.

5. Put toothpaste down.

6. Bring toothbrush to mouth.

7. Brush front teeth.

8. Brush chewing surfaces of right side.

9. Brush outer surface of right side.

10. Brush inner surface of right side.

11. Brush chewing surfaces of left side.

12. Brush outer surfaces of left side.

13. Brush inner surfaces of left side.

14. Spit toothpaste into sink.

15. Turn on water.

16. Rinse out brush.

17. Rinse out mouth.

18. Wipe off mouth.

19. Put toothbrush away.

20. Put toothpaste away.

21. Wipe off sink.

If needed, this sequence can be further broken down into smaller steps. As training continues, if progress stalls at a given step, this step can also be divided into smaller components. The secret to task analysis is to break the sequence down into easily obtainable steps, so that training progresses smoothly.

Skill analysis

The above examples consisted of tasks that were broken down into a chain of behaviors. Not all training consists of chaining simple responses. For example, teaching discrete behaviors, such as discrimination training (e.g. color, size, shape, objects, etc.), may not require the chaining of sequential steps, by which performance of one step is dependent upon the preceding step. Task analysis for these types of tasks usually consists of analyzing the sequence of skill development. In other words, training is sequenced by level of difficulty or skill complexity. An example of this might be teaching sorting or matching by shape or color.

As with task analysis, skill analysis also breaks the objective down into sequential steps. Both types of analysis are designed to develop a skill by gradually adding small increments of new learning at a time.

Task analysis procedures

When performing task analysis, there are six primary factors to consider:

1. Identify and operationally define the desired terminal behavior. Be specific in defining your objective in observable and measurable terms.

2. Break the task down into small, easy-to-obtain steps. It is usually beneficial to break the task or behavior down into the smallest possible steps since this will minimize frustration and reduce the need for re-analyzing steps during training.

3. Arrange the steps in sequential order.

4. Define the steps clearly, so that both the trainer and child know what is expected.

5. When defining the steps, consider any specific deficits that might inhibit learning. As with all training techniques, task analysis needs to be individualized to the specific child.

6. Identify the child's current skill level so training can start there and build from that.

Although it may take a little more time and practice to develop task-analyzed programs, the benefits received clearly outweigh the costs incurred. The result is usually a program with greater probability of success.

Backward and forward chaining

Once you have task analyzed the skill or task and identified the child's current abilities, then the most common training strategy is to use either backward or forward chaining. With both chaining techniques, the strategy is to teach one step at a time while chaining the steps together. The most popular strategy is using backward chaining. With this strategy, the trainer (parent, teacher) completes all the steps for the child except for the last step. While using assistance as needed, the child actively performs the last step of the chain and then immediately receives reinforcement (praise, tangible reward, etc.). Once this last step is learned, then the child is taught to do the second to last step, plus the last step that was already learned. Again, the trainer does all the steps up to the target step and then prompts/assists the child to finish the task. The child continues to learn each step, going backwards through the chain of steps until he can complete the whole sequence independently.

As you might guess, with forward chaining, training starts with the first step in the chain and continues one step at a time until the entire chain is learned. Again, the same principle is being used: only teaching one simple step (behavior) at a time, while chaining the steps together. Which chaining should you use? I find that backward chaining often works best because the child learns the last step first, which is completing the task. Reinforcement always occurs at the same predictable step: finishing the task. This way, the child feels the mastery of completing the task, which can motivate more independence in learning the rest of the steps.

Verbal prompting: don't over-use it!

It is very common for parents and teachers to continually repeat requests and directions over and over until the child responds. And it is also common to hear the sound of their voices get louder and angrier with each repetition. With any type of prompting, the more you use it without producing the desired response, the weaker the prompt becomes. Each time you have to repeat the verbal command (because the child is not responding), the weaker the command becomes and the less effective verbal commands are in the future. Eventually, you reach the point where you are nagging, yelling, and arguing!

Also, what people do not understand is that many children have auditory processing problems and delayed information processing, which weaken the effectiveness of verbal prompting. Often the child is only picking up on small pieces of what is being said. So, the longer the prompt, direction, or explanation is, the more confusing it becomes. Most of us are used to talking, so we give long verbal statements. Most children on the spectrum do better with very short phrases—literally to the point.

For children with delayed processing, it may take the child 10–30 seconds to process what you say. While in the middle of a direction, if you repeat the request, the child has to start processing all over again. This can lead to frustration, resistance, and opposition from the child, and in turn increase the tone and volume of the parent's voice.

So, when requesting and/or directing the child, try to avoid repetitive verbal prompts. I would recommend the following:

1. When giving a verbal prompt, do not do it from across the room. Walk over to the child, get face to face at eye level, and then give a short verbal statement (e.g. "time to eat").

2. If the child has auditory processing issues, and is inconsistent with verbal prompting, try pairing the verbal prompt with a visual (show him the spoon or gesture for eating).

3. Give your child 10–15 seconds to respond. If there is no response, then pair the verbal command again with a physical prompt of guided assistance to jump-start his action. Use only enough touch to initiate

movement, and then back off as action begins. This way, the child learns that he needs to respond to your initial request; otherwise, you will up the assistance.

The point is not to continue restating a prompt that is not working. It only weakens the effectiveness of that prompt. If your child has an auditory processing disorder, pair with a visual cue. For some kids who become overwhelmed with verbal prompting, I may only use one word (e.g. "eat") instead of a sentence and provide the gesture/visual cue. If they have severe delayed processing, you might want to wait even longer for the child to process the prompt.

You will notice when you use less repeated verbal prompting you will see greater results and feel better (less irritated and angry).

Physical guidance! Teaching a new skill

For many young children and those with severe learning abilities, physical guidance is often used as a training tool. With physical guidance, the trainer (teacher/parent) uses physical touch (e.g. hand over hand) to guide the child through the desired movement, until the child learns to do it without guidance. As the child learns what is needed, the physical guidance is gradually faded out until the child can implement the response on his own. This procedure is often used when the child does not respond adequately to verbal prompting, visual prompts, gestures, or demonstration (modeling what to do).

For example, when prompting the child to brush his teeth, the parent may say "brush teeth" (verbal), show child the toothbrush (visual), or model the response (brush their own teeth). If there is no response, the trainer might place the brush in the child's hand and physically guide the moment, either to start the response or assist the child to brush part or all of his teeth. Usually, for longer, more complex skills such as tooth brushing, the task is broken down into simpler steps (pick up brush, wet brush, put paste on brush, etc.) and taught only one step at a time.

The use of physical guidance can bring with it inherent problems. First, some children are tactile-defensive and find touch distracting or extremely uncomfortable. Their brains will react negatively to the touch and they will resist the guidance. Also, some children have a defensive reaction to anyone physically forcing movement. Unless they have total control over the action, they may resist it. Other children may be passive and allow others to physically guide them without making any active attempt to do it on their own or to learn from it. Lastly, unless faded quickly, many children become overly dependent on the physical guidance and will not respond without it. On the positive side, using physical guidance maximizes success by minimizing errors (errorless teaching).

It allows the children to feel the correct response, so they have a mental map of how to do it.

There are different techniques in using physical guidance. Some people provide prompt fading, which may require full physical assistance and then systematically fade the location of the assistance as the child becomes more independent. Usually, guidance starts out with hand-over-hand guidance to allow the child to feel the right motor pattern. Once the child has a chance to experience the motor pattern, we start to change the location of our physical guidance to give the child more responsibility in implementing the response (e.g. brushing teeth, washing hands, dressing, etc.). Usually this consists of gradually moving our location of guidance up the hand to the wrist, then forearm, elbow, upper arm, etc. By moving the location of guidance further up the arm, the child takes on more responsibility for the action.

Another strategy for fading the hand guidance is to keep the location of the guidance the same, but lessen the amount of pressure and guidance that you provide. While keeping the guiding hand in the same location, the trainer slowly releases his pressure from full guidance to partial guidance, until he is simply shadowing the child's hand as the child more independently performs the action.

The approach I prefer is called "graduated guidance." With graduated guidance, you use the least amount of assistance, at any given moment, to initiate the response and keep it going through completion. In essence, my hands shadow their hands. I may provide light touch to nudge them to initiate the response, and use only enough pressure to get them moving. Once moving, I immediately fade back the pressure and guidance, as long as they are moving on track. If they stop, I reinstate only enough pressure to reinstate the desired movement. I keep my hands shadowing theirs. If they start to steer off course, I am framing their movement to redirect them back on the right path. From moment to moment, my touch and guidance will fade in and out, providing touch and pressure only if needed, allowing them to "do it themselves." I steer their response, rather than physically do the response.

What I like about the use of graduated guidance is that (1) I am framing the response with my guidance to ensure the correct action, (2) the child is actively initiating the movement (I just direct the child's willful movement), and (2) the child feels himself mastering the response (rather than allowing me to do it for him). I also am fading my touch at all times, rather than waiting and trying to fade it out later. There is less chance for the child to become conditionally dependent on the guidance. I am assisting by framing the child's movement, rather than doing it for him.

For tasks that require both hands, I often work from behind the child (only if he feels comfortable with it). I shadow both his arms and hands with my arms and hands. He can better see the framing, even though I may not be touching him. I may start by framing my arms and hands only an inch outside his, so as to block any erroneous movement or gently nudge forward movement, so he can see and feel himself doing the correct response. However, he always feels himself doing it, while feeling the mastery of completing it.

My preferred choice of teaching is demonstrating and modeling, doing the task together, in "we-do" fashion. We do the task together, with the child learning by observing and doing it together with me. The child learns by doing with me, referencing and learning through watching and copying my actions. However, if the child does not have the ability to learn that way, or the response is too complex for him to learn by observing then doing, then I will use graduated guidance. If done correctly, it is very effective. However, it is important to respect the child's responsiveness to such guidance. If the child is actively resistant to such an approach, I avoid using it.

Block, ignore, and redirect! Keeping the child on task

I work a lot with young, disorganized, and often very anxious children on the spectrum. They often have sensory processing issues, poor emotional regulation, and trouble focusing on task. They are not used to following the lead of someone else, struggle to stay focused on tasks, and get anxious and resistant when others try and guide them. For many of these children, it is not about intentional noncompliance or purposeful opposition. It is more about (1) not seeing and understanding what is going on, (2) not understanding what is expected of them, and (3) not feeling competent doing what is expected. Between both sensory and information processing difficulties, many young children often do not understand what is happening and what is expected of them, and become anxious in situations of uncertainty. They feel vulnerable and insecure. They get overwhelmed easily, which results in anxious, disorganized behavior, or, when overloaded, the fight-or-flight panic response.

For the child who resists following their lead, many parents, teachers, and caregivers will either back off and allow the child to escape or force participation until meltdown occurs, both of which do little to help the child feel competent following the adult's lead in learning. Backing off and allowing the child to escape teaches the child to avoid all new learning situations, and forcing follow-through instills fear of following the lead of others.

To help these vulnerable children learn to trust following your lead, we need to (1) increase their understanding of what is occurring and what is expected, and (2) provide supportive assistance in guiding them through it. It is very important to prepare the child before entering into tasks. This means previewing (1) what the children can expect, (2) what is expected of them, and (3) what boundaries or rules are in place. This is often called "framing" or "scripting" the event for the child, making it very clear. This increases understanding and reduces the confusion and anxiety.

The second part is providing guided participation to coach the children successfully through the activity, so they stay on course and master the uncertainty. I usually recommend that the adult and child do the activity together, side by side, learning by doing together. This takes the pressure off and allows the child to feel competent by following the lead of the adult. However, for many young children who have not yet learned to follow the lead of the trainer, this approach does not work well. For these children, we usually coach them through the action by first modeling or demonstrating what the child will do, then using guidance to assist the child to through it. Because the child initially feels anxious and has difficulty staying focused, we need to frame our guidance to maximize keeping the child focused and staying on track. We often frame performance by working directly behind the child, with our arms extending out to each side of the child to produce a "frame" that keeps him moving forward. Our arms are not touching the child unless needed to guide, just providing a frame to show the child that he moves forward, staying on path. This way, we (1) can use our hands and body to guide the child as needed, (2) block the child from getting off task, (3) provide ongoing encouragement and reinforcement, and (4) are less visually distracting for the child since we are working from behind him. Many parents try to work from in front of the child where the child is more visually distracted by the parent, or from the side where the parents cannot adequately frame and assist the child to stay on course. Working from directly behind the child, with our arms framing each side of him, allows us to shadow his arms and body to keep him on the correct path, and provide immediate guidance to his arms and hands, if needed to stay successful. We only touch the child briefly as needed to initiate, block, or guide a movement; we immediately withdraw the touch once the action is on track. You want the child to feel himself doing it, rather than you doing it.

If the child displays mild resistance, we tighten the framing with our arms to each side of the child, increase our guidance, and verbally focus on what we want the child to do. We minimize attention given to the resistance and focus attention on what we want him to do. If necessary, we may pause and briefly reassure the child, but keep the focus clearly on what the child needs to do. This is very important so the child does not get distracted off course. We want the child to clearly see the path, so he can stay on course. We block and ignore mild resistance and clearly state what to do, making it clear for the child. Typically, when a child gets a little anxious, his attention is immediately shifted to escape, and he loses his focus on what to do. By framing yourself around the child, and immediately keeping your focus directed on what to do, the child can more easily stay on task. As the child moves, we guide that movement in the right direction, keeping him on track and focused. We block, ignore, and redirect the child back on track so he feels himself staying on task to success.

It is important that we don't physically force the child's action. This will immediately increase anxiety and panic. When the child physically resists, we block escape with our framing, gently hold the child if needed, restate what we want the child to do, and wait for the child to move on his own. Once the child begins to move, we guide that movement in the direction of staying on course. If the child tries to sit down, we block the child, halfway from dropping, restate what to do, and calmly wait for the child to start movement again. It is important not to scold, counsel, coax, or argue with the child; simply state what you want the child to do so the child can keep his focus on what is needed.

Once the child begins to move on his own, praise him and keep the focus clearly on what is needed to do. Make sure you provide frequent praise, as long as it doesn't distract the child off course. Once the child successfully completes the action, walk around in front of him, face to face at eye level, praise with animated facial expression, and celebrate with high fives! The feeling of mastery and doing it together will not only teach the skill but also teach the child to feel competent following your lead.

This technique works well for children who are very anxious, disorganized, and have difficulty following your lead. It may not work for older and larger children who may become severely aggressive when guided. Some children will immediately melt down with this technique, which would not be appropriate with such children. This technique only works if you can successfully block, ignore, and redirect the child's resistance to stay on track.

Support, do not pressure!

Autism is an information processing difference that often consists of delayed information processing. This often occurs because the child has to consciously process what may come intuitively for other children. Because of brain wiring differences, their processing is different and needs certain accommodations to match our expectations to the processing needs of the child. Listed below are some guidelines for bridging these processing differences:

1. Give the child time to process. With delayed processing, it is important to give the child at least 10–20 seconds to respond (even longer for some children). If you keep repeating the prompt before processing is completed, the child has to start processing all over. This is very frustrating and exhausting.

2. Let the child pace this performance. We cannot push him faster than his brain can process. If we do, the brain panics and reacts in fight or flight.

I see this all the time. We are constantly trying to speed these kids up, pushing them faster than they can process.

3. Shorten your words! Provide very short, concrete directions. Use short phrases and sentences with only the main point. Many of the children have auditory processing problems. The longer the sentences and the more words used, the greater chances the information will get jumbled and lost. Only use the important words, getting to the point.

4. Use visuals whenever possible. Demonstrate (model) what you want. Give visual directions. Write out a couple of directions for school topics, instead of relying on verbal directions. Words are fleeting, whereas written instructions are constant and can be easily referenced.

5. Break it down; slow it down. Break tasks down into smaller parts and give them each step sequentially. If possible, give them a checklist to mark off as they do each step. *Do not* expect the children to multitask! Allow them extra time to get it done, but let them finish! It is important to finish one task before going to another.

6. Use visual templates. Give the student outlines, laying out the important points so the student can categorize the information you give him. A simple outline will highlight to him what information is important to focus on, and give him mental "files" for categorizing, organizing, and storing the information. Consider using worksheets, outlines, and other templates that help him organize and categorize important information.

7. Prepare by previewing. If possible, preview the learning ahead of time to give a mental framework of what is being presented. Many of the children have difficulty sorting out the relevant information from the irrelevant. This highlights the areas of importance to help direct their attention and gives them a frame of reference to organize the information.

8. Allow children to use their preferred way of communicating what they know. Many children have problems writing. If that is the case, let them give verbal answers. If you require them to write, they cannot think about how to write and what to write about at the same time. If you want to find out what they know, let them pick the method of telling you.

When in doubt, let the child set the pace!

I don't know how many of you have noticed! Your child has a processing speed and pace at which he will do things. You cannot rush it. Many kids on the spectrum have delayed information processing and slow responding. We often try to hurry them along, but it never works. They freeze or resist the pressure, which often makes things worse. The harder we push, the stronger they resist. That is because the brain cannot move faster than it processes. It goes into panic, freeze mode, or fight-or-flight. We always need to be respectful of that and let the child pace the speed of action. Unfortunately, it is uncomfortable for us, but necessary for them. It is a natural tendency to want the child to match our pace, but that is often not possible. Let them set the pace to feel comfortable and competent!

Don't force; invite! If I don't respond, find out why!

In our own impatience and frustration, we tend to push, prompt, direct, and pressure the child to perform. However, many children on the spectrum will freeze, avoid, and, if necessary, act out if forced to respond. We tend to move too fast for many on the spectrum. They usually process dynamic information more slowly than we allow them time to. Most likely, if the children are not responding, they either do not understand what is expected, don't know how to perform what you are asking, or are scared, overwhelmed, and feeling incompetent. If they don't understand, we need to clarify and verify. If they are overwhelmed and scared, we need to back up, slow down, and make the demands simpler. If they do not know how to perform what is expected, we need to support and guide. In almost all cases, if the child is not responding, pressure and force will only produce fear and panic.

We need to let the child pace the learning and feel safe in knowing we will not demand, force, or pressure him to respond. Invite, do not demand, engagement. If the child does not feel safe, accepted, and competent enough to respond, we need to back up, understand why, and then provide the support needed for the child to feel safe and competent enough to engage. If the child is not responding, it is *our* responsibility to change, not his. As impatient as we may be to move on, we must take the responsibility to make the change and allow the child time to respond. The more rigid the child's response, the more flexible our approach must be. Listen, learn, respect, and provide. We need to meet resistance with compassion, and listen to what he needs. Unless he perceives us as a working partner with him, he will not accept us as a trusted guide.

Mentor/apprentice relationship

In Relationship Development Intervention (www.rdiconnect.com), Steven Gutstein (2000, 2002a, 2002b, 2009) emphasizes the importance of the master/apprentice relationship. In my material I often use the label "mentor," rather than "master." The fear of uncertainty and the all-important drive to avoid it lead to the obsessive need to control everything. This strong drive drastically interferes with learning and is probably the most significant roadblock to development. Most child development comes from the mentor–apprentice relationship that is established between the parent and child. During early infancy, the infant becomes emotionally attached to mom and dad, and wants to learn from them. Most learning occurs as a result of the child becoming an apprentice to mom and dad. He sees mom and dad as the mentor/master of trade, so to speak, and learns by watching, imitating, and emulating mom and dad. For that to occur, the child has to follow the lead of the master (mom and dad) and feel comfortable allowing the parent to lead and control. Children on the spectrum often miss this milestone early in life and do not develop the emotional security to give up control and become an apprentice to mom and dad. Since these children often resist following the lead of a more experienced master (mom and dad), they are not exposed to the thousands of learning opportunities that occur in normal child development.

Most parents, if they watch closely, can see that their children actually control most of the interaction and activity in their family. The child is rarely following the lead of the mom or dad, and usually the parents are patterning their interaction to help keep the child from feeling anxious, melting down, or acting out. Although we may be able to make the children's lives easier for them and help them to feel a little safer, they never learn to feel competent in tackling uncertainty and taking risks that are inherent in learning anything new. They will not learn how to regulate interactions with others, go with the flow, or follow the lead of the more experienced mentor. The greatest insecurity I see in these children is an overwhelming feeling of incompetency, the inability to feel competent in coping with the uncertainty of daily living. This leads them to control everything and to melt down/act out when they cannot control it.

This is a very serious topic and can be a very emotionally charged issue. My focus has recently become tackling the core deficits of autism to teach the child the rewards of emotionally connecting with others, to feel competent and comfortable with giving up this obsessive need to control in order to avoid uncertainty. Once the child learns to follow the lead of the parent and to trust the parent to lead them successfully through uncertainty, they learn to feel competent and enjoy tackling the uncertainties that normal everyday life presents. In essence, most child development consists of constantly facing and learning to adapt to novel uncertainty. The child places trust in the parents to keep him safe and to allow them to lead him through the uncertainty. If we can back up and establish this milestone with children on the spectrum, they also can establish this mentor–apprentice relationship.

"Learning" through "relating"! Activate the right-side brain!

Children on the spectrum have weak neurological connections between the different brain centers. This weakens communication between the different brain centers. Poor brain integration interrupts major brain functioning. One of these integrative functions is integrating the left brain (logical, analytical, detail/factual) with the right brain (intuitive, creative, social/emotional relating). For people with autism, it is well known that they are weak in the area of social referencing, perspective taking, reading nonverbal communication, and emotion sharing, all of which are important in social relating. Not only is social relating compromised, but much of our early learning is through "social learning"— learning by referencing others for information, imitating, and following the lead of others. Most early learning occurs through relating with others. Many children on the spectrum do not learn by taking the perspective of others or by following their lead. They have to learn by individual exploration, missing out on all the learning through others that most children thrive on.

Recent research in the area of "brain plasticity" has shown that the brain is constantly rewiring itself through experience. With each new experience and repetition of experiences, the brain creates new neurological pathways. The brain can develop stronger neurological connections through repeated experiences that pave the way. Given this, it is important that we provide the child with constant exposure, through normal daily activities, to experience sharing with others, especially the primary caregiver (parents). This does not mean more rote social skills training (teaching discrete social scripts), or throwing the child into social groups and overloading him with trying to regulate with multiple peers. This is too confusing and overwhelming to him. Teaching the child relating skills occurs through the one-on-one daily interactions with the primary caregiver (parents). These social, relating pathways develop by doing things together and sharing the experiences together. These "we-do" activities set the stage for children to (1) reference you for information, (2) share emotion together, (3) reference your perspective, and (4) learn to coordinate and co-regulate interaction with others. This joint attention and experience sharing with another can occur through shared engagement in normal daily activities.

By doing it together in "we-do" activities, we incorporate this essential learning into all daily activity. By doing together and learning through relating, we bring into play the parts of brain responsible for relating and develop stronger neurological pathways to these regions. We bring into play the right side of the brain that needs further strengthening. Also, by changing from *praising* performance ("Good job, Johnny") to *celebrating* doing it together (give five, thumbs up, etc.), we are developing social reciprocity (the social dance of sharing an experience). This learning through sharing an experience with others provides constant exposure and activation of these neurological pathways, creating stronger social/emotional relating. While we are teaching essential life skills by doing it together, we are also teaching social referencing, emotion sharing, and relating skills. The child is learning through doing with you, referencing your guidance and feeling competent learning through you. It builds stronger emotional attachment, greater relating skills, and stronger social learning skills.

Start by building relating into your normal daily routine activities with your child, by doing them together, helping each other out, and becoming an essential element in the activity. In addition, move from praising task performance to celebrating doing it together, with a three-step social reward (physical contact, gesture, and declarative statements). By doing so, you are bringing the social areas of the brain into play and developing greater neurological pathways through these experiences.

Mentoring through guided participation

Steven Gutstein (2000, 2002a, 2002b, 2009), founder of Relationship Development Intervention (RDI), popularized the "guided participation" model of teaching. I prefer to call this form of teaching "mentoring" or coaching. Mentoring is about guiding rather than instructing. It is about doing the task together, guiding and assisting each other through the challenge. Mentoring is about knowing and understanding your student, then framing the assistance so the child feels just the right challenge—just enough "newness" to feel the challenge, but not so much to overwhelm. Mentoring is about continually reading the child and appraising the amount of guidance needed to maximize the child being able to feel himself mastering the challenge. Mentoring is as much about relating, connecting, and celebrating companionship as it is about teaching. It is through this working partnership that the child feels competent through doing *with* and alongside the coach. It is not about prompting, instructing, or directing, but about doing it together, and gradually developing competency through sharing the experience.

With guided participation, both partners are actively participating and doing it together, with the mentor framing the activity for success—showing by doing! At any given time, the mentor continually adjusts his guidance to match the competence of the child. It is about staying in sync with the child, continually appraising and adjusting the guidance to match the performance of the child. At first, the child may only be able to do 20 percent of the performance, with the mentor matching the other 80 percent. As the child develops greater competence, the mentor gradually reduces the guidance, providing just enough challenge for the child to feel himself tackling it. With effective mentoring, this delicate balance between what the child can do and what the mentor provides is continually adjusted based on what the child is displaying at any given time. The child may be at 50 percent on one day and time, but, due to sensory issues, cognitive drain, and accumulated stress, may fall to 35 percent on another. Mentoring is about finding the "just right" challenge at that given period of time, and matching the amount of guidance to scaffold the "just right" challenge. It is not about demanding a certain level of performance and withholding reinforcement if the child doesn't perform to expectation. It is about "matching" the guidance to the competency at the moment. It is about becoming a working partner with the child, to become a trusted guide for him. So, next time you want to teach, mentor instead.

Teaching visual strategies

The importance of using visual strategies has been well documented in the literature for teaching, communicating, organizing schedules, and conveying information. However, when parents first introduce the use of visuals, their child often resists. If these visuals are so important for the children, why would they resist? The reason may lie in the way they are introduced. Kids on the spectrum often resist anything new that is imposed on them. Any new uncertainty will often result in immediate resistance, especially if it is initiated by others. Since they are not initiating the strategy, they are very defensive toward it. In other cases, resistance may occur because the children do not understand the value that the visual strategy has for them. Often the children (1) have not learned to associate that the pictures represent their favorite items or (2) do not understand that they can use the picture to request the item. The following guidelines can be used to introduce the use of visuals without causing anxiety and resistance.

1. Establishing association and meaning

To avoid the initial resistance when introducing something new like using pictures/photos, start off by pairing the pictures with the desired objects. Begin by placing pictures of the items right next to the actual objects around the house: picture of juice on the refrigerator, picture of toothbrush next to the toothbrush in the bathroom, picture of bath next to bath tub, etc. Throughout the day, each time you go to give the child the item (juice) or do the tasks with him (tooth brushing), point to and show him the picture as you give him the object. This way, the child learns to associate the picture with the object/task—giving the pictures meaning.

2. Picture exchange

Next, once the child seems to connect the picture to getting the item, we now give the child the picture to exchange for the desired item/event. Each time the child wants something, you hand him the picture and ask for the child to give it back (or you take it back), and immediately provide the item. This way, he learns to connect exchanging the picture of the item/event to obtain the desired item.

It is best to start off with only items of strong interest, since we know the child will be motivated to ask for those items. I also like to start with items where I can give multiple trials to establish the connection. For example, if the child likes juice, I will use a small glass with one swallow of juice in it. I give the child the picture of juice, say "juice," and immediately take the picture back and provide the juice to drink. Then I refill the glass with another swallow and give another trial; again I give the picture, prompt "drink," take the picture back, and provide the juice. This way, I can get in about ten picture exchanges for juice. Giving multiple trials consecutively provides mass practice of exchanging the picture for the desired item. I will also do this with favorite activities. Let's say the child likes to be picked up and swung around. I will provide the child with a picture representing "swing" (photo of dad swinging the child) and have him give me the picture back. I immediately say "swing!" and pick him up and swing him. Then I put the child down and hand him the picture and say "swing, again!" This provides multiple trials of picture exchange for swinging. I will do this repeatedly for approximately ten trials.

3. Portable picture boards

Over time, the child gets used to exchanging a variety of pictures for items/ activities. Next, we want to teach the child to take the picture to the item and exchange it. If it is time to take a bath, we give the child the photo of bath, say "bath," and take the child to the bathroom. Once in the bathroom, we have the child hand the picture to the parent who puts it up next to the picture near the tub, and say "bath." Same for asking for juice or other preferred items or activities.

If we are planning on using portable picture boards, we may start using them now. The portable picture board is usually a small 2 inch by 10 inch thin board or thick cardboard with a strip of Velcro on it. This board can usually hold up to four small pictures in sequence on the Velcro strip. At this time we simply put the picture of the desired item/event on the Velcro board, have the child pull the picture off (or the parent pulls it off and hands it to the child), and walk with it to the area to exchange for the desired item/event. This way, the child learns to take the picture to the desired event.

4. Now and next boards

Once the child learns to pull off the picture, take it to the desired area, and exchange it for the preferred item/event, then we move on to "now and next" boards. Another name for this is a "first, then" board. We use a portable Velcro board with two pictures on it. The two pictures are placed in order of sequence, representing "First we do ____, and then we can do____." The sequence usually includes a task that we wish him to do ("now" activity) to obtain the preferred item ("next" activity). We usually start with short and simple activities for the "now" activity, to make it easy to earn the "next" (preferred activity) activity.

For example, first we take a bath and then you have a snack. When the bath is complete, the photo is removed and the next activity is snack!

If the child is too resistant to do the "now" (non-preferred) activity to obtain the "next" (preferred activity), then we often start off with two "preferred events"—for example, first on play the computer (now) and then have a snack (next). By starting out with two preferred activities, we increase the likelihood of cooperation. Then, once the child starts doing two items in sequence and learns that he can get this by doing that, then we move on to using non-preferred events (bath) to earn the preferred event (snack).

Then the "now and next" sequence has the first picture being a non-preferred activity and the second a preferred activity.

5. Chaining

From there, we simply start chaining together one additional activity (picture) at a time (e.g. two activities to earn the preferred activity) while always ending the routine with the preferred activity. We move from the "now and next" sequence to a three-picture sequence (homework, bath, then computer time). As time goes on, we try to keep routine sequences with up to three or four activities, with the last picture being the preferred event. These items are placed in order on the portable Velcro board, and the child removes each picture as he completes them. This way he can see himself getting closer to the preferred event.

We usually start with one routine of three to four pictures that stays pretty consistent each day (e.g. coming home from school routine). Each routine always ends with a preferred activity/item as reinforcement. Once the child learns to follow the routine, then we start building in another routine of three to four pictures at some other time during the day (e.g. before bed routine). Over time, we build in several short picture routines throughout the day. Usually, we have the family do only one routine at a time and eventually add other routines (morning routine, coming home from school routine, going to bed routine, etc.) as each routine is established.

6. Master schedule

Eventually, these short picture routines can be added to a master picture schedule for the day. This schedule usually consists of a reinforcing (preferred) activity for every two or three non-preferred activities (the routines above). The master schedule is often hanging on the wall with a running list of the activities the child will do for the next couple of hours. On this master schedule will be a series of three to four picture routines, each ending with a preferred activity. As the child does each task, he removes the picture and puts it on the "done" strip of Velcro or places it in an envelope. As each task is completed, he sees himself getting closer to the preferred event (watching TV, playing on the computer, snack, etc.).

You can also continue to use the portable picture board along with the master schedule. This way, the short routines can be portable while the master schedule is not. Simply take three to four pictures off the master schedule and place them on the portable board to take with the child. As he completes each board, he returns to the master schedule for more pictures. This way, the child has a schedule for the day, but only works on one routine at a time. Remember, each routine should always end with a reinforcing, preferred activity.

7. Pictures for choices

Once the child learns to exchange pictures for items/activities, then we go on to teaching the child to make choices by picking between two or more pictures of choices. We usually start with giving the child choices between two items/activities. We present the two pictures of preferred items, name each one, and then ask the child which one he wants. This gives the child the choice between what he wants to do or have. Over time, we add more items to the choices, increasing his options to choose from. Often we will put together a "reinforcer menu" with a variety of available "preferred" events/items (snack, TV, computer, game, book, etc.). This way, the child can pick out what he wants to do for the preferred activities. Over time, we will make a chore menu, snack menu, preferred activity menu, community outing menu, and so on. We may put all the menus in a book so the child can choose and communicate what he wants to do. This allows the child to pick out want he wants to do and what he wants to earn.

Stop, think, and act; then check!

Most children have weak executive functioning. It is the last part of the brain to fully develop. Kids are usually impulsive, act without thinking, and often have difficulty appraising what is needed. When deciding to act, they also forget to evaluate what the future consequences of their actions will be.

The ability to inhibit our impulses, appraise what is needed, think about what we are doing, and monitor our effectiveness is part of the function of the frontal cortex. Until this part of the brain is working strongly, parents must provide these functions for the child. Parents slow the children down, interrupt them before acting dangerously, require them to stop and think it through before acting, and then monitor the children's actions as they do them. This "stop, think, then act" format works well for neurotypical (NT) children. Eventually, they internalize the process and do the steps simultaneously with minimal conscious effort.

For children who are on the spectrum, we need to teach these steps by slowing the children down and encouraging them to think about what is needed (appraising), then have them slowly step through the action, while evaluating how they are doing. For ongoing action, they need to periodically pause to evaluate and adjust their actions as needed. Children will often jump right into the activity without appraising what is needed and deciding a course of action. They dive right in without thinking, then melt down when things go wrong and they struggle. For example, when you take the child to the playground, he may impulsively run up and unsuccessfully jump on the equipment (without first appraising what is needed). He may not have a clue what to do, but jumps right in and starts doing it. He falls and gets hurts, becomes upset, and throws a tantrum for ten minutes.

We need to frame new situations by having the child "stop, think, then act." Prompt him to look and think about what is needed, what he needs to do, and how to do it. At the playground, before he starts climbing on the equipment, have him pause and think it through with you (hold on with both hands, take one step at a time, etc.). This provides him with a mental map. Next, have him pattern his actions based on this appraisal (start climbing, one step at a time, with both hands secure on the bars). Assist as needed, guiding his actions to be successful. If the child gets off track, pause him again and have him think about what adjustments (corrections) he needs to make. Once he has climbed over the equipment, then talk about how it went (evaluate). Finally, have him repeat these steps for several successful trials to ingrain the new learning.

Children on the spectrum need to have a script (stop, think, then act) to help them remember what to do. As you go through the day, model this script during your actions ("OK, I need to stop, think, then act!"). Then stop and remind the children of this frequently throughout the day. Until they learn the actions themselves, children need to have the parent coach them through it, framing and scaffolding the new learning. For example, with the child who is climbing on the playground equipment, the parent is thinking through it with the child and shadowing his actions, assisting him to do it correctly, and bridging what he may struggle with. We need to always encourage the child to cognitively think about what he is doing, before he does it, as well as while he is doing it. The parent demonstrates it, does it with the child, and helps the child monitor his progress. This ability to appraise and monitor takes a lot of time to develop, but is essential as the child gets older.

Many children on the spectrum have trouble inhibiting their impulses to act long enough to appraise what is needed. Also, while doing the action they have difficulty simultaneously monitoring their actions to match that expectation. They will either refuse to try something new or immediately jump in without first appraising what is needed and whether they have the ability to do it. Once they jump in, they cannot step back and monitor what they are doing to make sure they are doing it right. Consequently, they jump in too quickly, start to flounder, and then melt down when unsuccessful. The child with ADHD may also have these same problems. Again, we would stop the child first, think it through with him (appraise what is needed), coach and monitor the child through it, and then evaluate together how it went.

Let's look at an example of a child who wants to put together a model. Typically, he might jump right in and start haphazardly putting it together without following the instructions or appraising what is needed. Making matters worse, he probably will not monitor his work, checking to make sure he is doing it correctly. The parent needs to coach the child along these steps (stop, think, then act) as well as help him monitor how he is doing as he is doing it. The parent will think through it with him, help him check how he is doing, and provide support while doing it. Complete a step, evaluate if it is correct, and then appraise what is needed for the next step. Pause, check, and appraise! This way, the child learns how to appraise, evaluate, and adjust his actions to stay successful. This takes a lot of time and hard work to make automatic. However, appraising and self-monitoring are important functions to learn.

The first response I get from parents is "What if my child refuses to let me assist?" This is a prerequisite step for becoming a mentor for your child. If your child is resistant to your help, do not try to direct. Simply do it with him while letting him lead, or passively observe what he is doing. Think out loud as you appraise what is needed, and label what he is doing. Be a passive coach, without directing him. Let him do it his way, but provide "thinking" guidance as he is doing it. He is hearing you. Just don't tell him what to do, or try to direct what he is doing. Once he gets accustomed to your passive thoughts, then he will start to trust following your guidance. Trusting you as a mentor takes a lot of time and exposure (trials). Use this process frequently throughout the day in all normal daily activities, teaching the child to appraise first and frequently check how well he is performing. This will not happen quickly, but will occur through repetition over numerous activities. If the child is resistant at first, simply stay consistent and hang in there. It will come over time if you stick with it.

The challenges of tooth brushing!

Tooth brushing is very intrusive. When teaching staff to train tooth brushing, we used to have them brush each other's teeth so they see could feel how intrusive it is. When we brush our own teeth, we know how hard to brush, where we feel sensitivity, how to miss our gums, and how fast to brush. To have someone shove a toothbrush into your month and brush your teeth, without you controlling it, can be really discomforting. In addition, many of these children have strong sensory sensitivities. Kids who tend to be tactile-defensive (touch) are often orally sensitive. There are a variety of strategies we can try; however, we always need to start by validating that you recognize that the brushing causes discomfort for him and that it is understandable. Then, from there, try one or more of the following strategies:

1. Work slowly and talk him through it, telling him which side is next.

2. It often helps to have a set number of strokes you use for each side (top, bottom, side, front, etc.)—for example, five back and forth strokes. Count out each stroke. Counting gives the child a definite end. This provides predictability to the brushing, allowing him to see that it will not last long, and also provides a distraction.

3. It is best to give the child as much control over the brushing as possible. Brush five strokes on one surface, then pause and wait for child to let you know when he is ready for the next.

4. Let the child do as much of it as he can. Even if he does it poorly, you can go over it.

5. Throw away your toothbrush; the bristles may be too hard. Use a soft baby toothbrush or a sponge toothbrush called a toothette. These are good if the child has sensitive gums.

6. Experiment with different toothpastes to find which the child likes the best. Or don't use toothpaste at all. Simply use water. Some children will accept a mouth rinse on their brush.

7. Work slowly and pause whenever the child shows discomfort. Continually show the child you are working with him, pausing when discomfort occurs, and letting him control the pace of brushing.

8. Many children with oral sensitivity like to use a battery-operated, vibrating tooth brush. The vibration tends to dull their oral sensitivity.

9. Have fun with it. Brush together or you brush his teeth and let him brush yours.

10. Reinforce the child with a strong reward once the brushing is complete.

11. Put up a chart and let the child get a star for each time he brushes. After he fills up the chart (five squares, one for each star), he gets a special reward.

12. If the child doesn't like the taste of toothpaste, start off with just water, no toothpaste. Then slowly put a little on. There are liquid washes that you can substitute for those who do not like paste.

13. For some kids, we actually use a soft washcloth over our finger to rub the teeth and gums, instead of a toothbrush.

When in doubt, stay supportive and try not to force. I know it takes time, but having someone force a toothbrush around your mouth can be very intrusive.

Toilet training: ten-step habit training

Toilet training is one of the most asked-about concerns of parents with children on the spectrum. There are a variety of issues (physical, sensory, exaggerated fears, etc.) that can interfere with effective toilet training. Although we are all "creatures of habit," children on the spectrum are even more so. Once in a habit of voiding in their diaper, the children are often comfortable staying with that habit. This is routine to them and they may resist changing that routine. To the children, there are really no good reasons for them to stop their current habit. To reduce a habit (eliminating in the diaper), we need to first create a new habit (eliminating in the toilet). To create a new habit, you need to have a very structured, scheduled routine that occurs frequently and consistently across time. Also, we need to make it as enjoyable as possible and rewarding when followed. The following procedures are a basic toileting program using habit training:

1. Keep a journal of what times your child has toileting accidents. Over time, you may see patterns of when your child typically eliminates in his diaper or has wetting or bowel accidents.

2. The first step is to create a schedule of when to sit the child on the toilet. There are two ways of doing this. From the step above, by knowing the times when your child typically eliminates, create toileting trials that are approximately 15 minutes before the times when elimination usually occurs. The other, more popular schedule, is to toilet the child on a schedule of every 90 minutes, after meals, and before and after going places. The more toileting follows routine events in the child's daily schedule (e.g. after meals, before leaving the house, etc.), the more of a routine habit toileting becomes.

3. Make sure toileting is comfortable for the child. If he is young, make sure he can sit comfortably on the toilet and that his feet can rest on the floor. If he is small, you need to use a potty seat and a stool to place his feet on. If your child has known sensory issues, try to purchase a potty seat, or modify the current one, so it accommodates his sensitivities.

4. For each toileting trial, take the child to the toilet, assist him through the process, sit him on the toilet, and make sure he is comfortable. Stay right there with him and encourage him to "pee" or "poop" in the toilet. For most children, it is easier to first work on peeing in the toilet, since this function is usually easier for them to control. You can increase the understanding of what to do by having either a picture sequence for

using the toilet on the wall next to the toilet, or reading a social story about using the potty. Some parents will even model/demonstrate for the child by having the child observe them using the toilet. Remember, the child may not know that it is OK for him to poop or pee in the toilet. They are used to eliminating in their diaper. They may not associate that they are supposed to eliminate in the toilet.

5. Set a time timer (visual timer) for 3–5 minutes (for some children longer), so the child knows how long to sit on the toilet. Stay with him to help occupy his time and to tell if he eliminates in the toilet. Some parents will run water to help initiate peeing, and some will actually pour a little water between the child's legs to simulate urinating. Make it fun and have a good time. Encourage him to pee in the toilet. When he does eliminate in the toilet, clap and praise, and make a big deal of it! If needed, use a concrete reward for voiding in the toilet. If he doesn't eliminate at the end of the time, do not scold or counsel; simply end the trial and try again next time. Keep toileting positive and fun.

6. If children are not used to sitting on the toilet for at least three minutes, then you may need to first focus on teaching them to sit on the toilet. Try to make toileting time fun. You can purchase a portable table that can be place alongside and over the child sitting on the toilet, so he can play with toys or favorite games. You might play his favorite music. You may also want to invest in a visual timer (time timer) so he can see how long he needs to sit on the toilet. If your child will sit on the toilet for only 30 seconds, then start the time at 30 seconds. Once the time is up, praise heavily and end the trial. After three straight successful trials, expand the time by 5–10 seconds. Gradually keep adding longer and longer times as long as the child is successful.

7. If praise is not strong enough to motivate eliminating in the toilet, then use more concrete reinforcers (favorite snack or drink, video, favorite toy, etc.). Have the item right there to give immediately. Draw attention to the pee or poop in the toilet, give the reward, and immediately praise. If the child associates the toilet with eliminating, and he is old enough to delay, then using a reward chart (e.g. star chart) can be helpful. For example, for a child who has the understanding, you might put up a star chart with five squares on it. The child gets a star in one square each time he voids in the toilet. When he fills up the chart (five stars), he earns a special outing, rents a video, buys a small toy, etc. Keep it positive and fun!

8. While implementing the toileting program, keep a chart that tracks when the child uses the toilet, if he voids in the toilet, and when he has accidents. You may want to adjust the times for toileting if you still see a

pattern of accidents occurring. By increasing the frequency of the child eliminating in the toilet, you will hope to see a corresponding decrease in toileting accidents.

9. Once the child learns to eliminate in the toilet, if he still is having accidents, then implement "dry checks." Midway between toileting trials, check the child to see if he is dry. Build in reinforcement for being dry (earn points, tokens, access to favorite toys, etc.).

10. Try to avoid scolding, counseling, or punishing the child when he has an accident. You want to keep toileting positive and fun. When accidents occur, simply help the child clean up with minimal emotion given to the accident. It is fine to have the child help you clean up.

Remember to keep to the schedule and stay very consistent with implementing the procedures. It takes time to learn a new habit, especially when it has to replace an old one. Some children may have more sensory or physical issues that may cause barriers to successful toileting. Get extra help by consulting a professional or purchasing a book on toilet training for children with special needs.

Can my child ever learn to live on his own?

Parents often ask me, "Can my child ever learn to live on his own?" The answer for many of these children is yes. Not all children will be able to; however, many can if provided with the right opportunities. The three main things that hold them back are (1) the limited expectations of those teaching them, (2) the way we go about teaching, and (3) not starting early enough to teach them independent living.

At all ages we need to be teaching "life skills," whether it be basic personal care (dressing, eating, etc.) when younger, or advanced daily living skills (cooking, writing a check, etc.) when they get older. The problem I see is we tend to do way too much for these children (rather than allowing them to learn) and we start way too late (waiting for the time NT children learn them). We over-compensate for their delay in learning by doing for them, rather than teaching them how to. We need to assume the ability to learn and provide supportive coaching to teach them. We also need to project ahead to what they will need to function on their own, and then start teaching toward those objectives at an early age (both in school and at home).

How to teach!

Teach the child through "we-do" activities, doing them together, learning by doing with you. This is called "apprentice learning." The child learns the functions and skills by doing the activity with you, side by side, helping you out, while you scaffold the activity for learning to occur. He learns by actively doing, while you frame the activity for learning. Instead of standing back and instructing the child through these tasks, do them together, modeling and guiding as you go along. The child learns these needed skills during his natural daily routine of the day. He is always an active participant (rather than you doing it for him), so learning occurs naturally as he learns to reference, imitate, and follow your lead.

Starting now is important. Get him involved in cooking, meal planning, grocery shopping, laundry, dusting, vacuuming, putting away clothes, fixing simple things, and so on as early as possible. Make a list of everything he will need to learn to live on his own (open a savings account, budget money, plan meals, do dishes, etc.) and get him started on it now. Although it is never too early to teach basic functional skills, I would start projecting ahead to what is needed for him to be a functioning adult, and arrange the curriculum around this long-term goal. Make a list of skills to teach over time, then sit down with the child to prioritize where to start. Depending on the child's learning abilities, tackle no more than three or four skills at one time until they are mastered (only one skill at a time for less capable children). Once learned, build these skills into his daily routine (once the skill is learned, keep it in his daily routine). In Appendix E there is an Activities of Daily Living (ADL) assessment form which allows you to evaluate where your child's skills are at, what needs to be worked on, and task-analyzed steps to make training easy. This form is good for evaluating and monitoring progress in personal care, household tasks, leisure activities, community skills, and self-management skills.

Make a "My Independence Book" to track the child's progress. In the front of the notebook, put the list of skills to learn, followed by photos of him learning each skill as he does them. When he learns each skill, check that skill off his list as learned and move on to the next. Never stop doing the task once it is learned. Keep it in his routine so he continues to practice the skill. Learning by doing is so important for these children. Checking off the list helps him see what he has already learned and helps develop self-esteem and confidence.

What to teach

At school, academic tasks should be functional to daily living. For example, doing math should be hands-on learning to teach a daily skill (make change, balance a check book, etc.). Connect the new learning to functional living to give value for the child. Also, combine skills such as reading labels/instructions and measuring ingredients for cooking, cleaning, putting things together, etc. Don't limit learning to the home. Also teach functional skills in the community (shopping, banking, safety skills, etc.). Remember, what you do for him now, he has to learn to eventually do on his own. Do these activities together, side by side, giving him a small part to play (finding the items on the grocery shelves, handing money to the cashier, putting groceries away at home, etc.). Even if the child is not capable of doing the entire task independently, give him a part to do and learn. Set the expectation for learning to occur and gradually give more responsibility as the child learns.

Make a curriculum for both home and school. For each skill taught, ask yourself, "What function does it serve?" If the skill does not have immediate utility value, ask yourself, "Why do it?" All reading, writing, problem solving, and math need to be concrete and have functional utility for the child to grasp them. Teach by doing, rather than sitting at a desk, learning it. These children do not generalize well, so teach by doing.

The curriculum should look at what daily living skills (household chores, money handling skills, meal planning, personal care skills, driving a car, etc.) will be needed to live independently; what social skills are needed to meet these daily living skills (carry on a simple conversation, teamwork in activities, obtaining help, patiently standing in lines, following basic social rules, etc.); vocational skills (general work skills such as being on time, following directions, coordinating with co-workers, as well as skills specific to vocational interest); and basic organization skills for planning, organizing, and carrying out the daily activities (checklists, visual schedules, visual organizers, etc.).

Teach driving skills now. Let the child learn to feel comfortable steering, accelerating, and regulating a moving vehicle similar to a go-cart. Use golf carts, riding lawn mowers (blades detached), and four-wheel vehicles to give them "safe" experiences learning the perceptual motor skills of driving. Then when it comes to learning the cognitive aspects of driving on the road, they have the perceptual motor skills down. If the child can ride a bike, cycle together around the neighborhood while teaching him to look both ways, yield to oncoming traffic, follow road signs, and so on.

Who can live on their own?

Most children on the spectrum can learn to live in a setting that matches their needs—if not independently, then at least in semi-independent living. They just need very structured learning, with lots of repetition and guided participation. They need to learn by doing and thinking their way through things (rather than rote learning). Put them in real-life situations, every day, day after day, with your supportive guidance, and allow them to think their way through it (appraise what is needed, come up with options, and evaluate the alternatives). Slowly teach them how to *do* and also how to *appraise* what is needed. This takes time to learn, so start projecting ahead to what they will need to learn to be functional, independent adults. It is not good to wait until they are 16 years old to be considering these things. Start them as early as possible, 10–11 years of age or sooner, and build gradually to success! Get together with the school and provide guidance to a curriculum that will maximize independent learning.

What if my child will never be independent? For those who will need varying degrees of supervision and assistance all of their lives, many can still live on their own, in supervised living arrangements (apartments, small homes, and community group homes). If you live in America, many individuals are living in apartment settings with staff supervision, supported by government funding. These settings can be tailored to meet the goals and dreams as well as the sensory needs of the individual. We still want them to be as independent as possible, regardless of the degree of supervision required. However, staff should always be assisting them, rather than doing for them!

Making it happen! Promoting independence

We often make the mistake of assuming that if a person cannot do every step of an activity independently, there is no need to teach him that skill. This often is discussed during transition planning for adult living. "My son is low functioning, so he will have to live in a residential program for the rest of his life." "He cannot cook, because he will burn himself." "He needs someone to shop for him, because he does not have money skills." These types of statements often result in "He can't, therefore he shouldn't!"

In person-centered planning, we assess the person's goals, dreams, desires, and preferences, then build a quality of life around that profile. Regardless of the functioning level or capabilities of each individual, they all have goals, dreams, desires and preferences. Like all of us, they all deserve to live in a setting that helps them actualize those goals and dreams. First, we identify the types of activities (work, leisure, community, household, etc.) the person may value, and then build active participation around those activities. The person might be able to do some of these activities independently; however, for many he may require varying degrees of assistance. However, the need for assistance does not exclude the person from engaging in the activities.

We first outline what "quality of life" means for the individual. Then we build in the types of activities that will provide that quality of life. We next need to look at how to make that participation happen and how to promote as much independence as possible. However, regardless of skill level, the lack of independent skills should not exclude the person from participation. Participation should be a given, with us providing assistance where skills are lacking. The disability should not be a reason to exclude participation. Do not limit their vision or their dreams by their disability. Almost anything can happen with the right supports.

Making it happen!

For many parents, the thought of their child living on his own, away from them, is hard to envision. However, with good planning, the young adult can live a life that matches his needs and interests, a life where he is as independent as possible and the driver of his dreams. Many individuals live in their own settings with staff support. Staff assist them in skills they do not already know, and help train those skills that are possible to learn. The person is still fully engaged in daily living, just with supports as needed.

To help make this happen, we first assess what skills the person already has, those that are emerging, and those that he will need total assistance with. We use the ADL assessment form in Appendix E to evaluate their current skills profile. For each activity the person participates in, we identify (1) what steps the person can already do, (2) which ones he can partially do with assistance, (3) which steps he cannot do at all, and (4) what barriers make participation difficult. Often, the first questions center on the barriers. The person may have a variety of physical, sensory, social, and behavioral vulnerabilities that make participation difficult. This requires us to assess what types of modifications, adaptations, or accommodations we need to provide to make participation successful. This may include making physical adaptations, sensory modifications, or using behavioral supports to minimize these barriers. However, the goal of participation is a given; now, how do we make it happen?

Once the activity is chosen and the barriers identified, we need to break the activity down into simple steps (task analysis). From there we analyze (baseline) what skills the person already has, how independent the person is at each step, what barriers there are, and what type of assistance is needed to promote the highest level of independence possible. For the steps that the person cannot do independently, there are three levels of supports that we can provide.

1. *Teach.* Determine which skills can we teach successfully. Provide training to do these skills more independently.

2. *Modify or adapt.* For those skills that cannot be easily taught, can we modify or adapt the step so as to bypass the need for this skill? For example, if the person cannot make change, then he may be able to purchase items with a debit or money card. This still allows him to purchase things independently, without being able to make correct change. Many steps in an activity can be modified to lessen the need for assistance. Do not spend precious time teaching skills that can be accommodated for. Once the person is fully engaged in the activity, then go back and refine skills as desired.

3. *Assistance.* For any step that cannot be taught or modified, we provide assistance for successful completion. We can help guide the person through the step, or simply do that step for the person. However, we should always try to guide and assist, rather than simply do for the person.

The following are a few examples of how we use these three levels of supports when promoting engagement and learning.

Example 1

One of Sally's desires was to go into the store and purchase items on her own. In analyzing the barriers, it was determined that she could not correct change or remember what she needed to buy, and she got overwhelmed in large grocery stores. To make this activity successful for Sally, while allowing her to build independence, we tried the following:

1. Although Sally had difficulty making correct change, she could count to 30 by ones. We taught Sally the "next dollar approach." With this strategy, we taught Sally to look at the price of the item (e.g. $4.67). She learned to read the dollar amount ($4) and give one dollar more ($5) to the cashier. In this case she would give five one-dollar bills to the cashier, and wait for change back. If this was too difficult for Sally, then we gave her a large single bill (five- or ten-dollar bill) or a debit card. This way, until she learned to make correct change, she could still purchase independently. We simply bypassed the need to make change.

2. To help Sally remember what to buy (and to purchase nothing else), we either gave her a written list of items to cross off, or gave her a keyring with pictures of the items she needed to buy. She used the written list or pictures to find only the items she needed.

3. Since she got overwhelmed in large stores, Sally could do her shopping in small convenience stores. These stores are less crowded, and it was easier to find the items and for staff to monitor her from the car.

Over time, Sally was taught how to walk from her apartment to the corner store to buy small items. This helped her to build independence and self-confidence. From her daily trips to the store, she also began to build acquaintances. She frequently talked to neighbors on the way and became familiar with staff at the store. She was developing both independence skills and social acquaintances.

Example 2

Jack lived in his own apartment with assistance from support staff to help him cook dinner. He did not like to have staff stop by every day to help him cook dinner. It made him feel too dependent. He wanted to do this on his own. Staff and Jack's parents did not feel he had the safety skills needed to cook on the range without supervision. However, Jack could use the microwave oven independently. Jack agreed to have staff come in on Sunday morning and help him cook several meals. He would cook the food for the next week in advance, then portion out his meals in containers and refrigerate/freeze them. He would make out a menu of what to eat each evening, cook them on Sunday, and then warm them up in the microwave oven during the week. This way, Jack could live more independently without relying on staff coming by every day to watch him cook dinner.

Example 3

John lived in a group home with five other men. He did not like living in a group setting and wanted to get his own place. Staff felt that he never could live on his own because he could not remember what to do and when to do it. He simply did not have the organizational skills needed for living on his own. However, since this was John's dream, we wanted to help him realize it. We knew that John would need some visual system for organizing and following through with what he needed to do. John was used to having staff remind him what to do and when to do it. John would not be able to move out on his own if he needed staff supervision all day long. Instead, we set up a visual (picture) schedule for his morning routine (sequence of tasks in his morning routine) and another visual schedule for the evening routine. Everything that John needed to do was on the schedule. Instead of reminding John what and when to do things, staff simply reminded him to look at his chart. With an erasable marker, John would check off each task as he did them and simply follow the sequence of events. Over time, John learned to follow his routine without staff reminding him. John was strongly motivated to use this system because he knew it would lead to him eventually living on his own. Once he learned to set up and follow his own routine by using the visual schedule, John was ready to move into an apartment with staff stopping by twice a day to check on him and ensure he was following his daily routine. Instead of letting John's weaknesses stop him from realizing his dream, we simply made accommodations (visual schedule) for what he could not do independently.

Chapter 7

BUILDING ON STRENGTHS AND INTERESTS

Deficit model verses strength-based model

Parents, schools, and professionals usually focus on a "deficit model" of autism. They are often so focused on "treating" the child's deficits that they do not recognize the strengths and gifts that the child offers. Most diagnostic criteria for autism are a list of deficits or symptoms, all of which have negative connotations. Unfortunately for the child, the support we give is often driven to change the child, molding him to a model that doesn't fit his very nature. This places the child in a model that is constantly providing him with feedback on how deficient, damaged, or incompetent he is. Not only does this rarely work, but it often leaves the child feeling very anxious, insecure, and inadequate. Instead of focusing on what the child *is* and helping him develop his strengths, we often focus on what the child *isn't* and what we want him to be. We hope that by changing his behavior, or shaping him to act according to a given script, we can cure "autism."

Every child presents a set of strengths and weaknesses, with a cluster of interests, talents, and gifts. All children have natural gifts and strengths that, when supported and fostered, will grow into the person that naturally unfolds. We spend so much time forcing the children into a profile that doesn't match them that we ignore and suppress their true essence. This essence is what the child will naturally become if supported rather than changed. If we focus less on weaknesses and more on developing strengths, we help children build strong confidence and self-esteem, developing a strong sense of self-identity and self-worth. We recognize and value their unique essence and help them grow and blossom.

All children have a desire to feel safe, accepted, and competent. All human beings are motivated by mastery, success, and events that develop our strengths and interests. When children feel valued for what they are, rather than what we would like them to be, they develop and grow. There is a natural attraction to any event that helps us feel safe, accepted, and competent. Unfortunately, when we focus most of our attention on the child's weaknesses and molding him into what he is not, we place the child in situations where he often feels unsafe, unaccepted, and incompetent. No human being flourishes in these conditions.

Regardless of diagnosis or labels, we need to support the child to feel safe, accepted, and competent. This means identifying the child's profile of strengths, desires, and vulnerabilities. From this profile, we help the child feel safe and competent by lessening his stress, compensating for vulnerabilities, building off his interests, and developing his strengths. Matching our supports to the child's unique profile will communicate that we respect and value the child's sense of self and self-worth. For any child, regardless of profile or label, if we identify his natural strengths, interests, and vulnerabilities, and use this profile to help him feel safe, accepted, and competent, he will grow and develop, with strong self-esteem and gifts to offer the world.

When helping the child develop, we need to focus on three primary principles:

1. What helps the child feel *safe and secure*? What are the major sensory/ cognitive/social stressors that overwhelm the child? How can we modify and adapt the environment and conditions to minimize stress and respect his vulnerabilities? This gives the child a chance to feel safe to risk and grow.

2. What helps the child feel *accepted and valued*? Are the people who support the child engaging in ways that help him feel accepted and valued? Are parents and staff working partners in supporting the child, or are they trying to change the child? What interaction patterns (tone and volume of voice, intensity of animation, approach style, etc.) promote the feeling of acceptance and trust for the child?

3. What helps my child feel *competent*? What are my child's strengths, interests, and gifts, and how can we build on those to strengthen his talents? Build new learning around the child's interests and talents. Be aware of what learning style and teaching strategies the child responds best to. Give the needed supports to provide repeated exposure to mastery and success. Teach the child to feel competent by following your lead and trusting your guidance. Repeated exposure to success and mastery builds stronger confidence in tackling new learning. Mastery is motivating to all human beings. By building on their strengths/interests and providing guided participation, we enable all children to learn and grow.

These three principles are basic to all humans, regardless of labels and differences. When evaluating new teaching strategies for the child, first ask yourself, "How does this support help the child feel safe, accepted, and competent?" If it doesn't help, drop it. If it does, add it to the learning tools for that child. This child will learn, grow, and develop a strong sense of self and self-worth.

Differences vs. disabilities!

In previous posts regarding the controversy over the labels "high and low functioning" and "IQ and autism" (see Chapter 5), we explored that there are two main dimensions that have to be taken into consideration when talking about autism. There are two dimensions that interplay in how the person's ability to function will play out: (1) autism symptoms (sensory processing issues, rigid inflexible thinking, processing differences, executive functioning problems, communication differences, social and emotional difficulties) and (2) intellectual or cognitive impairment (limitations in being able to cognitively process information, understand, learn, and adapt to environmental demands). As discussed in previous posts, a person can be "higher functioning" intellectually, but still have severe symptoms of autism; on the other hand, a person can be more impaired cognitively (lower functioning) with less severe autism traits (more flexible, fewer sensory issues, easier time socially connecting, etc.). The whole confusion over low and high functioning has been because of the misunderstanding of how these two dimensions overlap. Granted, these labels are misleading and only tend to devalue the person. However, gaining a good understanding of these two dimensions (autism traits and cognitive impairments) is needed to truly understand how to help the individual.

There have been a lot of discussions and arguments around whether the autism traits are a disability or simply differences (different abilities). For the purpose of the discussion here, let's define "differences" as a different way of processing and adapting, and "disabilities" as limitations in being able to adapt. For example, there are both sensory differences in autism and sensory disabilities. Common sensory differences in autism would be better acuity of sensory detail, heightened sensitivity to sensory stimulation, strong perception of sensory patterns, unbiased perception of sensory stimulation, and strong sensory memory. Granted, some differences (e.g. sensory sensitivity) can be a strength in one situation but a deficit in another (sensorily overwhelmed). Whereas there are strong sensory differences in autism, there are also sensory disabilities. Deficits or disabilities can occur if the person has strong fragmented or distorted sensory "integration" difficulties, which interfere with the person's ability to effectively integrate his senses. This can greatly affect his ability to adapt to the world around him in any environment. When you cannot consistently integrate your senses, it greatly affects all other functioning. In autism, individuals almost always have sensory differences, but sensory integration disabilities (distorted, fragmented perceptions, integration problems) vary substantially in severity.

The same holds true for cognitive differences. People on the spectrum process information differently in that they are more concrete, factually based, detailed thinkers, with strong associative and static memories. In these areas they are stronger than the global, more inferential thinking patterns of neurotypical people. NT people tend to process from general to specific, and people on the spectrum tend to process from specific to general. People with autism tend to be more factual and less biased in their thinking compared with the more global, inferential thinking of NT people. NT thinking tends to be more abstract, whereas spectrum thinking tends to be more literal and concrete. These differences are neither good nor bad, just different.

In addition to the differences, there are some processing disabilities that affect autism in varying degrees. People on the spectrum often have strong disabilities in rapidly processing dynamic, multiple information simultaneously. They have difficulty processing information coming rapidly from multiple sources (or multiple senses) at one time. However, once the information flow slows down and is given sequentially, the processing improves drastically. Also, people on the spectrum have varying degrees of weaknesses in the areas of executive function which consists of the ability to control attention, inhibit impulses, organize, plan, and monitor a course of action, and multitask. These can be seen as a disability because they do greatly limit the person's ability to adapt. These too can vary in severity among people on the spectrum.

We all have strengths and weaknesses, and they come packaged a little differently. Unfortunately, since those with autism are a minority in society, their differences tend to be quickly labeled as deficits (disabilities) because they do not fit the general norm. Different often stands out as a deficit or weakness. This is where, as for many minorities, society can severely limit people on the spectrum. We need to embrace the differences and foster their development, not interpret them as deficits. Since their differences can be strengths that we miss, their value to society can be great. All we have to do is look at some of the major contributions people on the spectrum have made to art, science, and technology. The more we can learn from the way they view the world, the better our world can become. Their strong perceptual and detailed qualities can and have dramatically improved the quality of life for all of us.

So, in bridging the two cultures, we need to recognize the benefits that these qualities of autism present us. We need to help those on the spectrum accommodate and compensate for their disabilities (more sensory-friendly modifications, slowing down the information flow, respecting their tendency to become overwhelmed in our environment, avoiding strong social demands, etc.) and foster their valuable differences. By embracing everyone's differences, we can all benefit. We have to be open to these differences and embrace the different perspectives autism can provide us. Neurodiversity can benefit all of us.

Fixations = interests = strengths = learning!

Fixated interests serve a variety of functions for children on the spectrum:

- Fixations (interests, passions) often give children something they can control that is understandable and predictable for them. Categorizing, arranging, and learning everything there is to know about something helps the children feel safe in a world that is difficult to understand.

- Fixations help children bring order to a world that is often chaotic and confusing. They allow the child to hyper-focus on one or two things that he can understand, that are predictable, and for which he feels some degree of mastery.

- The ability to hyper-focus attention on an interest is a common characteristic of ASD. People often see this as a negative characteristic, but it can also be reframed and viewed as a strength. This hyper-focus on a passion is what drives learning and development of ideas. There have been many artists and inventors who have used these strengths to their advantage. These hyper-focused fixations have led to wonderful works of art, science, and technology.

- These fixations are often centered around static, unchanging information: objects, facts, rules, and physical qualities that do not change or change based on concrete rules. This allows children to learn facts about their passion and feel competent knowing everything there is to know. They understand their passions and learn facts about them, making them predictable and easy to control.

- Another ASD characteristic influencing fixations is the focus on detail. This focus on detail can drive children with ASD to stay hyper-focused on an interest to learn everything about it. This can also drive a strong need for knowledge of causation (knowing why something works). They want to break it down and understand each detail of why it works. In turn, this can lead to the drive to make things work better and make better products.

- These fixations also allow the children to hyper-focus on a narrow interest in order to block out, escape, and avoid overload from the fast-paced world that is difficult to process. It gives them an escape from the sensory overload, social insecurities, stress, and anxiety of their typical day. They can escape into a world that is understandable, predictable, and controllable—a world in which they feel competent.

- Fixations are often sensory-based and help calm and organize the nervous system. They soothe and feel good! They release stress chemicals and are great coping skills for tackling stress and anxiety. We all have sensory stimulation that we seek simply because it feels good!

- Socially, fixations give the child something to interact around. He feels competent about his passion and it gives him a topic to talk about. Also, the interest to find out more drives information seeking (asking questions). He is eager to share and learn with others.

Finally, it is important for parents and teachers to understand how valuable fixations are for the child. Use these fixations to engage the child and help him expand these fixations into greater strengths. Use the fixated interests to motivate greater learning. Expand on these interests to teach social skills, and coping skills for stress and anxiety, develop academic skills, further leisure interests, and create future vocational goals. Become part of these fixations, enjoy them, and develop them!

Preference-based learning!

I am a firm believer that with children on the spectrum your best motivator is to take their narrow interests and build them into teaching opportunities. Many children on the spectrum have to see value in what you are trying to teach in order to be interested in learning. To increase motivation, incorporate what they are interested in into the teaching. Often that may be a fixation on trains, Lego®, Super Mario, baseball statistics, fans, appliances, and so on. You can read and write about it, research it, categorize it, and build math, science, and history around it.

If your child is interested in vacuums, then build a variety of learning experiences around vacuums. You could help him look up the different brands online, read the different descriptions, research the pros and cons of each type, compare and contrast the various brands, learn the mechanics of how vacuums work, and categorize the brands based on the specifications. You can research the history and development of the vacuum, the advances over time, and contemplate directions the technology could go in the future. You could have him make his own catalog by categorizing vacuums by brand and model, what type of attachments come with them, what type of power train drives them, the amount of electrical power each uses, how much they cost, what type of replacement parts are available, which pick up water as well as dirt, what the consumer report ratings are, and which vacuums have the best guarantees.

You could pick up a broken vacuum at a junk yard and take it apart. Look at the different parts and what function they serve. He can learn how to take it apart and put it back together again, how to order parts and refurbish old vacuums, and even resell them! If he is younger, you can write simple stories around a make-believe vacuum cleaner and the experiences he has (the family that he is with, how each family member uses him, which room he likes to vacuum the best, how each carpet feels, what it feels like when he is filled up with dirt, etc.). Look for the video *The Brave Little Toaster*. It is a movie about a house full of animated appliances, and they have a character that is a vacuum. The learning opportunities are endless!

For older kids, there are books on how vacuums work, how to repair them, and how to sell them. There are instructional videos on how to use them and repair them. Google "vacuum cleaners" and you can come up with numerous ways of using vacuums to expand learning.

There isn't anything that you cannot build learning around. With kids on the spectrum, you often have to look closely to see what their passions are. We often want to ignore the fixations or suppress them because they are odd or different, in favor of something we value more. However, these passions are the key to their world and motivation. Find them and use them!

Turning deficits into assets! Rigid inflexibility expressed as commitment and dedication!

Many differences, which we often call deficits, can be true benefits. Many people on the spectrum tend to have all-or-nothing thinking, which is frequently labeled as rigid, inflexible thinking. This is often thought of in negative terms, because it leads to difficulty at times when flexible thinking is required. The thinking of those on the spectrum is often very black and white, either/or, or right or wrong. This type of thinking can also be an asset at times. When the person on the spectrum likes something or is committed to something, he will go all out and hyper-focus on it. He will commit wholeheartedly to whatever his passion or endeavor is. Therefore, he can excel in a preferred vocational interest or favorite activity. He will be very disciplined in practicing and persevere in the face of adversity. This all-or-nothing thinking can be very favorable when channeled in the right way.

The same is true for friendships. Even though relating can be difficult for them, most people on the spectrum, once they befriend you, will be among the most dedicated friends you will ever have. They will support you, help you out, and stand by you when things are not going well. If they are going to be your friend, they will be good friends. If they like something, they *really* like something. They don't go halfway.

Most of the so-called deficits in autism are simply differences. They can be viewed in a negative light (since they are not like ours), but can also be viewed in a positive light (strengths that we do not have). This is not to minimize the challenges that autism presents to both the person himself and to others. Yes, there are many struggles, but do not get stuck in automatically interpreting all differences as deficits. Do not stifle the unique qualities that autism can present.

Using your strengths to compensate for weaknesses!

I have found that many people on the spectrum have a unique form of logic that can be used to compensate for what they cannot intuitively read. We need to use the person's processing strengths (detailed, logical, analytically based) to compensate for their processing weaknesses (intuitive, social, contextually based).

I was once helping an adult on the spectrum learn to reduce stress that often resulted in overload and meltdowns. As can be expected, these emotional reactions affected both his employment and family life. Many people on the spectrum have poor sensory awareness of the internal body cues that warn us that we are becoming stressed and anxious. They often cannot feel the stress/anxiety building up in their nervous system. Consequently, they often do not realize that they are getting overwhelmed until they reach boiling point and their coping skills start to quickly deteriorate. When teaching emotional regulation, we teach people to recognize the internal cues (muscle tension, increased heart rate, etc.) that they are getting stressed, so that they can pull back and use coping skills to avoid overload. However, many people on the spectrum have difficulty sensing these body cues until they reach boiling point, which is often too late to control. Hence, if they cannot sense the early signs of being stressed, it is difficult to learn how to use coping skills early in the stress build-up.

For this individual, his lack of being able to sense the internal cues made it difficult for him to use coping skills to hold off overload. However, his strength was numerical reasoning abilities. He was very good with adding and subtracting numerical values quickly and easily. We found that he could compensate for his lack of internal stress cues by assigning numerical stress ratings to all of his daily stressors. The more stressful the event was, the higher the numerical rating. Each event in his daily routine was assigned a numerical rating based on how much effort or stress it presented.

Stress chemicals accumulate as the day goes on, and since he could not sense his body telling him that he was becoming stressed, he had to find another way of tracking how much stress his system was accumulating. He learned to assign numerical values as stress ratings of various events in his day. Since therapy usually focuses on teaching the person to recognize the early warning signs so he can activate coping skills, this person learned to numerically add up the stress ratings as they occurred throughout the day. He could quickly add his stress ratings as each event happened during the day. He learned that once his accumulated score reached a certain point (e.g. 100) he needed to escape to the bathroom and engage in his motor self-stimulation for 10–15 minutes to regroup and rebound. He found that he needed these breaks approximately once every couple of hours to reduce the chances of overload and emotional meltdown.

Even though he could not feel the stress chemicals building in his nervous system, he learned to trust his numerical ratings as an effective tool for emotional regulation. This made sense to him and utilized his numerical reasoning to control his emotional life. He was much happier and felt more competent in handling the daily stress on the job and in his social life. He was able to use his strength—numerical reasoning—to compensate for his inability to sense his internal cues.

In summary, individuals on the spectrum can learn to use their unique reasoning abilities to compensate effectively for the lack of intuitive social or emotional reasoning. Instead of trying to develop a weakness that may be fruitless, it is better to foster their reasoning strengths to compensate for their weaknesses. This does not mean that the person could not, at the same time, learn strategies for better recognizing his body cues (meditation, mindfulness, relaxation skills, etc.); however, this can be difficult given the sensory feedback systems of those on the spectrum.

Turning video games into strengths!

For many children on the spectrum, computer technology is a blessing. It fits their learning style perfectly (visual, focus on detail/patterns, minimal social interaction, immediate feedback, and very stimulating to the executive functioning part of the brain). Computers also allow the children to move at their own pace (fast or slow) and give them immediate feedback. Essentially, computers allow many people on the spectrum to let their talents shine and develop. It is natural that they would feel very safe and competent utilizing technology. Whereas for many NT children computer technology may actually be hampering direct social skills and possibly fostering a dependency on highly visual stimulation, for kids on the spectrum this technology can actually foster social skills and offer a medium to use their skills.

Remember that the best way to motivate individuals on the spectrum is to work with their strengths, interests, and what allows them to feel competent. I think the best thing to do with video games is to expand them into more functional learning games. I would go from regular video games into more educational software such as SimCity, history adventures, problem-solving games, and engineering (Lego® software). There are construction games, astronomy software, mathematical games, and so on. Try to find games that combine software with building something or researching a favorite topic. Find what skills and interests the child has and buy software that expands on it. Also, games for the Wii are great, especially if they involve physical activity and co-regulating with others.

You want to teach the children to use computers/video games to learn and expand themselves, rather than focus on simple arcade-type games. Video is a strong interest of kids on the spectrum, so we need to use this medium to expand their world. Drafting, engineering, graphic design, mechanical design, composing music, painting, and photography are all good ways to use video. There are apps, games, and learning software for just about any and all interests and needed skill development.

Also, interactive games for the Wii, which involve physical activity and co-regulation with others, are valuable. There are also newly developed software programs for teaching social skills, facial expressions, social problem solving, and video modeling. These are all great. Video interplay is a good tool that maximizes one of the strengths for many people on the spectrum. Yes, it needs to be controlled and integrated with other learning and activity, but it can be used to develop a number of skills. Since it is a medium that the kids feel very comfortable with, we should use it for development in many areas. Let's not suppress the main strength that they have; just steer it in the right direction.

For example, I was consulting with a family with a young man age 20. He is not allowed in school or work programs because of problematic behavior, and anxiety issues mean he is often confined to his home and immediate neighborhood. We were out at his house using a digital camera to make pictures for a picture schedule and he kept instructing us at what angle to take the pictures, what detail we needed to put in them, and how to use the lighting. He showed a great interest in photography just by his delight in making these household pictures. From there we took off on this strength. We are going to get him a digital camera and some photo software, have him sign up for an online photography course, and join a photography message board. He can develop, crop, and categorize photos, develop a website to display his photos, and eventually connect with some amateur photography groups in the community. His main interest at home is animals. He has a variety of dogs, exotic cats, turtles, and furless guinea pigs. Like many people on the spectrum, he connects better with animals than people. So my guess is he could become very skilled in taking photos of animals. Animals are another area we can use the internet to research and expand this interest.

Using preferences to safely engage

I have the privilege of consulting with many individuals who have severe impairments and multiple behavior challenges. They are often either living in institutions or community group homes. I use the exact same principles to teach safety in my presence and trust in my interaction. I start where they are at, identify their interests and comfort zones, and take what little leverage they give me to teach social engagement.

I had the pleasure of meeting one individual who was very aggressive and required one-on-one staffing to be within six feet of him at all times in order to protect him and others from being hurt. His name was Jeff. Most interactions between staff and Jeff were instrumental in nature (directions, prompts to do things or not to do something). Jeff did not feel connected with staff, so he obviously did not feel safe and accepted by them. He had to control all interaction and activity around him to feel that his world was safe and predictable. Jeff would typically refuse to engage with staff or comply with daily activities. He wanted to be left alone to engage in self-stimulation most of the day.

When I first met Jeff, I asked staff what he initiated on his own that he enjoyed doing. The only thing that staff could come up with was "ripping magazines." He enjoyed ripping pieces of pages in magazines and then dropping them in a pile on the floor. When I asked staff if he did this a lot, they reported no, because they kept magazines away from him. Since this behavior of ripping was not the norm, they defined it as being destructive and found it to be problematic. Unfortunately, staff did not see this as a strong interest that they could use to establish an emotional bond with Jeff. This behavior gave me a self-directed interest for this young man that I could use to create engagement ("we-do" activity) around.

I sat down next to Jeff, introduced myself, and put my hand out to shake hands. He refused. I shared that I had heard that he was good at ripping magazines and that I would like to see him do it. I gave him a magazine and allowed him to start ripping, perfectly straight, narrow pieces off the pages. I marveled and commented on how well he could do that, and expressed interest in doing it myself. I started slowly ripping paper right in front of him, face to face, within easy vision for him to reference me. As he ripped, I imitated him, animating how I was trying to do it as well as him. I would drop my pieces on the same pile as his. I commented on how good it felt to rip the pages, and he would look up at me as if he was amazed! Periodically, I would reach out my hand in gesture of acceptance and he would gradually reach out and lightly touch mine. I continued to follow his lead, imitate what he was doing, and celebrate with words of acceptance and frequently give "five."

After several minutes, Jeff seemed to feel comfortable with this level of engagement, so I decided to throw in a variation to stretch his comfort zone. I put my magazine down and asked him if we could rip together. I slowly reached over and started a small rip at the top of the page, and motioned for him to finish ripping it. He looked a little anxious, but followed my lead. We proceeded to tear and rip together, me starting the tear, and him finishing it. Now we had back-and-forth interaction, with both of us playing an active role in ripping. I would invite him to celebrate after every three or four rips by putting out my hand for him to reach out and give me "five." I continued to give animated emotional expressions that I enjoyed sharing this experience with him. A couple of times he smiled. We were using an activity that he felt comfortable with and enjoyed doing, to build reciprocal engagement around.

Next, I wanted to see if I could expand on this activity. My objective was to get him to sit up to the table to rip magazines. I knew this was a big step but felt that he was beginning to trust me. I had staff place two glasses of pop (which is his favorite drink) on the table. We went to the table and shared drinking pop together as I commented on how much fun I was having ripping magazines with him. I decided to try expanding it to make a collage of the bits of paper that we ripped from the magazine. As he ripped a piece of the magazine, I would paste it onto poster board to make the collage. He found it interesting that we could use the pieces of his ripped paper to make something. He ripped, and I pasted, sharing the experience. We continued to frequently celebrate with giving "fives" and emotion sharing. Next, he would rip and I would put glue on the piece and give it back to him to paste on the board. We filled up the paper and hung the collage on the wall, commenting on how nice it looked, and celebrating as usual.

In a matter of about 40 minutes we had established a social connection together around an interest that people were defining as bad and limiting his opportunities for ripping. I had started where he was at, engaged myself in an activity of interest for him, let him initially lead while I imitated his action, and frequently celebrated with giving "fives" and emotion sharing. Once he felt comfortable with that, I expanded on the activity by adding variations to it. This resulted in co-regulating back-and-forth interaction, where we helped each other in completing the collage together. This was a real eye-opener for staff to see that the avenue to socially connect with him was validating and engaging in the sensory preference (ripping) that he found rewarding. From there, the staff were given directions to bring in all the old magazines they could find and do this activity at least twice a day to build a social connection with him. Over time, both this young man and the staff started to feel more comfortable and connected with each other, and eventually expanded the "we-do" activities into a number of reciprocal, interactive activities together.

You can kill the weeds, or strengthen the grass!

Many people who are trying to grow a good lawn try to focus on killing the weeds. However, killing the weeds alone does not develop strong grass! By fertilizing the grass and helping it to grow stronger, the lawn overcomes the weeds, giving them little chance to grow.

This also applies to our children! At first, we tend to want to change our children, and focus on habilitating their vulnerabilities and weaknesses to make them "less autistic." We focus on the negative aspects of autism and want to change them. However, by focusing so much on their deficits, we often invalidate the children, unintentionally communicating that they are broken and need to be fixed. By focusing on changing their weaknesses, we often do not foster a stronger person. Instead, it often weakens their identities and self-esteem, just like killing the weeds will not necessarily create stronger grass.

We need to "fertilize" the children's strengths to make them stronger. We need to foster their strengths and preferences, that which truly defines them, to develop their true selves. By using their preferences to foster their strengths, we enable the children to grow and develop to the point where they can use their strengths to compensate for their weaknesses. Of course, we want to devise strategies for compensating for sensory issues, help alleviate immune system vulnerabilities, and provide for a healthier child. We want to teach them communication skills, life skills, and social skills, but do it in the framework of fostering their strengths and preferences. Help the children grow to their true potential. Support the child to blossom and let the flower unfold—not try to pattern a daisy into a rose!

All children, regardless of impairments, have strengths and preferences that define who they are. We must observe closely and listen to the children, and support them to blossom into what their potential will define. This is true with all children, not just those on the spectrum. Support who they are and help them become who they are meant to be. Help them develop their strengths and validate their interests to foster those strengths. You will find not only greater acceptance but also faster development and an emotionally stronger person. Focus on the potential, not the deficit, and you will see more potential!

Chapter 8

EFFECTIVE DISCIPLINE

Probably one of the most frequent questions I get is "How do I discipline my child?" Children on the spectrum often do not respond to the same disciplinary strategies that you use with children who are not on the spectrum. On the surface, this appears true; however, I think the principles below work with all children. The articles that follow lay out a foundation for effective discipline. Although each article can stand alone, these strategies work better when combined together.

Autism "explains" behavior, but does not "excuse" behavior!

Many of the past articles have focused on understanding, accepting, and validating the child, before attempting to change his behavior. One of the basic premises of the Autism Discussion Page is: assume the child is doing the best that he can, given the situation he is in, and his current skills to deal with the demands. Consequently, when the child is struggling, we need to lower the demands to better match his skill level, and/or provide greater assistance to support his performance. Hence, when things go wrong, we have often placed the child in situations which he cannot handle. We need to take responsibility for overwhelming him.

Now, in this premise, where does the responsibility lie with the child? Autism presents many challenges (sensory issues, information processing, emotional dysregulation, social relating issues, etc.) that overwhelm the child, and explain *why* he may melt down and act out. However, autism must not excuse the behavior. Of course, when the child is overwhelmed and disorganized, we need to recognize, understand, and validate how he is *feeling*, but not necessarily accept how he is *behaving*. All children need boundaries, rules, and expectations. We must communicate understanding when he is upset, but not accept physically attacking others, destroying property, and serious self-injury. Autism is not an excuse for aggression. The child needs to learn that there are a variety of ways that he can express frustration (even screaming, hitting a pillow, etc.), but attacking others and breaking property are not acceptable.

We, as the supportive adults, need to ask, "How do I want the child to express frustration?" Help the child to identify a couple of ways (coping skills) for him to appropriately express his anger and frustration (using his words, physical exercise, asking for help, engaging in regulating patterns—rocking, jumping, etc.). From there, we need to help the child practice these alternatives so he can adequately express his anger. However, we also must establish strong expectations of no aggression and have appropriate consequences, including making amends, for aggression. Boundaries and expectations need to be very clear with consistent consequences, so they are concrete and easy to understand. The child needs strong, black and white rules and expectations to make sense of the world, and understand what is acceptable and what is not allowed. Just as we need to understand and respect him, he also needs to learn to respect others.

Strong boundaries, with clear expectations and consistent consequences, implemented in a posture of understanding, acceptance, and validation allow us to respect the child, while changing his behavior. If we focus on teaching, practicing, and heavily reinforcing the positive alternative behavior, natural consequences for unacceptable acting out can be effective. However, before dealing with the behavior, acknowledge and validate the feelings underlying the behavior. Implement the consequence without degrading the child, so he views the consequence as the result of his behavior. Make sure the child knows and practices how to react appropriately, and always review what the consequence is before using it. This way, when you implement the consequence, it is understandable and predictable. Every child needs strong boundaries and consequences for his actions. Don't let the diagnosis excuse the behavior. At the same time, when the outbursts occur, we have more than likely placed the child in a situation that he could not handle. We still have the responsibility to re-evaluate the demands and provide greater assistance and support to decrease the likelihood of the situation occurring again. By doing so, we decrease the frequency of this unacceptable behavior by better matching the demands to the child's abilities and teaching the child acceptable ways of dealing with anger and frustration.

The world according to me!

When you are dealing with the rigid, oppositional child, he often patterns the world so it pacifies what he wants, how it he wants it, and when he wants it. The world revolves around him, and he becomes skillful in modifying the behavior of all of those around him. The household revolves around him! In severe cases, the family is held captive by the child's behavior. At this point, there is a total lack of reciprocity; I respond to you because you respond to me. As the child becomes bigger and stronger, this problem becomes greater and more dangerous. The child learns that he can use threatening behavior, aggression, and property destruction to force his parents to do anything and everything he wants.

We have to be careful when supporting children with challenging behavior that we do not inadvertently reinforce worse behavior. When the child is younger and has emotional regulation problems (tantrums), we need to make sure that those tantrums do not (1) get him want he wants or (2) allow him to escape things that he needs to do. We can identify and modify task demands, add assistance to provide greater support, and build in accommodations to deal with vulnerabilities, all to try to match the demands of the situation to the child's skill level. However, in the process we need to not give in and let the child have what he wants because he threw a fit, or escape common daily demands by acting out. We can validate how he feels, and provide help to support him through it, but in the end do not let his acting out gain control over his environment. We can teach more effective ways to get what he wants, but do not let the tantrums work. If we give in and let him have it, or escape it, on a regular basis, this acting out will become his main tool for manipulating what he wants. The longer this occurs, the stronger the behavior becomes, until the child automatically acts out whenever we block what he wants.

If the child throws a tantrum because he cannot have something that he wants, then we have to let the child throw his tantrum. We can review what happened afterwards to see if there are changes we can make to minimize it occurring again in the future; but once the tantrum occurs, do not allow the child to get what he wants from acting out. If the child screams for an hour, because he is used to getting what he wants from screaming, then keep him safe, validate how he feels, but let him cry it out. It is OK for the child to be mad! It is OK if it takes him an hour to get over it! We do not have to pacify every whim to avoid him being upset. Reassure the child he is safe, back off, and let him work it out. Even if you use a soothing technique to calm him, do not give in to what he wanted or what he is trying to avoid. If it was a simple daily task, then he goes back and tackles that task when he calms down. If needed, shorten the task or provide added support, but try to go back and finish the task. You can talk out the problem and understand why he was mad, plus talk about other more effective ways of getting what he wants, but do not give it to him after acting out. If you do, by time he is 12–14 years old, it could get dangerous.

The world is not according to them, us, or anyone. The world is about reciprocity and mutual respect for each other. We have to have boundaries and learn appropriate ways of getting our needs meet. Yes, the child can get mad and until he learns self-control may tantrum when upset, but don't reinforce it by giving in. I know, it sounds easy, but is so hard to do!

Set clear boundaries and expectations!

All children need strong rules, regulations, and expectations. All activity and interactions have boundaries that define the limits for which our actions are acceptable or unacceptable. They provide a mental map to keep us within expectations. Most of these boundaries are unwritten social rules, which are invisible but assumed. These boundaries provide the structure to guide our behavior and provide predictability to our world. These boundaries help provide the foundation for our sense of safety and security. Without these boundaries, we would be lost, anxious, and insecure.

Children on the spectrum have a hard time reading these unwritten, often invisible boundaries. Unless the boundaries are very clear and concrete, they do not have the mental map to structure what they are doing. Without these concrete boundaries, their behavior can seem haphazard and disorganized. Without clear expectations, the children often overstep the boundaries and behave in ways that are unacceptable to our standards. These children are often perceived as resistant and oppositional, with purposeful intent to be noncompliant. In many cases, they simply do not understand the expectations and limitations that are assumed by others. Since the world lacks the framework, they are often in free fall, with little organization to their behavior. With the lack of these invisible boundaries, the children become anxious and insecure, and often have a strong need to control all activity/interaction to create predictability to their world.

Children on the spectrum need very concrete, black and white rules and expectations (boundaries), with very consistent consequences for not following them. Once the rules and expectations become clear, consistent, and predictable, they provide children with a path to follow which decreases anxiety. At first, the boundaries need to be strong, concrete, and literal. If possible, provide them with visuals (pictures, written, or physical boundaries). Keep them short, simple, and black and white to begin with. To be understood, the expectations have to be very clear and consistent, with little flexibility. The child needs immediate, consistent consequences that are firm in the face of resistance. As the child's world becomes more consistent, flexibility can gradually be introduced.

We often go wrong by assuming that the child understands what is expected. Since these boundaries are intuitive for us, we forget that they are not for the children. To assist the child in meeting expectations, it is important for us to provide a concrete path to follow. Make it standard practice to implement the following:

- Before events, define the boundaries (rules and expectations) to provide the framework for understanding. Preview for the child what he can expect to happen and what is expected of him, and define the rules, regulations, and any consequences for not following them. Explain what seems obvious to us. Lay out a structured path for the child to follow.

- If it is a new activity, don't assume that the child will be able to successfully follow the path. Use guided participation, with close framing and guidance, to stay on the correct path. Don't expect perfection, but provide the guidance. It is easier to set the stage for success than correct him when going astray.

- When the child begins to steer off course, gently block and redirect him back on the path. Don't let him get far off track. This maximizes the likelihood of success. The further off he gets, the harder it is to get him back on track. It is easier to frame the boundaries to easily redirect him to stay on the path than it is to let him get off track and then reel him back in.

- Be a firm but loving guide. Stay firm to the boundaries and implement clear and consistent consequences for ignoring the guidance/boundaries. Consequences need to be implemented immediately and consistently. They have to be very concrete, and black and white.

- It is OK, beforehand, to collaborate with the child and negotiate as needed. However, once the boundaries are set, stay firm with them. When implementing consequences, stay consistent with what was discussed, and implement them with little emotion and no discussion, explanation, or negotiation.

- If possible, avoid creating new rules or changing the rules during the game! Once the expectations are set, stay consistent with them. Making up rules as you go along can cause strong resistance.

- Children respond best to what is routine and habit. Start with boundaries early on in life and make it a habit to follow the rules. Rules provide the path for guiding behavior.

Boundaries and expectations: principles of teaching!

Because young children on the spectrum can have a host of visual, auditory, and other sensory processes problems, they often have a hard time seeing boundaries, understanding them, or knowing how to respond to them. They may not understand the purpose of the rules or associate the consequences for not following the rules. If they don't understand the rules, connect their purpose, or associate the consequences for following them, then rules have little control over behavior. This can be very frustrating for parents. Parents may revert to punishing the child. However, if the child does not understand why he is being punished, then punishment will not change his behavior. Try the following suggestions to teach boundaries:

1. *Concrete rules.* First you need to create a rule or boundary and make it very easy to see. The child has to know that there is a rule and understand what it is. Do not work on more than one or two rules at a time. Make them literal and concrete, by writing them out or using pictures. When first teaching a rule, keep it very black and white (absolute), all or nothing.

Keep it short and simple. If the rule is not to do something (e.g. no hitting), also include what to do (e.g. say stop).

Rules for rules:

a. No more than one or two at a time.

b. Keep them short and simple.

c. Write them out and display them; use pictures if needed.

d. Review them regularly.

e. Implement them consistently.

f. Focus on what to do, as well as what not to do.

2. *Clear expectations.* When implementing rules and expectations, they have to be very simple, clear and concise, and be previewed just prior to the event. For example, when entering into the grocery store, we may set the rule (expectation) that the child must have both hands on the grocery cart. We defined a role that he will push the cart, and *rule* that his hands must be on the cart at all times (this eliminates the opportunities for the child to grab items or other people, run off, or engage in other problematic behavior). We would want to talk about the expectation before leaving the house, reminding the child just before entering the store and periodically while in the store. Clarify the rule and verify that he understands. We may even use a photo of the child with his hands on the cart, when reviewing the rule. When teaching expectations, clarify what is expected and what is not expected (when upset, no hitting, tell mommy). You want the expectations of what to do and what not to do to be as clear as possible. Once in the store, the parent's attention has to stay on the rule "keep hands on cart." Once a hand leaves the cart, stop the action, and prompt the hand back on the cart (enforce the rule). Do not let the child stray off course, and then try to reel him back in.

3. *Preview, review, role-play and practice.* When first teaching a rule, you must focus heavily on it until the rule becomes learned. Create many opportunities to teach the rule and practice the expectation. In doing so, discuss what is expected, next role-play it, and then practice it in different settings. Demonstrate the expectation and then have the child practice it. Have fun teaching it! Then preview the expectation just prior to entering the event, talk about it through the event, and then review how it went after the event is over. Sandwich the learning by previewing it before the event and discussing it following the event. Take pictures to make a picture story so you can frequently review the rule and read social stories to further explain it.

4. *Coaching and guiding.* During the event don't assume the child can implement the expectation in the heat of the moment (e.g. no hitting, tell mommy), even though he can verbally state the rule. It takes practice and repetition before the rule becomes a behavior habit. During the events, watch carefully for the opportunities when the rule/expectation applies, then remind the child to follow the rule, and help guide him as needed. As the behavior becomes instilled, then fade guidance.

5. *Immediate consequences.* It is important that you have very clear and consistent consequences for both following the expectations and for not following the expectations. The child needs to be reinforced immediately and consistently for performing the expectation (e.g. praise or concrete reward). In addition, let the child know exactly what will happen if he does not follow the rule (stop the action, redirect, time out, loss of a privilege, etc). This does not mean you have to use punishment, but if you do, make sure the child understands clearly what the punishment is (role-play and practice) and knows exactly what he should be doing correctly (again role-play and practice). Do not punish a behavior unless the child (1) knows what to do correctly, (2) has practiced and can perform the desired response, and (3) knows that the punishment will happen prior to implementing it.

6. *One hundred percent consistency!* When first teaching a rule make sure you implement the above procedures consistently, every time by everyone! You want to provide frequent opportunities to implement the rule, and follow the rule consistently every time. Regardless of time constraints, embarrassment, or negative reactions from others, you must implement it consistently every time. For parents, this means consistently between parents, grandparents, and teachers (if possible). It may be hard at first, but you have to implement the rules and consequences consistently.

Even for the most severely impaired children, rules and expectations can be learned as long as they are simple, black and white, implemented consistently, and practiced frequently. It is not always easy, but very important to teach.

Educate, don't just punish!

When the word "discipline" comes up, people often think of punishing someone for doing something wrong. This presupposes that the person (1) knew what he did was wrong, (2) knew what to do right, and (3) chose to do the wrong thing. Punishing only works effectively under these conditions.

However, children, when misbehaving, often do not know that the behavior is inappropriate or how to act more appropriately in that situation. Punishing a behavior will teach the child that it is undesirable, but does not teach the child what he should do instead (the appropriate alternative). In addition, even if the child *cognitively* knows what to do (because we tell him), it doesn't mean that he can *behaviorally* do it (execute the action in the heat of the moment). Knowing what to do is different from being able to do it. If the desired behavior has not been practiced and adequately demonstrated, there is a good chance it will not happen in the moment. Compounding matters, the child may cognitively know what to do differently, but not have the ability to inhibit his impulses long enough to use the forethought to act differently. He cannot check his responses long enough to (1) appraise what is needed, (2) see different options, and (3) evaluate what the effects and consequences of his actions are going to be. This is the child who feels remorseful after doing something and can tell you what he should have done instead, but was unable to do it in the heat of the moment.

So, when looking at designing effective discipline strategies, we want not just to suppress the undesirable behavior, but also to teach the child what he should do instead—a more desirable way of responding. When doing so, ask the following questions:

1. What is the child doing wrong?

   a. Does the child know that it is wrong?

   b. Does the child have good conscious control over it (impulse control)?

2. Why is the child doing it?

   a. What conditions trigger the behavior (antecedents)?

   b. Are the demands (sensory, cognitive, social, or emotional) greater than the child's skills in dealing with them? Can we lower our expectations or build in stronger supports?

   c. What are the gains or pay-offs reinforcing the behavior (gets what he wants, attention, escapes doing something unpleasant, etc.)?

   d. What purpose (function) does the behavior have for the child?

   e. Does the child know any other way?

3. What do we want the child to do?

   a. What appropriate response should the child do instead? (Don't suppress a behavior; replace it with a more appropriate one.)

   b. Does the child know what and how to do it?

   c. Has the child demonstrated that he can do it? In the heat of the moment?

d. If he doesn't know it, how are we going to teach it (role-play and practice when calm)?

e. Does the child have the ability to inhibit his impulse long enough to choose the appropriate response? If not, repeated practice will make it an automatic response (habit).

4. Why should the child do it (choose the appropriate response)?

a. What is the pay-off or reinforcement for choosing the new, appropriate behavior, instead of the original, inappropriate behavior? The new behavior should serve the same function (same pay-off), equal or greater in value.

b. How are you going to reinforce (praise, token, natural consequences, etc.) the new response?

Discipline should focus on teaching the children better ways of meeting their needs. Simply punishing an inappropriate response does not teach the child what to do instead. You may be successful in suppressing the undesirable response, but the child is left without knowing how to respond. However, once the child (1) understands that the negative behavior is unacceptable, (2) understands and can perform the appropriate behavior, (3) is reinforced for doing so, and (4) continues to choose the unacceptable behavior, then mild punishment may be used to increase the motivation for choosing the desirable behavior. Discipline should be educational, not simply punishing!

Be a "working partner" and "trusted guide"

It is important that we respect and validate the child, even when disciplining behavior. It is important that we work *with* the child, not force control on the child. Many children on the spectrum will react very strongly to external control when we try to force compliance. Uncertainty and following the lead of others can be very scary for kids on the spectrum. It is very difficult for them to give up control and trust following the lead of someone else. As for all children, it is beneficial to include them as much as possible in developing the strategies, and over time teach them to collaborate and negotiate the best that they can. It is important that we listen, respect their vulnerabilities and comfort zones, and always communicate understanding and acceptance, even if we do not agree with their behavior. We are still responsible for teaching them right from wrong, and general respectful behavior, but we can do so in an understanding and accepting way. We want the children to feel that we are working with them, to guide them, not to force control on them. Some basic tips for doing so include:

1. Be aware of the sensory, cognitive, social, and emotional vulnerabilities of the child. When evaluating the conditions that trigger the behavior, interpret them in light of these vulnerabilities. Their vulnerabilities do not excuse the behavior, but they do help explain the behavior. Understand the child's comfort zones and make sure you are not stretching them too quickly (asking for too much).

2. When possible, ask the child; seek their input to (1) understand the function(s) the behavior serves for him, (2) identify how he should respond (replacement behavior to teach), and (3) determine what consequences should be applied to both the desired behavior (reinforcement) and negative behavior (corrective action, mild punishment, etc.). Including the child in the planning process helps him to understand the connections, as well as feel he has a voice.

3. Try to understand and validate the feelings behind how the child is acting, although not agreeing with his actions. Validate how it is natural to be mad if his sister took his favorite toy; however, it is never OK to hit her. This way you are not invalidating the natural fact that he is mad (it is OK to be mad), but he needs to find a different way of responding. This leads you into collaborating on how else he can act (replacement behavior) to meet the same need.

4. Tailor the expectations, replacement behavior, and consequences to match the abilities of the child. For a child with poor impulse control, don't expect him to immediately be able to appraise a situation accurately, check his impulses, and use strong forethought before acting. He will need a lot of practice to learn to perform the desired response, and will need coaching to use it in the heat of the moment. Do not expect him to go from an awareness of what to do to being able to do it accurately in the heat of the moment. This is what I like about giving a warning first (allowing the child to check his actions), along with reminding him of what to do, before implementing a consequence. "Bobby, gently pet the dog, not pull his ears." Then model how to pet.

5. All behavior needs consequences to establish effectiveness. The positive behavior needs to lead to desirable consequences (either natural effects— get what I want, avoid what I don't want—or artificial reinforcers— tokens, privileges, etc.) and the inappropriate behavior needs to lead to lack of reinforcement, correction, or mild undesirable consequences. These consequences can be negotiated between the parent and child, but need to be clear and implemented consistently. These consequences should be discussed ahead of time and not sprung on the child in the heat of the moment (when possible). Consequences should become a

natural part of all learning, be partly under the control of the child, and be clearly defined.

6. Pick your battles based on the abilities and vulnerabilities of the child. Do not try to apply numerous rules and expectations about every little behavior. The more rigid the child, the more flexible the adult needs to be. Pick only one or two rules (or behaviors) to work on at one time. Negotiate if possible, then stay consistent to the rules. Let the smaller stuff go. Draw clear, black and white boundaries, but be flexible within those boundaries.

7. Always ask yourself, "Does my child feel supported or controlled?" Does he feel you are working with him or forcing compliance out of him? Are you trying to teach him or control him? Don't feel bad; we fall into the control trap very often. We always have to step back and ask ourselves whether we are teaching or controlling. Your child will feel more loved and accepted, even when fair consequences are being implemented for intentional transgressions.

We promote what we look for, spotlight, and highlight!

It is human nature to focus on the negative. Maybe it is our survival instinct to hyper-focus on the negative out of fear and anxiety. As a behavior specialist, one of the principles I learned over the years is that we tend to inadvertently promote what we focus on, that which we throw our attention at. This is very evident with our children who display challenging behaviors.

Everyone gets anxious and excited; they analyze and strategize! We meet, brainstorm, problem-solve, program, and document. We are hyper-focused on the challenging behavior—on high alert for it to happen, and ready to jump on it when it occurs. The challenging behaviors bring out the emotion in us, and we react with high intensity. What we often do not realize is that the more we react and give attention to the negative, the more value we give to it. The more we focus on it, the more we see it. The behavior and the emotions tend to spiral out of control, with all parties getting frustrated and angry. Sometimes, the more we try, the more behavior we get!

This is not just with children on the spectrum. This principle applies to everyone—whether it is marriage conflicts, employee/employer relationships, parent/child conflicts. When we focus on the negative, throw our attention at it, and intensively react to it, it tends to increase. When we hyper-focus on the negative, we spotlight and highlight it, and inadvertently foster it. As the vicious cycle continues, both the adults and children become more frustrated, angry, and controlling. Unfortunately for all, the problem often escalates.

What people often do not realize is the attention and emotion given to a behavior will often reinforce it to occur more frequently. This is often evident with giving praise for good behavior, but also for giving negative reactions to challenging behavior. Whether the child likes the negative attention or not, the attention often increases the frequency of the challenging behavior. The child feels the control he sees in the emotional reactions of others, enjoys manipulating what he wants by creating such attention, or hates the negative reactions and acts out more out of frustration. Regardless of the reasons for the challenging behavior, our attention to it often fosters it.

Another concept in psychology is that we tend to identify with what others highlight in us. If others tend to spotlight and highlight our negative qualities, we tend to identify ourselves with those qualities. If we are labeled and treated like a bad, lazy, oppositional, inadequate person, we will become that person. Our self-identities tend to mirror what others project on us. When we label a child a bully, we focus on his bad behavior and expect it out of him, and then he identifies with those expectations. If we expect the child to act out when working with him, we will look for the behavior, are quick to interpret all behavior in a negative light, expect it to occur, and then give added attention to it when it happens. The child begins to see himself as being that way, because that is him!

Often when meeting with parents, teachers, administrators, and professionals, I find that about 90 percent of the discussion is centered around the child's challenging behaviors (why is it occurring, what are the triggers, what consequences will reduce it, etc.) as if these behaviors define the child. I can get caught up in this myself. After listening to this discussion for some time, I usually have to interrupt the discussion and ask, "What does the child do right?" What are his positive behaviors and attributes? When he is not acting out, what positive things does he do, say, and engage in? We are often so focused on the negative behavior that we fail to notice the positive. We start to define the child as a problem. This is because our natural instinct is to react to the negative. It colors our vision and directs our focus.

In behavioral language, we often "baseline" the negative behavior (document how often it occurs, for how long it occurs, and how intense it is). We immediately start looking for it, expecting it, and sometimes inadvertently creating it. I find that it is often better to have parents and teachers first start with documenting what the child is doing right—what his good attributes are, when he is being good, and under what conditions he is at his best. Catch him being good, attend to it, and document it. Track throughout the day what things the child is doing right, when is he doing them, and under what conditions he does well. We write them all down, listing and comparing notes on what behavior we want to see, when it is occurring, and how we are attending (or not attending) to it.

People are at first annoyed by this, because of their hyper-focus on reducing the negative behavior. They want to turn the attention back to the negative behavior, as if that will somehow stop it. However, if they take a few weeks to simply focus on the good behavior, making an emphasis to praise and attend to it, and learning to create conditions for the good behavior to occur, not only does the good behavior start to occur more frequently, but the negative behavior starts to decrease significantly. When we tend to change our focus to spotlighting and highlighting the positive in the child, we actually become less reactive to the negative, stop hyper-focusing on it, and reduce the expectation for it to occur. When our attention is turned to the positive, what the child is doing right, and what helps him feel safe, accepted, and competent, there is little time, energy, or need for the negative behavior. When others feel good about you, and you feel good about yourself, there is little value in the negative behaviors.

Keep making your lists of all the good things you see from the child, and how you are praising and attending to them. Define your child by the good qualities in him, and more good things will come from him. Spotlight and highlight these good behaviors by creating a "Me" photo book of all the great things the child does. Use a digital camera to take pictures of times when the child shines, doing good things. Make a "Me" picture book of these events. Turn these events into "we-do" activities—doing them together, having fun, and sharing the experience together. Sit down with this "Me" book and review and highlight the positive moments. Reminisce and share the experiences. By valuing the positive, the child will begin to gleam and aspire to meet the expectations. He will begin to define himself by the positive, become more competent and confident, and build stronger self-esteem. Children with strong self-esteem rarely find the need to be negative.

When the negative behaviors do occur, stay calm, minimize your attention, give little emotional reaction, support and redirect as needed, then turn right back to accentuating the positive. You will find that when there is four times more attention and emphasis on the positive than the negative, you will start to see a good turnaround, both in your child and in yourself. Positive breeds more positive, and everyone benefits. This all sounds much easier than it often is to implement. In actuality, this can take a lot of practice to change our focus and attention. But you will find that you are happier, and so is your child!

Functional assessment: understanding the behavior

All behavior serves a function (purpose) for the person. Behavior occurs for a reason(s). It serves a function for the child. The child may be acting out to escape or avoid something uncomfortable for him, may be doing it for the attention or reaction he gets from others, for stimulation when bored, or to gain something that he desires. The child may be screaming because he has no other way of communicating that he is hungry, frustrated, or in pain. He may be screaming because the demands placed on him are greater than his current skills in dealing with them. He may be screaming because he is overwhelmed by the sensory chaos of the load noises, bright lights, and strong smells in the grocery store. He may be screaming because his sister just took his favorite toy from him, or because he just stepped on something sharp. Consequently, the same behavior can occur for a variety of reasons (under a variety of conditions), and several behaviors (screaming, biting self, hitting others) can occur for the same reason (e.g. to get out of doing something).

Identifying the function(s) the behavior serves gives us a good understanding of why it is occurring, the purpose that it serves for the child, what is maintaining the behavior, and some ideas of how to go about supporting the child and reducing the problem behavior. It can be troublesome to try to change a behavior before understanding the purpose that it serves the child and the conditions under which it occurs. Reducing the problem behavior may be as simple as modifying some of the conditions causing the behavior (reduce demands, provide added support, etc.) or changing the way we react to the behavior (support rather than demand, minimize our emotional reactions, redirect, etc.). Often we do not have to change the child at all, but modify the conditions (often our own behavior) surrounding the behavior. In other cases, we may need to teach alternative behaviors to replace the ones we wish to decrease.

When doing a functional assessment, we try to define the conditions occurring just prior to the behavior that may be influencing (triggering) its occurrence. These conditions are usually called "antecedents" to the behavior. They set the stage for the negative behavior to occur. By tracking (documenting) when and where the behavior is occurring, what is occurring, as well as with whom, we are can identify common conditions (antecedents) that trigger the behavior. It may occur when certain demands are placed on the child, under certain sensory stimulation (bright sunlight), when left alone with nothing to do, and so on. By noting these conditions each time the behavior occurs, we can isolate common patterns (conditions) that produce the undesirable behavior. Identifying under what conditions the behavior occurs can tell us a lot about what function the behavior serves for the child (escape demands, attention, getting something, etc.). Often we can reduce the frequency of the behavior simply by eliminating or modifying the conditions (antecedents) that elicit the behavior. If we can change the conditions triggering the behavior (reduce the demands, provide more frequent attention, give frequent breaks, etc.), we reduce the need for the child to engage in the behavior. Even if we cannot eliminate or modify the conditions, we can provide added support (greater assistance) or accommodations to help the child adapt to the conditions (e.g. sunglasses to minimize bright lights). Changing the antecedent conditions that trigger the behavior is often the best, and easiest, way to reduce the unwanted behavior. Change the conditions before trying to discipline the child.

We may also look at under what conditions the behavior does not occur. If the behavior does not occur when added support or assistance is given, then we may want to increase our support to minimize frustration. If the behavior is displayed when the activity occurs in the morning, but not when the activity is in the afternoon, then we may change the time of the activity to the afternoon. If we can identify times and conditions when the behavior is less likely to occur, then we may want to increase those conditions. So, by identifying when, where, and under what conditions the behavior does occur and when it reliably doesn't occur, we can make major modification in these conditions.

In addition to identifying the conditions triggering the behavior (antecedents), we also want to identify the effects (reactions) the behavior has immediately following its occurrence. What does the child get from the behavior? Again, we want to note what occurs (especially how people react and what effects the behavior has for the child) immediately following the behavior (e.g. withdraw demands, reactions of others, getting something he wants, escaping situation, etc.). These are the gains or pay-offs that the child receives from engaging in the behavior. These effects are often reinforcing the behavior and increasing the likelihood that it will occur again under similar conditions.

By identifying these effects, we can often modify the consequences so that the behavior does not provide the same pay-offs for the child, thus decreasing the likelihood of it occurring again under similar conditions. We may want to minimize our reaction to the behavior, if our attention seems to reinforce it. We may also want to make sure the child doesn't get what he wants by throwing a tantrum, or get out of doing things by acting out. In addition, we want to teach the child better, more adaptive ways of obtaining the same effects (saying "stop" or "help" rather than hitting when wanting to escape a difficult demand).

As you can see, by changing the conditions that elicit the behavior (antecedents) and the effects that occur immediately following the behavior (consequences), we can significantly modify the likelihood of the negative behavior occurring again. Emphasis should be on identifying the conditions that trigger the behavior and building in added supports to either eliminate or modify these conditions. This way we are reducing the stressful conditions that trigger the child's undesirable behavior.

In addition to changing the conditions, once we identify the function (purpose) that the behavior serves, we can also begin to teach other, more acceptable behavior that can achieve the same result (purpose, function). If the child chews on his shirt for stimulation to stay aroused, we might substitute chewing gum to take its place. If the child yells in class to get the teacher's attention, he might be taught to raise his hand instead.

Support and teach!

Once you have identified the conditions eliciting (antecedents) and maintaining (consequences) the behavior, you have a better understanding of the function(s) that the behavior serves for the child. With that knowledge, you now have the information needed to develop a comprehensive plan for supporting the child and reducing the problem behavior. The steps listed here provide the basic outline for developing a comprehensive positive behavior support plan.

1. Identify the triggers producing the behavior.

2. Build in added supports to lessen triggers.

3. Reduce the reinforcing consequences that maintain the behavior.

4. Identify the function the behavior serves.

5. Develop a more appropriate behavior (that serves the same function), to replace the inappropriate behavior.

6. Practice, preview, and review replacement behavior.

7. Watch for prime times; intervene early and cue/redirect to replacement behavior.

8. Reinforce heavily for choosing a desirable response.

9. Keep it as positive and supportive as possible.

Follow this outline and you have a well-designed positive behavior support plan. The two biggest components of the plan are (1) eliminating, modifying, and otherwise lessening the impact of the antecedent conditions presenting the behavior and (2) teaching better ways (alternative behavior) to obtain the same goal (function) as that of the negative behavior. Every good support plan should include these two variables.

1. Changing the antecedent conditions triggering the behavior

Eliminate the trigger. If possible and/or appropriate, eliminate the conditions that lead to the behavior.

- "If certain tasks lead to acting out, eliminate the tasks."

   Modify the trigger. If you cannot eliminate the trigger, can you modify it to reduce the negative impact it is having?

- "Can you modify the tasks to make them less stressful?"

   Build in added supports. If you cannot eliminate or modify the triggers, what support or assistance can you give the child to help them cope with triggers.

- "Can you add extra assistance to make the tasks less stressful?"

Always look for ways of changing the conditions to better match the needs and skill level of the child. Often the demands (expectations) of the situation are greater than the child's abilities to deal with them. First, reduce the demands, then teach better skills in dealing with them.

2. Teach more acceptable "replacement" behavior

Next, teach a more desirable behavior to replace the negative behavior. How do you want the child to act under these conditions? This new behavior should meet the same need, or function, as the problem behavior. What function does the negative behavior serve for the child (get what he wants, express frustration, get out of doing something, obtain attention, etc.)? Make sure the replacement behavior serves the same purpose. The replacement behavior needs to be at least as effective as the negative behavior, if not more effective.

Example replacement behavior

Anger/frustration	Talk with adult, ask for assistance, leave event, hit pillow, deep breathing/relaxation, physical exercise, problem-solve.
Escape/avoid	Raise hand, say "no," use break card, walk away, ask for assistance.
Obtain something	Raise hand, touch person, point, use picture board, ask for assistance.
Self-stimulation	Use fidget toys, filler activity, substitute activity providing same stimulation.

Role-play and practice the replacement behavior when calm. If possible, role-play common conditions (antecedents) to practice the replacement behavior. Make it fun and rewarding!

Before entering vulnerable situations (common antecedents), preview how to use replacement behavior to cope with the situation. Walk through it before experiencing it.

During the situation, help coach the child in using the desirable response. If negative behavior starts to occur, redirect to the desired behavior and reinforce heavily for responding. Make sure the desired response is reinforced much more strongly than the negative behavior. If the desired response is both more effective and more efficient than the negative behavior, then it will become the preferred response.

Afterwards, review how it went! Focus on the good points! Reinforce heavily with praise and positive attention.

If your plan does an effective job in modifying the antecedent conditions triggering the behavior, as well as teaching better ways of dealing with the triggers (replacement behavior), then you are on your way to reducing the problem behavior. Discipline should be educational in teaching better ways of getting your needs meet, not just punishing problem behavior!

Setting up your consequences

Probably the greatest gift that Applied Behavior Analysis gave us is the understanding of consequences (effects of behavior) and their influence on behavior. In its very simplest form, behavior that leads to desirable effects will be strengthened and more likely to occur again in the future, and behavior that leads to undesirable effects will be weakened and less likely to occur again in the future. Of course, it is not always that simple to figure out, because most behaviors have multiple consequences, some desirable and some undesirable. All behavior has pros and cons. With there being multiple consequences, the likelihood of a behavior occurring again will depend on whether the rewards received outweigh the costs incurred. When the pros outweigh the cons, the behavior is more likely to occur.

Every behavior has costs incurred, simply by the effort that it takes to engage in the behavior. For many children on the spectrum, since they have a variety of processing, motor planning, and learning difficulties, most actions take a lot more effort on their part, especially learning and practicing new behaviors. Since the costs incurred are usually much higher for children on the spectrum, they often appear to be less motivated to learn new behaviors. This is also compounded by the fact that when we ask them to do something, often they have no clue why it is important, and thus it has no functional meaning for them. When we take into consideration that the behavior we want them to learn not only takes a lot more effort to learn and produce, but also has little value (meaning) to them, it is no wonder that they display little motivation to learn it. Because these two negative factors add to the costs incurred, we often need to increase the rewards received in order to tip the balance so the pay-offs outweigh the costs.

We have talked about how it is important to teach more acceptable (replacement) behavior, to substitute for problem behavior we want to decrease, and that good discipline is educational and involves teaching appropriate behavior to replace undesirable behavior. In addition to focusing on what we don't want the child to do (stop screaming), we also need to focus on what we want the child to do (ask for help). To do so, we need to look at and modify the consequences of each response (the undesirable and desirable) so the rewards received vs. the costs incurred for the desirable behavior are stronger than the rewards vs. costs of the inappropriate behavior. If we expect to replace the one (negative) behavior with another positive behavior, we need to make sure it is highly rewarding to engage in the new behavior. However, you have to keep in mind that the established, old behavior already works for the child (otherwise it would not be occurring). Learning the new response will take a lot more effort to learn and produce than the old behavior, so the rewards received will need to be higher than those for the old behavior.

When looking at reducing a problem behavior that is already established, we can do it in two ways: (1) reduce the rewards received (e.g. reduce attention given for the behavior, or not let the child have his way when acting out) or (2) increase the costs incurred by imposing a penalty (e.g. time out, loss of privilege). Doing either one or both of these alternatives will help tip the scale of cost vs. rewards, until the behavior eventually stops.

Now, on the other hand, if we want to replace the undesirable behavior with a more desirable one, we have to ask ourselves, "Why should he want to do it?" What is the benefit for the child to choose the desirable behavior over the already established problem behavior? To do so, we have to ensure that the rewards received vs. the costs incurred are stronger for the new behavior than they are for the old behavior. Ensure that the new behavior is more "worth it" than the old behavior. Keep in mind that the cost of the new behavior is already higher because it takes more effort to learn. So, by making the old behavior less reinforcing (taking away the pay-offs or adding a penalty) and by reinforcing the new behavior, we can tip the balance in favor of substituting the new (desirable) behavior.

In effective disciplining, we need to weigh the pros and cons of each behavior (old and new) to tip the balance to the new behavior. Simply by minimizing the attention given to the old behavior and providing lavish attention for the new behavior, we often can tip the scales greatly. This is assuming that attention is reinforcing to the child. For some children on the spectrum, our attention has minimal positive value for the child. For those children, we need to build in other more instrumental reinforcers (favorite activity, toy, food, escaping undesirable events. etc.). When performing the functional behavior assessment, we identify what the child is doing wrong and why he is doing it. The second part of the equation is what we want the child to do and why he should do it. Usually, the child is engaging in the problem behavior because he either gains something he wants or gets to escape or avoid something that he doesn't want. So, when teaching the child to choose an alternative response, we need to make sure that the old behavior doesn't work for him (doesn't get him the desired results) and the new behavior does!

For example, Johnny screams whenever faced with a task or demand that he wishes to avoid. The more people press him, the more he screams until they back off and remove the task/demand. Now, since he is screaming to escape or avoid a task/demand, we could teach him a more appropriate way to do this. We could teach him to say the word "stop" or "no," or put out the palm of his hand to signal "stop." This would be a more desirable way to communicate "stop" than to scream. Now, since screaming already works for him and we want him to choose the new response, we want to make sure that the screaming no longer leads to the removal of the task/demand, but communicating "stop" does. We want to first teach him the correct response and then frequently practice it. Once he has learned the new response, when he starts to scream to remove the demand, we redirect him to communicate "stop," and only remove the demand when he does. We selectively remove the reinforcing pay-off for the screaming, but apply it to the new response. Once he learns that (1) the old behavior does not work anymore and (2) the new response gets him the desired results, then the new response will become stronger.

In conclusion, when disciplining we want to (1) teach more appropriate behavior by following it with strong pay-offs and (2) reduce the reinforcing pay-offs for the old (problematic) response and/or increase the costs incurred by adding a penalty (time out, loss or privilege, etc.). Once the new response has more rewarding costs/benefits than the old behavior, then the child will choose the new, more desirable behavior.

Making consequences clear and effective!

When implementing consequences, it is important that the child understands both the consequences for the desired behavior (reinforcement) and the consequences for the unwanted behavior (punishment). Often the effectiveness is lost because the child does not understand the associations between the behavior and the consequences (contingencies) or because the consequences are not implemented immediately and consistently. If a child acts out in frustration at school and you take away computer time at home that night, does he understand the association? When he is at school and in the heat of the moment, is he even thinking, "If I hit that child, I will lose my computer tonight at home"? If the child doesn't associate the consequence with the action, cannot use forethought to evaluate what the consequences of his actions will be, or does not have control over his behavior because of sensory overload, then the intended consequences may have little effect on his behavior.

It is so important to discuss, role-play, and emphasize the associations (contingencies) between the behaviors and their consequences. There are several strategies you can use to make this association very clear and easy to understand:

- Make a picture sequence displaying how the desired behavior leads to a positive reinforcer, which leads to a smiling face (happy child). Right under that, make another picture sequence displaying the unwanted behavior, leading to mild punishment (penalty), which leads to a frown face (unhappy child). Preview and review the chart daily until the child knows it well.

- Role-play both the desired sequence and unwanted sequence, so the child can behaviorally associate the consequences with the behavior. Have fun, and have parents and child switch places, role-playing each other as well as themselves. This makes the contingencies very familiar and predictable, keeping the parent viewed as a supportive partner, rather than a controlling force.

- Role-play various antecedent conditions (situations that trigger the behavior) so the child can practice doing the desirable replacement behavior and receiving the reinforcement for it. If there are multiple situations that trigger the undesirable behavior, make an index card with the problem situation described on one side and the desirable response described on the other side. Role-play one or two situations a day. If a penalty is given for the negative behavior, role-play that also. As new situations arise, add them to the cards.

- Make a picture reinforcer menu of all the different items/activities the child can earn. Allow the child to pick out what he wants to work for. Having him pick out the reinforcer before he engages in the activity puts the consequence at the forefront of his mind and wets the whistle for wanting to earn it. He can take the picture of the reinforcer with him to remind him of what he is working for.

- Using a visual reinforcement chart (e.g. star chart) is a great way to visually see what the child is working for. Place a picture of the reward on the chart, preceded by the number of boxes he must fill up with stars in order to earn it. This way, as he earns each star he can see how close he is getting to earning the big reward. This also helps solidify the association between behaving appropriately and earning the reinforcement. If the child will earn computer time for finishing an assignment at school, then place a picture of the computer on his desk so it stays fresh in his mind what he earns when he has completed the assignment.

- Before entering into situations that commonly trigger the negative behavior, discuss (or role-play) and preview the desired behavior and the reinforcement that will follow. This is a good time to use the picture contingency sequences (good and unwanted responses) to review what to do.

- When the undesirable behavior does occur, calmly but immediately implement the consequence. Once the situation is over, sit down and review what happened and how the child could react better (and earn the reinforcement) next time.

When in doubt, clarify and verify that the child understands exactly what is expected of him and what the consequences of his action are. Identify and clarify this before entering into the situation, so you are not springing something unexpected on him. When possible, role-play and practice the contingencies so that they are well ingrained before entering into the triggering situations. When the desired behaviors are displayed, praise and reinforce heavily, and when the negative behavior occurs, calmly implement the consequences, without scolding, yelling, counselling, or negotiating. Stay calm and let the contingencies teach the behavior.

Reaction strategies: redirection

What do you do when the negative behavior occurs? Many people scold, counsel, demand, and try to force the child to stop. That often leads to emotional chaos for both the parents and the child. There are four common reaction strategies that are used to intervene with negative behavior. The most common are redirection, social disapproval, time out, and response cost (taking away privileges). This article will take a look at redirection and how to use it effectively.

Redirection is the technique that I use the most and recommend to try first. It tends to teach, rather than punish. With redirection, we want to quickly interrupt the negative behavior and redirect the child to the desired replacement behavior, calming strategy, or into a distracting activity. The focus is on heavily reinforcing the child for appropriate behavior (being good). Then, when negative behavior or or occurs, we quickly interrupt the behavior, with minimal attention as possible, and redirect the child back to the appropriate behavior so he can continue to be reinforced. This procedure focuses attention on what you want the child to do. In the redirection model, we are trying to minimize the attention given to the negative behavior (thus reducing the pay-offs) while redirecting the child back to desired behavior so that he can continue to receive frequent reinforcement. The basic procedures consist of the following stages:

1. Teach the desired behavior by focusing on previewing, coaching, and reinforcing the child for the desired behavior.

2. When the negative behavior does occur, quickly interrupt it, redirect the child to what you want him to do (desired behavior), then reinforce with praise and positive attention.

3. Say very little about the negative behavior (no scolding, counseling, negotiating, etc.). Focus instead on what you want the child to do.

4. Use guidance and coaching as needed to help redirect the child to the appropriate behavior, while ignoring the inappropriate behavior.

5. Once the child responds to the redirection, reinforce cooperation with praise and positive attention.

This sounds easy to do, but it can be very difficult. Parents are used to scolding, counseling, directing, and trying to power their way to stopping the negative behavior. It can be difficult to show little emotion while redirecting the behavior back on a positive track. Negative behavior tends to draw our attention and takes it away from what we want the child to do. It can be hard learning to say very little about the negative behavior and focusing all attention on what we want the child to do. You need to focus attention on guiding the child through the desired response. This technique takes some practice to learn to do effectively.

Example #1

Sally frequently slaps herself when she gets frustrated with doing difficult tasks. We are trying to get her to say the word "help," so we can assist her in making the task easier. We role-play and practice saying "help" during activities, so she learns how to produce the desired response. Then, during daily activities, we remind Sally before doing tasks that if it gets hard to do, then say "help" and we will come and assist her. Of course, since slapping her face is a very established response to frustration, we cannot expect it to immediately go away. Before starting the activity, we preview saying "help" if she needs assistance and remind her again a couple of minutes into the task. If she starts to slap her face, we gently block the slapping and redirect her to say "help" (which she has learned to do with practice), and immediately assist her to make the task easier. We say nothing about the slapping, just redirect her to say help and immediately assist her. Once the task is completed, we review how well asking for "help" worked for her.

Example #2

Jackie has a strong self-stimulatory behavior of picking at her fingers, often until they bleed. This behavior occurs frequently and is difficult to control. The teacher will tell her to stop, which she will do for approximately one minute, but then she returns to picking. We try reinforcing Jackie for not picking, but she seems to do it without thinking about it. With further observation, we notice that this behavior occurs frequently when Jackie's hands are not occupied, and infrequently when her hands are kept busy. We decide to reinforce Jackie for keeping her hands busy: manipulating toys and fidget items, coloring, playing with cards, and drawing pictures. We place a box of these items at her desk. When she has completed her assignments, Jackie is encouraged and reinforced (with praise) to keep her hands occupied with her play items during her free time. When staff notice Jackie starting to pick at her fingers, they redirect her by giving her one of her play items to manipulate, and reinforce her if she cooperates. We also build in added reinforcement for playing with her toys. In addition, Jackie has a token card with three squares in a row, followed by a picture of a computer. During each down time, if she plays with her items, they give her a star on her chart. When she fills up the three squares, she earns 15 minutes of playing her favorite computer game. By increasing the amount of time her hands are busy, the picking is drastically reduced.

Example #3

Joshua has difficulty controlling his emotions when upset. Once he gets upset, he explodes into screaming, crying, and biting his hand. He will do this for 5–10 minutes until he exhausts himself. He will often make his hand bleed. We want to teach Joshua a better way of calming himself when upset. Joshua's parents report that Joshua likes to rock to soothe himself when anxious. With Joshua's help, we decide to try to teach him to chew on a piece of tubing periodically throughout the day to keep him more regulated. We also want him to learn to rock and bite/chew on the tubing to soothe himself when upset. We feel by having him become used to chewing on the tubing throughout the day, it will become a familiar tool to use when upset. We practice having Joshua rock and chew on his tubing when upset, encourage him to chew on his tubing during the day, and especially during times of high stress. This is easy to do since Joshua enjoyed chewing. When Joshua starts to get mad, his parents sit down with him, redirect him to rock and chew on the tubing, and model it by doing it right along with him. It takes several weeks for Joshua to inhibit his hand biting and substitute the tubing, but with coaching he is able to effectively make the switch. Over time, his parents learned the early signs that he is getting upset, and teach Joshua to take a break, sit, and rock while chewing his tubing. He learns to do this frequently when getting too aroused or overwhelmed, so it becomes a tool for regulating his emotional reactions. Hand biting is significantly reduced since it is substituted with the tubing.

Redirection alone only works if the behavior is easily redirected. If the child refuses and fights it, causing the situation to escalate, then this technique needs to be strengthened with additional strategies (pulling back until calm then redirecting, brief time out, etc.). This technique is often tried first, with other strategies added if redirection alone is not effective.

Reaction strategies: social disapproval

Children who simply have trouble with understanding boundaries and need the world to have clear and tight rules often respond to firm disapproval. Children often have difficulty reading the social cues and need strong feedback on what they are doing wrong and why it must be stopped. These children usually respond well to concrete, black and white rules, which add structure and understanding to an often confusing world.

Social disapproval consists of firm communication that behavior is unacceptable (e.g. "no hitting"), paired with facial expression of displeasure.

Procedures

1. Interrupt behavior.

2. Obtain attention (not necessarily eye contact, but face to face at eye level, within field of vision).

3. Firmly tell person "No__" or "Stop __." Pair verbal prompt with shaking of head no, and manual sign for no (or stop).

4. Show obvious displeasure (animated facial expression).

5. Keep statement short and clear.

6. Redirect without counseling/negotiating. Redirect by telling the child what you want him to do. Then focus all attention on what you want him to do.

Often for these children, you need to be very animated in your response for them to pick up on the obvious displeasure. These children often read most reactions from others as "fun" attention, and do not read the displeasure in others. Also, this technique can work for children who need firm feedback that you mean business. However, be prepared that you may need to back this up with additional punishment (time out or loss of privilege) if the child refuses to follow your lead. If you consistently back up this approach with further consequences, the child often knows you mean business and will respond to your firm prompt.

Reaction strategies: time out

One of the most widely used discipline procedures with children is the use of time out. Clinically, this procedure involves the temporary removal of positive events for engaging in the undesirable behavior. When the negative behavior occurs, the positive event is removed, or the child is removed from the event, for a brief time.

There are three primary forms of time out:

1. *Briefly removing the reinforcing event/item from the child.* Example: Johnny's mother is trying to teach him to swallow each bite of his food before taking another bite. She demonstrates for him and gently guides him to do the same. However, he is very impulsive and sometimes ignores her guidance, shoveling food into his mouth without swallowing between bites. When he is cooperative with her guidance, mom praises his responsiveness. If he ignores her guidance and begins to shovel food into his mouth, she briefly moves the plate of food away for one minute. This interruption is mildly annoying for Johnny, so he goes back to responding to her guidance. If Johnny becomes upset and resistant, she removes the plate away until one minute past calm.

2. *Removing the person away from, but in view of, the reinforcing activity (e.g. chair time out).* Example: Jessica will frequently take food from others at the lunch table at school. The assistant previews with Jessica, before eating, what is her food and what food belongs to the other children. The assistant also sits Jessica plenty of space away from other kids (to make sure she doesn't confuse her food with the others). Jessica is reminded to eat her food only, but she gets impulsive and wants to take the food of others. When she takes food from others, the assistant moves her chair several feet back from the table for three minutes. If calm, Jessica is allowed to go back and continue eating. If it occurs three times, she ends her lunch and finishes when others have completed eating.

3. *Removing the child away from the reinforcing area.* Example: At home, James will often get upset with his siblings when they do not play the way he wants them to play. He will scream, become demanding, and physically take things away from them. Mom tries to redirect James to give the item back and problem-solve with him. If James refuses to respond and continues screaming, mom has him sit in the bathroom for three minutes until he has been calm. Once he calms down, mom asks James if he knows why he was timed out (at first he may not know why). She briefly discusses how he should have reacted, and then he is allowed to rejoin the play. Mom sends him to the bathroom and not his bedroom, because there are too many fun things for him to do in his bedroom (a mistake that some parents make). However, if the child gets into things in the bathroom, another area may need to be identified.

There are some basic procedures to effectively use time out:

1. Only use if the child is actually in a positive situation to be timed out from. If the child is actually in a situation that he wants to avoid, removing him

from the event can actually be reinforcing (e.g. sending the child home from school, or sending him down to the resource room). If the task at hand is something he wishes to escape, then time out may be reinforcing. He will learn to act out to be removed from situations he does not like.

2. Discuss the use of time out with the child, and the conditions for which it will be applied, at a time when he is calm. If possible, review it frequently and role-play its use. It can be fun for both parties to switch roles and let the child time out the parent when role-playing. This makes the procedure very familiar and predictable for the child.

3. I typically try to give the child one prompt to stop the behavior before implementing time out. If the child does not comply, implement time out immediately with minimal attention or emotion. Simply implement the consequence, matter-of-factly. Do not argue, scold, or negotiate. Show minimal emotion and say nothing but "Go to ____." Try not to explain, justify, or counsel. Many kids will say they will be good or try to negotiate out of it. Say nothing but direct the child to the area of time out. Let the child know, "When you are calm for three minutes, then you can come out." Again, this should be a reminder, since you have already discussed this with the child when calm.

4. From that point on, provide no further verbal attention. Lead the child to the area of time out. Minimize all other attention and other rewarding activity. If the child keeps trying to come out, gesture or physically redirect back while minimizing speaking.

5. Time out does not have to last long; several minutes is usually good enough for young children. Children on the spectrum have difficulty with extended time. A good rule of thumb is one minute for each year of age. However, if the child has difficulty with extended times, keep it to about 3–5 minutes.

6. If the child is not calm after time elapses, wait until he has been calm for at least 1–3 minutes before ending time out.

7. Be prepared for all-out war! Ignore all negative behavior.

Often the child will act out in time out. If you choose to use this technique, you have to be prepared to provide minimal attention to the negative behavior. This procedure is not good for children who will potentially injure themselves (from self-abuse) or engage in extensive property destruction. You have to stay calm, show little emotion, and say very little. If you get emotional, or the child pulls you into scolding, counseling, or negotiating, this tends to give reinforcing attention and a sense of power to the child. If it cannot be implemented safely and with minimal attention, reconsider the value of using this technique.

As with all punishment procedures, I only recommend using them if (1) the child understands what he is doing is wrong, (2) knows what he should do instead, and (3) has demonstrated that he can perform the desired behavior. We also need to make sure that the child is reinforced heavily for appropriate behavior and that we are lowering our demands to match the current skill level of the child. If what we are expecting is too challenging and overwhelming for the child, then time out will not work and may even reinforce noncompliance (to escape events that are too demanding for him). We should only use punishment procedures as a last resort, and make sure strong proactive supports are built in to lessen the triggers and teach more appropriate behavior.

Once the child calms down and leaves time out, redirect the child back into time in again and reinforce all cooperation. However, it may be difficult to tell if the child is calm when letting him out. Many children will start yelling that they are calm as soon as you put them in the room, or stay quiet long enough to come out and then start all over again. In this case, we often require the child to do a simple task (e.g. relaxation exercise, coping skill, etc.) with us to measure if the child is actually calm, before leaving the area of time out. Usually, if the child is not fully calm, he cannot do the task cooperatively.

Reaction strategies: response cost; taking away privileges

Another popular discipline technique used by parents is "response cost," which is losing access to a positive reinforcer. This could be taking away a privilege, loss of computer time, taking away tokens, or losing the evening snack. Unfortunately, we often come up with these contingencies on the spot when angry, not as a planned intervention technique that is explained prior to the event and understood by the child.

Response costs procedures (losing something as a punishment for some behavior) can be more punishing for the parent than the child. It can backfire on you with children on the spectrum. First, children with ASD often have a hard time associating the consequence with the action, especially if there is a time delay before losing the event (act out and no TV later tonight). Second, once they have a thought in mind, it is hard for them to let go of it. They will perseverate on the loss and drive you nuts trying to get it back. If you give in occasionally, you will make it worse. Third (very important), children with autism need to know exactly when the item (or privilege) is going to be given back. So, when taking an item away, you need to be clear on when it will be given back, and hold to it. Fourth, children on the spectrum have a difficult time using forethought (reflecting on past memories and projecting on possible consequences) to control present behavior. Often they don't even consider ramifications of their actions (impulsive). So, the punishing experience may not control future occurrences, without frequent repetition.

When using a response cost with your children, consider the following:

- Make sure the child understands exactly what he did wrong, what is being taken away, and when it will be given back. "Johnny, because you hit your sister, you cannot play the computer until after dinner tonight." If he does not understand the association, it will not be effective and the child will simply hound you to death. It is often helpful to use visual pictures or written guidelines to make this association concrete. Go over it to explain the consequence as soon as the behavior happens, and then again when the item is given back. If the child is verbal, it is best to verify that he understands by asking him to repeat the association.

- If the negative behavior occurs frequently, I would make a visual picture sequence explaining the contingency and go over it frequently, not just when the behavior happens. Learning occurs better when everyone is calm. Take the picture sequence and review/preview it frequently. Also, make sure you go over how you want the child to act in that situation. I would make another picture story about how the child should respond, and the reinforcement he will receive for doing so.

- If possible, role-play and practice both the response cost when negative behavior occurs and the positive consequences when desired behaviors occur. Have fun and take turns switching roles (parent and child).

- When the child engages in the problem behavior and you have to implement the consequence (child loses the item/event), the child will inevitably question you about when the item will be given back. When the child questions you about the item, then tell him once, "You will get it back at (or when) _____." For children who repeatedly question about getting it back, refer them to the picture sequence, without further explanation. Sometimes, using a visual timer showing when the event will be given back helps reduce the anxiety.

- When removing the object, I would show the child where I put it so he sees where it is and that it didn't go away. Sometimes this reduces the uncertainty and lessens anxiety.

- Response cost can be implemented in one of two ways: the item will be taken away for a certain amount of time (losing computer for two hours) or the item will be given back once the child follows through with the desired request (get computer back once he completes what is asked of him), similar to time out. Either way, the child needs to know explicitly when he will get it back.

- When using time, remember that the longer the time between the problem behavior and the consequence (losing an outing tomorrow for hitting his sister today), the less he remembers the connection, and he may act up more out of frustration. I would keep it brief and immediate, since just telling the child it is removed will immediately make the child want it. So, I would not use a whole day or take away something that will not be occurring until later in the day. Try to make it something that the child loses immediately and lasts only a short time.

- I would pick no more than a couple of consequences (computer time, chair time out, etc.) and use them consistently, so they are familiar and predictable for the child.

- It often helps to interrupt the negative behavior early and give a warning, as well as remind the child how he should act. If the child stops with the warning and cooperates, then the consequence is not given. If he still continues the problem behavior after a warning to stop, then implement the consequence immediately.

- If the behavior is reoccurring and happens in certain conditions (e.g. he acts up in stores), then I would use the picture sequence and preview it just before going into the store. This visual sequence would include the reinforcement he receives for doing the appropriate behavior and the consequence he receives if he engages in the undesirable behavior.

- Watch for the triggers (situations that elicit the behavior) and intervene and redirect before the child engages in the negative behavior. Redirect him to the response you want him to do. Always focus heavily on what you want the child to do, and reinforce heavily when the child chooses that alternative.

1–2–3 warning

Use the 1–2–3 warning before implementing your consequence! This is an adaption of the "1–2–3 Magic" strategy that Thomas W. Phelan (2010) describes in his book *1–2–3 Magic: Effective Discipline for Children 2–12.*

Kids on the spectrum often have poor executive functioning (controlled by the part of the brain responsible for concentration, appraising situations, planning and organizing, self-monitoring, inhibition, etc.). This leaves them with weak impulse control and problems regulating their emotions. For these children, their brains have difficulty inhibiting impulses, so they frequently react immediately with little forethought (they act before thinking). Consequently, they often overreact and then feel badly for responding so strongly. Also, they act without thinking, then have to suffer the consequences of doing so. Discipline is only effective if it *teaches* the child, not just punishes the child. Punishing a child, when the child doesn't have good ability to stop, think, then act, can result in greater hostility and anger, further escalating the problem. For children with these weaknesses, it can be good to give them a chance to interrupt and control their behavior before implementing consequences.

For children who have difficulty inhibiting their impulses and act without thinking, using the "1–2–3 warning" approach can give the children a chance to interrupt their behavior, think, and shift gears. When the children are in the first stages of learning to control their emotions, we want to give them a chance to catch themselves, interrupt the behavior, and regroup without punishing them. Since they will initially have difficulty inhibiting the impulse, we want to give them that chance to stop, think, and then act. At this stage, we try to (1) interrupt the behavior, (2) redirect them to the alternative, replacement behavior (that is practiced when calm), before (3) implementing any disciplinary consequences. In other words, we want to give them a chance to regroup and do the desirable response before punishing.

When using this approach, you want to immediately interrupt the child and tell him what he should do (make sure to be short but clear on what to do, not just on what you want him to stop doing). Then be willing to coach him in what to do. With the 1–2–3 method, you are giving him until the count of three before implementing the consequence if he does not follow through. So, you interrupt and prompt what you want the child to do. Make sure you go to the child and get his attention before telling him what is expected. Do not tell him from across the room. Go to him, get face to face, and then tell him what to do. Give him 15–30 seconds to respond. If he does not respond, then repeat the instruction and say, "That's 1." Wait 15–30 seconds and then repeat the direction saying, "That's 2." If there is no response, then say, "That's 3," followed by the consequence ("That's 3; go to your room"). This way, you are giving the child a chance to stop, think, and choose the alternative behavior. Remember, this only works if you two have been practicing the alternative behavior, and the child knows how to do it. Then when you say, "3," immediately follow through with the consequence, with minimal emotion. Do not argue, counsel, explain, or justify what you are doing. Simply implement the consequence, with little emotion or talking. Once the child has calmed down, then go back and discuss how he could have responded, and what you both can do differently to make it better next time. You want to stay very supportive, validating how the child feels, but stay very clear and consistent in (1) what is expected and (2) implementing the consequences.

When implementing techniques like these, you want to make sure you decide upon and talk about the strategies ahead of time. Try not to haphazardly use techniques on the spot, with no advanced warning (changing the rules in the middle of the game). If you are going to use a simple time out or response cost (taking away a privilege), then talk about it ahead of time: what behavior it will be used for, what the expected alternative behavior is, whether you are going to give warnings, what the consequence is, how long it will last, etc. You want it to be clear before using it. That way, when you give a warning (and offer to help the child) and he is not cooperative, then he knows what to expect. You are building in proactive strategies for teaching, rather than simply punishing the child.

As a side note, some of our members have reported that their children become fixated on the numbers and continue to count past three. For these children, it is best to count backwards from three. That way, when you hit zero, it is the end! Always interesting with our children!

Let the consequences teach the behavior!

All behavior has consequences, either positive consequences that make the behavior more likely to occur again in the future or negative consequences that make it less likely that the behavior will occur again. You have heard me recommend many times matching the demands in the setting to the abilities of the child, and focusing on what we want the child to do, instead of what he is doing wrong. We need to remove unrealistic demands and teach better skills for handling the demands. Once we know that the child understands what to do and knows how to physically do it, all we have to do is make it more beneficial for him to do it than not do it! The same goes for replacing negative behavior with positive behavior. Once the child understands what he should do, as well as what he should not do, then we simply need to make the positive behavior more rewarding than the negative behavior.

When determining consequences it is important, if possible, to include the child in negotiating the consequences (positive reinforcers for good behavior, negative consequences for bad behavior, etc.). Sit down and make out an agreement on what consequences will occur to reinforce the good behavior, and what procedures/consequences (time out in room, loss of TV, etc.) will occur for negative behavior. If possible, make a written or picture contract, including these procedures. Do this when everyone is calm and can reasonably discuss the consequences. Set a time on a regular basis (e.g. every two weeks) to review the consequences and change or renegotiate the contract. These are also good times to discuss the "why" behind what is asked for, and what can be expected.

When implementing these consequences (both reinforcement and punishment), it is important to implement them immediately and consistently. These consequences should be black and white, clear, and consistent. Implement them strictly according to the agreement. If the child is to be reinforced for good behavior, implement them as soon as the good behavior occurs. Stay consistent with your promise. Often reinforcement procedures fail because they are not implemented immediately and consistently. If you implement them immediately and consistently, and the desired behavior is not increasing, then it may be that the reinforcer is not powerful enough and may need to be changed. The child needs to see the immediate connection between what he is doing right and the rewards received for doing it.

The same is true for negative consequences. Implement the strategies consistently and immediately. Once you have negotiated the consequence, implement it according to the agreement, without adding new rules, scolding, arguing, or negotiating. The main thing to remember about implementing punishment procedures, or withholding reinforcement (until the desired response occurs), is to implement them with little emotion, and not to counsel, scold, or negotiate in the heat of the moment. If the parent gets emotional (scolds, counsels, etc.) or allows the child to argue (renegotiate) conditions, then the child is distracted from the consequences and is reinforced by the sense of power from the attention he is getting. Usually, an argument and confrontation occur everyone gets emotional, then the consequences lose their effectiveness. Implement the procedures calmly and matter-of-factly, without much emotion.

The problem most people have is they expect the consequence to have an immediate effect and the behavior to improve immediately. However, many times the behavior will get worse before it gets better, and we have to give time for the child to experience the consequences, see that they are implemented consistently, and observe that they are not manipulating him. Often the child will test the consequences by fighting them, and then the parents get frustrated and desperately make changes. The child sees the parents' frustration and sees how his behavior manipulates the consequences, thus motivating the child to push the limits even more. Before giving up on the consequences, implement them consistently, with little emotion and no arguing, scolding, counseling, or negotiation. Give it some time for the child to experience the consequences and see that they are occurring consistently. Let the consequences teach the behavior!

Once the terms have been negotiated, simply implement the consequences with minimal emotion. Just refer to the agreement. For example, if the child has agreed to do his homework before watching TV, then simply hold him to it. If he whines and argues that he is too tired, acknowledge and validate that he may be tired and he can rest if he wants. However, calmly remind him that he cannot watch TV until the homework is completed. That is what was negotiated and written down. Do not get upset, argue, scold, or counsel. Simply step back and let the consequence teach the behavior. It is important for the child to (1) clearly experience the consequences and (2) and see that they are implemented consistently. Do not argue or fight with the child. Minimize emotion and don't negotiate. The child will initially argue to manipulate out of it, but simply remind him of the agreement. If, after a while, the procedures are not working for either side, then renegotiate the consequences (at a predetermined time).

Chapter 9

CHALLENGES AT SCHOOL

"Stop the world, I want off!"

An afternoon at school for a child with processing difficulties

The world is spinning and bombarding too fast! I try and try, until I cannot process any more. Help! My brain is drained, and my energy depleted. It is only noon and I have to somehow make it through the afternoon. Recess is chaotic; let me hide to the side. I have to somehow regroup and conserve, since I have little reserve. Like every afternoon, I will have to "shut down" to "shut out" the world. As I overload, my senses become heightened, hyper-sensitive, and impossible to tolerate. The sounds, the smells, the chaotic activity around me meshes into confusion. I have to hold it together and stay calm, as to explode would bring disaster. I will sit quietly, but stare off. To be aware will overwhelm.

Like most every afternoon, I will not remember what happened. It will be a blur. I will withdraw to survive, and gasp for air to not suffocate! I hurt all over, but cannot cry! I feel panic as the bright lights blind my eyes, the voices overwhelm me, and the smells make me nauseous. I can barely feel my arms and legs, let alone use them effectively. I am falling apart as I hold it in. I will withdraw and hide, sit quietly in my chair and hope that everyone forgets I am there. I want to hide in a corner, wrap up in a blanket, and withdraw to survive. I pray there will be no snags, or added demands, and hope that the teacher does not call on me. I cannot distinguish between what is said, what I did, or what is happening around me. Please, somebody! Stop the world and let me get off!

Always be aware that a full day at school can be very draining and overwhelming. The sensory bombardment, social strain, and academic demands can tax an already vulnerable nervous system. Our world presents too much, too fast, and too intensely for many on the spectrum. Many have delayed processing issues that make processing slow and taxing. They have to consciously think through much of what we process subconsciously and smoothly, with minimal energy. Slow it down, break it down, and give them a lot of breaks to rebound. Their energy supply drains fast, and they must have time to withdraw and regroup. Many have sleep disturbances, dietary concerns, and anxiety issues that leave them with a low reserve starting out the day. If they had an exhausting time the previous day, chances are they still have not replenished to full reserve. Do not pressure, do not demand—let them pace themselves. Develop a sensory diet with plenty of breaks, and most importantly allow them to escape when needed. Give them a voice, and make sure they know how, and feel safe, to say "no" and "I need help."

As a teacher or aide, help them feel safe in your presence, and trust that you understand. As the day wears on, be aware that stress chemicals accumulate and the child will be drained. Do not pressure or ridicule, but support and reassure. In the midst of chaos, they need to feel safe and accepted, and know that they can count on you to support them.

Change conditions first, before trying to change the child

When the child is acting out, behaving inappropriately, or not progressing as expected, it is very tempting to blame the child. The first tendency is to expect the child to change to meet our expectations, instead of changing our expectations to match the child. We somehow assume it is the child's fault if he doesn't match our expectations; therefore, it is the child's responsibility to change. This can be very damaging to children, especially since they often do not have the skills or abilities to make those changes.

To avoid this trap, we must start with the premise: Assume the child is doing the best he can, given the situation he is in, and his current skill level in dealing with it. Often, if the child is behaving inappropriately or not meeting expectations, then the demands of the situations are greater than his current abilities to deal with them. Given that assumption, then it naturally leads us to (1) re-evaluate our expectations and the demands we are placing on the child, in light of his current skill deficits, and (2) either lower the demands (expectations) or provide greater supports in helping the child meet the demands (or a combination of both). When the demands match the current abilities of the child, the child will learn and grow.

So, when faced with either behavior challenges or learning challenges, we need to evaluate three primary conditions to support the child:

1. Change the demands and expectations

First, look at gaining success by changing the demands. In light of the child's physical, sensory, cognitive, social, and emotional vulnerabilities, could the expectations and demands be changed to better match the child's current skills? The sensory demands of the environment could be overwhelming for the child, the social demands may be way too confusing for him, or the task demands may be way above what he can handle. Break it down, make it simpler, and build in extra support to help the child out.

This is where modifications and accommodations are important to match the environmental and task-related demands to the child. First, look at the physical settings that the child is in (classroom, cafeteria, gym, music room, hallways, etc.). Is there too much noise, too much activity, too much sensory stimulation that overloads or distracts the child? Are there modifications that can be built in to lower the sensory noise in the room, or accommodations such as seating arrangements, ear plugs, sunglasses, or other tools to mask the interfering sensory noise? Second, are the task demands too overwhelming for the child? Is there too much work, is the work too hard, or is it presented in the wrong way? Can the work be broken down, presented more visually, or assistance provided to lower the demands to match the processing needs of the child? Can the child handle the ongoing demands for a full school day? Once his mental energy runs out, he will become overwhelmed quickly and often shut down.

2. Change our interactions with the child

Once the demands/expectations are modified to match the child, then look at how we interact and teach the child. Does the child need assistance or guided support? Am I presenting the information favorably? Does the child feel supported and validated by me, or am I being too demanding? Does the child welcome my support? If the child is to be successful, we need to find the right approach that helps support his learning. We need to ask, "Does the child feel safe, accepted, and competent with me?" If the child is anxious, fearful, or insecure in our approach, he will naturally try to escape and avoid our guidance. Many behavior challenges are directly related to how the adult is interacting with the child. What interaction style (slow and quiet, upbeat and animated, etc.) does your child respond best to? How others are interacting and teaching your child will have a lot to do with him feeling safe and learning.

3. What skills do we need to teach the child to be successful?

Once we have lowered the demand, provided needed support, and changed our interaction style, then we need to concentrate on teaching the child better skills in dealing with the demands. If the child is struggling socially in school, then we need to teach better social skills. If he is having trouble with controlling his emotions, then we need to teach coping skills. If he is having trouble reading, then work more on teaching reading skills. This way, we are giving the child the tools necessary for meeting the environmental demands. Start simple, build gradually, provide support as needed, and develop the skills necessary for success.

Once we meet these three conditions, rarely do we need to blame, force, or punish the child. When the child is struggling, we are the ones who need to make the changes, not the child. We are the ones who are placing the child in situations that he cannot handle. So, let's look first at changing what we are asking of the child and how we are supporting the child, before looking at blaming or changing the child. Everyone will be successful and feel competent about what they are doing!

Building strong supports in school

Children need structure, predictability, and consistency of approach. Many children on the spectrum become overwhelmed very easily. You want to evaluate the sensory, academic, and instructional demands in the classroom. Try to make sure that the noise level is low, the lighting is not too bright, and academic demands are tailored to the learning style of the student. Try to keep a written or visual (picture) schedule for the day, and try to keep a consistent schedule each day. The more concrete, visual, and predictable the daily routine, the less the anxiety. Uncertainty is a major enemy of children with ASD. They can be very rule-bound interpreting things literally and following things literally. Post written rules and expectations, and review them frequently. Make sure you stay consistent in following them.

Be very careful of the social demands within the classroom. Children have difficulty interacting in a group situation, especially reading the fast-paced interactions among several people at one time. Invite, but do not push too hard, and then support them in group activities. They have trouble reading the unwritten rules of relating with others. They have trouble reading the thoughts, feelings, and perspective of others. They have difficulty fitting in. Try not to push them, but rather invite them into interacting. Children on the spectrum can be very different in their desire to interact. Either they tend to be indifferent or uninterested and need coaxing, or they are very social and very verbal, but do not know when to stop. The very social ones will often interrupt, talk nonstop about their topic of interest, dominate a conversation, and overwhelm other children. They do not know how their behavior is affecting others. They will need a lot of coaching.

Focus on their strengths and interests. Kids on the spectrum often have good awareness of detail and have one or two very strong interests. They can have very good memory for facts and detail, but not catch the gist of things. Identify what their strengths and interests are, and try to build them into the lessons. Like any child, if you build on their strengths and help support their weaknesses, they will develop.

Expect that they will have organizational problems very similar to children with attention deficit disorders. Break tasks down into manageable steps and give them a lot of visual cues. Set up organizers, color-code things, help them put their backpack together at the end of the day, and remind them to give you their homework at the beginning of the day. Try to give main instructions with written notes for them to refer back to when needed. Start where they are competent and build gradually.

Don't assume. Just because they are very verbal doesn't mean they understand. Also, because they are very literal, they often do not understand our multiple meanings and vague language. Don't assume they know. Be very careful to explain things very literally for them, and have them repeat it back to you. Be careful to clarify and verify everything. If the child does wrong, he probably misinterpreted the expectation. Look at how it was presented and how it was interpreted. Do not assume the child is purposely doing it wrong. Rarely is this the case. It is usually our fault, not theirs. However, do not expect to anticipate all problems; you cannot be that good.

These children are often very black and white, all or nothing in their thinking. The stronger their anxiety, the more rigid and inflexible their thinking. They can get upset with vague rules and expectations, and get very anxious, which may be displayed in obsessive/compulsive behavior or oppositional/defiant behavior. When highly anxious, they can be very perfectionistic and unrealistic in their own performance as well as their expectations of others. They can have a strong fear of being wrong, and need to make sure that they have completed it right.

Peer awareness is important. The better understanding the other kids have of the child, the better they can support him. There are some good videos and kids' books out for explaining autism/Asperger's. Some schools use videos to teach staff and peers about autism. Develop peer supports to help the child navigate the social life. Supportive peers (peer mentors) can sometimes be the best teachers. Watch very carefully for other children teasing and bullying the child.

Often, the hardest times during the school day will be the unstructured times, such as lunch, recess, between classes in the hall, locker room before gym. These transition times can be very difficult for them to regulate. When aides are not available, peer supports can really help out.

For many children with anxiety, stress chemicals will accumulate throughout the day. Give them frequent breaks during the school day to rebound and collect themselves. Also give them "break" cards that they can hand to you if they need to "get out of there" and rebound. I would also ask for an occupational therapist to evaluate them and give them sensory diets to help calm and organize their nervous system.

Each child is different, but assume that the everyday demands of school can be very overwhelming. Whether they tell you or not, their behavior will tell you how they are doing. Communicate that they are safe and accepted in your classroom, and provide proactive support. Become a working partner with them, and, most importantly, be flexible. Once they read that in you, they will use you for support and feel safe in your classroom.

Anxiety can be expressed in different ways. Some children will melt down and act out. Some children will shut down or tune out. They are just as overwhelmed and anxious. Some children use a very oppositional coping strategy. They often argue or resist much of what is going on. They will say something is stupid or boring, when they feel insecure and incompetent. Remember, the more oppositional the child is, the more inadequate he is feeling.

Because of their poor organizational skills, these children can appear lazy, oppositional, or that they have a poor attitude. Because they often have good verbal skills, the social and emotional issues are often more hidden. These children are not manipulative and oppositional by nature, only as a way of coping with uncertainty. Just always remind yourself, as the child becomes oppositional or defiant, that he is feeling more insecure and anxious.

For the children who become overwhelmed and melt down, do not scold or punish. Do not become controlling or demanding. When they are melting down, they lose coping skills and self-control. Back off demands, lower the stimulation, and lower your voice. Offer assistance, but be aware that many children need to be left completely alone to rebound. We often develop "safe areas" for the children to escape to in order to rebound. Communicate that they are safe and accepted with you. Respect their need to back away.

Be proactive rather than reactive. Provide strong proactive supports to minimize stress and build adaptive skills, rather than punishing problem behavior. This does not mean letting them get away with things. You can provide consequences for behavior, but focus heavily on identifying why the problems are occurring and building in supports to minimize the behavior.

Helping your child feel safe at school!

When assessing the safety factors at school, I look closely at the physical surroundings of the classroom (sensory issues, physical layout, seating arrangement, etc.), the instructional strategies that the teacher uses, the task performance demands, and the social interaction patterns with teachers and peers.

When looking at how to create a supportive school environment for your child, consider the following:

- Look to see if there are any sensory problems in the classroom (too many children, too much noise, too many distracting activities, etc.). Look to see if where he sits is a factor for him. Does he need to sit closer to the teacher, away from windows? Are other kids sitting too close to him?

- Children on the spectrum need strong organization in the classroom and schedule. They require strong predictability in their routine. The teacher should provide the class (or the child) with a picture schedule, and go over it at the beginning and middle of the day. The teacher should review the schedule frequently, and prepare the child ahead of time for transitions and changes. Also, use visual cues and visual instructions to what he needs to do.

- Remind the teachers to be very specific and very literal with their language. Don't assume that the child understands what is expected. Teachers need to clarify information and verify that the child understands it (ask him to repeat it back), and provide instructions in visual form (pictures, written words, etc.).

- Transitions between activities (ending one activity and starting another), especially if it means ending a preferred activity and going to a non-preferred activity, can be difficult for the kids. The children usually do better when they know what activity will follow the current one. Prepare them for the transition by giving a couple of warnings before transitioning ("In three minutes we will be cleaning up and begin ___," followed by a one-minute warning, etc.).

- Watch closely the interaction patterns with the staff. How do they support your child, what types of teaching strategies do they use, and how do they prompt your child to do things? Do they focus on his strengths and support him early when he is struggling? Does he feel accepted and supported by the way they assist him? If he gets overwhelmed and acts out, how do they support him at the time? Do they assist him to calm (e.g. back off demands, allow him to retreat to safe area, use calming strategies), or do they demand and command? Try to guide them in what techniques work best to lessen the overload, as well as to calm your son when overwhelmed. If needed, ask the occupational therapist to design a sensory diet to help your child stay calm and organized during the school day, and ask for a functional behavior assessment if your child is having behavior issues at school. Ask to be part of the team that will be assessing and designing any behavior strategies. You have a right to be part of all decision making.

- Also take a look at how the child interacts with the other children. This is often his strongest anxiety. Try to get the teachers/staff to support him during social, group activities. He will need help learning how to coordinate interaction with the other kids. He will need help navigating and interpreting social demands. He will not be aware of the reactions other children have to his behavior. He will not pick up on the cues other children give him, and will not be aware of the thoughts, feelings, and perspectives of the other children. Teachers need to help guide him in social interaction.

- Take a close look at how the work is presented. Kids with autism/Asperger's often need the work to be broken down into smaller parts, given to them one at a time, and they need to be given more time to complete their work. A good rule of thumb is giving half the work, in twice as much time. Also, many children need help getting started (even if they know what to do). They often have a hard time initiating that first step. Once they get started, they can attend better. The teacher might want to try assisting him through the first part of the task to get him started, and then return again midway through to reinforce working and redirect if needed. He will probably need occasional reminders and redirections to complete the task.

- Make sure the child knows how to ask for help and how to appropriately ask to get out of doing something. Even if the child is very verbal, he often does not know (or feel safe) asking for help. The child also might act out to escape a task he doesn't want to do (or feels uncomfortable doing). Sometimes by raising his hand for help and having a "break card" to use when he needs to take a break from the classroom, the child will do much better.

- Regardless of how bright your son is, he will find many of the normal daily demands of the classroom more stressful than the other children. Making his way through the normal interactions with other children and teachers will take ongoing conscious effort on his part. Much of what other children process subconsciously, with little effort, will require a lot of conscious thought from your child. Because of this, he will become overloaded very easily. He may need periodic breaks to rebound throughout the day, and chances to escape from the classroom demands and engage in an activity that calms and organizes him.

- Pay close attention to the unstructured times (lunch, recess, rest periods, etc.) and group activities that require more relating with the other children. The children are often lost in these activities, which will lead to them acting out to control them. They may need help from an aide or peer mentor during these times.

- Make a list of your son's strengths and interests, his fears and sensitivities, and what helps him feel safe, accepted, and competent. This helps teachers know the child better. The staff should focus heavily on his strengths, help compensate for his weaknesses, and adapt for his fears/sensitivities. At all times, focus your attention on what you want him to do and minimize attention on what he is doing wrong. Help the child feel competent by focusing on his strengths.

Helping the child feel safe, accepted, and competent at school takes many changes in the physical setting, task demands, teaching strategies, and ways of interacting with the child. Sometimes it takes a few years to isolate, analyze, and create the needed changes to make school successful.

Three conditions for matching the demands to the child!

Children do the best they can given the situation they are in and their current skills for dealing with it. If children are struggling, there is a good chance that the demands we are placing on them are greater than their skill level for dealing with them. In these cases, the first line of strategies should be to lower the demands or provide greater supports, so the demands match the skill level of the child. There are three factors you can modify in doing this: modify the environment, modify the task itself, and modify the teaching style, or assistance, given to the child.

1. *Modify the environment.* First, look at the environment to see if it interferes with your child's performance. Based on your child's sensory, social, and emotional needs, are there elements that threaten his performance? Let's take school as an example. Do the lights, noise, smells, or activity level overwhelm the child, so he cannot focus, process, and perform adequately? Does his seating arrangement need to be changed to allow him to concentrate? Would he be better off sitting on an air cushion or exercise ball to allow him to "fidget to focus"? Does he need to be facing away from the group or window to minimize distractions? Maybe he could benefit from chewing gum to maximize attention. Are there too many children sitting close to him who overwhelm or distract him? Or maybe there is a bully in the classroom teasing him? If your child has sensory needs, ask for the occupational therapist to recommend classroom modifications to accommodate his sensitivities, and a sensory diet to keep his nervous system calm and organized.

2. *Modify the task itself.* Is it too hard or asking for too much? Should it be downsized or broken up into smaller steps? Maybe placing only a couple problems on a page, instead of many, or providing more visual strategies to support his learning style would help. Could it be made more motivating by incorporating his favorite topic into the learning? There are a host of accommodations and modifications that can be done to better match the demands to the strengths of the child.

3. *Look at the interaction style of the teacher.* Is the teacher or aide too demanding, pressing too hard, giving too many verbal directions that confuse and overwhelm the child, or walking away without guiding the child? What are the best ways to provide instruction, guidance, and encouragement for the child? Maybe the teacher should use fewer words and more demonstration, or maybe she should support the child by doing the first couple of problems with him, or helping him outline what to do. Does your child respond to a soft, slow interaction style or an upbeat, animated style? Does your child feel safe, accepted, and competent with that teacher? If not, what can she do to change it?

These three factors can be modified to better match the demands to the child in any setting or task conditions (home, school, community setting, etc.). When your child is struggling, look at the environmental demands, task requirements, and instructional methods for ways to modify that and maximize success. Use the Comfort Zones Profile (Appendix B) to outline your child's strengths, vulnerabilities, and most effective strategies. Then provide the school and support staff with the profile to help them best support your child.

Match teaching to the child's learning style!
The three must-dos: input, output, and processing speed!
How does the child best receive information (input) and communicate what he knows (output), and at what speed can he adequately process information? Identify and respect these three processes and maximize the learning.

When advocating for your child at school, place emphasis on these three processing steps:

1. *Learning style.* Identify and cater to the child's primary learning style. Most children are either auditory learners (learn better through hearing), visual learners (better through vision), or tactile learners (learning by touching and doing). Many children on the spectrum have auditory processing problems, so they are often visual learners, processing information better through written words and pictures. For these children, verbal information can get jumbled up and lost before it is stored in the memory. Verbal information is too fleeting, whereas visual information is more constant and available to reference. However, some children have visual processing difficulties or visual learning disorders and receive information better orally. They do better *hearing* the information. Some children learn best by touching and manipulating, and need to physically explore what they are learning.

   Pattern how information is given by how they receive it best. If the child has auditory problems, he may struggle understanding or remembering verbal information and oral directions. He will learn better with written material combined with pictures. So, when the teacher is giving directions, she would be better off giving the child directions in writing. If the child has visual processing issues, then the child would do better with verbal instructions, or listening to a story instead of reading it. It is important to isolate which sense is the primary processor and if any of the other senses have processing limitations. It is often recommended that the children go to an audiologist or ophthalmologist for comprehensive evaluations if they appear to be struggling with learning from hearing or vision.

2. *Communication style.* In addition to learning style, we need to understand the best way for the children to express what they have learned. Many children on the spectrum have fine motor difficulties and struggle with writing. For them, having to write out what they know (tests, papers, etc.) can be a real struggle. If you want to test what the child knows, then we have to use a medium with which he can express himself easily. If the child struggles with writing, he has to focus so much on making the written symbols that he cannot concentrate on *what* he wants to say. He cannot concentrate on (1) how to write and (2) what to write about at the same time. He will get anxious and expression breaks down. Children who struggle with writing need accommodations built in to take tests orally, type out answers, or have someone else write out the answers. We want to use the easiest way for them to express what they know.

3. *Processing speed.* Lastly, allow the child to pace the amount and speed at which he learns. This respects his processing speed. Many children on the spectrum have delayed processing problems. It takes added time to process the information and then formulate and execute a response. If we push them faster, the processing breaks down and interrupts their understanding and performance. We need to let their brains dictate the amount of time it takes for them to complete their work. Often it is half as much work in twice as much time. You cannot force the child to go fast, and doing so will only create more anxiety, which will inhibit his performance.

It is very important at school, and elsewhere, that we recognize and respect the learning style, mode of expression, and processing speed of the children to maximize learning. So, have these three functions evaluated, identify the best way to learn and express what they have learned, and have those accommodations built into the IEP from year to year. Your child will do much better at school.

Dealing proactively with behavior problems at school!
Teaching, rather than punishing!

The following is an example of building in proactive strategies at school to decrease problematic behavior. It is my recommendations for a child who has a problem with swearing and name calling!

Although these strategies are focused on a child who is having increased problems with name calling and swearing at peers, these same proactive strategies can be used for a variety of problem behaviors. If your child is acting inappropriately, make sure the school does a functional behavior assessment to identify the conditions eliciting the problem behavior and then develops a positive behavior supports plan to teach more appropriate skills to replace the negative behavior. Teach before punishing.

Tracy is getting frequent reports about her son calling other kids names and swearing at them. He wants very much to fit in and make friends, so it is confusing as to why he would call them names and swear at them. Tracy reports:

? Tracy's question

Daniel is using bad language all the time. Calling kids names and telling them to kiss his @*#. and Bi**hes. His aide is getting quite concerned about this. He does it at lunch and on the playground. She has taken many things away from him. He does not like it when he gets called names and cries. I talked with him and told him that if I hear another bad report his TV is coming out of his room. He said he understood, went back to his room, and I heard him bawling his eyes out. I went back there and I asked him if he knew that he was in big trouble and he said yes and started to cry harder. So what do you do with this?

AUTISM DISCUSSION PAGE

Tracy, they need to collect information to determine the exact function that the behavior has for Daniel. Each time that it happens, they need to note what was going on at the time, where he was at, what he was doing, who he was with, and what was asked of him. Under what conditions is he swearing at others? When frustrated? When he doesn't know how to relate? When others tease him? Are kids laughing at him, or is he getting added attention when swearing? By keeping track of the conditions for which it occurs, you can identify the function the behavior serves for Daniel. More than likely, Daniel is swearing when he is in a situation of not knowing how to act.

What they have to find out is, "Why is Daniel swearing at the other kids?" Then the question becomes, "Does Daniel know how he should appropriately act in those situations?" If he doesn't know how to act, simply punishing him will not work. Punishing only works if the child knows how to act differently and is making a choice to act inappropriately. So, in these cases they will need to teach him better social skills when interacting with other kids.

This would be accomplished by developing social stories around the effects that swearing at other kids have. This usually includes an understanding of how other kids feel when called names, and how other kids will act towards him when he calls them names. This gives him an idea of the perspectives of the other kids and the consequences of their reactions.

Once staff have identified common situations when he swears at them, decide how he should respond at those times (being teased, not getting his way, etc.). Teach him specific statements to say, instead of swearing at them. Have him practice the responses and role-play situations until they become automatic. You don't want Daniel to be continually thrown into social situations in which he does not know how to act, and then punish him for acting inappropriately.

Once staff have made a list of common situations in which he swears, they can practice these situations and then remind him of how to act as they see him entering into these situations. If there is an aide, this person should help Daniel interact during these times, framing the situations to coach him how to act appropriately, and encouraging and rewarding the use of the practiced responses when playing with others.

It may also be good to provide awareness training for his peers to explain that Daniel may be nervous and need their assistance in helping him act appropriately. Facilitating appropriate play means working with both the child and the peers.

It is important to focus on teaching rather than punishing. Make it fun, frame the activities by being right there to facilitate the desired responses, and praise heavily. Daniel needs strong framing. When he is left to his own devices, he loses his boundaries and then gets into trouble. This is a problem. He needs tight boundaries with very clear consequences, but also needs very black and white expectations. So, if Daniel knows what to do, staff need to interrupt and redirect very quickly. If Daniel continues to swear or call names, then provide a clear consequence at that moment if he doesn't respond to the coaching.

Now, given the above, I would implement a behavior chart. For every activity that Daniel does not swear at someone, I would give him a sticker on a portable "reinforcement" board. When he earns four stickers, he gets to choose a reward. If he swears, he simply doesn't get a sticker. However, be aware that unless the staff teach him the appropriate way of interacting, no reinforcement or punishment can work.

Oh, by the way, I would not punish Daniel at home for what he is doing at school. Let them implement consequences there. If you want to do anything, set up a reward chart for good reports from school, not punishment for being put in situations in which he may not know how to act.

Maximizing motivation and learning!

One of the greatest frustrations for teachers and parents is trying to teach children who have little motivation to learn! They often appear to not have the natural motivation to learn, like that of most neurotypical children. In reality, they don't lack motivation for that which they value. Most NT children are motivated by the praise from others, leading them to want to learn in order to please others, to imitate and be like them. Learning is very socially based and socially motivated. For many children on the spectrum, the concept of pleasing another is often foreign to them. Or, if motivated by praise, they have difficulty associating what to do to get it. They are usually more motivated by things that have concrete value to them, rather than learning something because someone else desires them to. So, when teaching we need to be concrete in how this learning applies to them and what they value.

To maximize motivation and learning:

1. *Use their intrinsic interests.* Try to build the new concepts around their current interests (Lego®, videos, history, trains, etc.). When it comes to their specific interests, they are motivated and focused.

2. *Build off their strengths.* Like all kids, they are more motivated if you build off their strengths. Usually when building off their strengths rather than focusing on their weakness, teaching is easier, they feel more competent, and learning is fun! If the child is good at drawing, then have him draw many of the concepts that you are trying to teach.

3. *Make new learning closely connected to past learning.* Always build new learning onto what they already know, so they can easily associate the material to already established concepts. They will be less motivated to learn material that has no conceivable importance or reference for them. If it is not material they value, they have a hard time seeing the relevance and why they should learn it. So, always tie more abstract concepts to concrete reference points that have meaning for them. Do not assume they make that connection on their own.

4. *Frame the new learning, so they see it.* When incorporating a new concept into an activity, you need to highlight the new learning so the child sees it. Don't assume that they pick it up. If I am trying to teach "same but different," then I need to highlight how something is the same, or how it is different, so it stands out for them to see.

5. *Let them lead, then support them.* Some children on the spectrum have strong anxiety following the lead of another person. They need to lead and control the activity to feel comfortable. For these children, let them lead while you support by framing and scaffolding the activity to highlight the new learning.

6. *Let the child pace the activity or new learning.* Children on the spectrum will resist information or task demands that are coming at them too fast. Many have processing difficulties and become overwhelmed if the information, or actions, are coming at them too fast. Slow it down, break it down, and let them pace it.

7. *Tailor how you teach to the learning style of the child.* If they are visual learners, then provide the information visually (written or pictures of demonstration). If they are more kinesthetic, then use hands-on projects to teach new learning. Many kids on the spectrum have auditory processing problems, so verbal instructions are often difficult for them.

8. *Avoid putting them on the spot.* Many children on the spectrum have strong task performance anxiety and resist any tasks that put them on the spot to perform. For these children, you can lower this anxiety by doing it with them, providing guided participation to maximize success. Learning then consists of gradually fading out the assistance.

9. *Reward new learning!* For activity that has minimal value for the child, build in additional reinforcement. For example, follow new learning with participation in a preferred activity; first complete this worksheet, then you can play on the computer. For school, I like to use a reinforcer puzzle. If the child likes to play on the computer, I will cut up a photo of the computer into four pieces. For each activity that he completes, he receives one piece of the computer. Once he earns all four pieces of the computer (completed four activities), he has earned time to play on the computer.

In summary, children on the spectrum are motivated by different factors compared with many NT children. Whereas NT children are often motivated to please and imitate others, many children on the spectrum are motivated by what satisfies more intrinsic needs (sensory, favorite interests, etc.). Children on the spectrum have a difficult time building motivation/concentration on learning that has little concrete value for them. The new learning has to have value for them to be attracted to it. Consequently, we have to make learning relevant to what the child finds meaning in. The new information needs to be connected to or associated with concepts that already have meaning for him. If the new material has value to the child, is centered around his strengths and interests, is matched to his learning style, and has reinforcing value to him, the child will be motivated to learn. So, if you are having difficulty motivating the child, consider one or more of the possible suggestions above.

Homework

Getting kids to do homework is a challenge with all children, not just kids on the spectrum. The first question I would have is whether you know the reasons why he doesn't want to do his homework. There can be a variety of factors causing kids to want to avoid homework:

- Some kids connect school work with school and will resist doing school work at home. It is something they do at school, period! These children are very stimulus-bound, meaning the activities are very connected to a specific setting.

- If school work is very hard for them and/or they do not feel competent doing it, then they will resist doing it when at home.

- Many of the kids have executive functioning problems, making it difficult to organize the work, know where or how to get started, and be able to break it down and sequence the work to get it done. Often they do not know how much time it will take to do it or know when it is "good enough." When they think of doing it, they get overwhelmed.

- As with all children, there are often more fun things to distract them, which they do not want to leave. Trying to get the kids to leave a preferred activity (video games) to do a non-preferred activity (homework) can result in strong resistance.

There are several things you can do to increase responsiveness. Depending on the child, you may need to incorporate several of these strategies:

- Schedule set times to do homework for the same time every day. Also, pick a spot that is distraction-free to do their homework. It is important to set up a consistent routine that stays the same each day. If the child doesn't have homework for that day, have extra work that can be done at that time. This way, the child has homework time every day.

- Most kids do not have the attention span to do homework for long. I recommend that children have no more than one hour of homework a day. With that, you may need to break it down into two 30 minute sessions, one before dinner and one after dinner.

- Try to do the homework before more preferred activity—for example, doing 30 minutes of homework after coming home from school, before doing a fun activity. (However, many kids need 30–60 minutes of down time or physical activity to rebound.) Then set aside another 30 minutes right after dinner before free time in the evening. If the child is resistant, do not argue. I usually validate their feelings: "I can understand how you might not feel like doing it right now. That's OK. Take a break and do it when you are ready." However, fun activities cannot occur until the homework gets done. This way, it becomes the child's choice.

- Always have a set time, so the child knows exactly the beginning and end to the homework session. Kids on the spectrum do much better when there is a set time (e.g. 30 minutes) that is predictable and easy for them to see. For children who will simply avoid doing much work during this time, identify how much work needs to be done as the criterion for the session ending. Only put out what needs to be completed for the session to end. This way, when the work is completed the session is done.

- Break it down, keep it simple. Break homework down into simple portions so it does not seem overwhelming when the child looks at it.

It is better to break it down into small easy-to-do parts, so it does not overwhelm him. A good rule of thumb is no more than 15–30 minutes (depending upon how easy the subject is for the child) for each subject. A little bit of homework done well with interest is better than a lot of homework that was done with confrontation. You want the sessions to be successful and fun for it to be perceived as positive.

- Set up a consistent sequence, so the child knows when to move from one task to another, perhaps using a visual timer to notify the child when to move on.

- Help the child to get started since initiating activity is difficult for many kids. Help them get started, and if the task is hard, do it together, scaffolding the activity to make it successful.

- Make sure when the homework is completed that it is placed in the child's folder/backpack, so it gets to school. Also, make sure the teacher is reminding the child to turn it in. Many children struggle with being organized and will forget to bring home the work, put it in their backpack when completed, and turn it in. This is not laziness. It is actually due to a brain wiring difference in the frontal lobes of the brain. Build in supports (reminders) or use a checklist for the child to remember.

Parents as advocates

As parents, no one can advocate better for your child than you can. No one knows your child like you do or understands autism (as it affects your child) like you do, and no one loves your child more than you do! You are also in a unique position to follow your child from moment to moment, day to day, and year to year. No one can advocate for your child better than you can. You have to be considerate but assertive in working with all people in your child's life, whether they are teachers, professionals, relatives, friends, or the general public.

For many parents, it is hard to advocate because they may not be assertive by nature, or they may end up being too aggressive out of their passion for protecting their child. You have to be an effective collaborator, working alongside the teachers and professionals, understanding and patterning what they are doing. In our schools, there are many barriers for children with special needs, and you need to work with the teachers and staff to help them (1) understand your child, both his strengths and vulnerabilities, (2) design effective teaching strategies to match the learning style of your child, and (3) make sure these strategies are implemented and carried over from year to year. Empowerment and person-centered planning means *nothing for the person, without the person*. For all but the older teens, you are your child's voice. You are "the person." You need to drive and facilitate services, strategies, and educational supports for your child. You need to be there to provide awareness training for these people, and meet with them regularly to monitor progress and modify strategies.

To be a strong advocate, you need to know what your child is entitled to. Each country has its own set of standards. In America they are the IDEA regulations. Parents should have an understanding of these standards so they know what they are entitled to and how to go about advocating for the services their child will need. These standards are easy to obtain by googling them on the internet. There are many sources that summarize these standards for parents to easily read. Read them and take a copy of them to your IEP meetings. Knowledge is power.

The schools and professionals need to know that nothing is determined without you being there. All meetings and all decisions about your child need to include you (and the child if old enough). Recruit a team of professionals (occupational therapist, speech pathologist, social worker, teacher consultant, etc.) and meet with them at least once every 2–3 months to review progress and modify the plan as needed. At the beginning of every school year, have a meeting with all the teachers to provide awareness training about who your child is, what his strengths and vulnerabilities are, what supports and accommodations are built into the IEP, and explain that they can expect you to visit regularly to observe and help out. Be a working partner with them, but make them aware that you will be involved! Make sure to give them a copy of the Comfort Zones Profile (Appendix B) or a 2–3-page summary profile of your child. Establish how communication will occur and ask them how you can help them in any way. Be a working partner with them, but insist that the IEP will be implemented as designed.

Make sure you stay in touch with the principal and administrators in the school district. Advocate for increased supports for all children, as well as your own. Be polite, but persistent, in identifying weak areas in the system and possible solutions, and sit on any work groups organized to develop changes. Get together with other parents and organize a support group for kids at school with special needs. There is a greater voice in numbers; be visible and vocal. Have a representative from your group at each board meeting and PTA. When organizing a special education support group, make sure to include a teacher or school personnel if possible. This is very important if you want to be a working partner with the school.

Now, this can be very overwhelming for most parents. That is why it is important to be involved with a support group. If you have trouble being assertive, or need someone to hold you back, then take another parent from the support group with you. Whatever it takes, you are still the best advocate for your child. Know your own strengths and weaknesses, and build supports around you.

Change at school! Focus on the positive and expand the strengths

When supporting people, whether that is a child, parent, or teacher, the same principles apply. We all feel stronger when we feel safe, accepted, and competent. Because of this, focusing on what others are doing right, validating their frustrations, and developing their strengths is the position to take.

As a consultant, I stay grounded to the two basic premises that the Autism Discussion Page is founded on:

1.   Assume the person is doing the best that he can, given the situation he is in, and the skills that he has.

2.   Everyone does better when they feel safe, accepted, and competent.

Create change, not by focusing on what the person is doing wrong, but by supporting what they are doing right (i.e. strengths). Expand on what they are doing right and develop their strengths to compensate for their weaknesses.

As a consultant, I have several clients to serve. I have the child himself, the needs and skills of the parents, the needs and skills of the school, and the needs and skills of other professionals supporting the child. To be effective, I have to use the same premises above to support each of these people.

So, let's take the school staff. I assume (1) that they went into the teaching profession with good intentions of teaching and developing children, (2) that they are doing the best that they can given the situation they are in and their current skills level, and (3) that if I can help them feel safe, accepted, and more competent in helping the child, then everyone will grow stronger.

Looking at the school personnel the same way I would the child (since all humans have these needs), I have to start by (1) validating the staff's frustrations and challenges in dealing with situations they are not prepared for, (2) assuming that their negative behavior is the result of not feeling safe or competent in dealing with the situation, (3) helping them feel safe, accepted, and supported by both the parents and administrators (we are all in this together), and (4) identifying and focusing on what they are doing right, rather than complaining about what they are doing wrong.

As parents, you are naturally focused on looking at your child this way, and assuming that the teachers and professionals (1) actually know what to do, (2) have the ability and resources to do it, and (3) are willfully choosing not to do it. This is rarely the case. Teachers and professionals are often put in situations where they do not know the answer, even though they are expected to (same conditions your children are often in). In most cases, when I am consulting, when things are going badly, all parties are struggling in all three of these conditions. They are all in situations where the demands of the situation outweigh their current abilities to handle them, so everyone gets defensive, and spends more time fighting back (just like our kids) and digging a deeper hole.

The school environment, by its nature, is a very difficult setting to make autism-friendly. The task of meeting the social, emotional, sensory, and academic demands of all the children is almost impossible. The basic design of our school system is not meant to meet the vulnerable needs of children on the spectrum. We are essentially forcing our children into environments that assault their basic nature. In doing so, when things are not going right, we all point fingers of blame at each other (parent at teachers and administrators, teachers back at parents and administrators, etc.) and spend more time fighting among ourselves, since we don't know what to do.

My experience is (1) when we focus on the negative (what the child or personnel are doing wrong), we get defensive, oppositional, and sometimes act out (both from the child and staff); (2) even if we create compliance with force, it is never effective or lasting; and (3) punishment breeds hostility and further negative behavior. Research in human behavior has demonstrated that looking past the negative behavior, focusing on and reinforcing what the person is doing right, and expanding on the person's strengths are the strongest strategies for creating change.

As I tell my psychology staff, as a consultant your client has to first see you as a working partner with him, before he will see you as a trusted guide in helping him out. This is the philosophy I take with the child. The child has to first see us (parents, teachers, etc.) as a working partner (validating and supportive), before he will take us as a trusted guide. When we force, fight and, demand, he will not feel safe and accepted enough to trust following our lead. So, given that we are all this way, we need to become a working partner with each other, validate and accept that we are all in a situation we are not strongly competent in handling, and help each other feel safe and accepted tackling the challenges. Which means, as with our children, we often have to bite our tongues when behavior is going badly, validate and accept, focus on their strengths, and help support them.

In looking at the school, it is so easy to get focused on what they are not doing or not providing. Try to dig deeper and look at what little things they are doing right, and assume that they *want* to support the child and are doing the best that they can in the given situation. Now, that doesn't mean you want to accept the current status (just as we don't with our children). Look for what they are doing right, then praise and expand on it. Draw attention to every little thing they are doing right and provide assistance in making that better. It doesn't mean we simply ignore what they are doing wrong, but you must spend at least three times more attention on what they are doing right. When we focus on their strengths, they feel safe and accepted, and will work with you, trust following your lead, and grow better at meeting the needs of your child.

Building an effective team at school

Probably the greatest struggles parents have are getting the supports they need at school. It seems as if there are always constant conflicts and struggles from year to year. In all systems, there are usually several key "leader" staff who are strong advocates and potential "change makers." Find them and become a partner with them.

It is very important during the school years that parents seek out a couple of advocates for their children at school. These advocates can be a social worker, counselor, special teacher, para-pro, occupational or speech therapist, or teacher consultant. Find at least one, if not two, school staff who can advocate for your child from year to year, as well as day to day, especially when times get rough. Sometimes that means spending some extra time volunteering at school or providing extra awareness training for the staff. When things get rough with behavior issues, there can be all kinds of reasons for acting-out behavior at school. Just like all of us, school personnel get anxious when faced with issues they do not know how to handle. When feeling anxious and incompetent, they (like us) want to escape and avoid the issue.

You want to pull together a small team of advocates to isolate what variables at school are causing the child to feel overwhelmed and act out. Whether the academic demands are too challenging, sensory stimulation is overwhelming, or social struggles are causing stress, accommodations and supports need to be built in to help the child feel safe and competent at school. This might include making accommodations to the academic demands, rearranging the daily schedule, using visual supports, implementing a sensory diet, and performing a functional behavior assessment to develop a positive behavior supports plan. In order to indentify, develop, implement, and monitor these supports, you will need a couple of key figures at school to monitor and advocate for your child. Seek these people out, and use them as "leaders."

As a parent, in this situation I would do the following:

- If the child is displaying challenging behavior at school, I recommend writing a letter to the school district formally requesting a Functional Behavior Assessment and a Positive Behavior Support Plan, which they are required by federal standards to complete. Ask to meet with them to review the assessment and request to be part of the team for designing the proactive strategies.

- Each school district has a teacher consultant (sometimes called an autism consultant) as well as a behavioral consultant. Find out who these people are and ask to meet with them. Get them involved and invite them to your IEP meetings. Stay a working partner with these support people.

They can be a big support when the local school personnel are struggling with meeting your child's needs.

- Work closely with the occupational therapist and speech therapist to make sure that what they are working on in direct therapy is also being taught to the classroom staff to carry over goals into the daily routine. Having these therapists work with your child a couple of times a week for 30 minutes will not do much. Ask them to incorporate what they are working on into the classroom, as objectives in the IEP. Also have these therapists teach you what they are doing so you can carry it over at home. These procedures need to be implemented throughout the day.

- The staff in the classroom need to know how to arrange the academic, social, and sensory accommodations to lessen frustration. This may include sensory strategies as needed for keeping him calm and organized, communication strategies to foster effective expression of frustration, and ways to soothe your child when he is feeling overwhelmed. If you already know what works, then teach the school staff how to best support your child. When procedures are identified to help your child feel safe, accepted, and competent, make sure they get carried over from year to year. This is where it is important to know the psychologists, social workers, and teacher consultants who can ensure continuity from year to year.

- Meet with this support team at least once every 2–3 months, if not more frequently, even when things are going well. We tend to only meet when things are going badly. You want to get things on the right track and then keep them that way. Once you develop an effective plan of action, you want to meet regularly to identify what is going right and maintain it (especially from year to year when things get forgotten and fall apart with new classes, staff, etc.).

- Demand that you are actively involved in all assessments and plan development. You know your child better than anyone. You have the legal right to be actively involved as part of the team, with nothing being developed or implemented without being reviewed by you.

- Most importantly, be a working partner with the school, supporting them as best you can. Be persistent and assertive, but supportive. Make sure to praise all positive steps teachers, aides, and professional staff do.

Fitting a square peg into a round hole!
Making changes at school

I totally understand the passion and emotion that goes with struggling with the school systems. However, this is inherent in trying to fit children into a system poorly designed for them. The very structure and nature of the school day is not designed for the fragile nervous system of many children on the spectrum. Physically, socially, academically, and emotionally, the environment is very stressful. Whether it is the sensory bombardment, forced social regulation with peers and staff, task performance demands, informational overload, or emotional regulation problems, often the child on the spectrum is in constant stress in the school environment. Even if the child is meek and non-aggressive, their nervous system is forced to shut down in order to minimize the stress.

I understand that we expect the school district to somehow modify the environment and demands, and provide supports to meet the needs of the individual child. However, that is an incredible task for a large system that is designed to meet the needs of children without a fragile nervous system. When we choose inclusion, without ensuring that all the stressful variables are well defined and easily integrated into the overall system, we run the risk of placing the children in an environment that is constantly invalidating them.

In systems analysis, all systems will resist major changes that cannot be easily assimilated into the overall model. When we are asking schools to make very individualized modifications, it requires major changes to a system that has to meet the needs of thousands of children. Massive changes to systems take time to evolve. Unfortunately, I realize that, for your child, you do not have that time to wait. However, we have to remember that we are making the decision to place the children in a setting that is often invalidating to them. I understand that, for some children, inclusion can work really well, but for many children this requires many adaptations, accommodations, and modifications that have to be individually tailored to the individual. Large systems that are designed to meet the needs of the masses cannot easily adapt to individual disabilities. When I see all schools struggle with this, it is a major systems problem, not just individual attitudes of school personnel. People go into teaching and education to help children grow and develop. If all the school districts struggle, then there are issues inherent in what we are asking the system to do.

It is a shame that these kids often have to spend half their day in a setting that can be invalidating to their self-worth. Children, regardless of abilities, need to be in a setting that validates their uniqueness and fosters a sense of competence. Except for a few children on the spectrum, this is often not the case. Because of this unnatural fit, many of the children suffer increased anxiety and depression. By the time they make it through middle school, they often start to develop strong feelings of inadequacy that follow them for years into adulthood.

I understand why some parents choose to do home schooling. But that has its drawbacks and is not an option for many families. I personally think that schools should build a few curriculum tracks that are based on different learning styles, but are integrated together in the same building. All children have access to all resources, but these are tailored to their given learning styles. This way, all children can benefit from being integrated with everyone else, while their sensory, social, and academic needs are respected and satisfied.

Current federal and state guidelines list numerous supports that schools are required to offer, but have not given user-friendly ways for schools to utilize them. Many strategies make major modifications to the current class routine or cost the schools much more money than their budgets allow for. The teacher has the job of meeting the needs of the overall group of children, while somehow having to tailor the learning to the kids with different learning styles. Again, if the changes are too big for the system to assimilate, then they will naturally resist making the changes. Administrations see what is demanded, get overwhelmed and overloaded, and go into fight-or-flight mode. We have to start where they are at and stretch slowly, while keeping everyone feeling safe, accepted, and competent.

Making the most out of OT and speech therapy!

At school, children often get very limited occupational therapy (OT) or speech therapy, and often in a group (for speech). The therapists' caseloads are very large, resulting in little one-on-one, individual time. I think people miss the boat if they think that using this precious time in direct therapy is the most effective way to provide training. You would need more than the 15 minutes of one-on-one, once every week or two, to have good results.

Children on the spectrum need frequent repetitions to make good progress. Also, the skills need to be learned in the natural setting in order to aid generalization. I recommend that you ask for the following in the IEP.

Instead of worrying about how much individual therapy the child is getting, advocate for consultation in the classroom. Ask the therapist to develop goals and objectives for the teacher and aides to implement in the classroom (e.g. answering "wh" questions: who, what, where). This way, the teaching is occurring across the day with the teachers and assistants.

In these speech and OT classroom plans, have the objectives and strategies incorporated into repeated trials throughout the day to provide frequent practice (asking "wh" questions several times a day). The therapist spends part of the allotted time training and monitoring the classroom staff, and the rest of her time testing out these objectives in one-on-one therapy.

Ask to have the therapists train you in the strategies so you can implement them at home and sample the progress from the therapy. This way, the child is learning the skills both at school and at home.

If possible, ask to observe how the teachers are implementing the strategies in the classroom and share notes. Meet with the therapists at least once every couple of months to go over progress and troubleshoot any problems.

The classroom should be taking data to measure the progress of the objectives. Periodically ask to check the data and learn how to read it. You might want to keep similar data at home. You can compare data and also share it with the therapist.

If the school is using visual (picture) strategies, you may also want to incorporate them at home. Ask the therapist for copies of the pictures that could be used at home. They may also be willing to make up additional pictures for you to use at home.

Remember, not much learning can occur in brief individual therapy, once a week. However, if the skills are practiced throughout the day in the classroom, and also possibly at home, you will see good progress. Access to occupational and speech therapy is very limited, so use the consultation model to maximize effectiveness.

Build social goals into the IEP

Schools naturally focus on building in supports for teaching academic skills. Although that is important, many children on the spectrum struggle as much, if not more, socially than they do academically. Also, it is not their lack of academic skills that makes it difficult to get a job and function independently in adult life, but their lack of social skills. From the moment the child starts school, his IEP should include at least one social goal that focuses on (1) engaging the child in "safe" social activities, (2) encouraging reciprocal, cooperative interaction skills, and (3) teaching social cognition skills (perspective taking, social problem solving, etc.). These goals should (1) parallel age-appropriate interaction skills, (2) be taught during typical peer activity through the day (recess, lunch, after-school activities, etc.), (3) be facilitated and monitored by an adult, and (4) include peer awareness/acceptance and/or peer mentoring strategies.

Although social skills can be taught via books, videos, and role play, the child still needs to have numerous safe opportunities for "learning by doing," experiential learning in the natural social setting with their peers. Except in the early grades, most socializing does not occur in the classroom. Learning opportunities are recess, lunch, locker room, hallway, informal activities, and extracurricular activities. However, these are often the times when teacher assistants are not with the child. These unstructured times during the school day are when most socializing occurs, but also when most teasing and bullying occurs. These are the prime times to teach valuable social and life skills. You want to include strategies in the IEP for taking advantage of these learning opportunities. These strategies should include (1) graded exposure that matches the comfort and skill level of the child, (2) clear objectives for facilitating reciprocal interaction (for both child and peers), and (3) close monitoring to minimize teasing and bullying.

Strategies should also be built into the plan to have the facilitator prepare your child before the events by previewing what he can expect to happen, what is expected of him, and any boundaries or social rules that may be specific to that situation. Once in the event, the facilitator should help facilitate and coach the child (and peers) through the event, and then review how it went with the child afterwards. By (1) previewing, (2) coaching, and (3) reviewing afterwards, this process increases the likelihood of success and maximizes learning.

If possible, parents and teachers should try to include at least one social integration goal in the IEP. It is better to have one well-framed activity than a bunch of unstructured, poorly guided events. My experience is that using the one event to highlight the objective and training (taking turns, sharing, initiating interaction, etc.) often gets generalized into other social opportunities during the day. Making safe social learning opportunities part of the IEP should start in the earliest grades and continue through high school. As the child progresses into middle and high school, these opportunities should expand to extracurricular activities (dances, basketball games, clubs, etc.) and include peer mentors as the coaches.

Inclusion/mainstreaming

This is one of the most heated discussions I see people get into. There are definitely both pros and cons. In theory, it is great. However, it works well only if the right resources are there to support your child. Many school districts implement the model, but know very little about autism, and do not know how to support the child, or cannot adequately fund the resources. I have seen some children blossom in inclusion, and others withdraw and regress. If the child does not feel safe, accepted, and competent in the classroom, he may withdraw and shut down, or possibly even melt down or act out. If the child doesn't feel safe and accepted, he will frequently shut down during class (may even seem fine behaviorally) and then melt down once he gets home.

I have seen inclusion do wonders when the cognitive, social, emotional, and sensory vulnerabilities are recognized and compensated for. If the classroom, academic demands, or social pressures, are too overwhelming for the child, however, inclusion can do more harm than good. I am a firm believer that any child will develop in a setting where he feels safe, accepted, and competent. If you are going to include your child, become very active in monitoring the process. Become a working partner with the teachers and aides, and help them along. It can be a very rewarding experience, but one you have to be in charge of, helping to guide the teachers and monitoring your child's progress.

School or home school? Education is not just an either/or process!

Self-contained classrooms for children with special needs or mainstream inclusion? Formal schools or home school? We tend to look at education as an all-or-nothing decision. When it comes to full days at school, it is plain that, for many children on the spectrum, it is simply too mentally and emotionally draining for their nervous system to handle. If you have followed the series of posts on cognitive issues in autism, we discussed how the brains of people on the spectrum have difficulty processing multiple information simultaneously. Essentially, this means that 80 percent of what the NT child processes subconsciously, with minimal mental energy, children on the spectrum have to process consciously (think it though), which is mentally draining. Everything about school—sensory bombardment, task performance demands, and ongoing social/interaction requirements—is very overwhelming for many on the spectrum. Their brains often become taxed and overloaded, requiring them to shut down in order to avoid overload. A child cannot learn in shutdown mode!

What to do? Is home school alone the answer? For some, yes, it has worked out really well. However, for many families this is not an option. It requires parents to stay home, have the ability and learn to teach, and have the money and connections to pull it off. The nice thing about home schooling is that the teacher (parent) is very committed and can tailor all teaching to the strengths, preferences, and learning style of the child. Many argue that it limits social learning since the child is not in a class. My advice to all who home school is to join a home schooling group. They get together on a regular basis for social activities, community outings, and field trips. You can tailor play dates and group activities to match the child. The child gets the "just right" dose of social stimulation because the parent can control it. You can set up and facilitate social activities tailored to the objectives for your child. This is the ultimate for many children who find regular school simply too demanding and overwhelming. However, this is not an option for the majority of parents in our current society.

What other options are there? It doesn't have to be an either/or question (regular school or home school). For most, the best option may be a little of both. Many children can handle part-time school (2–3 hours a day), especially for courses that they like and can handle. The children can avoid being overwhelmed by the cafeteria, gym, change of classes, assemblies, or other events that overwhelm them. Also, for short durations, school can be mediated with peer mentors who can help include the child in the school activities, facilitate social interaction, and protect from bullying. Outside the classroom, the child can utilize online classes. Online classes are an awesome alternative for children on the spectrum. They can learn in the comfort of their safe home, in their own time, and at their own speed. Part-time also allows the child to learn many of the skills in his natural settings (home, shopping, banking, etc.), rather than the artificial setting of the classroom. Between home school groups and curriculums, online classes, and part-time school, you can design a mix that matches your child's learning style and processing abilities. Learning can be fun, and the child can feel safe, accepted, and competent in learning!

Navigating the IEP meeting!

The day has come and you arrive at school for your child's IEP (Individualized Education Program) meeting. If it is the child's initial IEP, then you will probably be totally clueless about what to expect or what your role is. If this is not your first, but one of many, you may be more seasoned, but still intimidated about how to advocate for your child. Either way, you need to prepare yourself and know what you are entitled to and how to go about getting it. The following are some suggestions for making the most of your IEP meetings.

Prepare ahead of time. Ask in writing to obtain copies of all the multidisciplinary evaluation team (MET) assessments, so you can review them ahead of time. These may include psychological, occupational therapy, and speech and language assessments. Once you review them, if you have questions (which you should), request a meeting with the professional to clarify information and recommendations, and answer any questions you may have. Do not go to the meeting without first reviewing these assessments.

In addition to the MET assessments, ask in writing to obtain a copy of the Present Level of Academic Achievement and Functional Performance (PLAAFP) assessment. This assessment includes information on the child's current performance (skill level) in all areas of education. The PLAAFP provides current performance levels in each area of deficits and academic achievement. From this assessment, goals and objectives are derived, as well as special accommodations and supports. Review this document ahead of time, ask questions, and talk to key figures in assessing your child.

Review your school district's IEP form before the meeting. Get a blank copy and review the outline, make notes, and ask questions. They will usually follow this outline during the meeting. Make sure each area is covered and that you have jotted down any suggestions you made for each area. Don't let them gloss over any areas. Many schools come with a draft IEP already written. Be prepared for this. When requesting the assessments (in writing), also request to review the "draft IEP." If the school does not supply you with either the assessments or drafts, and in turn comes into the meeting with either of them, ask to reschedule the meeting until you can review the documents. There should be no documents that you haven't reviewed ahead of time. In all fairness, only do this if you had first requested in writing to obtain copies. Do not let them slide something by you or pressure you to complete the meeting due to time constraints.

With your teacher and professionals as assigned, review the progress toward last year's goals and objectives. In reality, you should be aware of these goals and be monitoring the progress regularly throughout the year. Ask to see how the progress is measured and how much progress your child made. If there is no apparent progress, question why it would be continued or make revisions to increase likelihood of progress.

To summarize, before you walk into the meeting you should have reviewed all MET assessments, the PLAAFP assessment, the IEP format, and the draft IEP. Review all the areas of assessment, current goals and objectives, and your child's progress. Also, obtain a summary list of common accommodations and modifications which your child may be entitled to. If you have access to an advocate or a more experienced parent who knows the system well, ask to review these documents with them for clarity and suggestions.

You have the right to invite whomever you wish to attend the meeting. I would strongly suggest that if your child has a para-pro (assistant) working with him, demand that person be at the meeting. He or she is the most important person in your child's day-to-day adjustment to school. He or she knows more about your child than most everyone else at the table. Also, make sure all the supporting disciplines will be there (not on vacation).

I highly recommend that you bring someone with you, either a formal advocate or experienced parent who knows how to navigate these meetings. Not only can they help you advocate, but they also will be an objective observer. You will be filled with a variety of emotions, miss a lot, forget or misinterpret what is said. Have them take notes. You also have the right to tape-record the meeting if you choose. Be careful in relying on the teacher consultant as the advocate at the meeting. This person is usually an employee of the school district and will feel pressured not to say certain things or push for certain supports.

If at any time during the meeting you feel confused, request to take a break, talk to someone individually, or reschedule the meeting until further information is provided. Parents often feel pressured, confused, and intimidated during the meeting. Slow things down, ask a lot of questions, get clarification, and reschedule if needed.

Go in knowing what you want, which modifications and accommodations you are requesting. Be prepared that these supports have to directly relate to the individual goals. It is the goals that drive the accommodations and supports.

Ask how each goal and objective will be measured so you can question the validity of how progress will be measured. Request to have periodic review meetings with the team (at least once every couple of months) to evaluate progress toward these goals. If progress is not being made, then request changes in either the objectives or teaching strategies to increase the likelihood of progress. Do not let them continue with goals that are showing no progress.

For each goal and objective, question the functionality of the goal (skill), how it is being measured, and what strategies will be used to teach it. Know your child's learning style and question any strategies that do not match that.

Complete the Comfort Zones Profile or other learning profile sheets to summarize at the meeting what your child's strengths and challenges are, and what accommodations and learning strategies best support your child. Build these strategies into the IEP to ensure others use them. You want the IEP to include all that is needed to maximize that your child feels safe, accepted, and competent at school.

Before the meeting ends, make sure all agreements are written into the IEP. The school is not accountable for anything that is verbally agreed upon, only that which is in writing. Don't let them get by with saying they will build them in later, or as needed. Also, don't let them say that "we provide this as normal routine." Get it in writing!

Most importantly, be firm and assertive, but avoid being aggressive! Don't back down, but stay calm and supportive. You want to be a working partner with the school and maintain a working relationship with them. If everyone is on the defensive, nothing seems to work well. Just because you get it written into the IEP doesn't mean that it will happen, or be effective even if you get it. Collaboration is the best tool to use to gain the most effective implementation of the IEP!

What to ask for in an IEP

It can be really challenging knowing what to ask for at the IEP meeting. There are many articles and books written that explain the legal aspects of the IEP, responsibilities of all parties, federal standards and regulations, and so on. It can get very confusing and overwhelming. You hear words such as accommodations, modifications, strategies, and supports thrown around with little awareness of what they mean.

To keep it simple and to the point, as a parent you want your child to feel safe, accepted, and competent at school. You want the academic, physical, social, and emotional demands of the school day to match what your child can handle. Unless your child feels safe and accepted, he will have a difficult time learning. Ask yourself (and your child): What is difficult for your child? What areas (sensory, academic, social, transitions, riding the bus, lunch, gym, bullying, etc.) is he struggling with? Is the work too hard or too much? Does he have too much homework to handle? Is he overwhelmed by the physical, social, or sensory demands in gym or during lunch/recess? Does he not feel safe when transitioning in the halls between classes? Does he get distracted when sitting at the back of the room or by a window? Does he feel safe and accepted by the teachers, aides, and peers? Does he need breaks to escape and regroup, or a sensory diet to stay calm, alert, and regulated? Does he need the work broken down, presented visually, or instructions read to him to make the tasks easier? I tend to look at five main areas when categorizing supports that may be needed in helping the child to be successful at school.

Physical/sensory

Does your child have physical or sensory challenges that may need accommodating for in the classroom or other areas of the school? Does where he sits in the classroom affect his ability to focus (front of classroom, near or away from a window or doorway, etc.)? Does he need special adaptations or accommodations for lighting and noise that may overwhelm him? Does he need a cushion on his seat, because he cannot tolerate the hard surfaces? Does he need a sensory diet to keep him calm and alert? He may need sensory breaks throughout the day to escape and rebound from the demands of the classroom. Does your child have any physical disabilities that will need to be accommodated for in order to be successful at school? Does your child struggle with fine or gross motor skills, and need direct therapy to help with that? Usually, the occupational therapist can be a big help in evaluating and providing recommendations in these areas.

Social

This is often a major area for children on the spectrum. What accommodations need to be in place for your child to feel safe and accepted by those around him, both teachers/staff and other students? Usually, I break these down into four categories: (1) disclosure and awareness training, (2) supervision, (3) facilitation, and (4) mentoring/skill teaching. How much are you going to disclose about your child's vulnerabilities, and how should awareness training for staff and peers be done so that they understand your child? What type of supervision, and how much, is going to be needed to keep your child socially feeling safe and accepted at school (especially during the unstructured times of lunch, recess, locker room, hallways, etc.)? Does your child need to be supervised and assisted during these times, possibly leave class a little early when transitioning between classes? Does he need supervision to protect him from being teased or bullied? Next, what strategies and supports will be used to help facilitate cooperative interaction with peers? What social skills will need to be taught so your child can adequately regulate in these social interactions? Are there peer mentors who can help supervise, support, and coach your child socially during the day? Are there formal social skills groups that your child can join? Usually, the social worker or speech and language therapist can be of help in this area.

Communication

Is your child struggling to communicate his wants and needs, or communicate what he knows? Does he need augmented communication (pictures, sign, electronic communication device, iPad, laptop, etc.) to effectively communicate what he knows and needs? Does he need direct speech and language therapy to develop more effective communication, and how will that be integrated into the school? Does he need visual supports to understand and expressively communicate? The speech and language pathologist is the person to assess and make recommendations in these areas.

Scheduling/organizing

Most children on the spectrum have problems organizing themselves and function much better with a predictable structure. Visual schedules, picture sequence boards, color-coded organizers, and so on can be a great help for many on the spectrum. Calendars for events, check-off lists, homework reminders, appointment books, and color-coded course separators can be useful in helping the child organize. These systems help the child transition and navigate the events and demands of the day. When the child is having trouble transitioning between activities and classes, remembering to turn in, or bring home, his homework, or keeping his work organized, these strategies will help significantly.

Emotionally/behaviorally

Is your child displaying high anxiety, depression, opposition, or behavior challenges at school? What are his major stressors and/or the triggers causing the difficulties? What coping skills does he need to emotionally cope with the demands that are challenging him? What behavior skills does he need to learn to better communicate and cope with his stressors? What supports need to be in place to reduce the anxiety, teach him to communicate his needs better, and cope emotionally? If he is exhibiting ongoing challenging behaviors, then you want to request, in writing, a functional behavior assessment to create a positive behavior support plan to address these challenges. Although the actual behavior support plan is often only an addendum to the IEP, make sure it is listed in the IEP that such a plan will be developed.

Academic

What challenges does your child have with learning and expressing what he has learned? Is the work too hard, or too much, or does he need more time to get it down? Accommodations can include how the material is broken down and presented, and also how your child can best express what he has learned. Does he need to present what he knows orally, instead of in writing? Does he need to type it out instead of writing it out? Does he need instructions given orally, or the material previewed ahead of time to help him organize what he is learning? Does he need more time to take tests, and does he need to be taken to a quieter area to take them in? What accommodations need to be made for homework?

Does your child need a para-pro to assist and support him through the material and tasks? There are a host of accommodations and modifications that can help in this area. If your child is struggling with the course work, ask how they plan to support him. What strategies will they use?

There are numerous types of accommodations that can be built into the IEP. You most likely will not know all the supports that could be provided. That is OK! However, make a list of the different challenges (sensory, social, communicative, academic, organization, emotional/behavioral, etc.) that your child is experiencing and use those to discuss what strategies will be put in place to support and assist the child with these challenges. You don't have to have all the answers (know what supports) going in, but don't leave the meeting without them! If there is not enough time, schedule another meeting! Next, make sure there is a goal in the IEP to address each one of these challenges and supporting strategies. If it is not listed under a goal, it may well never occur. So, if your child has challenges with sensory issues, task assignments, social concerns, and behavior, make sure there is a goal to address each area. List out the strategies in the IEP. Get it in writing! If you go prepared, then you will feel more successful when you leave! Lastly, it is often best to develop a core team including a social worker, occupational therapist, speech and language therapist, behavior specialist, and special education coordinator, to help assess the areas of challenges and design the goals and strategies for supporting these concerns. That way, you can periodically meet with them individually to assess and measure progress. The teacher will not have the time, and often the knowledge, to assess and develop all the strategies that may be needed to help your child feel safe, accepted, and competent!

Beyond the IEP meeting

The child's IEP (Individualized Education Program) plan is an ongoing process throughout the year. The goals, objectives, accommodations, and supports need to be implemented, measured, and evaluated as the year goes on. The parents' role should not stop at the meeting. You are a member of the IEP team and have the right to meet periodically with individual team members and/or have periodic progress review meetings with the team. The following suggestions can help frame an outline for supporting the plan over the course of the year.

Keep a copy of the plan and know the goals, objectives, and teaching strategies. As often as possible, stop by the school and ask how it is going. Stop by the classroom and stay connected with the teacher. Keep the teacher notified of any concerns you have with your child, what challenges he is having, health issues, homework concerns, and so on. Also ask about the goals and objectives, and what help you can provide. If you cannot visit the school, many schools give you email access to the staff.

If possible, be a classroom volunteer, either in the classroom itself or periodically for field trips and special events. Help with decorations or baking items for holiday events. Be visible as often as possible. This way, you can keep a positive relationship going with the teacher, as well as keep an eye on how your child is doing.

As much as possible, focus on the positive. Draw attention to what is going right or well. Look for positive things to praise the teacher and staff. If the teacher, assistants, and professionals are doing a good job, write a letter of appreciation to the principal. Don't just complain when things are not going well. If you focus on the positive and stay supportive, the school will be less defensive when you have concerns.

Every couple of months, ask to sit down with the team or individual team members to discuss your child's progress. Each goal and objective will have concrete data to measure how the child is doing. Ask to see the data and discuss the progress with each individual team member. I find that individual contact is the best, unless there are very strong issues that need formal meetings. If you want to have formal review meetings, make sure you get that written into the IEP. If your child is not progressing with a given objective, help the staff brainstorm what changes could be made to increase the likelihood of progress. If needed, change the goal and objectives, break things down a little more, or move on to another goal.

If changes come up, the IEP can be addended at any time. If there is a change of status, new goals need to be developed, or new supports put in place, the IEP can be addended at any time. The addendum can be made without a formal meeting, or, if needed, the school or parents can request another IEP meeting. If there is a major change of status, new assessments can be requested. Place the requests in writing.

When there is difficulty identifying learning strategies, or behavior issues crop up, ask for the teacher consultant (TC) to do an evaluation to give suggestions to the staff. Usually, the school district will have a school consultant who has a good understanding of disabilities and can work with the staff to design successful strategies. Once the assessment is completed, ask to have a meeting with the consultant and the team to discuss the recommendations.

If, at any time, the school is uncooperative, you can file a formal appeal to the school district and your state's department of education. I prefer to take this step only when everything else has failed. Make sure you keep copies of all your written requests and their responses in writing. If you submit your request in writing, request an answer in writing. You want to keep a paper trial of all contact. When filing a formal appeal, make sure you know specifically what you are asking for and what the school is not providing.

Remember, as the year moves on, you are an active member of the IEP team. Take that responsibility seriously and be sure to monitor closely and be a working partner with the school. However, stay persistent in what your child needs and what the school agreed. Stay supportive, but persistent!

Chapter 10

EMPOWERMENT

Does your child understand his autism?
Self-awareness equals empowerment!

It is very important that children on the spectrum learn to understand what autism or Asperger's is, and how it affects them—both its strengths and challenges. It is important that they learn how they are different from others, not only in terms of how *they* experience the world, but also how *we* experience the world. Life will always be a struggle for them, since the world is based on how we process information, and does not match how they experience the world. Learning about their differences from us allows them to better adapt and advocate for themselves.

For most people on the spectrum, daily living is a constant struggle, since they are always trying to navigate a world that is not a good match for them. This struggle can be handled more effectively if the person begins to understand how their differences impact these challenges. Learning about their differences is twofold. First, they have to understand how they process information and, second, they have to understand how we process information, so they can understand the differences. This allows them to understand why the world is often confusing and allows them to better adapt to it. From this awareness, they can learn to maximize their strengths and compensate for their differences.

I usually break these differences down into sensory, cognitive, social, and emotional differences. Once people on the spectrum begin to understand how we are different, their challenges start making sense to them. From there, they can make accommodations to minimize the daily challenges they face, develop coping strategies to face stressors they cannot avoid, and learn to regulate their nervous system so they do not get overwhelmed. They can identify what physical, social, and emotional challenges tax their nervous system so they can build in accommodations to avoid and/or modify these conditions to lessen the negative effect. They can learn how to adapt to the work setting, navigate around social issues, independently follow their daily routine, and build a home environment that allows them to escape the confusing world, regroup, and rebound for the next day. They can do an analysis of each daily setting/event (work, school, family, recreation, etc.) to identify possible challenges/stressors, and then build in modifications, adaptations, and accommodations to minimize these challenges and maximize their independence and emotional wellbeing. They learn how many of their strengths can be used to maximize their success, and how to build on their preferences to improve quality of life. So, as early as possible but definitely in the teen years, try to build on the importance of the child learning about his differences and how to identify and design strategies for maximizing his ability to adapt to the settings he is in.

It is very important that we focus on strength-based parenting and teaching. Once the person learns what his sensory, processing, emotional, and social needs are, he has to embrace these needs and find ways to support and protect these needs, learning how to modify, accommodate, and adapt his environment and daily routine to meet these needs. It is important that the person doesn't feel the need to "fix" or "change" what his needs are, but to use his strengths to better meet those needs.

At what age should you start? The earlier the better! My experience is usually around eight or nine, if they seem to notice differences. You want to catch them as they are first noticing differences, before they start setting up defenses that are hard to break down. Often by the time the children are 13, if this hasn't been discussed, they have built in defense mechanisms that deny and refuse to recognize it. Focus on discussing all aspects of the child, his strengths and weaknesses, interests and personality traits, with autism just being one small area of it. In reality, it is good to have this type of discussion with all kids. We all need to be able to have strong self-awareness, know what our strengths and weaknesses are, and how to develop our strengths to help support any weaknesses.

Don't let them tell you "he can't"!

At one time it was thought that 90 percent of people with autism were intellectually impaired. Over the years, we have realized that typical intelligence testing cannot accurately reflect the intelligence behind the ASD symptoms. Many people who have been labeled as "low functioning" have surprised the world with unique abilities and risen to much greater heights than were anticipated. We still seem to equate the lack of verbal skills with poor intelligence and very limited abilities. Unfortunately, the label renders us having lower expectations and providing fewer opportunities for growth. Consequently, the child has reduced chances for development.

We do not know how intellectual a child on the spectrum truly is as long as he experiences significant sensory and communication challenges. If we listen to the child's needs, his current method of communication, and foster his strengths and preferences, the child can grow and develop past these limitations. Assume the child has the ability, even without the current skill. Understand his learning style, how he relates and communicates, accommodate for his sensory vulnerabilities, and use his interests as motivation. And most importantly, keep your goals high, but your short-term objectives realistic. Don't say "he can't and he never will"; say "he doesn't now, but can learn with support." Give him the same opportunities as every child; just frame them for success and provide the accommodations and guidance needed to support him.

There are several people on the Autism Discussion Page who were considered severely impaired, who have risen to great accomplishments (managing technological teams, teaching, getting married and having children, becoming an autism speaker and advocate, working on doctorate degrees, etc.), and who still have severe autism traits, but are fully functioning independent adults. I salute them. Given the barriers they face, and the pain and struggles they have experienced, they have the strength to show us all how people can rise past the diagnosis and limited expectations!

Do not let professional testing lower your expectations. If the child is not learning, change the way you are teaching. Do not assume the child cannot learn; assume we need to teach differently. Do not exclude a child from participating in an activity due to limited skills. Let him participate while providing the supports necessary for him to succeed. Give him the same opportunities as any child. Our limited expectations hold these children back more than their disabilities do. Let them taste the opportunities to grow their skills. Support them, do not exclude them. Make it happen, but keep it safe and supportive! Facilitate, rather than isolate. We need to learn from them as much as we need to teach them.

If you want them to communicate, give them a "voice"!

For many kids on the spectrum, communication presents many challenges. Whether it is difficulty formulating what to say, how to say it, or feeling safe saying it, trying to communicate an idea, feeling, need, or experience can be challenging and frustrating. First identifying the right words and then producing these words in structural content so others understand them can be exhausting. Even for those who have verbal speech, the anxiety of expressing themselves socially can be overwhelming.

In the early years, communication starts off very instrumentally. Children communicate that they want something or protest that they don't like something. For many children on the spectrum, because the world is very chaotic, confusing, and scary for them, much of their first communication is to escape and avoid situations that overwhelm them. In the professional sector, this is called "protesting." However, their first method of protest is usually behavioral (hollering, throwing things, hitting, kicking, biting self, etc.), rather than using words. Because we often try to punish and suppress such behavior, we often ignore the protesting, invalidating the intent of their communication. We often ignore or punish their communication intent, further frustrating their beginning attempts to communicate. Even as they get older and establish spoken words, we often do not listen to them. Since we want them to do certain things, stop doing other things, and behave in certain ways, we often ignore or suppress their attempts to communicate their position, especially if it is not what we want to hear. We want them to talk and communicate, but often do not give them a voice.

Since we want the children to learn to communicate, we need to give them a voice! Whether it be through spoken words, gestures, manual signing, written words, vocal noises, pictures, or other behavioral actions, we need to allow the children to express what they want, don't want, feel safe with, and feel comfortable doing. We need to give them a voice, no matter how complex or refined the method of communication happens to be (gestures, sounds, facial expressions, behavior, etc.). We have to establish (1) communication intent and (2) safety and acceptance in expressing oneself, before the child will be motivated to learn more complex forms of communication. At a very early age, I recommend that we start doing the following:

1. From the earliest years, listen to the child's behavior and assign communication intent to it. Whether the child turns and looks at something, picks something up, throws something, makes cooing vocal noises, or screams, assume intent to communicate and assign meaning to it. For example, when Sally reaches for an object, assume intent to communicate; say, "Sally wants ____" and immediately give it to her. If Johnny pulls away and hollers when you present something, say, "Johnny doesn't like ____" and withdraw it. Assign intent to any communication the child gives. In turn, verbally state this implied intent to the child, so he begins to connect that his actions have an effect on changing the behavior of others. At first the child may not be attempting to communicate. However, if we assign meaning and intent to it, the child learns the cause-and-effect connection from his actions having impact on his environment. This will both establish the meaning of intent and increase motivation to communicate.

2. Find the best method for your child to communicate. Although we all want our children to speak, speech may not be the first and best method of communicating at this time. Use a "total communication" approach, employing a variety of methods (vocal noises, gestures, pictures, etc.) to establish communication. Many parents worry that using augmentative methods of communicating will inhibit their child's use of speech. This is not true. Establishing communication in any form will increase the likelihood of speaking, if that modality is something they are capable of. All children first learn to communicate with vocal noises, gestures, and facial expressions before learning to talk.

3. Give the child a "voice" in everything. Ask his opinion or what his preferences are. Give him simple choices (between what to eat, what

to wear, what to do first, etc.). If he does not respond, take a guess and watch his reaction ("I bet Sammy would like the juice!"). Take whatever his response tends to be (reach, vocal noise, turning away, etc.) as communication, and reply back how you interpret it. Ask him his opinion, give him choices, and pause to give him a chance to respond. Once he responds, reply with how you interpret it. This will establish the connection of your response to his action.

4. Understand and respect the child's "protest." If he doesn't like something or something scares/overwhelms him, first acknowledge that you understand and validate that he is scared or doesn't want something. This is important for the child to feel safe expressing his needs. If possible, withdraw the demand, modify it to meet his needs, or provide extra support to help the child through it. With the adult acknowledging and validating the protest, then withdrawing or modifying the demand or providing greater support, the child is learning that his opinion is (1) important, (2) listened to, and (3) has a positive effect in assisting him.

5. In addition, when your child is expressing emotion (happy, sad, angry, scared, etc.), label the feeling that you see and connect it to what is causing it: "Johnny, you look angry because you cannot have the toy." This way, the child begins to connect his emotion to the event and realizes that you read his response as communication (which can help him deal with it). It connects the emotion to the event, and then his communication to your action.

6. Lastly, "nothing for the child, without the child." Give him a voice in everything happening to him. Regardless of what that voice is (verbal or nonverbal), listen to it, acknowledge it, and respect it. This does not mean that you have to give in to all the child's demands. Just make sure you (1) give him a chance to voice his opinion, (2) acknowledge and validate his feelings, and (3) try to modify, adapt, or provide greater assistance to make it better. When we listen, the children will feel safe to express themselves, and develop better communication skills.

Once you have established the above conditions, make sure to advocate the child's right to a voice in all settings that he is engaged in (e.g. school). Advocate for your child to have a voice and to use his voice!

Teach the words "no" and "help"!

(Although this post references self-injurious behavior, it also applies for all acting-out behavior including aggression and property disruption. It is included here because teaching the words "no" and "help" are very important for promoting empowerment.)

I have worked with many children who exhibit severe self-injurious behavior, usually in the forms of hitting or slapping themselves, head banging, or biting themselves. Self-injurious behavior is often an attempt to escape or avoid a situation that is unpleasant for them. It can also be a response to pain or discomfort. Self-abuse, as well as other forms of acting out (aggression, property destruction, etc.), is often the result of adults placing children in situations that overwhelm them. Often the children do not know how to communicate the need to escape, or people are not listening to them. They become overwhelmed, panic, and fight or flight sets in. This intense behavior often reduces once the children develop speech or other forms of communication. Once the children can communicate their needs and wants, and can effectively protest, then acting-out behavior often lessens. Unfortunately, for many children we often do not listen to them or respect what they are telling us. If they are not allowed to protest, then acting out will occur.

Much self-injurious behavior and other forms of acting out can be reduced by (1) understanding the child's sensitivities and comfort zones, and (2) respecting these comfort zones. Often the child is not just being oppositional, but may be in "panic" due to sensory overload. The child may be refusing the broccoli because the texture, taste, or smell may be too overwhelming for him. Once the brain goes into panic mode, there is nothing you can do to change it. The same can be true for placing the child in situations of uncertainty. Uncertainty can set off extreme anxiety panic. In addition, these extreme reactions can also occur when the expectations or demands are much greater than the child's ability to cope with them. Task performance anxiety can cause a lot of self-injurious behavior. Finally, trying to force children into situations where they do not feel safe will trigger extreme behavioral reactions.

Children with autism are often pressured into situations that are overwhelming for them. Frequently, they do not know how to communicate their distress, or we ignore their protest and try to force compliance. All of these situations mentioned above are usually due to adults pressuring the child into situations that overwhelm them. That is why we must identify their "comfort zones" (see Comfort Zones Profile, Appendix B) and make sure the adults in their lives respect these comfort zones. Identify the vulnerabilities and their safe zones, and stay within these comfort zones as you slowly stretch them. As parents, one of your primary responsibilities is assuring that adults in your child's life have a good understanding of the child's sensitivities and comfort zones. Until the child becomes old enough to advocate for himself, we need to be his voice.

Teaching the child a way to communicate his needs and wants is a must for reducing self-injurious behavior. Even if the child is nonverbal, teach him to use gestures, sign language, or pictures to communicate what he wants and to protest what he does not want. Once he is capable of basic communication, teach the child to say "no" and "help." To help empower your child to escape overwhelming demands, teach him to say "no" and "help." This way, he can protest and escape overwhelming demands, or ask for help. Many children are afraid to ask for help, so it needs to be encouraged and reinforced.

In addition, we also need to respect the child's protests in whatever way he can communicate them. We often either ignore his pleas, or treat him as noncompliant and force compliance. The child feels either incapable or scared to protest, and releases his stress by harming himself. Unfortunately, when his acceptable protest is ignored or denied, his self-abuse allows him to successfully escape the demands. Since it is often severe, we back off from the demands. Consequently, self-abuse is reinforced, while protesting appropriately is denied. We need to make sure each child knows how to communicate "no" and "help" so that he can either escape the situation or seek assistance in dealing with it. From there, we need to make sure people respect and honor the protests. So ask yourself: (1) do I know what my child's vulnerabilities and comfort zones are, and (2) does my child have a way of consistently communicating "no" and "help"? From there, advocate that everyone knows and respects the child's comfort zones, and honors his protests and requests for help. These are the two primary means of respecting and validating the child's need to feel safe, accepted, and competent.

Teaching children to advocate for themselves at school!

Many parents try to teach their children to "speak up" when they are stressed at school, and to advocate for what they need. Often parents will talk to their children at home about what to do, but the children don't speak up when at school. I find that, on their own, the kids will typically not speak up unless it is facilitated by school staff. There are six primary reasons why they do not speak up for themselves:

1. The social anxiety of initiating the interaction.

2. The fear of not knowing how the teacher is going to react.

3. Not wanting to bring attention to themselves.

4. The inability to feel and recognize the stress build-up in their nervous system.

5. The poor ability to remember (working memory) what they are supposed to say in the heat of the moment.

6. The weak executive functioning skills of organizing what to say and then to initiate saying it.

To help reduce all these problems, work with the school to identify the events that cause the stress, then work on a plan to (1) make a written or picture list of these stressors (so the child has a visual in front of him) and what accommodations he should ask for at these times of stress, (2) have the teachers cue him in at those times when he appears stressed (because he may not notice it), and then (3) help him speak up for what he is feeling and say what he needs. Between using the written list of events and what accommodations to ask for, and having the teachers cue and support him to use it, he begins to (1) recognize the events that are stressful, (2) identify and label when he is feeling stressed, and then (3) advocate for himself to reduce the stress.

Usually, the child is going to need support in implementing the above during the time the stress is occurring, until it becomes a routine behavior for him.

Teaching self-advocacy! Promoting "voice" and "choice"!

Many parents fight hard for accommodations and supports while their children are in grade school. Then, once out of school, parents arrive at the rude awakening that their advocacy has less impact. Once an adult, the person on the spectrum is expected to advocate for himself. Whether entering the workforce, college, or vocational schools, young adults on the spectrum are expected to advocate for their own needs. The two main differences in the adult world are (1) the person is not entitled (by government standards) to automatically have these institutions (work, college, government services, etc.) seek them out and provide needed services, and (2) they are expected to be their own voice and advocate for their own needs (instead of their parents). The service providers will listen and talk to the young adult himself not his parents. Unless preparation ahead of time is done, this can be a very rude awakening for both the parents and the young adult.

Self-advocacy skills do not come overnight or simply arrive at the child's 18th birthday. It takes time to develop and foster the skills needed for advocating for your own needs. Since early childhood, parents have been the protector and strong voice for the child, and have made all the important choices and decisions. However, it is so very important that parents and teachers learn to transfer these skills to the child as he grows through his teen years and into adulthood.

How do you do this? Not only is it scary for the parents who have grown used to feeling more secure making these decisions for the child, but also the child becomes dependent on relying on the parents making the choice and being the voice. First, we must take a look at what self-advocacy skills consist of. There are many skills, but several fundamental ones include the following:

- Before you can advocate for your own needs, you have to have an awareness of what those needs are! People on the spectrum need to have a good awareness of what their vulnerabilities are. These include sensory vulnerabilities, emotional regulation difficulties, cognitive processing problems, social weaknesses, and communication issues. Often parents become very competent in identifying these issues, but never teach the child to be aware of his own vulnerabilities.

- Not only does the person need self-awareness of his own vulnerabilities, but he also needs to recognize (1) what environmental conditions cause problems for these vulnerabilities and (2) what accommodations are needed to lessen their negative impact and allow him to cope with the challenges. He needs to be aware of what situations cause him the most challenges, and learn how to recognize them. From there, he can learn what to avoid, how to compensate, and how to advocate for what he needs.

- Next, the person needs to have a keen awareness of what his strengths are, so he can use them to compensate for the vulnerabilities that he has. He also needs to use these strengths to develop social, leisure, and vocational skills. We all have strengths and weaknesses. The person needs to learn how to make the most of his strengths and gravitate to areas that showcase them.

- Lastly, the person needs to know how to communicate these needs to others effectively, ask for the accommodations that he needs, disclose his disability (if he chooses to), and negotiate inevitable social conflicts that will arrive.

How do we teach these skills? When do we start the teaching? This should start as early as possible, even in early childhood.

1. As parents begin identifying and defining these vulnerabilities (sensory, emotional, cognitive, social, etc.), they need talk to their child about them. It doesn't matter if the child is verbal or not; he can understand if you keep it simple. Be his "inner voice." Describe what you see him experiencing, especially his emotions: "Billy is sad." Next, connect it to the event that causes it: "Billy is sad because daddy is going to work." Keep it simple and as literal as possible. This will help the child begin to label his feelings, connect them to events, and learn to regulate his emotions.

2. In addition to labeling and connecting what the child is thinking and feeling, also verbally describe what you are thinking and feeling and what you see others thinking and feeling, again connecting these thoughts and feelings to specific events. This running dialog helps give the child an

awareness of the thoughts, feelings, and perspectives of those around him, and how they may be different from his own.

3. As you accommodate for the child's vulnerabilities, talk to him about what you are doing. This could consist of (1) modifying the environment ("I am turning the light down because it may hurt your eyes"), (2) adapting to the environment when it cannot be modified ("Let's wear sunglasses, because the sun is bright and hurts the eyes"), and (3) coping strategies for when overload occurs ("If the noise becomes too loud, tell mommy 'go' and we will leave"). This way, the child is learning to recognize his vulnerabilities and connecting them with making needed accommodations.

4. Next, you have to listen to your child and give him a "voice" in what he thinks, feels, wants, and needs. He has to learn how to communicate his needs and wants, and we have to learn how to listen. Whether he communicates with spoken words, pictures, signs, gestures, facial expressions, or typed words, we need to give him a voice. In addition, once he has a voice, we need to listen to him, and respect his voice. This can be hard to do, but must start as early as possible. Start by giving him simple choices in his daily routine. Give choices between two snacks to eat, two shirts to wear, two toys to play with. Start with just two items and gradually move up. Before jumping in and deciding for the child, let him participate and voice his opinion. Nothing for the child, without the child!

5. Throughout the years, teach your child to negotiate and collaborate, first with you and then with others. Teach him to (1) communicate his concerns, (2) listen to the other's concerns, and then (3) collaborate and compromise to meet both needs. This is hard for us, because it means taking time to collaborate and also compromising our position. However, this is a necessary skill to learn. Start early and start simple—first with you (where errors can be tolerated) and then with others.

6. Then, finally, teach him to how to problem-solve. Similar to negotiating and collaborating, teach the child to (1) label what the problem is, (2) identify several options for solving the problem, (3) assess the pros and cons of options, (4) pick and try out an option, then (5) evaluate the effectiveness of the choice. Of course, this will have to start with the parent coaching the child through the steps, and also thinking out loud for simple decisions that the parent typically makes throughout the day. Include the child in these simple decisions and mentor the decision-making process. As the child becomes older, teach him to use a problem-solving worksheet, with the above steps on it, to list and use the steps.

These skills must be fostered throughout childhood. Once the child is in school, include him in assessing the classroom setting needs and academic and social accommodations, and describe and connect all accommodations to the given vulnerabilities: what and why! Have the teacher help coach him in voicing his needs as they arise throughout the day. The teacher needs to teach and coach him when and how to ask for help, say "no," and when he needs a break. As he gets older, he should know each of the accommodations in his IEP and how to ask for them if people forget. In addition, as he starts into middle school, give him more and more of a voice in the IEP process itself. By the time he is in his last couple of years in school, he should be the main voice at his own IEP meeting. Self-advocacy skills should be of prime importance in the high school years. Parents need to push for this, but teachers need to be the mentors (prompting and coaching the child).

Empowering teens and adults

Understanding the four challenges to quality living!

As teens begin to reach adulthood, it is vital for them to understand and advocate for their own needs. The ability to do so will be determined more by their cognitive abilities than by the severity of their autism. However, regardless of the cognitive skills, most on the spectrum share these four core challenges that they must understand and learn to cope with. Speaking directly to older teens and young adults, these four issues will be presented by discussing the challenges, how to accommodate, and how to advocate for your needs.

1. Sensory processing issues

CHALLENGES!

Since sensory sensitivities to light, noise, touch, and smells can bombard and overwhelm the nervous system, you have to become keenly aware of and learn how to accommodate for your sensory sensitivities. Nothing sets off the panic fight-or-flight response more than sensory overload. The neurotypical (NT) world is filled with blinding artificial lights, overwhelming noise from motors, blaring ads, horns, alarms, and vacuums, noxious chemical smells, and irritating fabric textures. Whereas NT people can filter out and tone down these stimulations, your nervous system takes a direct hit, becomes overwhelmed, and breaks down quickly.

ACCOMMODATE!

You must understand what your sensitivities are, how to avoid them, or modify your immediate environment to lessen their impact. You have to be able to appraise new environments for the sensory threats that are inherent. If you can tone down the stimulation (modify the lighting, sounds, smells, and visual "noise") and/or learn coping strategies for masking them (e.g. wear brim hat, shaded glasses, ear plugs, face desk toward the window for natural lighting, use partitions to block out light and distracting activity, etc.), you can learn to make adult living more tolerable. You also need to know how much you can handle and when to back away and give your nervous system a break. Modifying the environment, masking what cannot be modified, using simple strategies for coping with sensory bombardment, and giving yourself frequent breaks are the pillars to protecting your nervous system!

ADVOCATE!

You will no longer have parents and teachers adapting the world for you! You are on your own. You must be able to appraise the environment for what accommodations will be needed, and know what to disclose and what to advocate for. You need to build your home or apartment to be a sensory-friendly, safe haven for you to escape to and rebound from the hectic outside world. You cannot avoid the bombardment outside the home, but you can develop a sensory-friendly, soothing environment at home. If you live with others who still irritate your nervous system, set aside one room that is your sensory-friendly escape. It is a must if you are going to allow your nervous system to rebound.

At work, you have to be able to make modifications and accommodations to the work setting, or build in accommodations to mask and tone down the stimulation in order to excel at work. You may need to disclose what your sensitivities are, and advocate for what accommodations you need. If you don't, more than likely you will not be successful at the job. You have to be clear about what you need, and use your voice to advocate how to get it.

2. Information processing challenges

CHALLENGES!

You must realize that much of the dynamic world simply moves too fast, with too much information, for your nervous system to process. Whereas NT people can filter out and process most of the information simultaneously and subconsciously, with minimal mental energy, you do not filter out the stimulation. It all comes in, bombarding the nervous system. You must process it sequentially and consciously, which can be very taxing and quickly drains your mental energy. As the day rolls on, the simple daily activities that NT people take for granted require intense processing from you. What comes easily for them is a constant struggle for you.

Accommodate!

You have to be conscious of how much mental energy you have at any given moment of time, appraise how much mental drain each activity or event will have for you, learn what to avoid, tone down the flow of information, and understand when your metal energy reserve is being depleted and how to pull away and re-energize. You have to eat a good diet, get plenty of sleep (and rest), and exercise regularly. These three conditions significantly affect your ability to process information. You need to slow the world down, give yourself plenty of time (which is hard for you to estimate), give yourself frequent breaks, and learn to escape the bombardment before you hit overload. This is an ongoing problem for many adults on the spectrum. Don't wait until you feel yourself melting down; slow it down, tone it down, and give yourself frequent breaks.

Advocate!

As with the sensory challenges, you need to be able to accommodate for yourself. Be able to appraise an event for how draining it will be, position yourself to buffer yourself from much of the overload, and take frequent breaks to rebound. Those breaks might be going for a brisk walk or going to the bathroom to engage in five minutes of your favorite self-stimulation. If you choose to go to a party with friends on Friday night, assume it will exhaust you and plan ahead to stay home all day Saturday to rebound from the stress.

At work, be honest with your boss about what you can effectively handle and what you cannot. It will come back to haunt you eventually if you don't. Tell him you will not be able to multitask and will need information given to you sequentially and visually (written instructions rather than verbal). Be clear on working in a distraction-free setting so you can focus on your work, break the work down into simple steps, pace yourself, and have frequent mini-breaks. Tell your supervisor that he needs to be clear and to the point, and that you may need to clarify and verify expectations. You need to find a job where you can advocate for your needs, so you can be productive and successful.

At home, again create an environment where you can slow down, pace the information flow, and build in a lot of isolative activity to re-energize (rest, exercise, favorite hobbies, etc.). It is essential that your home gives you plenty of opportunities to regroup and re-energize, otherwise, your energy reserve will not be enough for the next day. Eat well, get a good night's sleep, and get some exercise!

3. Executive functioning challenges

CHALLENGES!

It is a given, if you are on the spectrum, that you will have a hard time organizing yourself to get things done, forget to do things or where you put things, forget to make and keep appointments, have difficulty judging how much time things will take, have problems multitasking several jobs at one time, and struggle transitioning from one activity to another. You will either have a hard time keeping your home clean and organized or be compulsive in doing so. You will struggle to make deadlines, know how to plan out events, organize what is needed, and follow through with things. This is due to the weak neurological connections in the frontal lobes of the brain. Get used to it and learn to accommodate for it.

ACCOMMODATE!

Lists, calendars, outlines, and written instructions are your savior. You need rigid routines to make everyday activities "habits," so you can do them automatically without thinking about them. Build in strong structure and consistent routines, and adhere to them religiously. They become your lifeline, the foundation for your security. You need predictability to feel secure; otherwise, anxiety will overcome you. Without a predictable routine filled with set rituals, you will become disorganized and risk falling apart.

Today's technology can drastically help with this. PDAs, smartphones, iPads, and wristwatch alarms can all help you schedule your day and cue you in when it is time to do things. Electronic calendars, "to do lists," and alarms from your watch or phone can cue you in to what and when to do things. At home and work, make sure you have set spots to keep everything, so you do not lose them. Color-code files, notebooks, and information so that you can categorize and easily retrieve information when you need it. Pay your bills, do your shopping, clean your house at the same day and time of the week to keep them routine. For larger projects such as house cleaning, break them into smaller tasks (make bed, do laundry, clean bathroom, etc.) and do them separately, each with their routine day and time.

Make sure you preview and prepare for all events that are not routine and done automatically, out of habit. Know what you are entering into, appraise what is needed, and develop a script, or map, for how to do it. This is very time-consuming and energy-draining, but much better upfront than trying to organize yourself once in the event. Lay out the course of action before entering the event. Know what your exit plan will be ahead of time in case it becomes overwhelming for you.

Advocate!

This is where you may need to build in a few supportive people to help you out. Life at work can be much easier if you disclose these challenges with planning, organizing, and timeliness with your supervisor and possibly a close co-worker. You will need help with reminders, visual outlines for breaking work down, sequencing work out, making timelines for completion, and providing constructive feedback to maximize success. If you cannot trust your supervisor and/or a close co-worker, more than likely the job will be a bad match for you and will not last long.

Often, at home it is good to have a roommate, spouse, or friend who is good at what you are weak at. If you are scattered, forgetful, and disorganized, it is good to have a spouse or housemate who is strong in those areas. If you cannot do it yourself, it is helpful to have someone who can do it for you, or, at best, remind you to do it. You will struggle in these areas for the rest of your life. Accept it—we all have strengths and weaknesses. Learn how to compensate for what you need and advocate for getting it.

4. Social challenges

Challenges!

Face it, you will always have a hard time reading social cues, reading the thoughts, feelings, perspectives and intention of others, and learning how to emotionally please others. You are pragmatic, factual, and intellectual, not social, emotional, and relational. What comes naturally and intuitively for NT people requires intense processing for you. You cannot regulate small talk and the give-and-go flow of spontaneous conversation. You may get good at interacting with one person at a time, but will always struggle regulating group interaction. You will not be able to keep up with the nonverbal communication, read between the lines, understand the invisible social rules, and understand the social context. Your brain is just not wired to do so smoothly and effortlessly.

Accommodate!

This does not mean you cannot have friends and a marriage. You love and care for others in your own way, and can be a very committed friend, spouse, parent, and co-worker. However, more than likely you will express your love very pragmatically, not emotionally. You will be there and do things for others, but struggle at supporting others emotionally. You will never be good at guessing what others need and providing the emotional support that NT people often desire. This doesn't mean that you cannot have a healthy relationship with others, but they will have to know and accept you for who you are. Once you trust someone, you have to be upfront with them in disclosing what your strengths and weaknesses are. You have to be clear that you cannot read their thoughts, feelings, and needs, and that they will have to clearly spell them out for you. Both you and your partner will have to learn to clarify information and verify meaning, and not to assume understanding. You both will have to mean what you say and say what you mean. They will have to value you for who you are, and the strengths that you have, not hope to change you.

ADVOCATE!

You will have to be upfront with your boss and close co-workers. They need to know that you may seem rude and overbearing at times, without realizing it may hurt their feelings. Let them know that you feel uncomfortable with small talk, and will not join in with informal conversations. Let them know that regulating team work and group interaction is very draining for you, and that you may not take part, or do so only for brief periods of time. You have to be very aware of how taxing interacting is for you and what situations you need to avoid. Don't try to be more than you are and pretend to be something you are not. It will only invalidate your identity and wear you down. Be you, accept you, and only stay in situations in which you are accepted for that. Yes, you may have to sample many settings, events, and jobs before you find the right fit.

You need someone at work (supervisor or close co-worker) and a spouse or close friend to be a tutor and social navigator for you. They need to be honest and give you clear, concrete feedback on what is expected, how you are acting, and what changes you need to make. Temple Grandin has been very clear on how important it was for key figures in her life to tell her very clearly when she was stepping out of line and what she needed to do. These people need to be able to stop you quickly, tell you not only what you are doing wrong but also what you need to do right. They can help interpret the invisible social rules, expectations, and behavior of others for you. They can help you navigate the often chaotic and confusing social world.

WHERE TO GO FROM HERE

This book is one of a two book series of discussion posts from the Facebook page, the Autism Discussion Page, www.facebook.com/autismdiscussionpage. The sister book, titled *The Autism Discussion Page on the core challenges of autism: A toolbox for helping children with autism feel safe, accepted, and competent* (Nason 2014), provides a comprehensive discussion of the four main areas of challenges: sensory, cognitive, social, and emotional. It provides the reader with a very good understanding of how the child processes information and experiences his world. By understanding how the child perceives the world, it becomes easier to understand his behavior and help support him through these daily challenges. It systematically goes through each major area of vulnerabilities, with easy-to-read, step-by-step strategies for supporting the child with these challenges. It is an essential reference book for parents, teachers, and professionals who provide services to children on the spectrum.

In addition to these books, we invite everyone to visit and "like" the Autism Discussion Page for further information and strategies. We have more than 50,000 members from all over the world who ask questions, provide suggestions, and share their experiences. On this page we also have more than 40 slide presentations on all the topics covered in these books. These books provide a manual to the page, allowing members to discuss each article further, seek extra advice, and view slide presentations that expand this information further. Additionally, in the following appendix section, appendices B, D, E, F and G are available to be downloaded from www.jkp.com/catalogue/book/978184905994/resources (they have been marked with a ★).

FRAGILE WORLD ON THE SPECTRUM

My world is "confusing" and "overwhelming!"

Overwhelming environmental demands →	Weak and fragile nervous system →	Stress overload! →	Fight, flight, or freeze!
• Too much, too fast! • Too loud, too bright! • I don't understand! • What do they mean? • I don't know how to act! • What is expected? • How should I respond?	• Sensory-defensive; overreacting to stimulation. • Poor registration of information. • Problems integrating senses. • Becomes overloaded easily. • Poor digestive and weakened immune systems. • Areas of brain do not work well together to give meaning to event.	• Build-up of stress chemicals. • Feeling confused, overwhelmed. • Feeling frustrated, anxious and scared. • Breakdown of thought processes and ability to regulate emotions.	• Shutdowns: withdraw; unresponsive; nervous system shuts down in order to rebound. • Meltdowns: tantrums, aggression, property disruption, self-abuse, all in attempt to release stress chemicals and to escape/avoid stressors.

Please help me to understand and feel safe, accepted, and competent!

SOURCES OF STRESS

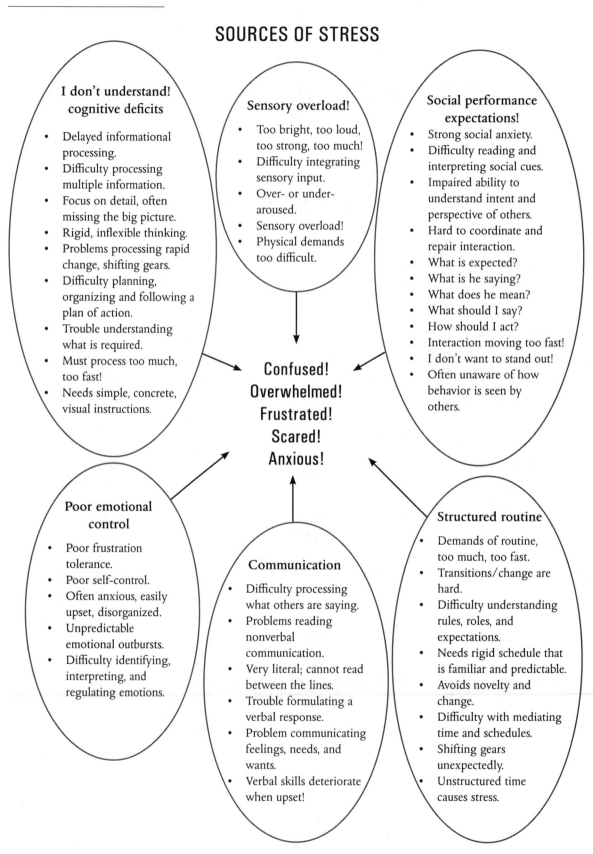

I don't understand! cognitive deficits

- Delayed informational processing.
- Difficulty processing multiple information.
- Focus on detail, often missing the big picture.
- Rigid, inflexible thinking.
- Problems processing rapid change, shifting gears.
- Difficulty planning, organizing and following a plan of action.
- Trouble understanding what is required.
- Must process too much, too fast!
- Needs simple, concrete, visual instructions.

Sensory overload!

- Too bright, too loud, too strong, too much!
- Difficulty integrating sensory input.
- Over- or under-aroused.
- Sensory overload!
- Physical demands too difficult.

Social performance expectations!

- Strong social anxiety.
- Difficulty reading and interpreting social cues.
- Impaired ability to understand intent and perspective of others.
- Hard to coordinate and repair interaction.
- What is expected?
- What is he saying?
- What does he mean?
- What should I say?
- How should I act?
- Interaction moving too fast!
- I don't want to stand out!
- Often unaware of how behavior is seen by others.

Confused! Overwhelmed! Frustrated! Scared! Anxious!

Poor emotional control

- Poor frustration tolerance.
- Poor self-control.
- Often anxious, easily upset, disorganized.
- Unpredictable emotional outbursts.
- Difficulty identifying, interpreting, and regulating emotions.

Communication

- Difficulty processing what others are saying.
- Problems reading nonverbal communication.
- Very literal; cannot read between the lines.
- Trouble formulating a verbal response.
- Problem communicating feelings, needs, and wants.
- Verbal skills deteriorate when upset!

Structured routine

- Demands of routine, too much, too fast.
- Transitions/change are hard.
- Difficulty understanding rules, roles, and expectations.
- Needs rigid schedule that is familiar and predictable.
- Avoids novelty and change.
- Difficulty with mediating time and schedules.
- Shifting gears unexpectedly.
- Unstructured time causes stress.

Stress reaction

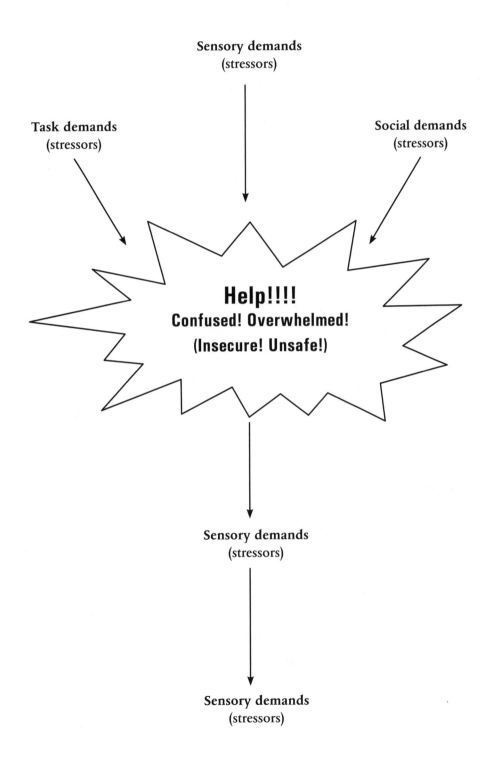

Stress reduction

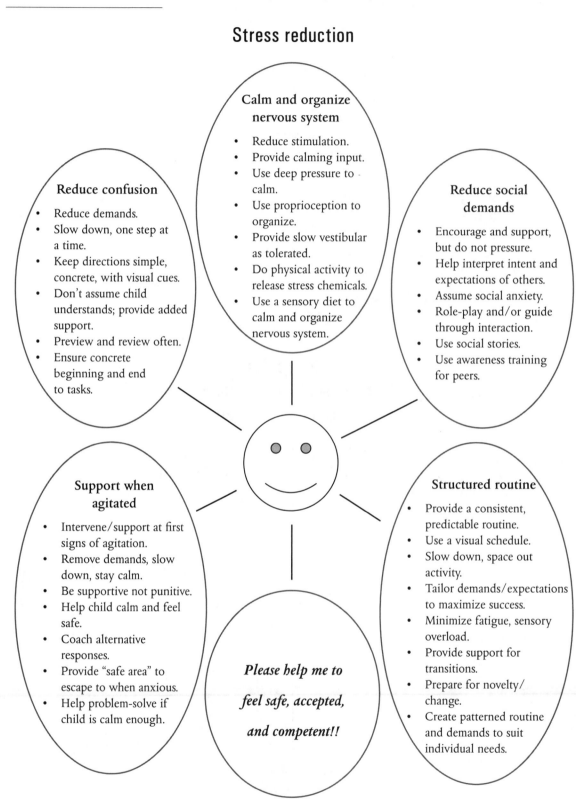

Calm and organize nervous system
- Reduce stimulation.
- Provide calming input.
- Use deep pressure to calm.
- Use proprioception to organize.
- Provide slow vestibular as tolerated.
- Do physical activity to release stress chemicals.
- Use a sensory diet to calm and organize nervous system.

Reduce confusion
- Reduce demands.
- Slow down, one step at a time.
- Keep directions simple, concrete, with visual cues.
- Don't assume child understands; provide added support.
- Preview and review often.
- Ensure concrete beginning and end to tasks.

Reduce social demands
- Encourage and support, but do not pressure.
- Help interpret intent and expectations of others.
- Assume social anxiety.
- Role-play and/or guide through interaction.
- Use social stories.
- Use awareness training for peers.

Support when agitated
- Intervene/support at first signs of agitation.
- Remove demands, slow down, stay calm.
- Be supportive not punitive.
- Help child calm and feel safe.
- Coach alternative responses.
- Provide "safe area" to escape to when anxious.
- Help problem-solve if child is calm enough.

Please help me to feel safe, accepted, and competent!!

Structured routine
- Provide a consistent, predictable routine.
- Use a visual schedule.
- Slow down, space out activity.
- Tailor demands/expectations to maximize success.
- Minimize fatigue, sensory overload.
- Provide support for transitions.
- Prepare for novelty/change.
- Create patterned routine and demands to suit individual needs.

Appendix B

COMFORT ZONES PROFILE

Name: Age: Date:
Reporter:

Sensory profile

a. Sensory stimulation the child avoids/is defensive to:

b. Sensory stimulation the child is attracted to, seeks out:

c. Sensory stimulation that alerts the child:

d. Known sensory situations that overwhelm the child:

e. Sensory stimulation that calms the child:

f. Sensory accommodations, or sensory diet, currently used to support the child:

g. Favorite sensory activities for engaging the child in interaction:

h. Other:

Cognitive (information) profile

a. Information processing problems the child experiences:

☐ delayed processing   ☐ processing multiple information
                                       simultaneously

☐ processing auditory information   ☐ processing visual information

Explain:

b. Best way to present information to the child:

Type: (visual, pictures, written, verbal, etc.)

How much? (Short phrases, broken down into small portions at one time, etc.)

How fast? (Needs 15–30 seconds to process, etc.)

c. Information (topics) that tend to be easy for the child? Difficult?

d. The child tends to have problems:

☐ concentrating   ☐ organizing materials   ☐ initiating a task
☐ staying on task   ☐ finishing task   ☐ turning in completed work

Explain:

e. Accommodations/supports that have worked well in helping the child learn:

f. Other:

Social profile:

a. What type of interaction style works best to:

Engage the child (animated, calm, non-demanding, slow-paced, physical contact, etc.):

Soothe the child:

b. Types of interaction to avoid with the child:

c. Types of interaction that overwhelm the child:

d. How the child handles interacting with:

Familiar adults:

★

Unfamiliar adults:

Other children:

Group activities:

e. The child's interaction skills:
Sharing:

Taking turns:

Following directions:

Referencing others to stay coordinated in action with them:

Sharing enjoyment with others:

f. Social situations to avoid for the child:

g. Accommodations and supports that help the child feel safe and accepted with others:

h. Other:

Emotional profile:

a. The child's general level of emotional stability (fairly calm, emotionally overreactive, etc.) is:

b. How the child expresses:
Excitement/pleasure:

Frustration:

Unhappiness:

★

Sadness:

Fear:

c. The child's abilities to:

Identify and label his emotions:

Control and regulate his emotions:

Calm after getting upset:

Situations that the child becomes overwhelmed by, or overreacts to:

d. Supports/accommodations that can be used to keep the child from becoming emotionally overwhelmed:

e. Best ways to calm the child when upset, overwhelmed:

f. Things to avoid when the child is emotionally overwhelmed, upset:

g. Other strategies that help the child feel "safe" in general, and in times of stress:

Other comfort zones (medical, dietary, physical activity, etc.) important to the child feeling safe:

Given the above information, the child functions the best under the following conditions:

The child struggles the most under the following conditions:

Summary of strengths and preferences
The child feels the most confident and learns best when we focus on his strengths and preferences.

★

a. The child's strengths include (what are his best qualities? What is he good at? What does he feel most competent doing?):

b. Favorite interests (topics, hobbies, music, activities, toys, etc.):

c. Ways of incorporating interests into learning opportunities. List any ways that have been used to incorporate the child's interests and preferences into learning opportunities (reading, writing, math, researching topic, etc.), to build social engagement around (peer play, group activities), and to soothe and cope with stress. Possible ways of expanding on these interests. Build the child's strengths, preferences, and interests into as many areas of learning as possible.

★

Appendix C

FUNCTIONAL ASSESSMENTS OF CHALLENGING BEHAVIORS

Functional behavior assessments are frequently used when trying to identify the conditions controlling problematic behavior. They are typically performed when strategies are needed to reduce challenging behaviors. Although they are a clinical tool, it is important for parents and teachers to understand what a good assessment consists of and how to provide necessary input. This may be more theoretical and clinical than most articles in this book, so for some of you it may be difficult to comprehend or a little overwhelming to understand. However, if you have a child or adult who displays severe behavior challenges, you may find this information valuable when helping the school or professionals complete these assessments. If you are new to functional behavior assessments, then I recommend that you read the post *Functional assessment: understanding the behavior* in Chapter 8, Effective Discipline.

This article will go into more depth about how to incorporate a functional behavior assessment (analysis of behavior) with a core deficit assessment (analysis of the autism vulnerabilities) to arrive at a more comprehensive understanding of your child's behavior challenges. The documents that are included are meant for professional evaluations, but are helpful for everyone. The information assumes a good knowledge of the core deficits of autism that are thoroughly covered in the companion book, *The Autism Discussion Page on the Core Challenges of Autism: A toolbox for helping children on the spectrum feel safe, accepted, and competent* (Nason 2014). It is my opinion that only when the observable antecedents, consequences, and functions identified in the functional behavior assessment are interpreted based on the core challenges of the person's autism, can the adaptive function of the behavior have true meaning.

Functional behavior assessment

In the post *Functional assessment: understanding the behavior* (Chapter 8, Effective Discipline), we discussed the importance of performing a "functional behavior assessment" to identify the functions or purpose that a challenging behavior has for the person. Usually functional behavior assessments focus on defining the A–B–C model of behavior: A (antecedent triggers), B (target behaviors), and C (consequences following the behavior). From close observations and from documenting details of the circumstances surrounding each episode, we can start to pick up patterns and identify *why* the behavior is occurring. Usually, detailed journaling for each episode includes where the incident occurred, time of day, what activity was occurring, and who was involved. This looks at what conditions were occurring when the behavior occurred and what changes in the environment occurred as the result of the behavior. By analyzing these factors, usually we start to pick up patterns to explain *why* a behavior is occurring.

The "why" is the functional value that the behavior has for the person: what benefit he derives from the behavior (gets him something he wants, gets to escape something he doesn't want, communicate frustration, etc.). Sometimes the behavior may have multiple functions for the person (communicate frustration, pain, hungry, doesn't like something, etc.) and often the person may have several behaviors (scream, hit, bite self, break things) that serve the same function. Once we can identify the variables (antecedents and consequences) surrounding the behavior, we often can change the behaivor by modifying the variable surrounding it, or we can teach a more adaptive response to replace the unwanted behavior. Table A.1 provides a summary of the common questions that make up a functional assessment.

Appendix D provides a brief functional behavior assessment form that can be used to help identify the variables listed in Table A.1 (it is also available to download from www.jkp.com/catalogue/book/9781849059954/resources). There are many versions of functional behavior assessment forms that you can search for online. This form provides an outline for defining the challenging behavior, identifying antecedent conditions (triggers), appraising the consequences that follow the behavior, and assessing the possible functional value the behavior serves the child. However, this assessment should not occur in conjunction with assessments of the child's communication skills, adaptive skill development, strengths and weaknesses, preferences and desires, social and emotional skills. Often the challenging behavior occurs because the child lacks appropriate means of communicating or functionally adapting to the demands of his surroundings. It is very important to look at the child's total skill set as well as his vulnerabilities when interpreting the functional behavior assessments. This table lists the issues that need to be identified and defined for each step of the assessment.

Table A.1 Functional assessment flow chart

A	B	C
• Conditions that trigger the behavior: *When:* What times does the behavior occur? *Where:* Where does it occur? *What:* What is happening at time of the behavior? What is person doing, the demands are placed on person? *Who:* Who is involved (parent, staff, peers)? • What other activity is going on in the area? • What are the common patterns that trigger the behavior? • When (what conditions) does the behavior not occur? • What characteristics of the conditions make them triggers (micro-analysis)?	• Define the behavior in observable and measurable terms. • Describe the course of the behavior from start to finish. • Does the behavior occur in a chain of behavior? • Are there precursor behaviors that signify the likelihood that the target behavior will occur?	• What happens following the behavior? • What does the person gain? What are the pay-offs? • What effects does the behavior have? • How do parents/ staff/peers react? • How does the person react to how others intervene? • What is the person gaining or escaping from?

Understand first; change second!

Functional behavior assessment: understand the "adaptive" function, not just the "observable" function

We need to look at the strong function that all behavior serves before deciding to suppress or change it. In ABA (Applied Behavior Analysis) they talk about doing a "functional analysis" to identify the function(s) that a behavior serves. This has been a standard protocol in treating behavior challenges. However, we often have to look not just at the observable, more immediate variables, but also at underlying physical, sensory, or emotional functions that the behavior is actually satisfying. For example, if a child acts out to escape certain situations, we need to have some idea of why he is trying to escape these situations (sensory overload, doesn't know what to expect, demands too hard, etc.) in order to support the issues underlying the behavior. On the surface, if we do not look closer, we can assume this behavior is an "escape" behavior that is reinforced by the child being allowed to escape (get out of) the unwanted situation. "When people ask me to do things I don't want to do, I scream and hit, and they back off the demand and I do not have to do it." To remove this reinforcing consequence (extinction), we might choose to force the child to stay with the distressing event so that he does not "escape" the situation (doesn't get reinforced by escaping the situation). Although we might be successful in removing the reinforcing consequence, we are doing nothing to help the child. We must know why the child finds the need to escape the situation (sensory overload, confused about expectations, too hard demands, etc.). By actually looking further at *why* these events trigger the behavior, we can (1) help support the vulnerabilities that are overwhelming the child and (2) teach the child another more acceptable way of communicating that he needs out of a situation. We need to look not only at the *observable function* (escape) but also the *adaptive function* (reduce sensory overload) in order to effectively support the child.

Autism presents so many processing difficulties (sensory sensitivities, integration difficulties, delayed information processing, processing overload, social thinking differences, etc.) that we have to look past the observable variables to understand how the person is experiencing the event to truly understand the meaning the behavior has for him. You have to understand how the person is experiencing the world before you can truly understand what function a behavior serves. The emphasis should not just be on changing behavior, but on supporting/helping the person. The therapist needs to focus first on becoming a working partner with the individual, before deciding which, if any, behavior needs to be changed. A good therapist should help the individual better adapt to his world, rather than simply change his behavior.

Core deficit assessment
Understand the core deficits of the disability to interpret the function of behavior!
For most of us, the extreme reactions we see in children on the spectrum can look bewildering. We are taught to look at the observable triggers of the behavior and the observable effects that the behavior has, in order to understand the function that behavior serves. However, what we see on the observable surface is not enough to understand the function the behavior serves. We often are quick to punish or extinguish a behavior, before understanding the adaptive function the behavior serves the child.

It is important to understand the core deficits of the disability to understand the true functions that the behavior serves (what the behavior is communicating). You have to understand the (1) sensory challenges (sensory defensiveness, overload, arousal issues), (2) cognitive differences (inflexible, black and white thinking, difficulty shifting gears, limited ability to evaluate consequences, poor empathy, etc.), (3) emotional deficits (poor frustration tolerance, limited emotional regulation, emotional overload, etc.), (4) social difficulties (difficulty reading social cues, reading effects their behavior has on others, etc.), (5) communication issues (difficulty expressing thoughts, feelings, and perspectives), and (6) medical/biological issues (digestive, allergies, weak immune system, etc.) in order to understand the adaptive function that drives the behavior. Once we understand the core deficits of the disability, the behavior is much easier to understand. In addition, once this function is identified, then we can provide the proactive supports needed to lessen the stressors driving the behavior, and teach more acceptable, alternative behavior to serve the same function. Table A.2 provides a summary of core deficit areas.

Table A.2 Core deficit areas

Sensory

- Over- or under-sensitivity to stimulation.
- Sensory overload
- Sensory seeking
- Under-aroused nervous system

Emotional

- Exaggerated emotional responses.
- Goes from 0 to 100 quickly.
- Difficult to calm.
- Poor frustration tolerance.

Medical

- Eating or sleeping problems.
- Chronic infections, congestion.
- Digestive, gastrointestinal problems.
- Constipation, loose stools, etc.
- Allergies, arthritis, migraines.

Cognitive

- Information processing problems (delayed, multitasking, etc).
- Rigid, inflexible thinking (shifting gears, transitions, change, etc.).
- Executive functioning problems (attention, organization, follow through).

Social/communication

- Difficulty communicating needs/wants.
- Problems understanding directions.
- Problems making friends.
- Difficulty reading thoughts, feelings, perspectives of others.
- Has to control all interaction.
- Difficulty sharing, taking turns, etc.

Psychiatric

- Mood swings, over-activity.
- Withdrawn, inactive, few interests.
- Rapid, pressured speech.
- Anxious, apprehensive, fearful.
- Compulsive, repetitive behavior.
- Hallucinations.
- Delusional ideations.
- Preoccupied thoughts.

If your child is having problems at home or school, make sure those who are designing strategies for changing the behavior understand your child's unique vulnerabilities and core challenges, which will help explain the behavior. Until you understand how the child experiences the world, you will often misinterpret what the behavior is communicating. When working with parents and teachers I will use the document Fragile Word on the Spectrum, in Appendix A, to explain some of the common vulnerabilities in the different core areas (sensory, cognitive, social, emotional, etc.) and provide them with possible ways of supporting those vulnerabilities. Once we complete the assessment, I return to this document to show them what strategies we are using to support their child.

Next, I use the Core Deficit Assessment, in Appendix F, to help identify the child's specific vulnerabilities. If you understand these vulnerabilities, then you can accurately interpret why certain events result in such extreme reactions from the child. Once completing the assessment then we return to the Fragile World on the Spectrum to fill in pages 2 and 4 with the child's specific vulnerabilities and possible strategies for supporting him. Using these two documents helps first to explain what the common vulnerabilities are in autism, next to assess what vulnerabilities the child exhibits, and then to discuss some possible strategies for helping the child.

Comprehensive behavior assessment (combining functional behavior and core deficit assessments)

Table A.3 provides a summary sheet for completing a comprehensive behavior assessment. This assessment combines the typical functional behavior assessment with a core deficit assessment. This is a summary sheet of what variables should be considered when evaluating behavior issues that occur with our children. At the top is the functional behavior assessment (ABC) and at the bottom is the core deficit assessment. The ABC section identifies the antecedents (triggers) of the behavior and the consequences (possible pay-offs) of the behavior. However, the core deficit assessment is what allows us to give meaning to the ABC analysis—to understand what adaptive function the behavior serves, what the behavior is communicating. It allows us to design positive behavior supports (accommodations, adaptations, modifications, and skills to teach) to lessen the stressors, and teach better coping skills.

Turning comprehensive behavior assessments into positive behavior support plans

The above framework gives us a better understanding of the adaptive function that the behavior serves in light of the child's vulnerabilities related to his autism. If the child acts out under certain conditions, we need to understand *why* the conditions elicit the negative behavior, not just recognize that they do. Why does the person feel the need to escape and avoid given situations? The function that a behavior serves for the individual is determined by the unique vulnerabilities that may be driving the behavior (sensory issues, cognitive confusion, emotional overreactivity, excessive anxiety, etc.).

Over the years, behavior plans which focused heavily on changing behavior by changing its consequences have evolved into positive behavior support plans which focus more on interpreting the child's behavior in light of their vulnerabilities and building in proactive supports to better match the demands of the environment to the current abilities of the child. This reinforces the premise that the child is doing the best that he can, given the demands that he is under, and his current skills to deal with them (Greene 2010). This premise assumes that when a child is acting out the demands are greater than the child's current abilities to handle them. Thus, our first obligation is to lower the demands and/or provide greater assistance to support the child to be successful. It assumes that we need to first change the conditions around the child, rather than change the child. Once the conditions provide a comfortable match for the abilities of the child, we can begin to teach stronger skills for handling the greater demands.

Figure A.1 displays a flow chart summarizing how interpreting the antecedents (triggers) of behavior in light of the "core deficits" of the disability leads to providing a list of positive, proactive strategies to lessen the demands and stress and provide greater assistance to support the child to be successful. In this example, Jimmy is a seven-year-old child who displays "tantrums" consisting of screaming, hitting himself, and hitting his parents. These behaviors occur most frequently when asked to do something (especially homework), during bathing and tooth brushing, and often during community outings. The functional behavior assessments identified these situations as the antecedents for the screaming and hitting.

Table A.3 Comprehensive behavior assessment

A — B — C

A

- Conditions that trigger the behavior:
  When: What times does the behavior occur?
  Where: Where does it occur?
  What: What is happening at time of the behavior? What is the person doing, demands placed on person?
  Who: Who is involved (parent, staff, peers)?
- What other activity is going on in the area?
- What are the common patterns that trigger the behavior?
- When (what conditions) does the behavior not occur?
- What characteristics of the conditions make them triggers (micro-analysis)?

B

- Define the behavior in observable and measurable terms.
- Describe the course of the behavior from start to finish.
- Does the behavior occur in a chain of behavior?
- Are there precursor behaviors that signify the likelihood that the target behavior will occur?
- Describe frequency, duration, and intensity of the behavior.
- What is the person communicating with behavior?

C

- What happens following the behavior?
- What does the person gain? What are the pay-offs?
- What effects does the behavior have?
- How do parents/staff/peers react?
- How does the person react to how others intervene?
- What is the person gaining or escaping from?

Core deficits

Sensory

- Over- or under-sensitivity to stimulation.
- Sensory overload.
- Sensory seeking.
- Under-aroused nervous system.

Cognitive

- Information processing problems (delayed, multitasking, etc.).
- Rigid, inflexible thinking (shifting gears, transitions, change, etc.).
- Executive functioning problems (attention, organization, follow through).

Emotional

- Exaggerated emotional responses.
- Goes from 0 to 100 quickly.
- Difficult to calm.
- Poor frustration tolerance.

Social/communication

- Difficulty communicating needs/wants.
- Problems understanding directions.
- Problems making friends.
- Difficulty reading thoughts, feelings, perspectives of others.
- Has to control all interaction.
- Difficulty sharing, taking turns, etc.

Medical

- Eating or sleeping problems.
- Chronic infections, congestion.
- Digestive, gastrointestinal problems.
- Constipation, loose stools, etc.
- Allergies, arthritis, migraines.

Psychiatric

- Mood swings, over-activity.
- Withdrawn, inactive, few interests.
- Rapid, pressured speech.
- Anxious, apprehensive, fearful.
- Compulsive, repetitive behavior.
- Hallucinations.
- Delusional ideations.
- Preoccupied thoughts.

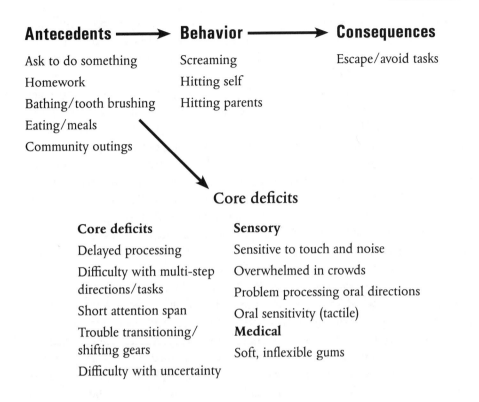

Antecedents ➔ **Behavior** ➔ **Consequences**

Antecedents	Behavior	Consequences
Ask to do something	Screaming	Escape/avoid tasks
Homework	Hitting self	
Bathing/tooth brushing	Hitting parents	
Eating/meals		
Community outings		

Core deficits

Core deficits	**Sensory**
Delayed processing	Sensitive to touch and noise
Difficulty with multi-step directions/tasks	Overwhelmed in crowds
	Problem processing oral directions
Short attention span	Oral sensitivity (tactile)
Trouble transitioning/ shifting gears	**Medical**
	Soft, inflexible gums
Difficulty with uncertainty	

Figure A.1 Comprehensive behavior assessment—Jimmy

When looking closely at some of the "core deficits" the child displays (determined by the core deficits assessment), we get a better view of why the child has difficultly during these times. Jimmy's core deficit assessment identified that he had processing problems (both sensory and cognitive) that made following directions difficult. He displayed auditory processing difficulties that could render verbal directions confusing. He also had problems processing multi-step directions, and displayed delayed information processing (took 10–15 seconds to process directions and produce an adaptive response). During the time, if the parent restated the verbal direction, Jimmy had to start his processing all over again. The more prompting the parents used, the more frustrated Jimmy became. In addition, the parents would use lengthy statements to prompt, direct, explain, and justify why Jimmy had to do something. Given his processing difficulties, this created more confusion and would overwhelm him. Jimmy needed instructions to be broken down into one-step directions, presented in short three- to four-word phrases. He also did better with information that was given visually (gestures, pictures, demonstration), and when he was given up to 15 seconds to respond. These modifications made directions much more understandable, expectations clearer, and allowed more time to respond.

Homework was another trigger. The amount of Jimmy's homework was overwhelming given his attention span and processing abilities. By recognizing and accommodating for these issues, Jimmy was successful when homework was broken down into smaller amounts and given in shorter sessions. Since Jimmy had difficulties initiating tasks, his parents offered assistance to jump-start the homework. This made homework easier to handle, and also allowed the parents to get him started on the right track. It wasn't that he did not like doing the homework; it was simply overwhelming for his current adaptive skills.

Further analysis of Jimmy's acting out during bathing and tooth brushing made sense in light of his tactile defensiveness and processing difficulties. Jimmy was defensive to touch so the physical contact that was required to assist Jimmy was very alarming for him. Also, the intrusiveness of having someone else doing these things to him, with little self-control, overwhelmed Jimmy. Further investigation led to the realization that Jimmy had very sensitive gums which made brushing his teeth painful. Based on his sensory sensitivities and processing problems, we needed to modify these tasks to (1) give Jimmy more control over the activity, (2) clarify exactly what was going to happen next, (3) use a soft sponge toothbrush, instead of a firm bristle brush, (4) use soft soap, instead of bar soap, and (5) let Jimmy lather himself instead of parent lathering him. These modifications reduced his acting out substantially.

Because of Jimmy's sensory sensitivities, he often had problems in community settings that were crowded and noisy. He also had difficulty in new, novel situations, or when uncertain about what to expect and what was expected of him. Like many children with disabilities, Jimmy had difficultly with unexpected changes or snags in what he expected. Knowing these vulnerabilities, we requested the parents to prepare Jimmy before outings by explaining (1) what he could expect, (2) what was expected of him, (3) how long it would last, and (4) what was occurring following the outing. We also used simple picture sequences to make these outings very predictable for him. As we knew that he had problems with crowded, noisy settings, Jimmy was provided an MP3 player to listen to music, or ear plugs which helped to block out noise.

By understanding Jimmy's behavior in light of his vulnerabilities and processing differences, we were able to provide accommodations and greater supports to make daily activities easier for him. In Figure A.2, you will see how the strategies we used not only supported Jimmy's vulnerabilities, but also reduced the antecedents (triggers) that elicited the acting out behavior. Table A.5 lists the strategies used to treat each antecedent. In parentheses next to each strategy are the core deficits each strategy was supporting.

As you can see, each strategy not only reduced the negative impact of the antecedent but also supported the core deficits of the disability. Each accommodation reduced a core deficit that was underlying a trigger for the behavior, effectively treating both the antecedent trigger and the core deficit underlying that trigger. Once we identified the core deficits making these conditions triggers, we were able to reframe *why* they were triggers for Jimmy's behaviors. Without analyzing the antecedents in terms of the core deficits, many of these strategies would have been missed.

Once we had identified the accommodations and supports needed to match the demands to Jimmy's processing needs, we were then ready to put together a positive behavior supports plan.

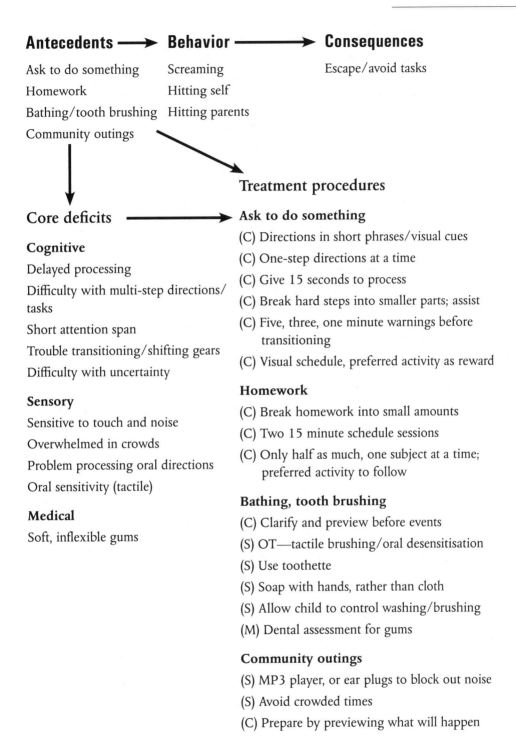

Antecedents ——→ **Behavior** ————→ **Consequences**

Ask to do something	Screaming	Escape/avoid tasks
Homework	Hitting self	
Bathing/tooth brushing	Hitting parents	
Community outings		

Treatment procedures

Core deficits ————→ **Ask to do something**

Cognitive

Delayed processing

Difficulty with multi-step directions/ tasks

Short attention span

Trouble transitioning/shifting gears

Difficulty with uncertainty

Sensory

Sensitive to touch and noise

Overwhelmed in crowds

Problem processing oral directions

Oral sensitivity (tactile)

Medical

Soft, inflexible gums

Ask to do something

(C) Directions in short phrases/visual cues

(C) One-step directions at a time

(C) Give 15 seconds to process

(C) Break hard steps into smaller parts; assist

(C) Five, three, one minute warnings before transitioning

(C) Visual schedule, preferred activity as reward

Homework

(C) Break homework into small amounts

(C) Two 15 minute schedule sessions

(C) Only half as much, one subject at a time; preferred activity to follow

Bathing, tooth brushing

(C) Clarify and preview before events

(S) OT—tactile brushing/oral desensitisation

(S) Use toothette

(S) Soap with hands, rather than cloth

(S) Allow child to control washing/brushing

(M) Dental assessment for gums

Community outings

(S) MP3 player, or ear plugs to block out noise

(S) Avoid crowded times

(C) Prepare by previewing what will happen

Figure A.2 Positive behavior supports—Jimmy

Core deficit assessment to Comfort Zones Profile

The most important document to give schools!

Once the child's vulnerabilities are identified using the Core Deficit Assessment (Appendix F) we need to establish the child's comfort zones and develop a Comfort Zones Profile (Appendix B) for each core area of deficits (sensory, cognitive, social, and emotional). The comfort zones are under what conditions (sensory, cognitive, social, and emotional) the child is at his best, feeling safe, comfortable, and competent. For example, if the child has strong sensory sensitivities, then define under what conditions he feels the safest (limited visual distractions, low lighting, minimal noise, etc.). For cognition, you define how to he processes information and how to best present information to him (slow down, break it down, give it visually, give ten seconds to process, etc.). Socially, it will include what types of social interaction (calm and quiet, excited and animated, etc.) your child responds best to. It also defines what types of social activities he can regulate, and for how long. The Comfort Zones Profile defines what helps the child feel safe and accepted, what is the best way to relate and engage with him, what are his strengths and interests, and what is his primary learning style. This profile is the most important information to share with your teachers. Don't leave it to chance! Build these strategies into the IEP, and review them frequently.

Appendix D

FUNCTIONAL BEHAVIOR ASSESSMENT

Name: Date:

Person interviewed:

Description of Behaviors

List behaviors of concern *(Be specific, hitting face, not self-abuse)*	Frequency and duration: how often and for how long	Intensity of behavior: damage done, injury involved, etc.	How long has behavior been occurring?

Do any of the behaviors above occur together or in a chain of responses? Describe behavior from start to stop.

What are the early signs that the person is getting upset or is about to begin the behavior?

What is the history of the behavior (when did it start, how has it changed over time)?

What may the person be trying to communicate with the behavior?

Program considerations

Can we intervene early in the chain, redirect, or support the person? How?

Is there another appropriate alternative behavior we can teach to replace the problem behavior? If so, can we use practice, role-play, or staff modeling to teach?

How do we make it more reinforcing to use appropriate alternative behavior?

Antecedent analysis

Under what circumstances does the behavior occur? What events seem to trigger the behavior?

Does the behavior occur at specific times during the day? With specific people?

Are there times/circumstances during the day when the behavior is less likely to occur?

Antecedent conditions

Check any of the following that present (trigger) the behavior:

❐ wants something
❐ told cannot have something
❐ something is taken away
❐ not receiving attention
❐ staff/parent withdraws attention
❐ when attention is turned to others
  behavior stops soon after attention or
  desired item is obtained
❐ requested to do something
❐ frustrated with difficult task
❐ pressured into unwanted events
❐ someone tries to control or lead his activity
❐ asked to stop doing something
❐ novel/new situations
❐ unexpected change
❐ when left alone or during downtime

❐ doesn't understand expectation
❐ doesn't know how to respond
❐ transitions
❐ pain/discomfort
❐ something scares him
❐ noisy, active settings
❐ peers are pestering him
❐ others are disruptive
❐ experiencing pain/discomfort
❐ difficulty communicating need/want
❐ happy/excited with upcoming event
❐ before, during, or after an outing
❐ during group activities
❐ riding in car
❐ prior to or during menses

★

Program considerations: eliminating/changing antecedent conditions
Can the triggers/conditions be eliminated/modified to reduce the behavior?

Can supports be added to minimize the impact of antecedents?

When these conditions occur, how do we want the person and/or staff to respond?

Can we increase the conditions for which the behavior does not occur?

Plan should include a list of specific antecedents and strategies to reduce their impact.

For identified antecedents, list more specific characteristics of the triggers: (Who, what, where, how, etc.)

Consequences of behavior: How people react to the behavior, the effects the behavior has on the environment, and the pay-offs the behavior has for the person
How do staff/family typically respond (intervene) when the behavior occurs?

How do others (peers, other adults, etc.) around the person respond?

How does the person respond when staff intervene/redirect?

What benefits does the person seem to gain from the behavior?

❐ Get out of doing something
❐ Obtain attention/ reaction
❐ Get back at someone

❐ Avoid/escape unwanted event
❐ Left alone
❐ Obtain stimulation

❐ Get something he wants
❐ Gain control
❐ Release tension/ frustration

Other:

What interventions have you tried so far?

★

What techniques have shown some success?

How does the person respond when:

Verbally redirected?

Physically redirected?

Behavior is ignored?

Removed from the group?

Asked to restore property disrupted?

Does the person seem to respond better to firm, neutral, or calm direction?

Program considerations:

We want to reduce the reinforcing pay-offs for problem behavior and increase positive pay-offs for behavior we want to see (e.g. replacement behavior, or simply lack of problem behavior). Goal is to interrupt problem behavior quickly with minimal reinforcing benefits. We need to focus on what we want the person to do, not on what he is doing wrong.) How should staff/family respond to calm, protect, and/or redirect the person?

How can we reduce the immediate reinforcing benefits of the problem behavior?

What do we want the person to do, and why should he do it (pay-off)?

Can we prompt and reinforce a replacement behavior?

Medical analysis

Acute medical problems: (e.g. constipation, ear infections, headaches, any acute discomfort)

★

Chronic medical problems: (e.g. ulcer, hernia, hypertension, allergies, diabetes)

Psychiatric concerns:

Medications:

Communication skills

Can the person adequately communicate the following:

Needs and wants:

Asking for help:

Saying "no," I don't want to:

Is communication a source of frustration?

Social skills

Is the behavior problem related to poor interaction patterns with peers and staff?

General ability to interact with others:

Relates/gets along with peers:

Relates/gets along with staff:

(Look closely at interaction patterns between the person and staff (how the person gets attention from staff, how staff request/prompt, how staff reward.)

How do we want staff to interact with the person (quiet/animated, tone/intensity of voice, touch, etc.)?

★

Daily routine

Is there enough structure, predictability, flexibility, stimulation, and choice in the daily routine?

Level of participation in:

Self-care:

Household tasks:

Leisure/free-time activities:

What changes do we need to make to the daily routine?

Are there possible sensory processing issues?

Reinforcement menu

Food/liquids:

Activities:

Toys/Objects:

Social:

Can the person mediate tokens, reinforcement charts?

★

ACTIVITIES OF DAILY LIVING (ADL) ASSESSMENT

Name: Date: Evaluator:

Scoring   2—The individual performs the task independently, without assistance.
criteria: 1—The individual actively performs the task with some assistance.
             0—The individual performs the task; requires complete assistance.

Directions: Rate steps of each task using the above criteria. Following each task,
             recommend possible step for training. Under comments, note any
             information regarding the individual's responsiveness to the task, factors
             interfering with training and other considerations.

Example: Removes   2—Takes pants off independently.
             pants.   1—Actively attempts to remove pants with prompting.
                        0—Requires total guidance; makes no attempt to remove pants.

1. Eating	Comments
❏ Swallows ground food.	
❏ Chews food before swallowing.	
❏ Bites.	
❏ Finger-feeds snack items.	
❏ Picks up spoon.	
❏ Scoops food to mouth.	
❏ Removes food from spoon with lips.	
❏ Places spoon on table.	
❏ Feeds self with spoon with minimal spillage.	
❏ Drinks from glass when glass is held.	
❏ Holds onto glass when drinking.	
❏ Drinks without gulping.	
❏ Drinks with minimal spillage.	
❏ Takes appropriate size bites.	
❏ Feeds self with minimal spillage.	
❏ Eats at appropriate pace.	
❏ Eats without choking.	
❏ Eats with fork.	
❏ Wipes mouth with napkin.	
❏ Cuts meat with knife.	

Recommended training step(s): _____

_____

2. Undressing

☐ Unties shoes.
☐ Removes shoes.
☐ Removes socks.
☐ Removes coat.
☐ Removes pullover shirt.
☐ Unbuttons shirt.
☐ Removes button-down shirt.
☐ Unzips pants.
☐ Removes pants.
☐ Removes dress or skirt.
☐ Removes underpants.
☐ Removes undershirt.
☐ Removes bra.

Recommended training step(s): _____

_____

_____

Comments

3. Dressing

☐ Picks out clothes.
☐ Puts on underpants.
☐ Puts on undershirt.
☐ Puts on bra.
☐ Fastens bra.
☐ Correctly orients clothes before putting on.
☐ Puts feet into pants.
☐ Pull pants up.
☐ Puts on pullover shirt.
☐ Puts on button-down shirt.
☐ Buttons shirt.
☐ Tucks in shirt.
☐ Fastens pants.
☐ Zips up pants.
☐ Loops belt into pants.
☐ Buckles belt.
☐ Puts on socks.
☐ Puts on shoes.
☐ Ties shoes.

Recommended training step(s): _____

_____

_____

Comments

★

4. Toileting

- ❏ Stays dry for two hours.
- ❏ Stays dry during the day.
- ❏ Stays dry at night.
- ❏ Has two or less BM accidents a week.
- ❏ Rarely has toileting accidents.
- ❏ Unfastens pants.
- ❏ Pulls pants down.
- ❏ Sits on toilet.
- ❏ Voids within 15 minutes.
- ❏ Wipes self.
- ❏ Pulls underpants up.
- ❏ Pulls pants up.
- ❏ Fastens pants.
- ❏ Flushes toilet.
- ❏ Washes hands.
- ❏ Goes to toilet with reminders.
- ❏ Self-initiates toileting.

Recommended training step(s): _____

_____

_____

Comments

5. Hand washing

- ❏ Turns on water.
- ❏ Adjusts water temperature.
- ❏ Wets hands.
- ❏ Applies soap.
- ❏ Lathers hands.
- ❏ Rinses hands.
- ❏ Turns off water.
- ❏ Obtains towel.
- ❏ Dries hands.
- ❏ Hangs up towels.
- ❏ Throws paper towel away.

Recommended training step(s): _____

_____

_____

Comments

★

6. Bathing

☐ Obtains towel and washcloth from closet.
☐ Gets clothes.
☐ Undresses.
☐ Turns on water.
☐ Adjusts water temperature.
☐ Wets washcloth.
☐ Soaps washcloths.
☐ Washes self.
☐ Rinses self.
☐ Wets hair.
☐ Obtains shampoo from container.
☐ Puts shampoo on hair.
☐ Rubs shampoo into hair.
☐ Rinses hair.
☐ Turns water off.
☐ Obtains towel.
☐ Dries self.
☐ Takes dirty clothes and towels to laundry.

Recommended training step(s): _____
_____
_____

Comments

7. Toothbrushing

☐ Obtains toothbrush.
☐ Obtains paste.
☐ Unscrews cap from paste.
☐ Wets brush.
☐ Puts paste on brush.
☐ Actively attempts to brush teeth; make brushing motion.
☐ Brushes front teeth.
☐ Brushes top back teeth.
☐ Brushes bottom back teeth.
☐ Rinses brush.
☐ Puts brush away.

Recommended training step(s): _____
_____
_____

Comments

★

8. Shaving

- ☐ Obtains razor.
- ☐ Holds razor.
- ☐ Plugs in razor.
- ☐ Turns on razor.
- ☐ Makes movement with razor on face.
- ☐ Shaves face area.
- ☐ Shaves throat and neck area.
- ☐ Turns razor off.
- ☐ Puts razor away.

Recommended training step(s): _____

_____

_____

Comments

9. Hair combing/brushing

- ☐ Holds comb/brush.
- ☐ Moves comb/brush through hair.
- ☐ Combs/brushes top of head.
- ☐ Combs/brushes sides of head.
- ☐ Combs/brushes back of head.
- ☐ Combs/brushes hair neatly.

Recommended training step(s): _____

_____

_____

Comments

10. Make-up

- ☐ Obtains make-up.
- ☐ Applies lipstick.
- ☐ Applies eye shadow.
- ☐ Applies eye liner.
- ☐ Applies mascara.
- ☐ Applies brush.
- ☐ Puts make-up away.

Recommended training step(s): _____

_____

_____

Comments

★

11. Meal preparation | Comments

☐ Obtains food from refrigerator.
☐ Carries items to counter.
☐ Obtains cooking utensils/dishes from cupboard or drawers.
☐ Opens box, bag, or other food containers.
☐ Pours ingredients from container into bowl/pan.
☐ Unscrews lid of jar.
☐ Pours liquids with minimal spillage.
☐ Uses measuring cup to scoop and transfer ingredients from container to bowl.
☐ Mixes with spoon.
☐ Mixes with hand beater.
☐ Mixes with electric mixer.
☐ Spreads butter on bread.
☐ Cuts bread with knife.
☐ Rinses vegetables.
☐ Cuts up vegetables with knife.
☐ Combines ingredients into dish as directed.
☐ Prepares cereal.
☐ Makes simple sandwiches.
☐ Makes simple drinks (juice, tea, koolaid).
☐ Operates electric can opener.
☐ Operates blender.
☐ Operates toaster.
☐ Operates oven.
☐ Operates range.
☐ Reads labels, written/pictures directions.
☐ Understands measurements.

Recommended training step(s): _____
_____
_____

12. Table setting | Comments

☐ Gets placemats, napkins, dishes, and utensils from cupboard or drawer.
☐ Carries dishes, utensils, etc. to table.
☐ Places dishes/utensils on placemat where staff point to.
☐ When given a placemat with pictures or drawings of dishes/utensils on it, can match items.
☐ Sets complete setting independently.

Recommended training step(s): _____
_____
_____

★

13. Serving

☐ Pours liquid into glass.
☐ Transfers hot food from cooking container to serving dish.
☐ Carries food without spillage.
☐ Carries liquids without spillage.
☐ Spoons out food from dish to plate.
☐ Takes appropriate size potions.
☐ Passes serving dish to others.

Recommended training step(s): _____

_____

_____

Comments

14. Meal clean-up

☐ Takes dishes to sink.
☐ Clears table.
☐ Cleans food from plate.
☐ Rinses dishes.
☐ Places dishes into dishwasher.
☐ Puts soap in dishwasher.
☐ Turns dishwasher on.
☐ Removes dishes from dishwasher.
☐ Washes dishes in sink.
☐ Dries dishes.
☐ Puts dishes/utensils in appropriate cupboards and drawers.
☐ Wipes off table, counter, or chairs.
☐ Takes protective clothing to laundry.
☐ Sweeps floor.

Recommended training step(s): _____

_____

_____

Comments

★

	Comments
15. Laundry ❏ Takes dirty clothes to laundry. ❏ Helps sort clothes by placing clothes in piles pointed to by staff. ❏ Sorts clothes with minimal assistance. ❏ Puts clothes into washer. ❏ Obtains detergent from cupboard. ❏ Measures out detergent. ❏ Pours detergent into washer. ❏ Sets dial, starts washer. ❏ Transfers clothes from washer to dryer. ❏ Folds clothes. ❏ Takes clothes to bedroom. ❏ Puts clothes in drawers. ❏ Places clothes on hangers. ❏ Hangs clothes up. Recommended training step(s): _____ _____	Comments
15. Bed making ❏ Takes blankets/sheets off bed. ❏ Spreads sheets/blankets across bed. ❏ Smoothes out sheet or blanket. ❏ Places pillows appropriately. ❏ Spreads bedspread across bed. ❏ Completely makes bed. Recommended training step(s): _____ _____	Comments
16. Vacuuming ❏ Obtains vacuum from closet. ❏ Turns vacuum on and off. ❏ Pushes vacuum back and forth. ❏ Vacuums small area with supervision. ❏ Vacuums entire room. Recommended training step(s): _____ _____	Comments
17. Dusting ❏ Obtains furniture polish, cloth, etc. ❏ Sprays polish. ❏ Actively attempts to dust; makes motion across surfaces. ❏ Completely dusts furniture. Recommended training step(s): _____ _____	Comments

★

18. Other domestic tasks

❏ Helps gets out and puts away activity materials.
❏ Gets mail.
❏ Cleans windows/mirrors.
❏ Cleans bathtub.
❏ Empties wastepaper baskets.
❏ Takes out trash.
❏ Puts groceries away.
❏ Washes vehicle.
❏ Shovels snow.
❏ Rakes yard.
❏ Mows yard.
❏ Sweeps garage.

Recommended training step(s): _____

_____

_____

Comments

19. Money skills

❏ Understands money has value.
❏ Can identify coins.
❏ Understands cent value of coins.
❏ Can make simple change.
❏ Understands denomination of paper money.
❏ Carries money without losing it.
❏ Can purchase simple items up to $10.00
❏ Can purchase items over $20.00.
❏ Saves for simple items.
❏ Can plan and follow a simple weekly budget.
❏ Uses savings account; fills out deposit.
❏ Uses credit or debit card.
❏ Takes care of own savings/credit accounts.
❏ Writes a check.
❏ Has addresses and phone numbers of creditors.
❏ Pay bills on time.
❏ Avoids money scams.
❏ Understands and takes care of entitlement funds,
     and social security.
❏ Takes care of tax returns.

Recommended training step(s): _____

_____

_____

Comments

★

20. Shopping

	Comments

❏ Can purchase simple items, and wait for change.
❏ Gives the correct amount of money.
❏ Can purchase multiple items adding correct costs.
❏ Can find items in store.
❏ Can find items from a list.
❏ Knows how to ask for help to find something.
❏ Finds way around store.
❏ Waits in line without difficultly.
❏ Gives money and waits for change.
❏ Shops at convenience store.
❏ Shops at grocery store.
❏ Shops at malls.
❏ Shops at specialty stores.
❏ Can go shopping in several stores without
    supervision.
❏ Can shop online.
❏ Purchases own clothing.
❏ Purchases own personal items.
❏ Can use public restroom.

Recommended training step(s): _____
_____
_____

21. Community/leisure

Comments

❏ Can order simple fast food.
❏ Can order food from a menu.
❏ Eats appropriately in public.
❏ Waits effectively in line.
❏ Goes to the movies, pays for ticket, orders food.
❏ Rents videos.
❏ Schedules and attends community events (concerts,
    sporting events).
❏ Attends community recreation.
❏ Goes out with group of friends.
❏ Uses library.
❏ Has leisure interests to occupy time (reading,
    television, computer, etc.).
❏ Adequately organizes own leisure time.

Recommended training step(s): _____
_____
_____

★

22. Social behavior in public

☐ Doesn't approach strangers inappropriately.
☐ Greets others appropriately.
☐ Avoids saying rude remarks to strangers.
☐ Doesn't talk loudly at library, church, or movie.
☐ Dresses appropriately for public.
☐ Willing to help others if needed.
☐ Controls anger in public.
☐ Avoids obvious stereotypic, self-stimulation behavior in public.
☐ Understands simple manners in public (please, thank you, and sorry).
☐ Doesn't touch people inappropriately, or invade personal space.

Recommended training step(s): _____

_____

_____

Comments

23. Community mobility

☐ Can walk simple distances, with adequate safety skills.
☐ Can cross street safely.
☐ Can read street and community signs.
☐ Has adequate stranger-danger skills.
☐ Knows how to seek help.
☐ Carries ID.
☐ Knows own address, telephone number, and emergency contacts.
☐ Can ride public transportation.
☐ Can schedule Your-Ride or taxi.
☐ Can find way around immediate area.
☐ Can find way to frequently visited settings (store, post office, barber shop, etc.).
☐ Can drive.
☐ Can travel around town, within limited distance.
☐ Can travel outside town using a map.

Recommended training step(s): _____

_____

_____

Comments

★

24. Safety/medical	Comments
☐ Tends to minor cuts. ☐ Takes own medications. ☐ Uses thermometer to take temperature. ☐ Recognizes when medical attention is needed. ☐ Knows who to call in emergencies (911). ☐ Can call and make medical appointments. ☐ Can fill prescriptions. ☐ Is careful with hot objects. ☐ Is careful with sharp objects. ☐ Understands and avoids dangers of electricity. ☐ Understands dangers of gas and heat (stove, furnace, etc.). ☐ Understands dangers of simple tools. ☐ Understands dangers of household chemicals. ☐ Can put out simple fires (use extinguisher). Recommended training step(s): _____ _____	
25. Communication	Comments
☐ Can use telephone. ☐ Keeps list of important phone numbers. ☐ Can use and maintain a cell phone. ☐ Can use internet to find information. ☐ Knows email address. ☐ Can seek out help when needed. Recommended training step(s): _____ _____	
26. Time/reading/writing	Comments
☐ Knows how to tell time. ☐ Knows the days of the week. ☐ Knows the month and year. ☐ Reads simple stories. ☐ Reads newspaper articles. ☐ Reads labels. ☐ Reads store signs and street signs. ☐ Can write or print name, address, and phone number. ☐ Can write or print simple notes. ☐ Can write or print letters. ☐ Can fill out applications. ☐ Can do simple addition and subtraction. Recommended training step(s): _____ _____	

★

27. Self-direction

☐ Remembers to eat all meals.
☐ Goes to bed on time, gets enough sleep.
☐ Gets up on own in the morning (e.g. alarm).
☐ Gets through morning routine and out the door for school or work independently.
☐ Plans out day and follows routine.
☐ Handles changes in routine.
☐ Remembers to do personal maintenance (change clothes every day, use deodorant, brush teeth, etc.).
☐ Remembers to run errands and do simple chores.
☐ Makes and keeps appointments.
☐ Follows a planner, monthly calendar or other planning tool.
☐ Remembers to follow through with responsibilities/comments.
☐ Keeps things organized enough not to lose them.
☐ Thinks about consequences before acting.
☐ Uses simple problem-solving skills when faced with a simple problem.

Recommended training step(s): _____

_____

_____

Comments

28. Self-advocacy/legal/financial

☐ Understands own disability including strengths and interests.
☐ Is able to communicate his disability to others.
☐ Can ask for support if he needs it.
☐ Understands own vulnerabilities and can advocate for accommodations.
☐ Can assess new situations in light of his vulnerabilities (sensory issues, social challenges, etc.).
☐ Knows to avoid situations that are above own skill level.
☐ Avoids getting taken advantage of by strangers, salesmen, or phone solicitors.
☐ Understands what he is entitled to by the American Disabilities Act.
☐ Understands contact sources for disability services.
☐ Can give informed consent for financial, legal, and medical matters.
☐ Knows how to apply for and correspond with Social Security, Medicaid, and other disability funds.

Comments

★

❏ Knows how to contact important government services (Secretary of State).
❏ Knows names and phone numbers of treatment support team members (case manager, vocational support, psychologist, doctor, etc.).
❏ Facilitates and collaborates in self-determination and treatment strategies.
❏ Understands legal responsibilities and knows how to obtain legal services.

Recommended training step(s): _____

_____

_____

	Comments

29. Work/school

❏ Gets up and to school/work on time.
❏ Calls if missing or going to be late.
❏ Follows time and simple work/school rules.
❏ Organizes and turns in homework.
❏ Organizes school or work schedule.
❏ Is typically on time to classes, from breaks, lunch, etc.
❏ Knows who to ask for help.
❏ Can fill out work applications and handle interviews.
❏ Can sign up for classes at school.
❏ Completes assigned school or work tasks.
❏ Listens and takes directions well.
❏ Handles criticism.
❏ Gets along with co-workers/students.
❏ Avoids making rude comments.
❏ Dresses appropriately for work/school.

Recommended training step(s): _____

_____

_____

★

Appendix F

CORE DEFICIT ASSESSMENT

Name: Date: Age:
Informant: Evaluator:

I = Infrequent   O = Occasional   F = Frequent

Core deficit	I	O	F	Examples/ comments
Sensory deficits				
1. Either under- or over-sensitive to touch.				
2. Either under- or over-sensitive to sounds.				
3. Either under- or over-sensitive to light.				
4. Either under- or over-sensitive to smells/tastes.				
5. Shows apprehension in movement activities.				
6. Withdraws or hits when approached or touched.				
7. Becomes overwhelmed in loud or crowded settings.				
8. Dislikes certain clothing, or layers clothing.				
9. Resists grooming: face washing, bathing, tooth brushing, combing hair, etc.				
10. Has problems understanding/following spoken directions.				
11. Sometimes appears not to hear when spoken to.				
12. Is frequently seeks out stimulation (touch, deep pressure, crashing, movement, smells, etc.).				
13. Frequently on the move; overactive.				
14. Is frequently touching/grabbing/hanging on others.				
15. Is slow, sluggish, with little energy.				
Other:				

Core deficit	I	O	F	Examples/ comments
Cognitive deficits				
16. Displays delayed information processing; delay in responding.				
17. Has difficulty processing multiple information simultaneously.				
18. Gets confused with multiple-step directions.				
19. Needs tasks broken down into small steps.				
20. Has problems multitasking.				
21. Has a short attention span, concentration, is easily distracted.				
22. Has trouble starting and finishing tasks.				
23. Has poor planning and organizing skills; scattered.				
24. Often loses or forgets things.				
25. Has poor impulse control, acts without forethought.				
26. Has problems monitoring actions to stay coordinated with others.				
27. Doesn't understand the effects of his behavior.				
28. Has difficulty shifting gears with minor snags or changes.				
29. Shows rigid/inflexible thinking; can only see his way.				
30. Displays black and white, all-or-nothing thinking (cannot see gray areas).				
Other:				
Emotional deficits				
31. Displays intense emotional reactions; often over-exaggerated.				
32. Goes from 0 to 100 quickly, difficulty calming down.				
33. Seems to lose control, becomes overwhelmed.				
34. Has poor frustration tolerance (has to have it now!).				
35. Has trouble identifying/labeling emotions.				
36. Often appears anxious, scared, or apprehensive.				
37. Changes moods quickly, difficult to predict.				
38. Laughs or cries for no apparent reason.				
39. Becomes over-excited easily.				
40. Shows emotions that often don't match situation.				
41. Shows little emotion.				
42. Has difficulty recognizing emotions of others.				
Other:				

★

Core deficit	I	O	F	Examples/comments
Social/communication deficits 43. Has difficulty communicating needs and wants. 44. Gets frustrated when others don't understand. 45. Has difficult time understanding spoken directions. 46. Needs to have directions repeated several times. 47. Gets upset when given directions. 48. Has difficult time making friends. 49. Has difficulty reading social cues. 50. Shows poor regard for (difficulty reading) the thoughts, feelings and perspectives of others. 51. Has to control all interactions. 52. Has difficulty sharing and taking turns. 53. Has difficulty coordinating back-and-forth interaction. 54. Has poor awareness of how his actions affect others. 55. Seeks out frequent attention. 56. Seems anxious, apprehensive when interacting. 57. Tends to avoid social contact. Other:				
Medical/psychiatric 58. Eating or sleeping problems. 59. Chronic infections, congestion. 60. Digestive, gastrointestinal problems. 61. Constipation, loose stools, etc. 62. Allergies, arthritis, migraines. 63. Mood swings, over-activity. 64. Withdrawn, inactive, little interests. 65. Rapid, pressured speech. 66. Anxious, apprehensive, fearful. 67. Compulsive, repetitive behavior. 68. Hallucinations. 69. Delusional ideations. 70. Preoccupied thoughts. Other:				

★

SUMMARY SHEET

If used in conjunction with functional behavior assessment, which core deficits impact the target behaviours in question?

For each core deficit area, list possible compensations, accommodations, or skills to teach.

Sensory:	Emotional:
Cognitive:	Social/communication:

Medical:
Psychiatric:

★

Appendix G

EVALUATING STRENGTHS AND PREFERENCES

Child's name: Age: Date:
Informant: Relationship to child:

All good treatment plans should focus on identifying and fostering the child's strengths and interests. We all develop stronger and faster when focusing on our strengths, and centering engagement around what interests us. Often, we find ourselves hyper-focusing on weaknesses and negative behavior. This is a mistake and often leads the child down the path of more negative behavior. In this assessment we want to identify the child's positive qualities; his strengths and preferences.

Favorite activities:

These can be functional activities like toys or games, TV, computer games, etc; but also ritualistic, repetitive behaviors (humming, rocking, lining up objects, etc.). Also include sensory seeking preferences and/or obsessive compulsive behavior; any activity that the person seeks out and occupies his time with. Nothing is too unusual; list any and all behavior that interests the child.

What does he/she most like to do?

Favorite topics to talk about:
Favorite TV shows:
Favorite Music:
Favorite video games or Internet searches:
Favorite topics to read about:
Favorite foods/liquids:
Favorite toys/objects:
When by himself what does he seek out and/or self-initiate?
Does he have any fixated interests or topics?
Hobbies:
Any repetitive, fixated behavior (rocking, lining up cars, spinning things, watching fans, etc.)?

What types of physical activity does the child enjoy?

Favorite outdoor activities:
Favorite community activities:
Preferred social activities:
What activity helps the child shine? What helps him feel the most competent?
When is the child at his best? What is he doing?

What activities does your child like to engage in with you? (can be simply sensory play or more complex activities).

What activities does your child help with around the house (laundry, yard work, dishes, etc.)?

Does he/she like: (Yes/No/sometimes)

Draw/paint:	Build things:	Take things apart:
Put things back together:	Read or Write:	Art projects:
Sports:	Play an instrument:	Research favorite topic:
Science:	Mechanical things:	Cars/trains:
Pretend/Drama:	History:	Super Heroes:
Science fiction:	Video Games:	Internet:
Pets/Animals:		
Other:		

School Activities

Favorite activities

In classroom:

On the playground:

(check any of the following that are the preferred interests for the child)

Gym, art, drama, and music:

Sports, band, chess club, debate, etc.

Favorite subjects at school (history, math, science, etc.)

Social activities he/she engages in with peers:

Any afterschool clubs or activities:

Vocational Interests (what does he want to do for work):

Goals and dreams for adult living: Where to live, what to do, who to be with, etc.

Sensory Preferences

Many individuals have strong sensory preferences (touch, smells, visual patterns, movement patterns, etc.) which can be used to expand into other functional activity.

Sensory preferences: What does he seek out, what calms him, what excites him?

Touch: fidget toys, feel things, sifting sand through fingers, smearing with hands, playing with clay, deep pressure touch, light stroking, tickle, soft vs. firm touch, etc:

Alerts him, seeks it out:

Calm and soothes him:

Avoids, dislikes

Movement: Jumping, running, swinging, rocking, spinning, riding, etc:

Alerts him, seeks it out:

Calm and soothes him:

Avoids, dislikes:

Proprioception: This involves any tension, resistance, rough-housing; gross motor activity involving pushing, pulling, carrying, lifting, hitting, running, jumping, crashing, squeezing, etc.

Alerts him, seeks it out:

Calm and soothes him:

Avoids, dislikes:

Auditory: Repetitive vocal noises, humming, repeating scripts, singing, sounds of equipment, environmental sounds, music, auditory patterns, etc.

Alerts him, seeks it out:

Calms and soothes him:

Avoids, dislikes:

★

Visual: Staring at lights, visual patterns, finger flicking in front of eyes, staring at mirrors or items that reflect light, spin objects, etc.

Alerts him, seeks it out:

Calms and sooths him:

Avoids, dislikes:

Olfactory: Smelling everything, attracted to odors, like materials with heavy scents, etc.

Alerts him, seeks it out:

Calms and sooths him:

Avoids, dislikes:

Does your child have favorite sensory self stimulation (rocking, humming, staring at light sources, etc.)?

Social Activity: Any activity the child likes to do with others

Preferred activities he does with familiar adults:

Preferred activities to do with peers:

Does he/she enjoy doing things for others?

Any social clubs or group activities?

Strengths

Consider anything that the child is good or considered a strength; even if it is unique, unusual. What is your child good at?

Is your child strong in any of the following areas? Yes/No

Focus on details ❏	Remembering facts ❏	Mechanical ❏
Perceiving sensory patterns ❏	Hyper-focusing on task ❏	Persistent ❏
Committed ❏	Drawing; graphic design ❏	Science/Math ❏
History ❏	Computer technology ❏	Video ❏
Games: Electronics ❏	Writing/Reading ❏	Art ❏
Sports ❏	Building things ❏	Automotive ❏
Other ❏		

Please give a brief description of your child's skills in each area below:

Communication skills:

Social skills:

Academic Skills:

Vocational Skills:

Using Strengths and Preferences:

How can we use these strengths and preferences to expand in the following areas:

Academic (e.g. If he likes race cars, he can read about cars, research them, write about them, etc.):

Vocational (if he likes animals he could volunteer or work at an animal shelter):

Leisure (likes science, purchase chemistry set):

Social (join clubs or play dates around special interest):

List at least three major ways we can foster your child's self esteem by expanding on his strengths and interests:

List at least three major ways we could increase his/her engagement with others around his special interest:

List at least two activities you could do with your child to have fun and relate around; simply to share the experience together:

★

REFERENCES

Dunn Buron, K. and Curti, M. (2012) *Incredible 5 Point Scale: The Significantly Improved and Expanded Second Edition; Assisting Students in Understanding Social Interactions and Controlling their Emotional Responses.* Shawnee Mission, KS: AACP Publishing.

Greene, R.W. and Ablon, S.J. (2005) *Treating Explosive Kids: The Collaborative Problem-Solving Approach.* New York, NY: Guilford Press.

Greene, R.W. (2008) *Lost at School: Why Our Kids with Behavioral Challenges are Falling Through the Cracks and How We Can Help Them.* New York, NY: Simons and Schuster.

Greene, R.W. (2010) *The Explosive Child: A New Approach for Understanding and Parenting Easily Frustrated, Chronically Inflexible Children.* New York, NY: HarperCollins.

Greenspan, S.I., Wieder, S. and Simons, R. (1998) *The Child with Special Needs: Encouraging Intellectual and Emotional Growth (A Merloyd Lawrence Book).* Reading, MA: Perseus Books Group.

Greenspan, S.I. and Wieder, S. (2009), *Engaging Autism: Using the Floortime Approach to Help Children Relate, Communicate, and Think (A Merloyd Lawrence Book).* Reading, MA: Perseus Books Group.

Gutstein, S.E. (2000*) Autism Aspergers: Solving the Relationship Puzzle—A New Developmental Program that Opens the Door to Lifelong Social and Emotional Growth.* Arlington: Future Horizons.

Gutstein, S.E. (2002a) *Relationship Development Intervention with Young Children: Social and Emotional Development Activities for Asperger Syndrome, Autism, PDD and NLD.* London: Jessica Kingsley Publishers.

Gutstein, S.E. (2002b) *Relationship Development Intervention with Children, Adolescents and Adults: Social and Emotional Development Activities for Asperger Syndrome, Autism, PDD and NLD.* London: Jessica Kingsley Publishers.

Gutstein, S.E. (2009) *The RDI Book: Forging New Pathways for Autism, Asperger's and PDD with the Relationship Development Intervention Probram.* Houston, TX: Connections Center Publishing.

Nason, B. (2014) *The Autism Discussion Page on the core challenges of autism: A toolbox for helping children with autism feel safe, accepted, and competent.* London: Jessica Kingsley Publishers.

Phelan, T. (2010) *1–2–3 Magic: Effective Discipline for Children 2–12* (Forth Edition). Glenn Ellyn, IL: ParentMagic.